the 13 gates
of the
Necronomicon

Praise for Donald Tyson

Necronomicon
"Tyson isn't the first writer to attempt a full 'translation' of the forbidden text, but his may be the most comprehensive."—*Publishers Weekly*

"Occult nonfiction author Tyson remains true to Lovecraft's spirit in this tribute to a master of horror."—*Library Journal*

"Scholarly horror, marvelously illustrated."—*Kirkus*

"This exhaustively researched volume reproduces and connects the details of the mythology originally created by the eldritch author."—www.Fangoria.com

Grimoire of the Necronomicon
"*Grimoire of the Necronomicon* is a classic treatment of an esoteric subject, and it deserves a wide reading audience. As an active Master of the Temple in the Golden Dawn, I found the information Tyson shared with the reader both educational and entertaining."—Lee Prosser, www.GhostVillage.com

Alhazred
"[For any reader] who appreciates Lovecraft's mythos, this homage to his work is a respectful tribute as well as an entertaining novel with a good mix of adventure and horror. —www.MorbidOutlook.com

Necronomicon Tarot
"Anne Stokes has done an excellent job of bringing together the essence of H.P. Lovecraft's work, along with the storyline presented by Donald Tyson, into a stunning deck."—Aeclectic Tarot, www.Aeclectic.net

"[Necronomicon Tarot] is most pleasantly creepy, and Lovecraft would have loved it." Colin Wilson, co-author of *The Necronomicon: The Book of Dead Names*

Portable Magic
"This is a refreshing change from deck-specific tarot guides or those which assume lots of room to lay out cards or lots of time to interpret results, and will attract any Wiccan with a small space and little time."—*Midwest Book Review*

Enochian Magic for Beginners
"[This is] a must read for anyone interested in the origins of our modern day practices . . . a valuable first study and basic reference book on the Magic of the Angels."—The Wiccan/Pagan Times, www.twpt.com

About the Author

Donald Tyson is a resident of Nova Scotia, Canada. After graduating university, he developed an interest in the tarot, which led him to study all branches of the Western esoteric tradition. His first book, *The New Magus*, was published in 1988. He has written about such varied subjects as the runes, crystal and mirror scrying, astral travel, spirit evocation, spirit familiars, the theory of magic, the Kabbalah, and the *Necronomicon*. He designed the popular *Necronomicon Tarot* card deck, illustrated by Anne Stokes, and is the inventor of rune dice. In his spare time he enjoys hiking, kayaking, and woodworking.

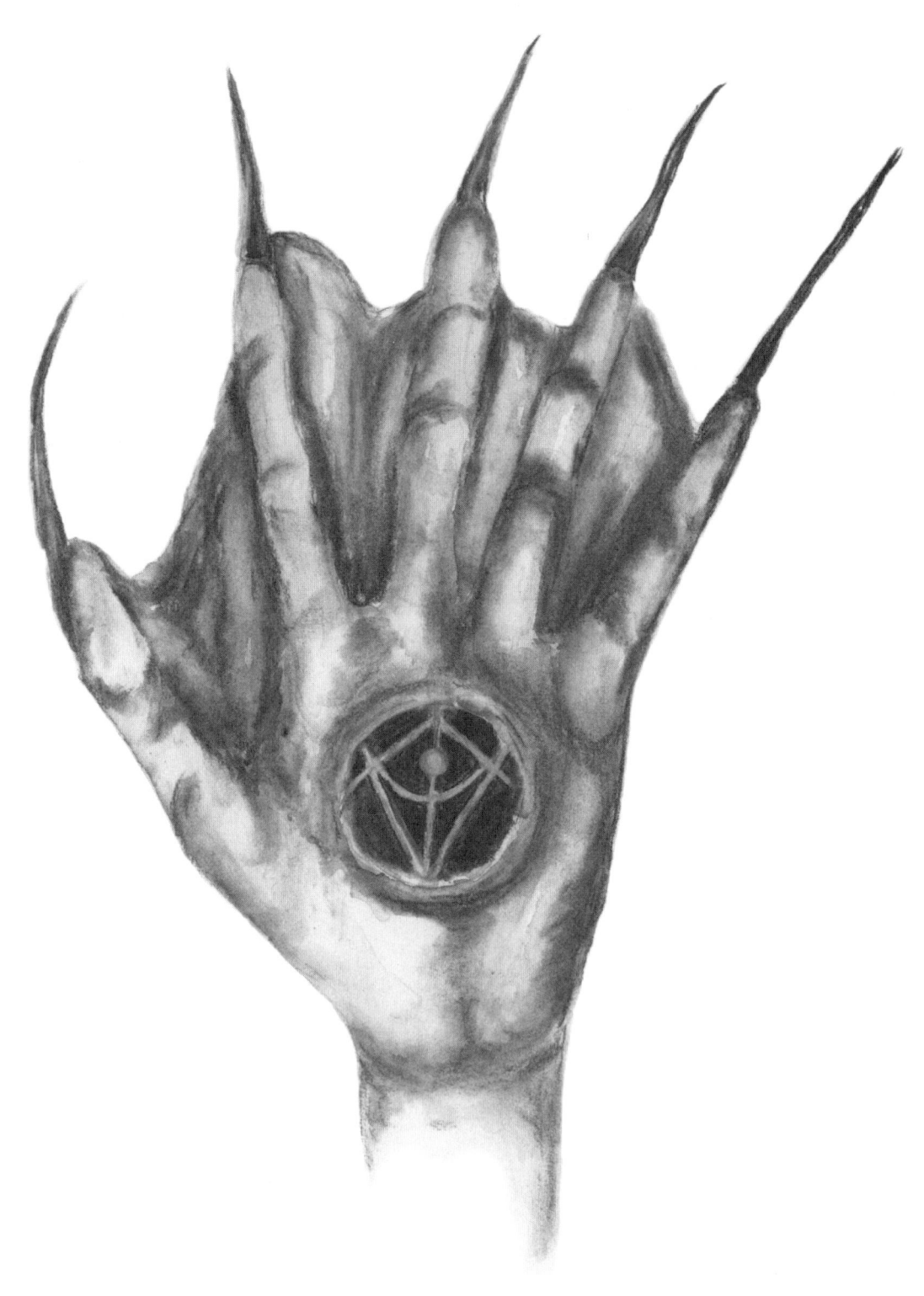

the 13 gates of the Necronomicon

Donald Tyson

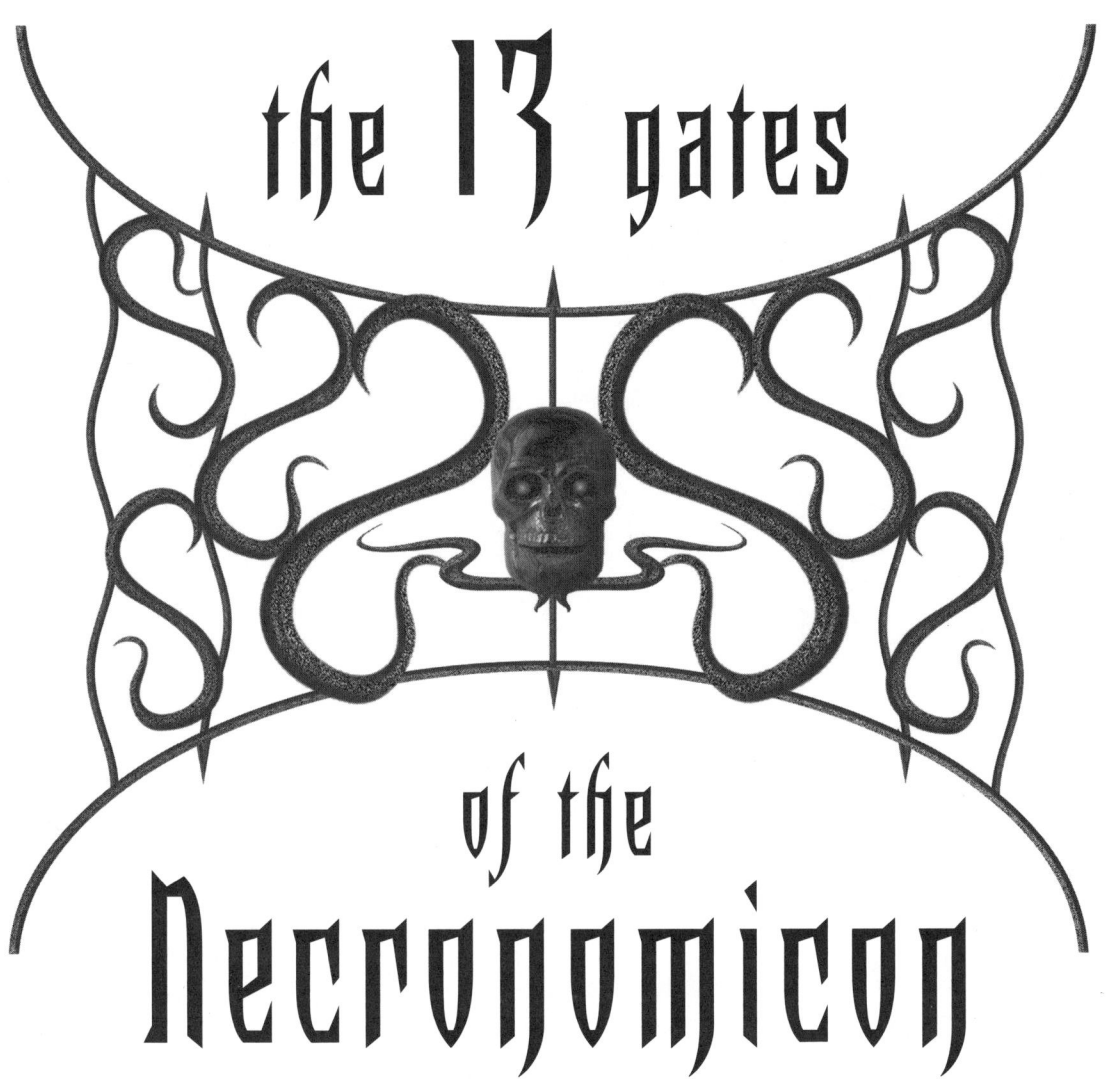

A Workbook of Magic

Llewellyn Publications
Woodbury, Minnesota

The 13 Gates of the Necronomicon: A Workbook of Magic © 2010 by Donald Tyson. All rights reserved. No part of this book may be used or reproduced in any manner whatsoever, including Internet usage, without written permission from Llewellyn Worldwide Ltd., except in the case of brief quotations embodied in critical articles and reviews.

First Edition
First Printing, 2010

Book design by Donna Burch
Cover art: Background clouds © iStockphoto.com/Borut Trdina
Cover design by Kevin R. Brown
Editing by Tom Bilstad
Interior illustrations on pages 16, 40, 44, 102, 106, 144, 148, 168, 172, 212, 216, 226, 230, 248, 252, 264, 268, 292, 296, 310, 314, 340, 344, 360, 364, 380 © Jenny Tyson, and interior illustrations on pages 8, 15, 42, 104, 146, 170, 214, 228, 250, 266, 294, 312, 342, 362, 382 © Donald Tyson

Llewellyn is a registered trademark of Llewellyn Worldwide Ltd.

Library of Congress Cataloging-in-Publication Data.
Tyson, Donald, 1954–
  The 13 gates of the Necronomicon : a workbook of magic / Donald Tyson.—1st ed.
     p. cm.
  Includes bibliographical references (p.   ) and index.
  ISBN 978-0-7387-2121-7
  1. Lovecraft, H. P. (Howard Phillips), 1890-1937. 2. Necronomicon (Imaginary book) I. Title. II. Title: Thirteen gates of the Necronomicon.
  PS3523.O833Z877 2010
  813'.52—dc22   2010010537

Llewellyn Worldwide Ltd. does not participate in, endorse, or have any authority or responsibility concerning private business transactions between our authors and the public.

All mail addressed to the author is forwarded but the publisher cannot, unless specifically instructed by the author, give out an address or phone number.

Any Internet references contained in this work are current at publication time, but the publisher cannot guarantee that a specific location will continue to be maintained. Please refer to the publisher's website for links to authors' websites and other sources.

Llewellyn Publications
A Division of Llewellyn Worldwide Ltd.
2143 Wooddale Drive
Woodbury, Minnesota 55125-2989
www.llewellyn.com

Printed in the United States of America

Other Books by Donald Tyson

The Messenger
(Llewellyn January 1990)

Ritual Magic: What It Is & How To Do It
(Llewellyn January 1992)

Three Books of Occult Philosophy
(Llewellyn January 1992)

Scrying For Beginners
(Llewellyn February 1997)

Enochian Magic for Beginners: The Original System of Angel Magic
(Llewellyn September 2002)

Familiar Spirits: A Practical Guide for Witches & Magicians
(Llewellyn January 2004)

The Power of the Word: The Secret Code of Creation
(Llewellyn March 2004)

1-2-3 Tarot: Answers In An Instant
(Llewellyn October 2004)

Necronomicon: The Wanderings of Alhazred
(Llewellyn December 2004)

Alhazred: Author of the Necronomicon
(Llewellyn July 2006)

Portable Magic: Tarot Is the Only Tool You Need
(Llewellyn October 2006)

Soul Flight: Astral Projection and the Magical Universe
(Llewellyn March 2007)

Grimoire of the Necronomicon
(Llewellyn August 2008)

Runic Astrology
(Llewellyn 2009)

The Fourth Book of Occult Philosophy
(Llewellyn 2009)

Acknowledgement

The hand-painted grayscale illustrations in this book were created by my wife, Jenny, who is a better graphic artist than I am. They were done according to my specifications, so please direct any praise to her, and any blame to me. The black-and-white line drawings are my own work.

Contents

Introduction . . . 1

Eastern Gates: Persons

First Gate: The Great Races . . . 17
Second Gate: Unique Personalities . . . 45
Third Gate: Gods and Devils . . . 107
Fourth Gate: Monsters . . . 149

Southern Gates: Places

Fifth Gate: Human Habitations . . . 173
Sixth Gate: Alien Dwellings . . . 217
Seventh Gate: The Dreamlands . . . 231
Eighth Gate: Other Worlds . . . 253

Western Gates: Things

Ninth Gate: Books . . . 269
Tenth Gate: Talismans . . . 297
Eleventh Gate: Oddities . . . 315
Twelfth Gate: Abominations . . . 345

Northern Gate: Sorceries

Thirteenth Gate: Rites and Incantations . . . 365

Mythos Works by Lovecraft . . . 385
Bibliography . . . 403
Index . . . 405

Introduction
The City of the Book

*"For he who passes the gateways always wins a shadow,
and never again can he be alone."*
—H. P. Lovecraft, *The Book*

The unique mythology created by the American writer of horror fiction, Howard Phillips Lovecraft (1890–1937) will in this work be referred to as the Necronomicon mythos. The more common title, the Cthulhu mythos, is inaccurate since Cthulhu is not the central figure of the tales, nor does he represent all aspects of the mythos. Lovecraft intertwined four thematic threads in his stories, only one of which directly concerns Cthulhu. However, the *Necronomicon* book touches upon all four of them. These threads cannot be easily separated since they cross over at various points like a woven fabric, but they can be distinguished.

Four Threads of the Mythos

One thread, of which Cthulhu is a part, concerns alien races from distant star systems or other dimensions of space and time that contested with each other for the rule of the primordial Earth long before the evolution of mankind. They still wait in secret places for the stars to "come right" in the heavens so that they can emerge and displace us as masters of this world. These beings are not evil. They are merely aloof from the concerns of humanity. They regard us as we might regard a species of bacteria.

Another mythic thread involves ancient sorceries, demons, witches, and the dark doings of magicians. Even though Lovecraft himself claimed to have contempt for occultism and a disinterest in religion, he was inherently mystical in his thinking. His stories are filled with references to witchcraft and black magic. Lovecraft looked upon magic as a kind of alien science. A handful of human beings were capable of manipulating it, but could never truly understand it, and if they tried, they usually went insane.

The author of the *Necronomicon*, Abdul Alhazred, was characterized by Lovecraft as the mad Arab poet of Yemen—but whether his study of magic drove him mad, or whether his madness enabled his grasp of occult secrets hidden from sane men, is not made clear.

Another thread of the mythos is concerned with the exploration of the dreamlands by dream travelers—those who remain conscious and aware while dreaming. Today, this is known as lucid dreaming, and is generally accepted as a real phenomenon. In Lovecraft's time lucid dreaming was not widely recognized. Lovecraft wrote about men who consciously explore the mysterious and dangerous lands of their dreams in the same way that waking men embarked on expeditions to distant and unknown regions of the Earth. More powerful dreamers can go further into the dreamlands, and can learn arcane secrets available through no other source, for the dreamlands hold much lore of both men and alien races that has been lost to the material world over the centuries through neglect, decay, fires, wars and geological upheavals.

The final thread of the mythos is a dark one occupied with death, decay, corruption, the grave, ghouls, and the reanimation of the dead. These subjects fascinated Lovecraft to the point of obsession. By writing about them, he exorcised them from his own nightmares. Both his father and his mother had gone insane, and ended their days locked up in an asylum. Lovecraft always dreaded the possibility that his own mind, so strangely unlike the minds of other men, would eventually fall prey to this hereditary weakness. Related to his dread of madness was a horror of genetic degeneration from inbreeding, or breeding with things not quite human, resulting in deformity, idiocy, and even cannibalism. Lovecraft suffered from the neurotic conviction that his own face was hideously deformed, a fixation instilled into him at a young age by his mother. This caused him to avoid the daylight and crowds, and instead wander the streets of his native Providence late at night and linger alone in graveyards. He was fascinated with the past, with graves and monuments, and with old buildings, and half-believed himself the reincarnation of an Englishman from the eighteenth century.

Magic and the Mythos

There are many ways to approach this strange and often frightening mythological universe. It is possible to read all of Lovecraft's stories and poems for the details and hints of lore they contain. More prosaic minds might prefer to study the shelves of books of literary criticism that delve analytically into the artistic merit and psychological meaning of Lovecraft's fiction. Another avenue to understanding lies in the history of Lovecraft's personal life and his interactions with other fantasy writers of his period, expounded in such exhaustive detail in Lovecraft's thousands of letters and in his numerous biographies. Yet another approach is through role-playing games set within the Lovecraft mythos. Finally, there are those who choose to employ Lovecraft's writings as the basis for a system of practical magic, and as the foundation for a new religion.

The use of Lovecraft's story elements to compose a workable and coherent system of modern ritual magic is of comparatively recent vintage. Kenneth Grant, the leader of one branch of the Ordo Templi Orientis, may be regarded as one of the godfathers of this curious child of the mythos. In 1994 he published the book *The Outer Gateways*, which examines the Lovecraft mythos in a serious way as the partial basis for a new system of esoteric belief and practice. On the first page of the first chapter of the book, he made this bold statement: "Said to have been written by a mad Arab named Al Hazred, the Necronomicon actually exists on a plane accessible to those who either consciously like Crowley, or unconsciously like Lovecraft have succeeded in penetrating it."

Grant suffered a good deal of derision and criticism for asserting the reality of the *Necronomicon*. He is regarded as a serious occultist, and his ideas about Lovecraft's mythos caused him to lose credibility in some quarters. However, in retrospect it was inevitable that sooner or later Lovecraft's mythos would catch the attention of Western magicians. It is pregnant with meaning on all levels, and provides a cohesive set of gods and devils that are in many ways surprisingly modern. The Old Ones are beings that dwell in the spaces between the stars, and who travel through the aether of space, or through dimensional portals between worlds. They have much in common with the modern mythology of UFOs, which supposes that the Earth was visited in the past, and continues to be observed, by beings from other worlds who remain in the shadows, but who sometimes abduct human beings for study, or transport them to their worlds for instruction. Almost a century ago Lovecraft wrote much the same thing about the races he called the Mi-Go and the Yithians.

Those who claim to be abducted by UFOs sometimes vanish through portals, or are lifted up on beams of light into disk-shaped ships, just as in the Bible the Old Testament prophets were said to be lifted and carried through the sky to other dimensions of reality by whirlwinds or strange chariots of fire. The aliens subject those they abduct to scientific tests, probing them in a clinically dispassionate way as a human scientist might probe a white lab rat. The terror of the abductees does not touch the emotions of the aliens, who seem devoid of compassion. Similarly, Lovecraft's Old Ones are indifferent to the needs or fears of human beings. They use them for various purposes when humans are able to provide useful services, but just as casually discard them when they prove troublesome.

Another feature of the spontaneous modern mythology of UFO visitations and abductions is the use of human women to breed a race of hybrid children, who share genetic components from both species, and who possess physical characteristics both human and alien. This is a very ancient myth. Demons were said in early Christian lore to visit women in their beds and impregnate them, so that the women gave birth to monsters. Even earlier than this, the ancient Greeks and Egyptians believed that the gods sometimes engendered children on mortal women, and in the Book of Enoch mention is made of the Watchers who lusted after mortal women and who descended to Earth to take them as wives.

The same theme of human-alien hybrids recurs in Lovecraft's mythos. The Old Ones impregnate mortal women to breed hybrids that they can employ as their agents on the earth. The Deep Ones seek to breed children with the men and women of the town of Innsmouth, whom they take in marriage. Why they need these hybrids is not clear, but it may be speculated that they are required to reinvigorate the genetic material of the Deep Ones, to prevent it falling into decadence and decay.

These similarities between Lovecraft's mythos and the spontaneous modern mythology of UFOs serve to illustrate that Lovecraft's fiction contains material of deep significance on the subconscious level that may be employed for various purposes, among them religious worship and practical magic. Lovecraft, through his dreams, tapped into a wellspring of meaning, which he cloaked in terms of interactions between humanity and dwellers in the depths—not only the depths of the oceans and the earth, but the depths of space and time, the depths of other dimensions of reality. The true depths tapped into by Lovecraft were those of the subconscious mind.

The Necronomicon

Lovecraft's universe is epitomized in his greatest creation, the dreaded *Necronomicon*, a book of the dead that the modern world refuses to let die. The *Necronomicon* is the beating heart of the mythos, and to study the book is to study the mythos. The *Necronomicon* is neither wholly fiction nor wholly real, but an uncanny merging of truth and fantasy that is almost impossible for the mind to capture or express, since the boundaries that define it continue to evolve. No one can say exactly what the *Necronomicon* contains. It is a history of the ages on Earth before the rise of mankind. It is the xenobiology of alien races from beyond the stars. It is a textbook of arcane chemistry. It is a grimoire of the necromantic arts. It is poetry, it is philosophy, it is the blasphemous bible of Lovecraft's demon-haunted world.

Those who would dismiss the *Necronomicon* as no more than a fictional device created by Lovecraft on the spur of the moment to serve as window-dressing for his fantasies have failed to consider the history of this book of the dead that refuses to die. Why would individuals have taken it upon themselves to enter its title in the card catalogs of major world libraries and in the lists of rare book dealers and auction houses? As a mere joke? Perhaps that is what they told themselves at the time, unaware that they served as the instruments of a higher purpose.

What is true of the *Necronomicon* is equally true of the Old Ones, the race of gods from alien stars that ruled this planet for aeons before human beings stood erect and learned to fear them. The Old Ones are dismissed by cynics as no more than a fantasy of Lovecraft's, yet they continue to resonate with undiminished power in the human psyche more than seven decades after the death of their creator. Did Lovecraft really create the Old Ones, or did he merely glimpse them moving through the terrifying caverns and sea depths of his nightmares? Was the *Necronomicon* a fantasy, or the echo of a book that stands on the shelves of libraries not of this world?

There are many who believe that Lovecraft was a sleeping prophet who traveled between dimensions and across the gulfs of space and time in his dreams. Lovecraft himself mentions in numerous letters that he drew upon his dreams for the subjects of his stories. The very name "Necronomicon" was not invented by Lovecraft, but was heard by him in a dream. Its philological structure has defied analysis, leading to dozens of different interpretations, but it carries an undeniable resonance in the mind, as do many of the topics of Lovecraft's stories.

It may be that Lovecraft's lost cities and alien worlds exist, as does the *Necronomicon* itself, slightly out of phase with our mundane reality, yet accessible by sensitive minds in dreams, where the boundaries between dimensions are crossed. For Lovecraft, dreams were more real than reality. He wrote himself into several of his stories in the character of Randolph Carter, an explorer of dreams who possessed the ability to remain self-aware and travel where he desired. There seems little doubt that Lovecraft was engaged in unconscious astral projection, and that many of his vivid dreams represented travel across the astral planes.

The *Necronomicon* has astral reality. So do the Old Ones and their horrifying broods and servants, and the other races that ruled the Earth in its infancy. Whether Lovecraft perceived an existing reality and recorded it in his stories, or whether the power of his stories resonating in millions of human minds created the astral reality, is a chicken-and-egg puzzle that may never be solved. I suspect it is both—that the Old Ones and the *Necronomicon* existed in some form on the astral level before Lovecraft wrote them down, but that by capturing the popular imaginations of millions, Lovecraft was able to bring them more firmly into our local astral environment, where they presently subsist, so close to our physical reality that it is almost possible to reach out and touch them.

One of the purposes of this book is to gather the essential elements of Lovecraft's mythos that lend themselves to use in practical esoteric ways such as dream scrying, astral projection, and spirit communication. It is not a grimoire of mythos magic. Those looking for a grimoire will find it in my *Necronomicon Grimoire* (Llewellyn, 2008). The present book is a compendium of source material upon which such a system of magic can be built by those who wish to construct it. The material gathered here is the matrix for the *Necronomicon*, which existed only on the astral level until Lovecraft scried its name in his dream travels and recorded a description of it and a scattering of its contents in his fiction.

It is so simplistic to state that the *Necronomicon* does not exist. Of course it does not exist in the same way that the book *Moby Dick* exists. It was never copied onto parchment or printed on paper prior to Lovecraft's description of it. Yet to say that it does not exist accomplishes nothing. It ignores the continuing power and presence of the book, which only grows stronger with each year that passes. Does beauty exist? Does a mathematical theory exist? Does God exist? Existence is so much more than mere corporeal presence.

Real or Unreal?

It is not my desire to mislead readers as to the reality of fictional persons, places, or things—or at least, no more my desire than it was that of Lovecraft, who wrote of nonexistent books as though they could be borrowed from the local university library, and mythical towns as though they might be visited by bus. In my examination of these topics, I also treat them as real, since it becomes tiresome to constantly remind readers that they are invented. They are real within the context of Lovecraft's world, a world that has more substance on the astral planes than most imagine.

To avoid the confusion that invariably arises when Lovecraft's creations are discussed, some writers divide mythos topics into the categories "real" and "fictional." At first consideration this seems like a useful division, but it has significant limitations. Many of the fictional matters treated by Lovecraft are real, in the sense that they exist in the larger world, even though they are fictional in nature. The gods of ancient Greece are a good example. They are real in the sense that Lovecraft did not dream them from nothingness, but they are fictional in the sense that they are not corporeal beings.

Many of the books mentioned by Lovecraft are actual published works, but Lovecraft's references to them may be completely fanciful, and may have nothing to do with their contents. Should they be classed as real or fictional? For example, Lovecraft refers to the *Book of Dzyan*, which is part of the lore of Theosophy. Madame Blavatsky, the leader of the Theosophical movement, claimed to have read the ancient and lost *Book of Dzyan*, and pretended that she had published stanzas from this work in her own book *The Secret Doctrine*. As it happens, Blavatsky invented the *Book of Dzyan* just as surely as Lovecraft invented the *Necronomicon*—or perhaps, just as surely did not invent it, as Lovecraft did not invent the *Necronomicon*. Blavatsky claimed the ability to read books stored in the great astral library known as the akashic records. It was very likely here that she studied the *Book of Dzyan*. Similarly, Lovecraft did not so much invent the *Necronomicon* as dream it into existence, and for Lovecraft dreams were very real.

Lovecraft's brief references to the *Book of Dzyan* have nothing to do with the actual stanzas published by Blavatsky. Should the *Book of Dzyan* be classed as fictional or real? Blavatsky claimed it to be a real work. Certainly, a portion of it exists in her *Secret Doctrine*, so it is real in the sense that it has been published. It was regarded as real enough by Theosophists. Yet most scholars agree that the *Book of Dzyan* had no existence of any material kind before Blavatsky wrote about it.

Similar confusion might arise concerning the categorization of literary inventions of other writers borrowed by Lovecraft for inclusion in his Necronomicon mythos. For example, the Yellow Sign is a symbol or letter of dire portent described by the writer Robert W. Chambers in his short story of the same name. Lovecraft mentioned it, making it a part of his mythos. It might be marked as "real" because it was not invented by Lovecraft, but was taken by him from the greater world he inhabited. Yet it is not a real thing in the sense of something tangible or extant.

The gods mentioned by Lovecraft that exist in the mythologies of ancient Greece are real to those who worship them, even though most people of more prosaic minds might be inclined to dismiss them as imaginary. Yet are they any less real than Christ or Krishna? Whether God and the Devil are treated as real or imaginary depends on one's point of view. To a believer they are real; to an atheist they are fiction.

It seems to me that a more useful division of the contents of the Necronomicon mythos, for the purpose of minimizing confusion regarding the sources of the material, is to mark items as either Lovecraft's invention, or otherwise. Since most of the material is from Lovecraft fertile dreaming mind, it is sufficient to mark the material not of Lovecraft's invention with an asterisk (*) after the title, and to explain its source in the text. The asterisk merely indicates that the topic, or part of the topic, has existence beyond Lovecraft's invention—it does not signify that the topic is real in the usual materialistic sense.

The Gates and the Keys

For the purpose of exploration, the *Necronomicon* may be conceived as a walled Arabian city with many gates of entry. The pages of the book are its streets and buildings and marketplaces. Its inhabitants comprise the entire Necronomicon mythos as expressed in Lovecraft's stories and poems. We know the city is walled because of the mystery that shrouds the book. Its walls conceal what lies inside. To learn the byways of the city of the *Necronomicon*, we must enter into it through its gates, and to open the gates we must possess their keys.

It is of practical advantage to limit the gates of the city to a manageable number. Each gate is a unique avenue of approach that opens on a different section of the metropolis, some filled with palaces and noble houses, others having open vistas and green spaces, and yet others sustaining murky ghettos where it is dangerous to wander alone. The city is square, each of its four walls facing a different direction of the compass, each wall with its unique qualities that are expressed by its gates. Why square? Because it is our purpose to bring the astral *Necronomicon* down to our everyday reality so that we may delve into its mysteries, which are the wonders of Lovecraft's mythic universe. The square is the most material of geometric shapes. The city of the book is a kind of mandala that may be entered during ritual meditation. Graphically represented, it somewhat resembles a modern circuit diagram.

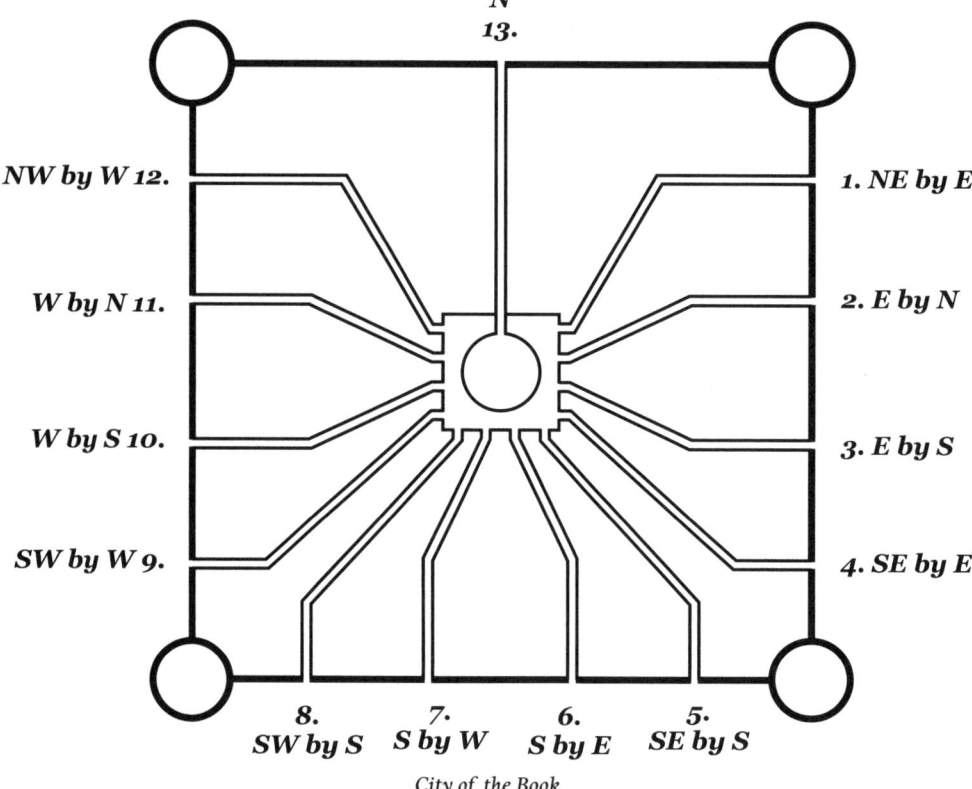

City of the Book

The layout of the gates is simple enough to describe. Each of the three walls that face east, south, and west has four gates. The gates of the eastern wall open on the topic of persons, both individual creatures and races of beings. They admit the traveler to the habitations and meeting halls of the city. The gates of the southern wall give access to those areas of the city that concern places, both of this Earth and beyond its boundaries.

They admit the traveler to the streets, public gardens, alleys, and catacombs. The gates of the western wall open on all manner of things both precious and noxious. They admit the traveler to the shops and marketplaces of the city. The northern wall has but a single gate in its center, the thirteenth gate of the city of the book. It gives entry upon a walled central garden in which take place all the rites and ceremonies of religion and magic, initiating travelers bold enough to use this lonely gate into the public rites of worship and the secret sorceries of necromancy and other forms of wizardry.

The illustrations of the gates that accompany the sections of the book are each distinctive and unique, so that during the rituals of opening the gates they may be more easily visualized and sustained in the mind on the astral level. For the same reason, the keys that open the gates are distinctively styled, so that each may be associated with its gate without confusion.

The Astral Gates

The city of the book is a construct of the imagination. It is difficult to manipulate a thing that exists purely on the mental level, where it remains uncontained and protean. For this reason it is useful to employ correspondences to the thirteen gates of the walled city that exist in the physical universe. As the great Hermetic maxim tells us, *What is below is like to what is above; and what is above is like to what is below: to accomplish the miracle of the One Thing.* Manipulation of the lower affects the higher; study of the higher reveals the lower.

There are thirteen zodiacal constellations that were recognized by the ancient Greeks—a zodiacal constellation is a constellation through which the sun passes in its apparent yearly circuit of the heavens. This may come as a surprise to those who have assumed, based on their understanding of astrology, that the zodiac consists of twelve constellations. In classical astrology, two of the thirteen, Scorpius and Ophiuchus, were combined into one under the name Scorpius, and each of the resulting twelve was nominally given an arc of the zodiac of exactly thirty degrees. In this way, the perfect order and harmony of Greek philosophy was imposed on the intuited chaos of the night sky.

It is convenient in astrology to reduce the number of zodiacal constellations to twelve, and give them zones of equal length. Indeed, the division of the band of the zodiac into twelve equal parts was made by the Babylonians a thousand years before the time of Christ. But like the perfect circle of Euclidian geometry, this division is artificial. You may raise the objection that the thirteen constellations themselves are artificial, imposed on the random pattern of the stars by the human propensity to find order in chaos. True enough, but this ordered chaos of thirteen irregular forms reflects an intuited level of perception that is more primal, and hence more potent, than the intellectual conceit that imposed on the heavens, by decree, an equal division of twelve zodiacal signs. The number thirteen is not arbitrary, but is integral to the yearly cycle. It should be noted that there are thirteen sidereal lunations in the course of a year.

The rituals of the thirteen constellations described at the end of each section in this book are not about astronomy or astrology, and no knowledge of these subjects is needed to work them. They are about opening astral gateways in the heavens, so that by occult sympathy the corresponding gateways of understanding are unlocked in the city of the Necronomicon, which is itself an astral construct. It is no accident that the term "astral" is based on the Latin *astrum*, meaning "star." The definition of astral is "of or from the stars." Astral archetypes are framed and delineated by the constellations and their brightest stars.

Most of Lovecraft's Old Ones came from the stars, but not from the common stars of our physical universe. Their origins were described as lying beyond the bounds of our universe, or as the places between the stars. It should be obvious to anyone who considers the matter that the Old Ones do not exist physically, in our material world. They would long since have been discovered by modern science were their bodies corporeal. No, the Old Ones are astral entities, and if they are to be communicated with, it must be through astral portals.

Men walk the streets of cities, but the gods dwell in splendor amid the stars. The night sky is a kind of black mirror into which it is possible to scry reflected aspects of the deep mind that hide below the level of conscious thought. The thirteen zodiacal constellations perceived in the heavens by the ancients are higher spiritual doorways that mirror the depths of the racial subconscious—what Carl Jung termed the collective unconscious, wherein lies concealed the city of the book. The stars in the night sky are used in these rituals to open the lower, more tangible gateways of the city, so that individual human awareness can pass therein.

The Fixed Stars

The Arabs, and the Persians before them, and the Babylonians before them, studied the natures of the fixed stars and attributed to each a unique identity and power over the Earth, which it was believed to exert through the rays of light it emanates. The fixed stars formed a significant part of Arab astrology, but modern astrology tends to discount and ignore their influence, perhaps because so many of the stars have unfortunate associations. Each constellation has a small number of relatively bright fixed stars that define its outline and parts. The brightest stars in each constellation represent, in a symbolic way, its active forces—the star of the feet its motion, the star of the head its mind, the star of the heart its strength, the stars of its appendages its power, and so on. Some stars are considered benevolent and beneficial, whereas others are regarded as malevolent and harmful.

In the rituals of the thirteen gates that follow each section of the book, two of the brightest stars in each constellation form the pillars or gateposts of its gateway. These two gateway stars of each constellation echo the myth of the two pillars that went before the Ark of the Covenant as it was carried across the desert by Moses and the Israelites, the pillar by day a column of smoke and the pillar by night a flaming column of fire (see Exodus 13:21). When Solomon erected the Temple to house the Ark at Jerusalem, he place two bronze pillars at its entrance in memory of these two spiritual pillars of the desert, the angels of God (First Kings 7:15). The right pillar was called Jachin ("he shall establish"), and the left pillar of the Temple was named Boaz ("in it is strength"). These pillars did not support any part of the Temple, but existed for one reason only—to open an occult gateway into the sacred space of the Holy of Holies by defining the limits of that gateway.

The gates are the thirteen images in the heavens crossed by the sun, and the pillars of those gates are the stars. In an occult sense, the gateway stars of a zodiacal constellation show the place where an aperture through the constellation can exist. They define the edges of its potential being. No gateway can come into being unless its limits are fixed. The ritual opens the higher celestial gate by means of the key provided. Meditation upon the nature of the key yields entry through the corresponding gateway in the lower astral realm of the walled city of the book. A resonance is created between the pattern of the fixed stars and the parts of the city. By projecting attention outwardly, access is gained within to the secret center. As above, so below. The constellations are archetypal concepts that resonate in the deep mind with great power for transformation.

If this course of study appears Byzantine in its conception, surely that is appropriate when dealing with a book supposed to have been written in the early part of the eighth century, a book that exists only in dreams and astral visions. I will be your guide and keeper of the keys as we visit in turn each of the gates of the dream city of the *Necronomicon*, following the course of the Sun through the year to the final solitary gate in the north. The Sun moves slowly against the backdrop of the stars from west to east, occupying each constellation and each astral gate for a unique duration of time. No two periods of occupation are exactly the same, although in this work they have been rounded to the nearest day. This differing duration of the solar passage helps define the uniqueness of each constellation and each gate. The actual dates of entry and exit vary slightly from year to year, and those given here should be understood as approximations.

The open source astronomy computer program Stellarium was used to determine the beginning and end dates for each gateway—when the Sun crosses the celestial longitudes of its right and left pillar stars. This program, or one like it, will also be found useful for determining the days and hours when the Moon occupies each gateway. The selection of stars for the pillars is based upon several criteria. One, the thirteen gateways must not overlap—the Sun can only occupy one gate at a time. Two, the stars must be named stars familiar to the ancient Greeks and Persians, each with a history of its own that gives it a unique identity. Three, they must be prominent stars readily visible to the naked eye in the night sky. Where possible, I have selected the brightest stars in each constellation for its gate pillars, but this was not always possible due to other conflicting factors. For example, sometimes the brightest stars are too close together in longitude to form a workable gate. Sometimes they overlap the longitude of the gates of other constellations.

Opening the Gates

We will begin at the northern corner of the eastern wall of the city with the constellation that marks the winter solstice, and will explore each important theme of the book in turn. The four keys of the east open upon the great alien races, the individual personalities, the gods and demons, and the misshapen monstrosities. The four keys of the south lead us inward upon the human landscapes, the alien realms, the dreamlands, and the worlds beyond this Earth. The four keys of the western gates open the ways to occult books, magic objects, curiosities, and abominations of the city. Entry through the lonely and dark northern gate allows us to reach the hidden garden at the center of the city, and experience the magical methods of the *Necronomicon*.

I have designed each key in a unique way, utilizing my power glyph system of occult symbols (see my book *Familiar Spirits* for a fuller explanation of the glyphs) to create a potent seal of entry for each of the thirteen gates. It is not necessary to understand the construction of the keys in order to use them effectively, but anyone familiar with my power glyph system will have little difficulty in tracing the manner by which the seals of the keys were composed. For the sake of those unfamiliar with the way in which the seals are made, who may have difficulty tracing their shape on the images of the keys, I have given the basic pattern for each seal in its ritual in the form of a graphic that shows the seal on the gate between the star pillars of that constellation. A chart showing the individual power glyphs is provided for reference at the end of this introduction.

It is useful to open the gates at a time or in a place of transition. For example, on the shore of the ocean or margin of a lake where water meets land; at a crossroads where one road meets another; in a doorway between rooms, or upon a threshold between inside and outside; in a hallway or entrance chamber that leads from one place to another. Times of transition include such times as at twilight when night gives way to day or day gives way to night; at midnight where one day becomes another; on the solstices or equinoxes of the year; on the last or first day of the month. It is not essential that the ritual be done at a time or in a place of transition, but it is conducive to its success. When no natural threshold exists, an artificial threshold can be created by the symbolic erection of gateway pillars.

To gain access through a gate following the ritual of its opening, the image of the gate should be visualized, and then built up in the imagination until it has a near-tangible presence. Bear in mind that the images of the gates that appear in this book are merely representations of the true gates of the astral city of the book. Your conception of the gates must be more detailed and more tangible. As you meditate upon the gates you will begin to see them with increasing clarity. The seal upon each key is to be traced upon the surface of its gate in a line of flickering white fire, using the key in the imagination as an astral wand, and the gate should be visualized in the imagination to open inward, allowing the astral traveler to pass through—for ritual entry into the city of the book is a form of astral projection.

A gate allows passage both in and out. The seals of the gates may be used as locks upon their portals to prevent the escape of the city's inhabitants. Even those gates that concern zones of the city related to places or things have numerous spiritual beings dwelling within who may seek to explore our world, just as we seek to explore the world of the mythos. It is better to seal the gates after leaving the city of the book. This may easily be done by looking at the image of the gate, imagining it to close, and then tracing in the mind the seal of the key on the surface of its gate. A key by its nature both unlocks and locks, so the same seal serves for both functions.

Such precautious are not necessary when merely reading this text with the conscious awareness, since at such times the passage through the gates is purely intellectual, consisting of ideas without tangible astral substance. Should the reader find that his or her mind drifts, and that an abstracted, daydreaming condition occurs repeatedly while reading this book, it would be a useful precaution to deliberately seal the gate after exiting the city, by deliberately closing the gate in the imagination and tracing the sigil of its key on its outer surface. A word to the wise is sufficient in these matters. The *Necronomicon* and the mythos it represents are not without their potency in the receptive mind. Any traveler passing through a strange city in a foreign land must remain watchful of its byways and turnings.

Those impatient to open a gate, and unwilling to wait for the Sun to enter it, may use the entry of the Moon for the same purpose. The Moon makes one complete circuit of the heavens against the backdrop of the stars (sidereal lunation) in approximately twenty-seven days, crossing all thirteen astral gates. The ritual of opening a gate may be worked while the Moon occupies that gate, or less effectively when the Moon occupies the constellation of that gate, but bear in mind that the Moon and the Sun are quite different in their natures. The Moon rules dreams, visions, and illusions. Working a ritual of opening while the Moon passes within a gate is especially effective when seeking a prophetic dream or a dream vision associated with the nature of the key used to open that gate.

The phase the Moon while passing through a gate, whether it be waxing, waning, or full, has a bearing on the general quality of the results that are likely to be obtained. The best result is obtained when the gate is occupied by the full Moon, or the waxing Moon. The waning Moon is less trustworthy. When the Moon is new, it is in conjunction with the Sun, and at these times the Sun should be used to open the gate, not the Moon.

The calculation for the location of the Moon in the actual zodiacal constellations (as opposed to the astrological signs of the zodiac) at any given hour is obscure to most of us. Fortunately, the Internet has sites that show the location of the Moon in the constellations in real time. For example, the website "http://heavens-above.com/" gives a sky-map of the constellation that contains the Moon for any given moment. By periodically refreshing this map, the motion of the Moon may be tracked across the constellation. The stars that form the gate of the constellation are labeled with their Greek letters, making it a relatively simple matter to determine when the Moon enters the gate. Probably the easiest way to learn these crossing days and hours for the Moon is by use of an astronomy program such as Stellarium, which can be easily installed on any computer.

Knowledgeable practitioners will divine another function of the gates and their keys—the manipulation of the matter of the *Necronomicon* mythos for the purposes of active practical magic. Such a use of this book is possible for a skilled occultist. Indeed, the system of the thirteen star gates of the actual zodiacal constellations need not be limited to Lovecraft's work, but is versatile enough to be used for general meditations, scryings, divinations, invocations, the making and empowering of charms and amulets, and even for the evocation of gods and spirits, particularly those who make their abodes beyond the planetary spheres amid the stars. Simply by using the power glyphs to creating different keys for specific ritual purposes, the gates may be employed in any form of magic, such as the magic of witchcraft, the Golden Dawn, Thelema, and even Enochian magic.

POWER GLYPHS

A	△	I, J	·	R	◎
B	∞	K	◎◎	S	S
C	∪	L	+	T	↑
D	∩	M	⋀	U, V	▽
E	—	N	◇	W	∿
F	|	O	○	X	⋈
G	⊕	P	◎	Y	⋎
H	□	Q	⊙	Z	⚡

Power Glyphs Chart

The First Gate

First Gate
The Great Races

The Necronomicon mythos is predicated on the assumption that the universe teams with alien forms of life, many of them intelligent yet some of them evolutionarily so far removed from the biological life that inhabits the surface of the Earth and its seas that we are scarcely able to recognize them as living beings. Aeons before the creation of humanity by the crinoid beings known as the Elder Race, our planet was populated by other alien species that had descended to its surface through space from distant star systems, or through dimensional gateways opened in the very fabric of space-time itself. These alien species built their cities and fought their wars with each other long before humans discovered the use of fire.

Over the vast expanse of geological history these species diminished in potency and prominence. The Elder Race was beaten back by warfare to its first colony in Antarctica, and suffered to see its mighty city sealed beneath the ice of an advancing glacier before retreating to a deep sea-filled cavern. The invisible Old Ones retreated from a malign alignment of the stars in the heavens into the spaces that lie between dimensions, while the related spawn of Cthulhu sought protection by sealing themselves in stone crypts under the surface of the ground, and were subsequently covered by the waters of the Pacific Ocean when their great island of R'lyeh sank beneath the waves.

In spite of these retreats, which left the world in the condition we presently know, the once-dominant alien races continue to maintain a presence on our planet, some beneath the seas, others under the ground, in distant aeons, or from the spaces between the stars. They watch and wait for conditions to change, when the stars will come right, and the Earth will once again be favorable to their natures, so that they can emerge from their places of waiting and resume their roles as masters. They once ruled where we now rule, and as Abdul Alhazred observed in the *Necronomicon*, they will rule again.

Throughout our history, these alien species have been classed as spirits, ghosts, monsters, angels, demons, and gods as humanity struggled to recast them into terms it could understand. Their sciences, so far in advance of anything we have achieved even in our modern age, were regarded as magic. They were by turns worshipped and shunned. The remnants of their cities became places of holy pilgrimage for the cults that adore them, or forbidden zones that none dared enter. Objects left scattered by the passage of their civilizations were cherished as icons of obscure religions, and fragments of their language were remembered in the form of magic chants and ritual observances.

Confusion can arise over Lovecraft's use of the terms "old ones," "elder race," "elder things," and similar terms, even for those well familiar with his writings, because Lovecraft sometimes used the same terms for different species. The Old Ones is a general term employed by characters in Lovecraft's fiction to refer to several alien races that occupy hidden corners of the Earth, or have occupied it in the distant past. It may be useful here to briefly distinguish between them.

Yog-Sothoth, who in *The Dunwich Horror* came through a dimensional gate above Sentinel Hill to breed with the mortal woman Lavinia Whateley for the purpose of producing hybrid offspring that could be multiplied to destroy all life on Earth, was one of an alien race of invisible Old Ones. It is to this race that the term is most commonly applied.

The crinoid race described in the story *At the Mountains of Madness*, which dwelt in a cyclopean lost city on a plateau of Antarctica, were called the Great Old Ones, but were also referred to as Elder Things. In order to distinguish them from the Old Ones of the *Dunwich Horror*, the general convention is to refer to this latter group of Old Ones as Elder Things or the Elder Race, since they were on the Earth prior to the coming of the invisible Old Ones, and hence from the human point of view are older than the Old Ones.

A third race to which the name Old Ones is applied occurs in the story *The Mound*, co-written by Lovecraft with Zealia Bishop. There is no question that the mythological aspects are Lovecraft's contribution. These Old Ones are much like human beings and live under the surface of the ground. They are deathless and do not breed. It is fabled that they came to this planet from the distant stars long ago and were the ancestors of all men.

In the *Whisperer in Darkness*, the name Old Ones is applied to the Mi-Go, an alien race from Yuggoth, the planet we know as Pluto. These elusive creatures are somewhat similar in appearance to crustaceans with pinkish bodies around five feet long, several sets of limbs, and membranous wings. They are composed of the same type of alien substance, so completely unlike ordinary living tissue, that makes up the Old Ones, and also Cthulhu and his spawn.

Lovecraft makes clear that the present conditions upon our world, in which the human race dominates—or appears to dominate—all other forms of life, are anomalous. They cannot and will not long endure. Humanity is living in a kind of bubble of conceit, the illusion of which may burst at any moment, precipitating a reign of horror unknown to us, but of common occurrence on the ancient Earth.

At any time, a geological upheaval may raise mighty Cthulhu from the floor of the Pacific Ocean. The stars may come right at last in the heavens, opening the dimensional gateways of Yog-Sothoth to pour forth the Old Ones into our reality. The Elder Things may choose to leave the protection of their subterranean world and seek the surface once again; or their one-time servants, the shoggoths, may abandon their places of concealment—and if they did, what power of man could stop them? The Mi-Go may return in greater numbers once more to our planet to conquer it, thereby securing access to the ore they cannot obtain on Yuggoth. It may enter the minds of the Deep Ones to conquer and rule the surface of the world, as they presently rule the oceans.

One or more of these various eventualities is not only possible, but regarded by Lovecraft as inevitable. The human race inhabits a kind of dream world that can be destroyed at any time as swiftly and easily as a man kicks apart an anthill. Those who take Lovecraft's visions seriously should regard the threat posed by the return of his fictional races as a metaphor for the very real threat to our continued existence as a species that is posed by the realities that lie behind those fictions. It is certain that in the vastness of space and time, and in the multiplicities of higher dimensions of reality, there exist many strange races of beings who might, at any moment of their choosing, obliterate not only the human species, but all life on this planet, and indeed, the very planet itself.

arachnid race

The ruling intelligent race of our Earth's final period, just prior to its destruction. The time-travelers of Yith sometimes visited their distantly future world.

(*The Shadow Out of Time*)

Ancient Ones

A race or sect of beings which the 'Umr at-Tawil (Most Ancient One) tells Randolph Carter are his "extensions" on Earth.

(*Through the Gates of the Silver Key*)

coleopterous species

The race of highly intelligent beetles that will rule the Earth after the passing away of the human race. The naked minds of the time-spanning Great Race of Yith will seek sanctuary in their forms in our future, after abandoning the rugose cones they inhabited in our distant past.

(*The Shadow Out of Time*)

cone-shaped race

A race of beings that flourished on the Earth from one billion years ago until around fifty million years ago. Their iridescent bodies were shaped like a cone, with a globular head having four eyes and arm-like appendages, two of which ended in prehensile claws. They stood approximately ten feet in height, and were ten feet broad at the base. Their native minds were displaced 600 million years ago by the invading alien minds of the time-spanning Great Race of Yith. In *The Shadow Out of Time*, Nathaniel Wingate Peaslee suffered the same fate, temporarily, and found himself in one of the cone-shaped bodies of the Great Race. He discovered that it was their habit to send forth minds to distant times and places, in order to learn alien sciences. When they did so, the minds of the beings they inhabited were transported into their conical bodies.

(*The Shadow Out of Time; The Challenge From Beyond*)

Elder Race

The Elder Race, Elder Things, or Elder Ones, as they are variously designated by Lovecraft, are formed of normal matter of incredible durability and toughness. This alien species was sometimes referred to by Lovecraft as the Old Ones, but it is very different in nature from the gelatinous, blood-sucking thing in the Whateley farmhouse that is described in *The Dunwich Horror*. Whereas the bodies of the beings who are more usually called the Old Ones are made up of substances not of this world, so that when their hybrid children die they simply evaporate into the air, the flesh of the Elder Race is described in *At the Mountains of Madness* as "leathery, undeteriorative, and almost indestructible." They cannot reshape or reform themselves as can the Old Ones and their kin. A measure of their durability is that a small number of the race lay in a dormant condition, frozen solid for forty million years, yet suffered no serious ill effects after they were revived.

Lovecraft has provided a detailed description of these beings. They stand upright and are eight feet in total length. The central six feet is made up of a barrel-shaped torso with five vertical ridges. Membranous wings seven feet long when extended are folded up between these ridges. Presumable there are five wings, although Lovecraft is not explicit on this point. From the center of each ridge extends a flexible gray tentacle that branches into five stalks, each of which branches into five more slender stalks, so that each tentacle has twenty-five thin fingers. These tentacles serve the creatures as arms and reach to a maximum of three feet from the barrel torso.

On the top of a blunt neck lighter gray in color than the body is a flat head shaped like a starfish. The neck is surrounded by gills. The entire head is covered with wiry cilia three inches in length that are every color of the rainbow. The head is two feet across, with a slit in the top for breathing when out of the water—for these beings are as much at home on land as in the sea. At the end of each of the five points is a short yellow stalk that terminates in a red eye. Between the points of the head extend longer reddish tubes that terminate in mouths that have small white teeth. Its vocal organs are adapted to a language that consists of shrill pipings similar to the notes of a flute.

The anatomy at the base of the barrel torso is similar to that of the head, but serves a different function, that of locomotion. A thick neck light gray in color extends downward from the torso, and terminates in a greenish starfish-like shape, from the points of which extend five flexible legs around four feet in length that end in flat, paddle-like feet. Each foot is green and shaped like a triangle eight inches long and six inches wide at its tip. From the inner angles of this lower starfish-like structure extend reddish tubes two feet in length with orifices at their tips that serve an excretory function.

The Elder Race propagates by means of spores. In place of blood, they have a thick fluid dark green in color. Their bodies emit an unpleasant odor described as pungent and acrid that causes dogs to react with intense hostility. Their brain is large and five-lobed, their nervous system advanced and complex. They have senses beyond the five with which we are familiar. These creatures cannot be classed as either animal or vegetable, but are a curious blending of the two categories. Lovecraft's narrator in *At the Mountains of Madness* connects them with the Elder Things referred to by Alhazred in the *Necronomicon*.

They are known as the Elder Race because they came to this planet before the coming of the Old Ones. When the Old Ones crossed space to reach our world, they found the Elder Race already well established, with mighty cities all over the face of the globe. The Elder Race colonized this world before it contained any life, when it was only naked lava flows and sterile seas. In the *Necronomicon* it is suggested that the Elder Things created all life on this planet, or at least all the beginnings of the life that later evolved. Alhazred was not clear as to why they did so. He thought that it had been done either as a great cosmic joke, or that perhaps it was merely a mistake. It may be presumed that Alhazred was recording lore already ancient in his time. Lovecraft's narrator characterizes the Elder Race as the "makers and enslavers" of earthly life.

The notion that life on Earth was a mistake, that it was not intended to exist in the greater scheme of things, is in harmony with the *Necronomicon* teaching, as related in *The Dunwich Horror*, that the Old Ones will one day wipe our planet clean of all biological surface life, before returning it to its former place in a higher dimension, from which it fell. If the Earth had been originally sterile, they would naturally view biological organisms as a kind of contamination or infection, to be washed away before this globe could be set back in its proper place. It might also explain in part the intense enmity between the Old Ones and the organic Elder Things—for these two alien races made wars against each other, contesting for control of this world long before humanity evolved.

The Elder Race came to our planet by flying across space on their membranous wings, which were able to push against the aether of space itself. They established their cities under the oceans of our barren sphere, and created various life forms familiar to them from their former worlds of origin to serve as their food sources and slave laborers. Chief among the workers were the shoggoths, enormous protoplasmic organisms similar to giant amoebas some fifteen feet in diameter that used their great strength to lift the enormous stone blocks of the submarine cities the Elder Race inhabited. Eventually they extended their habitations to the dry land, once it had been rendered less harsh by the growth of plant life.

Their original place of settlement was the Antarctic Ocean, and their first land cities were on the landmass of Antarctica, which was warm at this period in the history of the Earth. For a time they were driven back into the oceans by a war that they fought with alien invaders described in Lovecraft's story as "a land race of beings shaped like octopi" that Lovecraft identified as the spawn of Cthulhu. The two alien races made peace for a time, and the Elder Race returned to the older landmasses and kept the seas, while the spawn of Cthulhu occupied the newer volcanic landmasses rising up from the ocean floors. The Elder Race made its greatest city on a high plateau of the Antarctic, and regarded the land it occupied as sacred, since it had been the first place of settlement.

Eventually, the Pacific island of R'lyeh, upon which the primary city of Cthulhu and his spawn resided, sank into the sea, and the Elder Race once again reigned supreme and unopposed over the entire world. It was during this period that they made the biological experiments that eventually resulted in the rise of the human species. They fought a second war, this time a war of rebellion, against their own creations the shoggoths, which over time evolved advanced brains capable of resisting the hypnotic psychic commands of the Elder Race. Through the use of atomic weapons the shoggoths were completely subjugated—or so the Elder Race believed.

During the Jurassic Age, when dinosaurs walked the Earth, a new alien threat descended from the skies, the race known as the Mi-Go, beings with the general shape of crustaceans whose bodies were half-fungous in nature. Lovecraft speculated through his narrator that they are the same creatures known in legend as the abominable snowman or yeti. The Mi-Go were fearsome warriors and drove the Elder Race from all the landmasses of the Northern Hemisphere, but could not displace them from their undersea cities. In basic makeup the Mi-Go were similar to the spawn of Cthulhu—capable of reshaping and reintegrating their physical forms in ways impossible to the purely material Elder Race, which for all its toughness was made of ordinary matter.

The Elder Race gradually lost much of its advanced science as its civilization decayed. The ability to fly through the aether of space on their wings was lost, although they could still propel themselves through the air or the waters of the oceans. The ability to subsist indefinitely and function in a normal manner without eating was also lost. The Elder Race preferred to consume meat, either that of the sea which they ate raw, or that of land animals which they cooked. They eventually retreated to their most sacred place, the original settlement, which at the time the Elder Race arrived on the barren Earth had been deep under the sea, but which eventually was thrust up into an Antarctic plateau some four miles high. It was here that they perfected their final and most magnificent city.

Their greatest foe, the one that ultimately doomed them as a race, was the coming of the glacial periods. The relentless ice sealed their great city and made it into a tomb where some of them lay dormant through the ages. Others retreated back into the open sea, but most made their way into a great underground ocean beneath Antarctica, which they may perhaps still inhabit. Lovecraft's narrator does not offer a firm opinion as to whether they survived or perished. Their shoggoths, however, did survive in caverns beneath the surface of the city, and still remember the age-old hatred of their former masters.

(*At the Mountains of Madness; The Dreams in the Witch House; The Shadow Out of Time*)

Fishers from Outside

In Uganda are cyclopean ruins said by the local tribe to be older than mankind, and once an outpost of the "Fishers from Outside," as well as of the evil gods "Tsadogwa and Clulu." The first of these two names is probably a degeneration of the name "Tsathoggua," and the second is certainly a variant form of the name "Cthulhu." The Fishers from Outside would seem to be the Old Ones.

(*Winged Death*)

Great Ones

The gods of Earth, who have their habitation atop Kadath in the Cold Waste, in the dreamlands. They are watched over by the Other Gods.

(*The Dream-Quest of Unknown Kadath*)

Great Race of Yith

In *The Shadow Out of Time*, Lovecraft presented a race of time-spanning beings he called the Great Race. They dwelled upon the Earth from one billion until fifty million years ago, and had the curious ability to project their minds through time, both into the past and into the future, although it was much easier and also more useful for them to project into the future, where they could acquire future arts and sciences. When one of their explorers located a suitable host for its mind in the time period it had decided to visit, an exchange took place in which the mind of the host fell back into the past and took up resident in the body of the time-traveler, while the mind of the time-traveler entered and occupied the empty vessel of the host.

It was thus a kind of possession across time. The host organism remained outwardly unchanged, but its self-identity was that of the member of the Great Race that had entered it. Lovecraft asserted in his story that all of the great prophets in human history were the result of these time-spanning possessions by members of the Great Race. When a man suddenly became elevated by a higher genius, and gained remarkable abilities of which he had never before shown any sign, it was one of the Great Race inhabiting his vacant shell, while that man's mind resided in the body of the time-traveler not less than fifty million years in the past. Although Lovecraft did not dare to state such a thing, it would be reasonable to speculate that Jesus was a man possessed by the mind of a Yithian, which abandoned its host shortly before his crucifixion.

Sometimes the members of the Great Race who were on the point of death projected forward through time permanently, never meaning to return to their dying bodies. When they projected into a human being the result was outwardly a sudden and complete change in personality that remained for the duration of the human host's life. Usually, the possession was only temporary and was done as a way to explore the future. When the mind of one of the Great Race wished to return to the past and its own body, it used its host to build the machine it required to mentally travel across the ages. This was a mechanical device of rods, wheels, and mirrors, having one large convex and circular central mirror. The size of the device was not great—around two feet tall, by one foot wide, and one foot deep.

The members of the Great Race were described by Lovecraft as iridescent, rugose cones ten feet in height and ten feet across at the base, with four distensible limbs that contained the head and other organs spreading from the apex. They used the huge claws attached to the ends of two of these foot-thick limbs for communication, by clicking them and rubbing them. Another limb had on its end "four red, trumpet-like appendages" used to ingest a liquid nourishment, and on the final limb there was a yellowish round head some two feet in diameter, having three large, dark eyes spaced around its circumference. From the top of the head grew four thin, gray stalks with flower-like terminations, and from its bottom dangled eight greenish tentacles. It is these tentacles that were used to manipulate small objects such as a pen, not the claws, which were reserved for carrying heavier objects such as books. The beings moved after the manner of a snail, by means of a rubbery gray substance that fringed the base and provided locomotion by rhythmic expansion and contraction.

They needed no sleep, being of a vegetable nature. Their blood was a thick green ichor, and they reproduced by means of spores that grew in clusters on the fringe around their bases and developed only under water. There were few youngsters of the species since their lifespan averaged four or five thousand years.

These are not the original bodies of this race, which perished aeons ago on the distant and dead planet of Yith. When the Great Race foresaw the death of their planet, they sent their minds searching through space and future time for the best replacement bodies, and found the species of conical creatures in what to them was Earth's future, but is to us 600 million years in the past. The conical species was ancient even then, having existed for 400 million years. A vast mental migration took place in which the minds of the Great Race seized permanent control of their new bodies, and the minds of the displaced conical creatures were trapped in the old vacated bodies on dying Yith. Lovecraft described the original bodies as a "horror of strange shapes," though whether the horror was inherent in the shapes, or was only produced by unfamiliarity, is not clear. The minds of the Great Race inhabited their new conical bodies continuously until fifty million years ago, when they escaped destruction again by departing in another great mental migration into our future, where they will take up residence in the bodies of what Lovecraft described as a "coleopterous species," a race of intelligent beetles that will become the ruling race of this planet immediately after the passing away of mankind.

When they came from Yith, they found this world and three other planets of our solar system ruled by an alien race of "half-polypous" creatures from beyond our cosmos that were blind and only semi-material, so that at times they were not visible to the naked eye. Although wingless, they possessed the ability to fly through the air. It appears to be the same race known in the *Necronomicon* as the Old Ones. The Yithians found it impossible to reason with the Old Ones, or establish any common understanding due to their utterly alien natures and thought processes, so they used their knowledge of science to build weapons that drove the Old Ones from their windowless cities of black basalt and into caverns beneath the surface of the ground.

From their arrival on our planet until their departure from their conical bodies into the beetle race of our future, the Yithians kept constant watch over the gateways to the underworld where dwelled the remnants of the Old Ones. It was a subject they did not discuss with the captive minds that studied in their great library. Toward the end of their residence in the conical species, there was a sense among the Great Race that the Old Ones were growing more powerful and gathering their resources for some kind of retaliation. Lovecraft intimates that it was just such an attack from the Old Ones that was the disaster that drove the Yithians to see refuge in our future.

The Great Race traversed the ancient world in enormous air ships, or boat-like vehicles powered by atomic engines, which they drove along broad roads. Their libraries contained vast stores of knowledge culled from all ages. Indeed, they were said to contain the sum total of all knowledge of all the races that had ever existed both in the past and in the future. The mind of a host species that had undergone an exchange with the mind of a member of the Great Race, and found itself inhabiting one of these rugose cones, was permitted to study in the library at the capital city of Pnakotus once it understood its situation and grew reconciled to its fate, which was usually not permanent but temporary. This happened after the Great Race finished interrogating the displaced mind to learn all that could be readily gained from it that might be of any interest.

The study was a way for the entrapped alien mind to pass the time, while waiting for its return to its own body. It also served as a way for the Great Race to extract every possible bit of useful information from the alien mind, which was encouraged to write down its thoughts and memories in the library. For this purpose ink, paper, and pens were always provided. The books were printed on sheets of tough cellulose and bound in such a way that they opened from the top downward rather than from the side. Each book was kept in its own individual protective case of light, gray metal that was decorated with mathematical designs and marked with identifying hieroglyphics.

The library at Pnakotus was adapted to the bodies of the Great Race, having no chairs, but tall pedestals for the placement of the countless books that lined the walls in wooden shelves. The pedestals also held crystal lamps to facilitate reading and writing. The library was a vast stone building with high, vaulted ceilings of massive blocks and round glazed windows in its stone walls that were protected with heavy bars, to prevent escape attempts by the captive displaced minds from the future as they pursued their strange and unsought course of studies. Few tried to escape, since they recognized the futility of the attempt. They became reconciled to their situation. A human being who returned to his own body after the possessing mind of the Great Race had finished using it usually retained no detailed recollection of what he had learned in the library, but might remember vague impressions of the city of Pnakotus and the surrounding primordial jungle in later dreams.

The *Necronomicon* alludes to a secret cult of human beings that has a partial knowledge of the Great Race, and that sometimes gives aid to these time travelers in their explorations of their future, which is our present. The Great Race is also mentioned in parts of the text of the Pnakotic Manuscripts, and Lovecraft asserted that ruins of its cities can still be found beneath the sea, in the form of vast blocks of stone that outline giant causeways or foundations of colossal buildings, but appear too large to be artificially cut. The ruins of Pnakotus itself lie beneath the Great Sandy Desert of Australia, where remnants of the library survive in our own time, even after the passage of fifty million years.

(*The Shadow Out of Time; The Challenge from Beyond*)

K'n-yan, race of

The Earth of Lovecraft's weird fiction is not solid, but hollow, at least in part. In the story *The Mound*, co-written with Zealia Bishop, Lovecraft described three vast voids beneath the plains of Oklahoma, one above the other. The highest of the three, which is far below the surface of the ground, is blue-litten K'n-yan, a great cavern illuminated by a natural blue radiance that is so large the roof cannot be seen from the floor through the auroral glow. It is inhabited by a race of beings that somewhat resemble the Plains Indians, having copper-colored skin and high cheekbones, but their heads are elongated, whereas those of the Indians are round. Indeed, the human race may be genetically related to them. They were carried across the stars to our planet in the distant past by Cthulhu, who they continue to worship as a god along with the Father of All Serpents, Yig.

K'n-yan is connected to the surface by a number of narrow passages that exit the earth through ancient stone doorways. At one period in the distant past, the men of K'n-yan colonized the surface, creating the civilizations of Atlantis and Lemuria, but a great flood drove them back beneath the ground to their blue-litten home. They still occasionally appear near mounds that were erected at their doorways, to the bewilderment and terror of human beings, who regard them as ghosts. This error is promulgated by the ability of the men of K'n-yan to project their images to the surface during their dreams, and to make their physical bodies insubstantial or ghost-like for the purpose of walking through walls or other solid barriers. But those most often glimpsed are the ones placed as sentries at the doorways to warn off curious human beings, or capture those who will not heed the warning.

The local Wichita Indians who saw these apparitions called them "those people" or "the old people" or "they who dwell below." Chief Gray Eagle of the Wichitas specifically referred to them as "the old ones." Here we encounter again the generic use of the term Old Ones in Lovecraft's fiction to designate an ancient alien race.

The race of K'n-yan are intellectually advanced. They use telepathy for communication, although they have not forgotten how to speak with their voices. At one time their science was perfected to a high degree, but it was allowed to decay, so that in our own period they no longer use machines for transportation but ride on the backs of genetically modified beasts known as gyaa-yothn, which are carnivorous quadrupeds with hairy backs, humanoid faces, and a single horn in their foreheads. These disturbing creatures were bred from a genetic hybrid of the reptilian race of red-litten Yoth, combined with degenerate human beings captively bred by the race of K'n-yan for slave labor and as a food source.

The inhabitants of K'n-yan have ceased to be intellectuals and have become sensualists who seek only physical and emotional stimulation to relieve the tedium of their endless lives, for they have defeated death and can live forever unless they grow so weary of it that they end their own existence. One of their amusements is the torture of their human slaves, which they do before large crowds in enormous circular amphitheaters similar to those of ancient Rome. When the slaves die from this mistreatment, they are transformed by the ancient sciences of the race into animated corpses and used for purposes of field labor.

Two primary gods are worshipped by the copper-skinned men of K'n-yan, the octopus-headed Cthulhu who carried their race across the stars to Earth, and Yig, the Father of Serpents. However, there are temples in K'n-yan erected to Yig, Tulu, Nug, Yeb, and the Not-to-Be-Named One. "Tulu" is the local name for Cthulhu. At one time Tsathoggua the toad-god was worshipped in the form of black idols discovered in red-litten Yoth, the cavern world that lies immediately below K'n-yan. The men of K'n-yan, exploring the land of Yoth, discovered the cult of Tsathoggua preserved in the Vaults of Zin, chambers that lie beneath the largest ruined and nameless city of Yoth. They carried the black stone idols and written scrolls of the cult to their own world, where it waxed so greatly in popularity that their capital city came to be called "Tsath," in honor of Tsathoggua.

They learned that the idols of Tsathoggua were not native to the lost reptilian race of Yoth, but had been looted from the land of N'kai, which is called black N'kai because it has no natural illumination. Just as the race of K'n-yan had carried the idols up from Yoth, the race of Yoth had carried them up from N'kai, a cavern world below Yoth. When the men of K'n-yan began to explore N'kai with their enormously powerful atomic searchlights, what they found caused them to seal up all the entrances to N'kai, and to destroy every trace of the Tsathoggua cult in their own land. They discovered that N'kai was not deserted, but was inhabited by viscose beings of black ooze that moved by flowing along stone channels, and the terrible realization came to them that it was the looting of the idols of Tsathoggua that had brought about the destruction of the reptilian race of red-litten Yoth.

The primary building metal used in K'n-yan is gold, which they possess in great abundance. For this reason they value it scarcely at all, but cherish a metal carried with them down from the stars that is magnetic to itself, dark, mottled, and lustrous. This was transported by mighty Cthulhu across space in the form of various idols and cultic items, but at one point in the history of K'n-yan some of the metal was minted into coins and used as the basis for the monetary system of the land. These coins were around two inches in diameter, stamped with an image of the octopus head of Cthulhu on one side, and the serpentine body of Yig on the other. Gray Eagle possessed one as a talisman.

Tales of plentiful gold sometimes lure men to the mounds in the plains that mark the entrances to blue-litten K'n-yan, but those who find their way down the passages to the great cavern are never permitted to return to their own world. The insubstantial figures of the race of K'n-yan are sometimes seen walking on these mounds at twilight, either projected there as images during dreams by the powerful telepathic minds of the cavern-dwellers, or stationed there as guardians of the portals to the lower world. Those foolish enough to investigate these spectral sightings vanish without a trace.

(*The Mound*)

Mi-Go

Mi-Go, a word probably derived from the Nepalese Sherpa word *metoh* meaning "filthy or disgusting," is the name Lovecraft adopted for the abominable snowman or yeti of the Himalayan mountain range. *Metoh* is a partial and incorrect translation of the term actually used by the Sherpas in the 1920s, *meteh kangmi*, which means "wild man of the snow." At present the Sherpas favor the name *meh-the* for the yeti. Lovecraft in his fiction applied the name "Mi-Go" to an alien race, the occasional sightings of which in the Himalayas had given rise to the legends of the abominable snowman. He also associated these aliens with the hills of Vermont. Most of what Lovecraft has recorded concerning this race is contained in his short story *The Whisperer in Darkness*, but scattered hints appear elsewhere in his fiction.

The Vermont Mi-Go are described as around five feet tall, pinkish in color, their bodies resembling those of crustaceans such as the lobster. They have a pair of large membranous wings on their backs that they fold out of the way, and several sets of limbs. Their heads are "a sort of convoluted ellipsoid" that is covered with short antennae. The intended meaning seems to be that the head does not project much from the body and is without a neck. Lovecraft characterized them as "a sort of huge, light-red crab with many pairs of legs and with two great bat-like wings." Elsewhere in *The*

Whisperer in Darkness they are said to be "a great crab with a lot of pyramided fleshy rings or knots of thick, ropy stuff covered with feelers where a man's head would be."

In *At the Mountains of Madness* Lovecraft referred to the Mi-Go as "half-fungous, half-crustacean creatures." The interior of their bodies is composed of a kind of fungoidal matter; their blood is a thick green juice. They give off a foul odor. Several hours after death, they evaporate into the air and disappear, in a way similar to the bodies of the hybrid Old Ones. So alien is the matter that composes their bodies that they cannot be photographed, because they make no impression on ordinary photographic film. They are more vegetable than animal, but completely unlike anything that grows on this world. Even their atomic structure is said to have a rate of vibration different from common earthly matter.

Lovecraft intimates that there are several species of Mi-Go on Earth. The winged variety that lives in the wooded hills of Vermont is not as intelligent as those wingless Mi-Go that inhabit the remote mountains of Europe and Asia. Even so, the Mi-Go are the most intelligent living things on this planet, and the mental abilities of even the Vermont species is vastly greater than human intelligence. They speak in a strange buzzing voice that can imitate any human language, after they undergo a minor surgery that allows them to produce human speech at all, but among themselves converse silently by changing the colors of their heads, and also employ telepathy.

The Mi-Go first descended from space during the Jurassic Age, while R'lyeh was still above the waves. They fought a great war with the Elder Things and drove them from the northern hemisphere of our planet. They came to Earth seeking metals they could not mine on Yuggoth, the planetoid we know as Pluto, which they now inhabit. The race is not native to Pluto, but traveled across the gulfs of space, some species flying on their wings and others conveyed by machines, to make Pluto the latest planetary colony in their vast empire that extends beyond the bounds of our universe. These membranous wings also serve at times to carry them across the sky, but they are not skillful fliers in the air and prefer to use their legs, either walking upright on two hind legs when they have need of their other limbs to carry burdens, or employing all pairs of their legs to crawl along the ground.

Although the majority of those Mi-Go who colonized the Earth in its past have left it, a few still remain in remote places, such as the wooded hills of Vermont, and the mountains of the Himalayas, where they live in secret in deep mines disguised to look like caves, which they seal behind them with great stones. They continue to mine the metals their race needs but cannot obtain on Yuggoth. They could easily return to the Earth in great numbers and conquer it, but would rather avoid the effort if they can obtain their metals in secret.

In Vermont folktales they are commonly known as "those ones" or "the old ones," the latter being the general term used in Lovecraft's fiction for any ancient, alien race. The Puritan settlers of New England thought them familiars of the Devil, and the Irish and Scottish immigrants believed them to be malignant fairies, but the local Pennacook Indians asserted that they were not natives of our world, but had come long ago from the constellation of the Great Bear to dig the earth for a rock they could not find on their own world.

The Indians said that the Winged Ones, as they called this race, could not eat human food, but were forced to bring their own food down from the stars, as they carried away to their home world on their great wings the oar they dug from the ground. Their presence on Earth was of the nature of mining outposts. Animals shunned and loathed them. They did not harm human beings unless they were spied upon, and then they killed for their own protection. Although they knew the languages of all races, they had no need for language themselves, but communicated by the constantly changing colors on their heads. So claimed the legend of the Pennacooks.

In order to remain informed about the activities of humanity, and to protect their secrecy, the Mi-Go employ those who dwell alone in remote places as their agents, and these reclusive individuals have formed themselves into a cult of worshippers of the Outer Ones, as they call the Mi-Go. The human spies gather information of interest to the Mi-Go, and warn them when there is any danger that their existence may become known. This practice caused the local people of rural Vermont to regard any hermit with suspicion, due to the speculation that the man might be working for "those ones." The passage of the Mi-Go is sometimes betrayed by the distinctive claw-prints they leave in the ground over which they walk, and it is these trails of prints leading to blocked up cave mouths in the Vermont hills that are in large part responsible for the local folktales about these beings.

Perhaps one reason the Mi-Go have managed to remain concealed for so long is their power of mind control. They are able to hypnotize human beings and cloud their thoughts, taking away the force of their will and rendering them ineffectual to oppose the purposes of the Mi-Go, even when humans learn of the existence of this alien race. It is not the greater mass of humanity that the Mi-Go most fear, but a secret cult of human beings that worships Hastur and the Yellow Sign, and is in league with "powers from other dimensions" who seek to track down the Mi-Go. Just as the Mi-Go have enlisted individuals as their agents, so have these mysterious powers employed humans as their instruments in their efforts to persecute the Mi-Go. To elude this questing cult of Hastur, the Mi-Go conceal themselves.

It is the curious practice of the Mi-Go to extract the brains of other intelligent species and encase them in metal cylinders, for the purpose of carrying them through space to the alien worlds of their empire. Some of these worlds lie beyond the bounds of our universe. At these far destinations, the brains are given mechanical bodies in which to function. The Mi-Go do this, not as a torture or punishment, but as a kind of cultural exchange with alien races.

Lovecraft intimated that the discovery of Pluto by Clyde Thombaugh in 1930 was no accident, but was the result of telepathic instructions projected by the Mi-Go from Yuggoth. The Mi-Go believe that it will soon be necessary to reveal their existence to human beings, since the increasingly sophisticated technology of our race will make it impossible for them to remain concealed beneath the ground in their mining colonies. For this reason they have begun selective contact with certain human beings, with the purpose of forming bonds with men in positions of power and authority over whom they can exert their influence.

(*At the Mountains of Madness; The Whisperer in Darkness*)

Old Ones

"The Old Ones were, the Old Ones are, and the Old Ones shall be." So wrote H. P. Lovecraft in his short story *The Dunwich Horror*. It is part of a longer quotation from the *Necronomicon*, one of only a handful of direct quotes Lovecraft made from the dreaded book that he had seen during his dreams. From this quotation of Alhazred's text we learn that the Old Ones are invisible beings who walk between the spaces of men, or as we might say today, between dimensions. They are large and powerful beings, because they are described as having the ability to "bend the forest and crush the city."

It is not to be supposed that the Old Ones have left the Earth. They are still here, but slightly out of phase with our reality. They share this quality with the fairy race, which is supposed to live in the same places habited by human beings, but in another dimension that renders their bodies and their dwellings invisible and intangible, except under special conditions. According to Alhazred, the Old Ones walk the meadows and stand at the thresholds of our houses without us ever being aware of them, save sometimes by a foul odor that they carry with them.

Alhazred mentions several matters concerning these invisible beings. They can be called by seasonal rites and words of power in lonely places. Traditionally in magic, demonic spirits prefer deserts and wastelands where no human being lives. The reason for this is not evident, but wildernesses have always been reputed to be the haunts of evil spirits, particularly in Arabian mythology, but also in the myths and legends of Greece, Rome, and Judea. The link between evil spirits and wastelands goes all the way back to ancient Mesopotamia.

When the Old Ones are ritually called, the wind howls and the earth shakes. They are summoned through a dimensional gate that falls under the authority of a being known as Yog-Sothoth. It is through this gate of Yog-Sothoth that the Old Ones travel from their world to our world, and back again. The gate has the appearance of multiple intersecting spheres.

Alhazred wrote that Yog-Sothoth knows where the Olds Ones "broke through, and where they shall break through again." This implies either that there was some attempt to bar the entry of the Old Ones into our earthly reality, or that our world is naturally resistant to their intrusion and must be forcibly entered by them. Yog-Sothoth is described as the "key and the guardian of the gate" by the mad Arab, so it is possible that he must be bargained with before he will allow the gate to open.

The usual assumption is that Yog-Sothoth is one of the Old Ones, but this is not stated explicitly by Lovecraft, and Yog-Sothoth does not appear to be the same as these powerful, invisible beings. Perhaps he is a kind of lord or god of the gateway who is set over the Old Ones, somewhat akin to the Roman god Janus, god of comings and goings. It may be that the face he shows when he appears to men is only a symbolic representation of his function, and that no one has seen his true appearance, which is akin to the other invisible Old Ones.

Alhazred mentions that when these Old Ones come into our reality, they sometimes interbreed with human beings. This is in keeping with the medieval lore of demons, which in the legends of the Catholic Church were supposed to copulate with mortal women and engender unnatural children or monsters in their wombs. Angels were also supposed to have the ability to breed children from mortal women, but in this case the offspring were more beautiful and more intelligent than normal human beings. The hybrid children of the Old Ones varied widely in their nature from those who were, in childhood at least, almost indistinguishable from ordinary men to those who were almost identical to the Old Ones themselves.

Lovecraft's story involves the two extremes of such an unholy union, twin brothers bred upon Lavinia Whateley by Yog-Sothoth, ritually evoked for that purpose within a stone circle on Sentinel Hill by her father, the old Wizard Whateley. They were brothers under the skin, but not identical twins. They merely shared the same womb. One brother, Wilbur, was of normal appearance in early childhood but as he aged became less and less human. He grew and matured with abnormal rapidity. When he was killed by a dog at age fifteen, he was over eight feet tall and furry below the waist, with alien growths on his hips and abdomen, and a kind of tail that terminated in a mouth. The other unnamed brother was never remotely like a human being. He was kept imprisoned in the gutted Whateley farmhouse and sustained himself on blood sucked from live cows. Like his father, Yog-Sothoth, he was invisible.

The ultimate purpose of the Old Ones is sobering food for thought. They wish to strip the surface of our world of all corporeal life, both animal and vegetable, and then take the entire planet to another dimension, from whence it fall into our universe countless aeons ago. This transition would involve a sliding or shifting across the dimensional planes, so that the entire Earth became as the bodies of the Old Ones, imperceptible to normal senses, or as Alhazred puts it, "without shape or substance." Lovecraft implied that the Earth would also be taken from its orbit around the Sun, so it may be that a transition through space is also involved. The gate that would allow the Old Ones to initiate this purpose was to be opened by Wilbur Whateley with the voicing of the "long chant," which, as old Wizard Whateley informed his grandson, is to be found on page 751 of the complete English edition of the *Necronomicon*, the rare John Dee translation.

We might speculate as to why the Old Ones wish to return this planet to the higher dimension from which it fell, and how it came to fall to our lower reality. Is our Earth unique among the planets of our solar system, or perhaps even unique of all the planets in our great galaxy? Does the fall of the Earth from its higher place mirror the myth of the fall from grace of the rebel angels, who were cast down into a dark abyss for their disobedience? Is the fall of the Earth a punishment that the Old Ones seek to nullify? Or do they wish to correct an error? We may speculate about these weighty questions, but Lovecraft provided no information that would allow us to draw any firm conclusions.

The One Ones "cannot take body without human blood," so wrote Wilbur Whateley in his diary. This may be interpreted to mean that the Old Ones cannot become material without intermingling their seed with that of human beings, a rite that requires a sacrifice. The purpose for creating hybrids between humans and Old Ones is to use the hybrids as warriors in the army that will destroy all life on the Earth. However, until a great ritual had been enacted with the Long Chant from the *Necronomicon*, Wilbur's invisible brother could not be cloned. As Wizard Whateley told his grandson, only the Old Ones from beyond could make his brother multiply and do their work. Wilbur died before he was able to conduct the ritual, so the plan of the Old Ones for the destruction of all earthly life came to nothing, at least on this occasion.

Wilbur Whateley was able to glimpse the appearance of the Old Ones in the stone circle on top of Sentinel Hill during the rites of May-Eve, and he recorded in his diary that they looked very much like his invisible brother, who he could see in a dim way by using an occult gesture known as the Voorish sign, or by blowing over his brother's misshapen bulk the powder of Ibn Ghazi. No details are provided as to the nature of either of these devices of revealing.

When Wilbur's brother was made momentarily visible by Henry Armitage, he was described as larger than a barn, with a body made of squirming ropes of a jelly-like substance that are compressed together into an egg-shape, and dozens of legs as large as hogs-heads that extend and retract after the manner of pseudopods. The bulk of the thing was covered with numerous bulging eyes and ten or twenty mouths on stalks that ceaselessly open and shut. Its color was gray, with blue or purple rings. This may be taken to be the true appearance of the Old Ones, since Wilbur Whateley testified in his diary that his brother was very like those he saw on Sentinel Hill.

In *The Call of Cthulhu*, the members of a degenerate Cthulhu cult that held their rites in a wooded swamp south of New Orleans asserted when interrogated by the police that no man has ever seen the Old Ones. Strictly speaking Wilbur Whateley was not a man, so his glimpse of them does not violate this statement. According to the cult, the Old Ones came down from the sky when the world was young. They have lain dead beneath the earth and the sea since before the arising of the human race, but their dead bodies spoke to the first man in his dreams and told him secrets, giving rise to the cult. Cthulhu is described by them as a great priest, but they did not assert that the Old Ones resemble his carven images—they did not know if this was true or not.

One of the cultists, Old Castro, said that the Old Ones had ruled the world and inhabited great cities for aeons before the rise of mankind. They were all dead now, but the remains of their cities could still be seen on certain South Sea islands. There were practices known to the cult that could revive the Old Ones once the stars came around to the right positions in their celestial cycles. He said that the Old Ones had originally come from the stars, carrying their images with them. They were not beings of flesh and blood. They had shape but were not made of matter. When the stars were right they could travel from one world to another through the sky, but when the stars were wrong, they could not live.

Even though the Old Ones were not alive, Old Castro maintained that neither were they dead. They lay in their stone houses in the great undersea city of R'lyeh, protected by the powerful spells of Cthulhu, and would rise again once the stars came right. However, they could not break the spells that held them alone, but must have help from "some force from outside." Meanwhile, they lay in their stone tombs, awake and aware but unable to move. They knew what happened elsewhere in the universe by the power of their telepathy. When mankind evolved, they talked to those few of the first humans who were psychically sensitive in their dreams, and this is the only way they can communicate with human consciousness.

When the stars came right, the secret priests of the cult would liberate Cthulhu from his tomb, and then Cthulhu would lift his spells from the Old Ones and free them from their tombs. This time would be easy to know, said Old Castro. It would be when mankind was "beyond good and evil, with laws and morals thrown aside." Mighty Cthulhu would teach men new ways to kill and destroy. All the Earth would be engulfed in a holocaust of freedom.

Castro said that in ancient times, the dead-dreaming Old Ones had talked freely with chosen men in their dreams, but then the island that supported the city of R'lyeh had sunk deep beneath the Pacific ocean, and the great mass of intervening water had severed this psychic link. When the stars came right, the city would rise, and the link would be reestablished with the cult, who would come to the place and free Cthulhu from his tomb.

There are several points of interest between this account of the Old Ones and those of Wilbur Whatley and Abdul Alhazred. The Old Ones spoke to Wilbur from the sky, and seem to have been under the authority of Yog-Sothoth. By contrast, Castro believed that they would speak to his degenerate cult from the risen island of R'lyeh. Wilbur wrote that the Old Ones cannot take on bodies without human blood—without mingling with human blood to produce hybrids. Castro asserted that the bodies of the Old Ones lay in their stone houses in R'lyeh. Alhazred wrote that they walked the surface of the Earth unbodied and formless, and unnoticed save for the foul odor that follows them.

It may be that the sky-dwelling Old Ones of Yog-Sothoth and the water-sleeping Old Ones of Cthulhu are two different groups having different characteristics, but are at root the same race described by Alhazred. The revealed body of Wilbur Whateley's brother was described as gelatinous, and this description also applies to Cthulhu, as he appeared during his brief emergence from his tomb. Although Cthulhu may not be an Old One himself, in the strictest sense, he is said by Alhazred to be their cousin, indicating a close link with them. Perhaps it would be useful to think of them as two separate colonies of Old Ones that are bound to the Earth by the malign influence of the stars.

(*At the Mountains of Madness*; *The Dunwich Horror*; *The Mound*; *The Whisperer in Darkness*; *The Call of Cthulhu*)

Other Gods from Outside

Also known as the Ultimate Gods, the Other Gods from Outside are the "blind, voiceless, tenebrous, mindless" gods who dance around the black throne of the demon sultan Azathoth at the central vortex of all infinity, to the "muffled, maddening beating of vile drums and the thin, monotonous whine of accursed flutes." They are described as awkward and gigantic. Their soul and messenger is Nyarlathotep. In this regard they seem to be an extension of Azathoth.

In *The Dream-Quest of Unknown Kadath* they are called the Other Gods from Outside "whom it is better not to discuss," and are said to protect the gods of Earth, who rule feebly over our dreamlands and have "no power or habitation elsewhere." At least twice these Other Gods "set their seal" upon the granite of this planet, once in antediluvian times as illustrated by a drawing in that part of the Pnakotic Manuscripts that predates writing, and once "on Hatheg-Kla when Barzai the Wise tried to see Earth's gods dancing by moonlight."

The Other Gods are said to have many agents among men and among alien species that dwell in the dreamlands, agents eager to work their will in return for favors from Nyarlathotep. They are worshipped on the plateau of Leng by the High Priest Not To Be Described, who wears a yellow silken mask. The Other Gods generate nameless larvae in the aether, shapeless black things that lurk and caper and flounder, that are like the Other Gods "blind and without mind, and possessed of singular hungers and thirsts."

At one time the creatures of the dreamlands known as the gugs built stone circles in the woods and made "strange sacrifices" to the Other Gods and to Nyarlathotep, but they committed an abomination that so horrified the gods of Earth that the gugs were driven to dwell below the surface of the ground thereafter. It is not known what this abomination may have been.

(*The Dream-Quest of Unknown Kadath; The Other Gods*)

Outer Ones

Also called the Outer Beings, titles for the Mi-Go of Yuggoth, the planetoid we know as Pluto. It is the title used by members of their cult.

(*The Whisperer in Darkness*)

reptile people *

A reptilian race of Valusia, created by Lovecraft's friend, the writer Robert E. Howard. In the *Shadow Out of Time*, one of the minds stolen by the Great Race is the mind of a reptilian from Valusia.

(*The Shadow Out of Time*)

spawn of Cthulhu

Little is known about the minions of Cthulhu, other than they resemble their gigantic master in shape and substance. They were war-like, and vast in number. In *At the*

Mountains of Madness they are described as "a land race of beings shaped like octopi" that filtered down from cosmic infinity and precipitated a war with the crinoid Elder Things. They may resemble octopi only in part, or in one aspect, just as Cthulhu is like an octopus only in the sense that he has tentacles extending from his face.

Note that the spawn are not water-dwelling, but like mighty Cthulhu himself, were trapped beneath the waves of the Pacific Ocean when the island on which the city of R'lyeh was built sank to the sea floor. Prior to this cataclysmic event, when the stars in the heavens took on a configuration that was harmful to Cthulhu's spawn, they withdrew into stone chambers in R'lyeh, the city they had built from an alien green stone that shielded them from the rays of the stars, to await the coming right again of the constellations in the night sky. The sinking of the island took them by surprise, and the ocean became their prison.

It may be conjectured that the spawn are off-buddings from Cthulhu's own utterly alien substance, and in this sense his children—but only in the way that an amoeba born of cellular fission is considered to be the offspring of its originating cell, or as a mushroom grown from a spore is thought of as the offspring of the mushroom that originated the spore. Cthulhu may be likened to a queen bee, capable of generating countless smaller versions of himself to perform his labors and serve as soldiers in his wars. Most worker bees are never transformed into queens. Similarly, it may be that most or all of the spawn are never destined to develop into giants such as Cthulhu.

(*At the Mountains of Madness; Through the Gates of the Silver Key*)

Vaporous brains

A race of gaseous beings that dwell in the spiral nebula, and worship Yog-Sothoth in the form of an untranslatable sign.

(*Through the Gates of the Silver Key*)

Worm-like race

Around the year 1912 the Reverend Arthur Brooke Winters-Hall succeeded in translating a portion of the Eltdown Shards, which told of a race of worm-like creatures who had conquered their own galaxy through a mastery of interstellar travel and colonized its many star systems. Because they were unable to span the vast distances between galaxy in their ships, they scattered forth across the galaxies devices in the shape of a cube that had the hypnotic property of capturing the mind of any intelligent creature who looked at them, and sending that mind back to the home planets of the worm-like race, where it was investigated. If it was found to be of interest, the mind of one of the worm-like race would travel back along the channel formed by the cube to inhabit the living body of the creature while it investigated the alien world. If a race were discovered that seemed to pose a potential threat, that race would be exterminated through the power of the cube.

By pure chance one of these cosmic cubes fell to Earth 150,000,000 years ago, during the period our planet was ruled by the cone-shaped Great Race of Yith, who at once recognized its properties and the danger it posed. They killed all those of their own race who had looked upon the cube, then locked the cube safely away in a special shrine, since it was too valuable a scientific device to wantonly destroy. The worm-like race came to be aware of Earth and of the Yithians, but were powerless to vent their hatred because their cube had been rendered impotent. Over the passing aeons the shrine of the cube was lost amid warfare and general chaos, and the great polar city in which the shrine was located met with destruction. Fifty million years ago, the Great Race departed into the distant future to avoid the danger posed by the emergence of the Old Ones from the depths of the earth, where they Yithians had banished them. The forgotten cube was left behind in its lost shrine.

Lovecraft described members of the worm-like race as resembling gigantic gray worms or centipedes, as thick through the middle as a man, but twice the human length. Their eyeless, disk-like head is fringed with cilia and has a central orifice. The creatures glide along the ground on their rear legs, the front of their body raised so that they can use its two pairs of foremost legs as arms. A purple comb runs down the center of the creature's back, and its body ends in a fan-shaped gray tail. It communicates by means of a ring of flexible red spikes around its neck, which it manipulates to produce the clicking, twanging sounds that serve it as a language.

(*The Challenge from Beyond*)

Yoth, beings of

Yoth is the red-litten cavern world that lies below the blue-litten cavern of K'n-yan. Its native race has passed away, and of its civilization only ruins remain. At their height, the beings of Yoth could create life synthetically. They created various races of creatures for running their industries and transporting their goods, and also created grotesque living things for their amusement. The race of Yoth was believed to be reptilian or reptile-like quadrupeds by the physiologists of K'n-yan. The race of Yoth worshipped the toad-god Tsathoggua, which they learned about by raiding the black inner realm called N'kai that lies below their own red-litten cavern world.

(*The Mound*)

The Key to the First Gate

1st Astral Gate: Sagittarius—The Horse-Archer

Sun passes through Sagittarius: December 18–January 20

Constellation is represented by a satyr about to release an arrow from a drawn bow.

Right Pillar: Al Nasl (Arabic: The Point). Astronomical designation: Gamma Sagittarii. Astrological nature: Mars-Moon. Influence: penetration, failing vision, blindness. Magnitude: 3. Color: yellow. Sun crosses: December 23. Location: point of the arrow. Comments: The nature of this star is sharp and piercing.

Left Pillar: Pelagus (Latin: Sea); also known as Nunki. Astronomical designation: Sigma Sagittarii. Astrological nature: Jupiter-Mercury. Influence: truthfulness, optimism, spirituality, good fortune at sea. Magnitude: 2.1. Color: white. Sun crosses: January 3. Location: vane of the arrow. Comments: Always a star of good fortune.

The astral gate of Sagittarius lies along the arrow of the horse-archer, the star of its right pillar the point of the arrow and the star of its left pillar the vane or fletching of the arrow that is held in the archer's hand. The Sun enters the gate at the winter solstice, crossing the longitude of Al Nasl, the star of the right pillar, around December 23, at the time when the year is renewed and the days begin to lengthen. The transition of the gate takes eleven days, which contain what is generally considered the Christmas holiday season—from Christmas Eve to New Year's Day. The Sun exits the gate around January 3, when it crosses the longitude of the star of the left pillar, Pelagus.

The key to the First Gate opens Sagittarius, allowing entry into that part of the walled city of the Necronomicon that contains the great races. Use it for divining information or receiving dreams about the dominant alien races of the Necronomicon mythos, or for communicating with a representative of a hierarchy, race, or species when the specific name of an individual you wish to contact is unknown to you.

Seal of the First Key on the First Gate

Ritual of Opening Sagittarius

Face the direction of the compass ruled by the First Gate, which is northeast by east—that is, slightly to the right of the northeast. Visualize the closed gate of the walled city before you so that it is the full height and width of a real city gate, and large enough for you to walk through. Take the time to create on the astral level its shading and texture, the grain of its planks, the shape and patina of its hinges, straps, and nails.

With the image of the gate clear in your mind and projected upon the astral level to the northeast by east, speak the following invocation to Yog-Sothoth:

> Guardian of the Gate! Defender of the Door! Watcher of the Way! Who art the stout Lock, the slender Key, and the turning Hinge! Lord of All Transition, without whom there is no coming in or going out, I call thee! Keeper of the Threshold, whose dwelling place is between worlds, I summon thee! Yog-Sothoth, wise and great lord of the Old Ones, I invoke thee!
>
> By the authority of the dreaded name, Azathoth, that few dare speak, I charge thee, open to me the gateway of Sagittarius the Horse-Archer that lies between the blazing pillar Al Nasl on the right hand and the blazing pillar Pelagus on the left hand. As the solar chariot [or, lunar chariot] crosses between these pillars, I enter the city of the *Necronomicon* through its First Gate. Selah!

Visualize the key of the First Gate in your right hand some six inches long and made of cast gold. Feel its weight, texture, and shape as you hold it. Extend your right arm and use the key to draw upon the surface of the gate the seal of the key, which should be visualized to burn on the gate in a line of white spiritual fire. Point with the astral key at the center of the gate and speak the words:

> In the name of Azathoth, Ruler of Chaos, by the power of Yog-Sothoth, Lord of Portals, the First Gate is opened!

Visualize the gate unlocking and opening inward of its own accord upon a shadowed space beyond. On the astral level, walk through the gateway and stand in the dark space beyond. Focus your mind upon the aspect of the mythos you wish to investigate and open yourself to impressions concerning the alien races scried by Lovecraft during his dreams. In a more general sense, this ritual and this gate may be used to scry or communicate with unknown or unnamed representatives of any hierarchy, race, or intelligent species of ruling spirits, or to investigate unknown hierarchies of dominant spirits.

After fulfilling the purpose for which this gate was opened, conclude the ritual by astrally passing out through the gate and visualizing it to close. Draw the seal of the First Key on the surface of the gate with the astral key in your hand, and mentally cause it to lock itself shut, as it was at the beginning of the ritual. Speak the words:

> By the power of Yog-Sothoth, and authority of the supreme name Azathoth, I close and seal the First Gate. This ritual is well and truly ended.

Allow the image of the gate to grow pale in your imagination and fade to nothingness before you turn away from the ritual direction.

The Second Gate

Second Gate
Unique Personalities

The most unique personality in Lovecraft's stories was Lovecraft himself. He was forever finding ways to insert himself into his stories, so that he could experience them from the inside, as he had the dreams that gave rise to so many of them. The best example of this practice is Randolph Carter, a character who appears as the protagonist in several of the most important stories—*The Statement of Randolph Carter, The Silver Key, Through the Gates of the Silver Key, The Unnamable,* and what was perhaps Lovecraft's greatest work, *The Dream-Quest of Unknown Kadath.* He is also mentioned in *The Case of Charles Dexter Ward.* Carter is Lovecraft's alter ego, the kind of man he wanted himself to be in his dreams, and perhaps the kind of man he wished himself to be in waking life. He is bold, fearless, and forever questing after new experiences and more daring adventures.

Carter is by profession a writer of horror stories, an antiquarian by inclination, but his true vocation is dreamer. Dreams are more important to him than waking reality. This is true for a number of Lovecraft's characters, such as titular figure in *The Quest of Iranon*, and the keeper of the North Point lighthouse at Kingsport, Basil Elton, who appears in *The White Ship*, but none of the dreamers in the Necronomicon Mythos are as skilled or as practiced as Carter. None of them have gone so deeply into the dreamlands, or have dared to do so many things.

Besides the figure of Randolph Carter, Lovecraft inserted himself into his stories through various other less epic characters, such as the elderly Ward Phillips in *Through the Gates of the Silver Key*—Ward is the second half of Lovecraft's first name, and Phillips is his middle name. The short story *Ex Oblivione*, the narrator of which seeks escape from waking life in the land of dreams, was first published under the pseudonym Ward Phillips, as was the poem "Astrophobos," in which a man imagines how wonderful the distant worlds of the stars near the constellation of Ursa Major must be, only to perceive in a vision that they are terrible and horrifying.

The unnamed narrator of *The Outsider*, with his feeling of total alienation from all common human experience and his discovered delight in the things of the grave, is undoubtedly expressing some of Lovecraft's own alienation from normal society. The same may be said for Jervas Dudley, a young man in the story *The Tomb*, who nightly falls asleep outside the locked door of an ancient family burial crypt, and dreams that he consorts inside with the dead past. He ends up adopting the speech and mannerisms of one of his long-dead relations, even as Lovecraft himself as a young man affected the speech and writing style of an eighteenth-century English gentleman.

In addition to these various veiled versions of Lovecraft himself, the stories team with a myriad of strange and marvelous characters, most of them the product of Lovecraft's fancy, but some of them based on actual historical figures, or fictional characters created by other writers that Lovecraft chose to incorporate into his stories. The most notable is Abdul Alhazred himself, the mysterious mad Arab who composed the *Necronomicon*. Alhazred lurks in the background, lending his strange presence through his infamous book, but never coming center stage. Since the *Necronomicon* had its source in Lovecraft's dreams, it is possible that Alhazred himself was a dream character, although Lovecraft never stated this explicitly.

The man who translated the book from Greek to Latin, Olaus Wormius, was real enough—he was a Danish antiquarian of the seventeenth century. Lovecraft took the name but shifted him back in time four centuries or so, and made him the translator of the *Necronomicon*. John Dee, who in the mythos is said to have translated the book from Latin to English, was also a very real historical figure of Elizabethan England. It was this deft habit of merging reality with fantasy that makes Lovecraft's creations so realistic, and also makes it difficult at times to determine what is fact and what is fiction. Some characters, as in the case of the escape artist Harry Houdini, are both. Houdini, an actual stage magician and escape artist of Lovecraft's time, was placed by Lovecraft into *Imprisoned with the Pharaohs*, an adventure story set in Egypt that had him escaping from his bonds and viewing the ghoulish rites of an evil cult of the undead deep beneath the Pyramids of Giza.

Lovecraft was an amateur genealogist who enjoyed researching the forbearers of his relatives. This interest finds its way into his fiction in the form of family bloodlines for some of his major characters that span multiple generations. The Carters seem always to have been wizards. We read not only about Randolph Carter the antiquarian and writer, but about a distant ancestor who was captured during the Crusades and studied magic under the Saracens, and about a Sir Randolph Carter who practiced magic in the time of Queen Elizabeth the First. An Edmund Carter was almost hanged for witchcraft at Salem. The Carter line is even extended into the future by Lovecraft when he refers to Pickman Carter, who will use occult methods to turn back a Mongol invasion of Australia in the year 2169.

The line of wizards bearing the name Van der Heyl is particularly well detailed, as is the line of Van Kauran. Several generations of the Marsh family of Innsmouth occur in various of Lovecraft's tales, as do the Waites. In New England, the roots of wizardry and witchcraft run deep. Witches such as Goody Fowler and Keziah Mason may have lived centuries ago, but that does not necessarily mean that they are gone entirely, or that their power has faded. Their history and their presence lingers in the streets of Arkham, Kingsport, Innsmouth, Dunwich, and other towns steeped in the magic of the past.

Some of the most fascinating characters in Lovecraft's stories never set foot on our everyday world at all, but inhabit only the dreamlands, while others, such as the artist Richard Pickman and Randolph Carter, straddle the waking world and the world of dreams. It is possible to inhabit the dreamlands in three ways—by projecting the mind into them during sleep, by entering them bodily while still alive through some mysterious form of dimensional transition, and by becoming a part of them after death. Yet there are many living in the dreamlands who were never alive, in a corporeal sense.

Names with asterisks after them represent characters not wholly of Lovecraft's invention. They may be individuals from history that he has incorporated into his stories, or characters who were invented by other writers that Lovecraft adopted for his own use.

Afrasiab *

The semi-mythical ruler and warrior hero of Turan, an ancient kingdom that was bordered by the Oxus River (present-day Amu Darya), a river that runs along the southern border of modern Uzbekistan. The Oxus was the boundary between ancient Turan and Iran. Afrasiab made war against the Persians, and lost. He is remembered in the Persian epic *Shahnameh* (*Book of Kings*) written around 1000 AD. Lovecraft wrote in his story *The Nameless City,* "I repeated queer extracts, and muttered of Afrasiab and the daemons that floated with him down the Oxus." Lovecraft's reference is taken directly from a mention by Edgar Allan Poe at the end of his story *The Premature Burial*, where Poe wrote: "but, like the Demons in whose company Afrasiab made his voyage down the Oxus, they must sleep, or they will devour us—they must be suffered to slumber, or we perish." Poe derived the reference from the 1838 work *Stanley* by Horace Binney Wallace, who wrote (bk 1, p. 124): "The passions are like those demons with whom Afrasiab sailed down the river Oxus, our safety consists in keeping them asleep; if they wake we are lost."

(*The Nameless City*)

Alhazred, Abdul

The author of the dreaded *Necronomicon* is described as a mad poet from the ancient city of Sanaá in the land of Yemen. The date of his birth is not known, but Lovecraft indicated in his brief biography that Alhazred flourished around the year 700. He end is fixed with more exactness. He disappeared from Damascus in 738, when he was reported by his twelfth-century biographer Ebn Khallikan to have been caught up into the air by an invisible monster and devoured before a large number of horrified witnesses. Lovecraft wrote that concerning the disappearance of Alhazred "many terrible and conflicting things are told." However, he may have meant only that the reasons for Alhazred's disappearance are in dispute, not the manner of his disappearance, since he offers only the version of Ebn Khallikan.

The description of Alhazred's end, brief though it is, raises several questions. What was he doing in front of a large number of people at the time of his misfortune? Was it happenstance that he found himself in a crowded place at that fateful moment, or was he engaged in activity that precipitated the events described by Ebn Khallikan? It is possible that he was giving a demonstration of necromancy before an audience of people at Damascus, and that it was Alhazred himself who evoked the invisible being, either deliberately or accidentally, which devoured him? He may even have been performing for the caliph at the royal court.

Lovecraft in his brief biographical essay on Alhazred refers to the "death or disappearance" of the mad poet, so it is evident that Lovecraft himself was uncertain whether the events of 738 caused the end of Alhazred's life, or only his vanishing. If he was consumed, as Ebn Khallikan asserts, there can be little doubt that he was killed, but if he was merely caught up into the air and his body progressively obscured from sight, it is at least possible that the invisible creature took the poet through a dimensional portal. Lovecraft left the door open as to whether Alhazred met his death that day in Damascus.

Alhazred lived at Damascus during his "last years" and it was in this great city that he wrote his *Necronomicon*, the account of all the arcane history, geography, and necromantic art that he had acquired throughout the course of his life. As a young man he had been a wanderer, traveling to the ancient city of Memphis in Egypt, where he explored "subterranean secrets," and to the ruins of the city of Babylon in Persia. How he lost his reason is not revealed, and it may be presumed that it remains unknown to the historians. It was probably something he saw or encountered during his ten years living in solitude in the great desert of Arabia known as the Empty Space. This desert covers much of the southern part of the Arabian Peninsula and is one of the least hospitable lands on this planet. Almost nothing grows there.

The moment of his loss of reason may have come during his explorations of catacombs beneath the ruins of a nameless desert town, where he is said by Lovecraft to have discovered "shocking annals and secrets of a race older than mankind." Or it may have happened during his encounter with the fabled lost city of Irem, called the City of Pillars. In recent years the location of Irem was rediscovered through satellite photographs of the desert, which are able to show ancient and almost obliterated caravan roads that cannot be seen from the ground. Irem is presently little more than a shallow pit in the sand, but who knows what wonders lie beneath? It may even be that the nameless city and Irem are connected.

Whether Alhazred was truly mad may be questioned, since his reputation for madness stems from the incredible and scarcely believable things he wrote in his *Necronomicon*. If it chances that these matters are accurately reported by the poet, then he may have been as sane as any other man of Yemen. It is possible for a sudden shock to unhinge the reason for a temporary period, and for full rationality to be recovered at a later time. If Alhazred's mind was made mad due to some horror he encountered while wandering the Empty Space, he may have regained full clarity of thinking by the late period of his life when he sat down to pen his book at Damascus.

Alhazred was a man of some wealth or prominence, or at least had the benefit of a wealthy patron. The occupation of poet was not taken up by poor men, since it was an uncertain way to put food on the table. Poets, musicians, and artists required patrons to support their work. The only other way to earn a living as a poet was to recite in the marketplace for coins. Alhazred must have had money or he could not have traveled to distant lands. In the late seventh century, Egypt and Persia lay at the ends of the expanding empire of Islam. They were the boundaries of the civilized world—more distant and half-fabulous places such as Britain were no more than barbarian wildernesses as far as the learned Arabs of that time were concerned, lacking in both culture and history, and they would have regarded them as not worth visiting.

Lovecraft reported in his biographical note on the poet that Alhazred was an "indifferent Moslem" and also that he worshipped Yog-Sothoth and Cthulhu. Both the lack of devotion to Islam and the worship of alien gods would have earned Alhazred an execution at the hands of the caliph, had the ruler chosen to press the matter. Yet it is apparent that Alhazred was able to live freely at Damascus, and even to write what would have been a forbidden text, without suffering persecution from the mullahs of the city. He may have hidden his practices and beliefs during his life, and his book may not have begun to circulate publicly until after his death. Or, it is possible that he had the protection of a man of wealth and power to insulate him from persecution.

There are many examples of this selective enforcement of religious law in Christian Europe of the Renaissance. The magician John Dee, who lived in England during the reign of Queen Elizabeth I, was engaged in communications with spirits that could easily have resulted in his execution by hanging, had his sovereign chosen to pursue the matter, but Dee was protected from the malice of his enemies by the queen, who relied on him for horoscopes and for counsel in the arts of magic and alchemy. Elizabeth's successor, the Scotsman James I, was far less tolerant of Dee's studies and reviled him as a conjuror, but failed to get Dee hanged due to the vigor of Dee's self-defense and the fairness of English law.

The fate of necromancers was capricious during the Dark Ages. Some prospered thanks to shrewd dealings and powerful patrons, while others suffered the penalty for their practices under the law, which was almost invariably execution. Alhazred's reputation for madness, coupled with his outward profession of poet, may have conspired to shield him from the harshest criticism. His writings, if they became known during his lifetime, might have been dismissed as either the fantastic creations of an artistic genius or the ravings of a lunatic.

The name "Abdul Alhazred" is said to be an improper and even an impossible form for a true Arab name. The name came to Lovecraft in very early childhood. Lovecraft related in a letter that he had coined the name at age five after reading the Lang edition of the *Arabian Nights*. He was a precocious child and began to read adult literature at a very young age. He took the fancy to present himself as a little Arab, by giving himself what he imagined to be an Arab name, and dressing up in what appeared to him to be Arab robes, to the vast amusement of his family, who humored him in this caprice.

In another letter, Lovecraft admitted that he was not sure himself exactly where the name "Alhazred" had originated. He dimly associated it with the family lawyer, who sometimes visited the Lovecraft house, but was not sure if he had received the name from the lawyer, or had merely asked the lawyer to criticize his own selection of a name. Various attempts have been made to derive meaning from the name, even though it is improper Arabic. "Servant of the Devourer" seems to be the most significant, and raises the possibility that it is not a birth name at all, but rather a title bestowed on Alhazred through his cultic worship of the Old Ones.

We should not be too quick to dismiss the name merely because its construction appears to modern eyes faulty. During the Middle Ages many of the books of the great Arab philosophers and physicians made their way to Europe and were translated into Greek or Latin. The names of their authors were invariably corrupted by Europeans. For example, the philosopher Abul-Waleed Muhammad Ibn Rushd became in European common usage "Avarroes." Abu Yusuf Ya'qub ibn Ishaq became in European usage "Alkindi." It is entirely possible that the name "Abdul Alhazred" is a corrupt simplification of the mad poet's original name by a translator of his book, and that his original name has been lost. Perhaps this occurred when Theodorus Philetas made his Greek translation of the *Necronomicon* in the year 950 at Constantinople.

The identity of the invisible monster that caused Alhazred to vanish into the air is impossible to establish with certainty due to a lack of information, but there seems every likelihood that it was one of the Old Ones. Alhazred worshipped the Old Ones and had dealings with them. He may have earned their anger. The Old Ones are described as invisible by Lovecraft, and are able to fly through the air, even though they lack wings, by a form of levitation. They can be invoked by human beings, as they were by Wizard Whateley on Round Hill near Dunwich. The text of the *Necronomicon* itself testifies that the Old Ones are immensely powerful beings who can uproot trees and crush houses, so lifting a man into the air would be an easy task.

Yog-Sothoth, who appears to be one of the leaders of the Old Ones, controls the portals to other dimensions. Alhazred wrote about him in the *Necronomicon*, "Yog-Sothoth knows the gate. Yog-Sothoth is the gate. Yog-Sothoth is the key and guardian of the gate." It may well have been Yog-Sothoth himself who visited Alhazred at Damascus in the year 738, and who caught the necromancer up into the air and carried him away through a portal to another world. This would have given the appearance to the amazed onlookers that the poet was vanishing by degrees, or being devoured by space itself. Whether it was done in anger, or at the direction of Alhazred, who may have chosen to leave Damascus in a spectacular fashion, no man other than Alhazred himself can say.

(*History of the Necronomicon; At the Mountains of Madness; The Dreams in the Witch House; Out of the Aeons; The Call of Cthulhu; The Case of Charles Dexter Ward; The Descendant; The Festival; The Hound; The Last Test; The Nameless City; The Shadow Out of Time; The Thing on the Doorstep; The Whisperer in Darkness; Through the Gates of the Silver Key*)

Atal

A three-hundred year old priest of the dream city of Ulthar, who instructed Randolph Carter concerning the lore of the gods of Earth. He told Carter that "they are indeed only Earth's gods, ruling feebly our own dreamland and having no power or habitation elsewhere." Sometimes they answer prayers, but only if they are in a good humor. They are protected by the Other Gods from Outside, about whom it is best not to speak. Carter tricked Atal into drinking too much moon-wine, so that the old priest would talk about forbidden things. Atal told Carter where in the dreamlands to find a graven image of the gods of Earth, located atop "the mountain Ngranek, on the isle of Oriab in the Southern Sea," whereby he might recognize the gods by their features if he ever saw them.

(*The Dream-Quest of Unknown Kadath*)

Barzai the Wise

The companion of Atal, priest of Ulthar, who climbed the mountain Hatheg-Kla to see the gods of Earth dancing in the moonlight. For this transgression of divine dignity, he was drawn screaming up into the sky.

(*The Dream-Quest of Unknown Kadath*)

Borellus *

Pierre Borel (1620–89), a French physician and author of various works on scientific and historic subjects, who is more commonly known as Borellus, was born and grew to adulthood at Castres, a town in southern France. In 1640 he received his degree in medicine from the University of Montpellier. He moved to Paris in 1653 and the following year was named physician to King Louis XIV. In 1674 he was admitted to the French Academy of Science.

Borellus found his way into Lovecraft's short novel, *The Case of Charles Dexter Ward*, via Cotton Mather. Mather wrote of Borellus in his 1702 work *Magnalia Christi Americana* (bk. 2, ch. 12), asserting that the Frenchman had written that from the essential salts of human dust it was possible, without any criminal necromancy, to call up the form of a dead ancestor. What Borellus probably meant was the calling up of a shade or spectre of the dead by means of natural magic, which was not considered forbidden by most scholars.

In Lovecraft's novel, the technique is necromantic, and is based on an incantation in the *Necronomicon*. Joseph Curwen corresponds with other alchemists concerning their efforts to replicate the technique of Borellus. Curwen wrote, "I am foll'g oute what Borellus saith, and haue Helpe in Abdool Al-Hazred his VII. Booke."

(*The Case of Charles Dexter Ward*)

Bran

Bran Mak Morn, the last king of the Picts, was the hero in a series of short stories written by Robert E. Howard, who was the creator of Conan the Barbarian. Lovecraft and Howard corresponded, and Lovecraft liked to work references to the writings of his friends into his own stories, as a kind of wry homage. The name appears in *The Whisperer in Darkness* in a list of various esoteric references intended to evoke a mysterious atmosphere.

(*The Whisperer in Darkness*)

Buo

This wise resident of an alien race of wizards that ruled the planet Yaddith in the distant past is described as the Arch-Ancient Buo. It exchanged information with the wizard Zkauba, another member of its own species, while the body of Zkauba was inhabited by the consciousness of Randolph Carter.

(*Through the Gates of the Silver Key*)

Carter, Pickman

A future relative of Randolph Carter who, in 2169, will use "strange means" to repel the Mongol hoards from Australia. Randolph Carter became aware of him while traveling beyond the Ultimate Gate.

(*Through the Gates of the Silver Key*)

Carter, Randolph

The most prominent of Lovecraft's characters is the explorer of dream worlds, Randolph Carter. In many ways, Carter is a projection of Lovecraft himself, or at least an idealized version of Lovecraft as he wished himself to be. Lovecraft saw himself as an explorer of dreams. Much of his fiction is based on his dreams and nightmares. Lovecraft is the real Randolph Carter, but how extensively Carter's dream wanderings mirror those of his creator is not easy to determine. Lovecraft inserted many elements from his dreams into his stories, and a few of his shorter tales were entirely based on dreams.

We know this was the case for the story *The Statement of Randolph Carter*, in which the character of Carter appears for the first time, because on December 11, 1919, Lovecraft wrote a complete description of a recent dream in a letter to his friend, August Derleth, and it matches exactly the plot of his later short story, with one key difference—in the dream it is Lovecraft himself who is the protagonist, but in the short story the name has been changed from his own to that of Randolph Carter.

In the dream, Lovecraft and one of his many correspondents, a man named Samuel E. Loveman (1887–1976), opened a "flat sepulchre" in an ancient New England graveyard, and Loveman descended into the open sepulchre down a flight of stone steps to investigate the occult secrets of the regions below while Lovecraft remained on the surface, in communication with Loveman by means of a telephone wire that Loveman unreeled from a spool as he progressed. Lovecraft listened in horror as Loveman found more than he bargained for, and in a terrified voice declared that he was doomed, and that Lovecraft should flee from the open grave and save himself. Lovecraft, although paralyzed with fear, stated his intention to descend into the underground passage to help his friend, when a strange and inhuman voice came over the telephone wire, and spoke the fatal words, "You fool, Loveman is dead."

In writing the story based on this dream, Lovecraft did little more than change his name to that of Carter, and Loveman's name to Harley Warren. The location was moved from New England to Big Cypress Swamp in Florida. The story was published in 1920. In it is prefigured the *Necronomicon*, for Warren is said to carry in his pocket an "ancient book in undecipherable characters" when he descends into the opened sepulchre, and Lovecraft intimates that it was the possession of this dread book that was the cause of Warren's death. However, the *Necronomicon* is not named is this early story in Lovecraft's writing career, and it is unlikely that Warren's mysterious book was intended to be the *Necronomicon*.

At the end of his letter to Derleth, Lovecraft mentioned that he planned to turn this dream into a story, just has he had done with the dream that was the basis for his story *The Doom That Came to Sarnath*. He added, "I wonder, though, if I have a right to claim authorship of things I dream? I hate to take credit, when I did not really think out the picture with my own conscious wits. Yet if I do not take credit, who'n Heaven will I give credit tuh?"

This admission indicates very clearly to what degree Lovecraft was himself Randolph Carter, the explorer of dream worlds. It also supports the possibility that many readers of his works have suspected—that what he wrote about was not entirely fiction, and that Lovecraft was not merely dreaming but was engaged in a form of astral travel when he saw the incredible scenes and experienced the strange events he described in his writings. There are modern ceremonial magicians who take Lovecraft's Old Ones quite seriously, and who use Lovecraft's mythological ancient history of our world as the basis for a system of practical ritual magic.

According to the few brief mentions Lovecraft made of his idealized astral-projecting alter ego, Randolph Carter, he was descended from a long line of English occultists. One of his ancestors was a Crusader knight who studied magic from the Saracens while held captive and awaiting his ransom home. A Sir Randolph Carter was a magician in the time of Queen Elizabeth I. An Edmund Carter was almost hanged for witchcraft at Salem. Esoteric pursuits were an inherent part of Carter's bloodline. He was a resident of Boston in the house belonging to his paternal ancestors, a lover of the architecture of that city, and not surprisingly, a writer of tales of cosmic horror. He had graduated from Lovecraft's fictional Miskatonic University, so noted for its arcane library, and had served as a soldier during the First World War in the French Foreign Legion.

Randolph Carter appears in six of Lovecraft's stories: *The Statement of Randolph Carter*, *The Unnamable*, *The Silver Key*, *The Dream-Quest of Unknown Kadath*, *The Case of Charles Dexter Ward*, and *Through the Gates of the Silver Key*.

In the earliest two tales, Carter is more of an observer than a participant. The dream plot of *The Statement of Randolph Carter* has already been related. In *The Unnamable*, Carter and his friend, Joel Manton, are spending an autumn afternoon lounging in the old burying-ground in Lovecraft's fictional New England town of Arkham, gazing at the mold-covered tombstones and talking about horror in literature. Carter relates a monstrous birth mentioned by Cotton Mather in his *Magnalia Christi Americana*, of a thing more than beast but less than human, and casually elaborates on the history, saying that the monster did not die but lived to terrorize the town. He describes finding the bones of the thing in the attic eve of the dilapidated house that overlooks the graveyard. Suddenly something rushes out of the attic window of the house, where the misshapen, horned creature lived during its life, and both men awake in the hospital with injuries on their bodies. They were found in a lonely field beyond Meadow Hill, a mile from the burying-ground, unconscious. Carter remembers nothing of what transpired, but Manton describes "a gelatin—a slime yet it had shapes, a thousand shapes of horror beyond all memory. There were eyes—and a blemish. It was the pit—the maelstrom—the ultimate abomination."

The assumption may be made that the men were carried through the air to the field, upon which a slaughterhouse had once stood, by some sort of flying invisible monster, perhaps an early prototype of the concept Lovecraft would later develop into his Old Ones. Carter has on his body the bruise imprint of a split-hoof—the kind of print associated with the horned half-human monster of Carter's account. The Devil is noted for his cloven hooves, and the print is a sly acknowledgement by Lovecraft of the story *The Man Who Went Too Far* by E. F. Benson, at the end of which a corpse is discovered with such cloven footprints on its chest.

Only in the third story in which he appears does Randolph Carter become the active mover of events. The story is autobiographical, at least in an inner sense. It is quite obvious that Lovecraft was writing about himself in *The Silver Key* when he described Carter's revulsion with the materialism of modern society. Carter even went so far in his depression as to obtain a vial of poison, which he carried with him in case he decided to kill himself. This detail of the story is lifted from Lovecraft's own experience. While living in New York City, Lovecraft himself obtained a vial of poison and carried it with him for a time, so great was his unhappiness.

Lovecraft related that at age thirty, Carter had suddenly lost the key to dreams. He had been told so often by others that dreams were foolish and useless things that he began to half-believe these lies, even though in his heart he never could embrace the external material world or regard it as possessed of any importance. Carter subsisted in this unhappy state, neither a dreamer nor a materialist, for more than twenty years. For a time he wrote popular novels that sold well, but he sickened of their superficiality and burned in disgust the last works he had written.

Lovecraft described in *The Silver Key* Carter's attempts to recapture the magic of his youth through the study of both religion and conventional occultism, and how he ultimately discarded both pursuits as futile. His adventures with Harley Warren and Joel Manton are mentioned as part of this unrewarded quest for meaning during these middle years. At last, in disgust at his failure, Carter put aside all the esoteric trappings of his life and retreated into the past, redecorating his house in the Victorian style of his childhood. It was through the past that he remembered the way of dreaming. Not long after he turned fifty, he had a dream in which he talked in his old family house at Boston for long hours with his dead grandfather about his ancestors. His grandfather told him about Edmund Carter, who was almost hanged as a witch as Salem, and who before his death had hidden a great silver key in a antique box. The ghost of his grandfather indicated that the key was a legacy to Carter from the past.

Carter found this box in the attic of the Boston house where he was living. There is a curious lack of specificity as to whether the finding of the box occurs in the waking world or the dream world. Even before finding the box, Carter had begun to recapture the power of dreaming through his embrace of the things of his childhood. The box is presented in the story as a physical object, but the reader is never entirely certain that Carter is not still dreaming when he describes its discovery, and how its rusty iron lock was forced open by a fearful retainer of the family, who did not like the carved faces that leered at him from its age-blackened lid.

Inside this mysterious oaken box of mystery was an enormous key of tarnished silver, covered with arabesques, along with a scroll that was written over with the same indecipherable characters as were on a papyrus scroll in the possession of his ill-fated friend, Harley Warren, who years ago had descended the moldy steps into the rifled sepulchre at Big Cypress Swamp, never to return. Carter cleaned the key and kept it in its box beside his bed at night. His dreams became more real. He recognized that he was being called by them back into his own past. Lovecraft wrote of Carter, "Then he knew he must go into the past and merge himself with old things." Carter felt impelled to take the key to the ancient home of his maternal ancestors.

The maternal family homestead of the Carters is on the Miskatonic River not far outside of Arkham. The ruin of a white house occupies the crest of a hill, and from its windows it is possible to look across the river valley and see the spires of Kingsport in the distance, along with the ocean on the horizon. It is not far from the deserted and dilapidated farmhouse of Goody Fowler, a reputed witch who is remembered with dread in local legend. Lovecraft wrote that Carter's mother and her "fathers before her" had been born in the house, suggesting that at least four generations of Carter's family had occupied the dwelling, probably more. Carter had often visited the house during the first ten years of his boyhood. It was occupied until Carter was age twenty by his great uncle Christopher, and after Christopher passed away Carter allowed the house to remain vacant and untended for thirty years until it collapsed in upon itself. He returned to it at age fifty-four with the silver key, seeking to rekindle within himself the power of dreaming.

The silver key is the physical symbol for the key of the imagination that unlocks the gates of the dreamlands. In dreams, which are astral worlds, symbols have tangible substance. Lovecraft used the device of the key to indicate the intrusion of dream reality into physical reality, the merging of the real world with the dream world, just as the two were merged in Lovecraft's own life. As Carter climbed the hill to the abandoned family farmhouse, he saw sunlight glint from the old Congregational steeple on Central Hill in Kingsport. Suddenly he remembered that the steeple had been torn down years ago to make way for a new hospital.

With this realization, Carter was cast back in time forty-five years to 1883 and became once again a nine-year-old boy. He could not remember where he had obtained the key he carried in his pocket, but dimly recalled his uncle Christopher talking about it. All those who lived in the farmhouse, so many years dead, were alive once again. The next day, nine-year-old Randy Carter took the key to a strange cave known locally as the Snake-Den and entered it. What he did inside the secret depths of the cave was not revealed by Lovecraft, but when the boy emerged he was subtly altered, and had acquired the power of prophetic visions of the future.

The fifty-four year old Carter had vanished from the world on the night he sought to revisit his ancestral home near Arkham, while walking through the ancient woods. Lovecraft intimated that Carter was not dead, but had become a king of the dream city of Ilek-Vad, in the kingdom of Ulthar. In this way Randolph Carter achieved what Lovecraft himself always longed for but was never able to accomplish—he left the world of waking reality completely behind him, and went to live in the dreamlands—or so it appeared in this story.

Lovecraft's novel *The Dream-Quest of Unknown Kadath* is the longest of his mythos works. It relates a dream adventure that Randolph Carter experienced before the age of thirty, when he was still able to explore the dreamlands at will. It is astonishing and at times bewildering for the sheer complexity of the places, races, and individual beings it describes in the dreamlands. In this novel, Lovecraft lays out the entire geography of the dreamlands. How much of it is his deliberate invention, and how much is a description from his own dream explorations, it is impossible to know, but there are many elements that have been taken from Lovecraft's own dreams.

In order to find a way to return to a wonderful dream city that he had once known, but had forgotten how to reach, Carter undertook a convoluted quest of several months travel to the lofty and mystical mountain Kadath, which lies in the Cold Waste, so that he could consult the gods of the Earth who dwell on its summit. It transpired that the gods themselves had stolen Carter's city for their own to play in, so much did they love it. Carter took back his city and returned to the waking world the same night he had left it, for in the dreamlands time does not pass at the same rate it passes in waking life.

In the final story that directly involves Randolph Carter, *Through the Gates of the Silver Key*, we learn what happened to Carter when at age fifty-four he took his silver key and vanished into a grove of elms near ruins of the old Carter family farm. The tale is set in the New Orleans house of Carter's literary and financial executor, Etienne-Laurent de Marigny, who is described as "this continent's greatest mystic, mathematician, and orientalist," and takes place four years after Carter's disappearance. Friends of Carter have gathered to preside over the division of his estate among his distant cousins, who are represented by one of their number, Ernest K. Aspinwall of Chicago.

In addition to the executor and the cousin, there is present Carter's friend Ward Phillips, a mystic of Providence, Rhode Island, who was none other than Lovecraft himself under another name. He was described as "lean, gray, long-nosed, clean-shaven, and stoop-shouldered." He declared his conviction that since his disappearance, Carter had ruled in the dreamlands as king of the town of Ilek-Vad. The executor de Marigny also believed Carter to still be alive, but the cousins have forced the division of his estate by applying legal pressure. The final man present in the mansion is a mysterious turbaned figure who represents himself as Swami Chandraputra, an adept from Benares, India, and who claims to have information concerning the fate of Randolph Carter.

Chandraputra relates to the others that Carter conducted a ritual with the key while standing under the elms at twilight four years ago, involving nine turnings of the key accompanied by incantations. This carried him back to his boyhood, when he was only nine years old. The next day the nine-year-old Carter entered the Snake-Den with the key and, in the inner chamber of the cave, used the key again before a natural arch surmounted with a curious feature resembling a carved hand. This time the key opened a gate to an extension of the Earth that lies outside of time.

Carter confronted the Guardian of the Gate, a being known as 'Umr at-Twil, the Most Ancient One, called by Alhazred in the *Necronomicon* the "Prolonged of Life." Concerning this guide, Alhazred wrote, "they would have been more prudent had they avoided commerce with HIM." The Most Ancient One resembled a human form, but was half again as tall as a man, and shrouded entirely in a neutral-colored fabric in which there appeared to be no eyeholes through which he could see. He offered to show Carter the Ultimate Gate, and Carter accepted him as a guide.

Carter ascended onto a throne prepared for him atop a hexagonal pillar, alongside Ancients who served the Most Ancient One. With their help Carter was able to use the key to unlock the Ultimate Gate. As he passed through it, he looked back and saw that he had come through many gates of strange shape. He found his consciousness split into innumerable beings which he simultaneously inhabited. Yog-Sothoth, keeper of all gates, spoke to him and offered him access to the ultimate mystery, which he had in the past granted to only five other men.

Yog-Sothoth showed Carter the pettiness of the gods of Earth, who are wrapped up in the affairs of humanity. He taught him about higher dimensions, and conferred upon him a great truth: "That which we call substance and reality is shadow and illusion, and that which we call shadow and illusion is substance and reality." This was undoubtedly Lovecraft's own belief, the quintessence of his life philosophy. Past, present, and future exist only because of the limitations of the human mind. Even change itself is an illusion—all things and all conditions exist simultaneously. All the living beings in the universe are merely facets of the people of the Ultimate Abyss; formless, ineffable archetypes of whom the chief is Yog-Sothoth. On all worlds, all great thinkers such as Randolph Carter are expressions of the Chief Archetype.

Somewhat imprudently, Carter asked the Chief Archetype to send him into the past to the world of Yaddith, and suddenly found himself inhabiting the inhuman body of the wizard Zkauba, a creature with a shape "rugose, partly squamous, and curiously articulated," with claws and a snout. His consciousness did not immediately gain control, as he had expected, but was initially overpowered by the consciousness of Zkauba.

In time, and with immense difficulty, Carter assumed control over his new body, and used the wisdom of Yaddith to physically travel back to Earth in his alien shell. It was his purpose to decipher the parchment that had accompanied the silver key, and by its correct use regain his human body. Such was the account given by Swami Chandraputra, who was none other than Randolph Carter in disguise, his alien body concealed behind a mask and loose clothing.

As this revelation was made to the three men present at the hearing, the mind of Zkauba regained control of his form and was able to escape the Earth by means of a large, coffin-shaped clock with four hands that was in the house of Étienne-Laurent de Marigny. The wizard recognized the true function of the clock, as a portal through time and space, and entered its coffin-shaped case, never to emerge again upon the Earth. He left the silver key behind. The fate of Randolph Carter remains unknown. He may still be battling for supremacy over the consciousness of Zkauba as the two minds in one body travel from world to world. Lovecraft wrote nothing more on the matter.

In *The Case of Charles Dexter Ward*, Carter is mentioned only in passing as a friend to Doctor Marinus Bicknell Willett, who had once spoken to Willett about the power of the sign of Koth, a symbol which dreamers sometimes see fixed above the archway to a certain black tower in the dreamlands. Willett was made uncomfortable recalling the things Carter had told him, but what those secrets may have been, Lovecraft did not reveal.

(*The Statement of Randolph Carter; The Unnamable; The Silver Key; The Dream-Quest of Unknown Kadath; The Case of Charles Dexter Ward; Through the Gates of the Silver Key*)

Chandraputra, Swami

The mind of Randolph Carter, inhabiting the alien body of the wizard Zkauba, traveled to present-day earth from the distant past of the planet Yaddith through a time-space portal, as described in *Through the Gates of the Silver Key*. He called himself Swami Chandraputra, "an adept from Benares"—a guise adopted by Carter to conceal his alien form while he acquired the occult knowledge necessary to regain his human body. He appeared in Arkham in 1930, and from 1930 to 1932 lived in a flat in Chambers Street in the West End of Boston, where he pursued his researches. His speech had a hollow, metallic quality on the ear. His dark face was partially hidden behind a bushy black beard, and he wore the turban of a high-caste Brahman on his head, and mittens over his hands. His oddest feature was his deep-set eyes, which are described as "night-black, burning, almost irisless." In reality, his face was only a mask to hide Zakauba's alien features, just as the mittens served to cover his alien claws. When Zkauba regained control of his own body, he leapt through a time-space portal in the form of a tall, coffin-shaped clock with four hands, dragging the unwilling mind of Carter back with him to Yaddith.

Chandraputra was given a brief reference in the story *Out of the Aeons*, where he is described as a very strange character with a labored, unnatural voice and an expressionless face, who always wore mittens over his hands. He appeared in Boston at the Cabot Museum of Archaeology in November of 1932, where he quickly demonstrated that he was "unbelievably erudite in occult lore" and had some knowledge of the mysterious hieroglyphic scroll in the iridescent cylinder that was one of the prize exhibits of the museum.

(*Through the Gates of the Silver Key; Out of the Aeons*)

Churchward, Colonel James *

Colonel James Churchward (1851–1936), the author of the 1926 work *The Lost Continent of Mu, Motherland of Man*, and two other books on Mu, was drawn into the Necronomicon mythos when Lovecraft made him into a minor off-stage character of his story *Through the Gates of the Silver Key*. In the story, Churchward has been consulted about certain strange hieroglyphics on the parchment that was left to Randolph Carter along with an ornate silver key. Churchward offers his opinion that the hieroglyphics are not Naacal, the writing of lost Mu, nor do they resemble the symbols found on an Easter Island war club. Churchward is mentioned in passing in *Out of the Aeons*, along with Lewis Spence, as an authority on "lost continents and primal forgotten civilizations."

(*Through the Gates of the Silver Key; Out of the Aeons*)

Corey, Abaddon

A witch of Salem, Massachusetts. His daughter married Dirck van der Heyl, and the couple lived in Albany until 1746, when accusations of witchcraft drove them out.

(*The Diary of Alonzo Typer*)

Corsi, Bartolomeo

A Florentine monk of the twelfth century whose mind was imprisoned in the distant past in a cone-shaped body by the time-spanning Great Race of Yith. He conversed with Nathaniel Wingate Peaslee, a former resident of Arkham and professor at Miskatonic University whose mind was similarly trapped.

(*The Shadow Out of Time*)

Crom-Ya

A Cimmerian chieftain who lived circa 15,000 BC. Nathaniel Wingate Peaslee conversed with him while Peaslee's mind was held prisoner by the Yithians. This character is a minor tribute to Robert E. Howard, with whom Lovecraft carried on a friendly letter correspondence. Howard's greatest creation, Conan the Barbarian, was a Cimmerian, and the god of the Cimmerians was named Crom.

(*The Shadow Out of Time*)

Curwen, Joseph

An alchemist and necromancer born in 1662 at Salem-Village (now called Danvers), Massachusetts, not far from Salem. The full nature of his involvement in the Salem witch persecution is not known, but in 1692 when the witch trials were in progress, he was forced to flee from Salem to Providence, Rhode Island, where he settled and prospered as a merchant and slave trader. His true avocation was not trade, but necromancy. Working with the alchemists Edward Hutchinson of Salem-Village and one Simon Orne of Salem by means of written correspondence, Curwen perfected a technique for resurrecting the dead from their essential salts. He procured ancient corpses from the far places of the world, reduced them to their essential salts, and then brought the dead to life to extract by torture their secrets of magic. Through his alchemy he was able to prolong his own life and maintain his youthful appearance in Providence for almost eight decades, but in 1781 the townspeople of Providence mounted a raid on his lands and killed him.

In 1928 Curwen's descendant, the occult student Charles Dexter Ward, resurrected him from his essential salts. For a time the two studied together and resumed Curwen's necromantic work, but when Ward's horror began to grow at the monstrous evils they were committing, and at his ancestor's dark designs, Curwen murdered him and assumed his identity. This was made possible by a close facial resemblance between Curwen and his descendant that was not accidental, but the result of magic worked by Curwen during his first life to ensure his resurrection.

Due to his changed manner and the obvious gaps in his memory, Curwen masquerading as Ward was pronounced insane and locked into a mental institution. The Ward family doctor, Marinus Bicknell Willett, investigated the land where Curwen's old farmhouse had stood and discovered a catacomb of horrors in tunnels beneath it. Visiting the asylum, he reversed the necromantic spell that had given Curwen life, and returned him to his essential salts.

(*The Case of Charles Dexter Ward*)

Damascius *

Called the last of the Neoplatonists, Damascius (480–c. 550) is remembered chiefly for commentaries on the writings of Aristotle, Plato, and other Greek philosophers. He is mentioned by Lovecraft in *The Nameless City*, where the narrator speaks of "paragraphs from the apocryphal nightmares of Damascius" along with other dread works by Abdul Alhazred and Gautier de Metz. There is no evidence that Damascius ever wrote anything that might be described as "apocryphal nightmares."

(*The Nameless City*)

de la Poer, Gilbert

The First Baron Exham, he received the title to Exham Priory, just outside of Anchester, a village in Exeter, in the southwest of England, from King Henry III in 1261. In the year 1307 the family became cursed. The de la Poers entered into a black pact with an inhuman race of beings that dwelt in caverns deep beneath the ancient house, a pact that entailed human sacrifice and cannibal feasts.

(*The Rats in the Walls*)

de la Poer, Walter

The eleventh Baron Exham, he tried to lift the ancient curse that had hung over his family estate of Exham Priory for centuries by slaughtering his father, five of his siblings, and several family servants. He fled to the colony of Virginia, aided in his escape by the grateful people of the nearby village of Anchester.

(*The Rats in the Walls*)

de Marigny, Étienne-Laurent

The friend of Randolph Carter and a native of the old French Quarter of New Orleans. De Marigny met Carter while the two were both serving in the French Foreign Legion during the First World War. Both men shared an intense interest in occult studies. On a joint furlough, de Marigny took Carter to Bayonne, in the south of France, and revealed to Carter "certain terrible secrets" in the network of crypts beneath that ancient city. This act of trust sealed their friendship for life. Carter appointed de Marigny as the executor of his estate, should he die before the Creole. After Carter's disappearance at age 54, de Marigny prepared to handle the division of Carter's estate, and was present when the strange revelations of Swami Chandraputra were made in de Marigny's New Orleans home, as related in *Through the Gates of the Silver Key*. De Marigny is described in this story as "slim, dark, handsome, mustached, and still young."

Another reference is made to the "famous New Orleans mystic Étienne-Laurent de Marigny" in *Through the Aeons*, where he is said to have written an article in the *Occult Review* concerning the hieroglyphics on the scroll inside the iridescent cylinder that is part of the collection of the Cabot Museum of Boston. De Marigny contended that several of the hieroglyphs on the scroll corresponded with certain ideographs copied from monoliths or from secret rituals of obscure cults by Friedrich von Junzt, and recorded in his book *Nameless Cults*.

(*Through the Gates of the Silver Key; Out of the Aeons*)

De Metz, Gauthier *

French poet of the thirteenth century who wrote a poem about creation and the nature of the universe titled *"L'Image du monde"* ("Portrait of the World"). The narrator of *The Nameless City* characterized this poem as "delirious." It describes a spherical Earth, and part of the work is astrological.

(*The Nameless City*)

Dee, John *

The Elizabethan mathematician and cartographer Dr. John Dee is supposed to have made an English translation of the *Necronomicon*. A copy of the book was in the keeping of Wilbur Whateley, an inheritance from his grandfather, but it had become damaged and a portion of the text was missing. This caused Wilbur to attempt to learn the content of the missing pages by comparing his book with the Latin version of the *Necronomicon* in the library of Miskatonic University.

Had the *Necronomicon* existed in a physical sense during the Elizabethan Age, it is quite probable that John Dee would have possessed a copy. He was a renowned scholar, and his personal library was the largest in England. Men came from all over Europe to consult Dee and his books. Dee's primary interest was the use of magic to forward the geopolitical ambitions of his sovereign, Queen Elizabeth I, and to ensure his own financial prosperity. His library contained many forbidden books on magic, and Dee himself engaged for a period of years in an almost daily communication with a hierarchy of spirits identifying themselves as the angels who had instructed the patriarch Enoch in the occult arts. Dee was very much a practicing magician and an alchemist.

For the past three centuries, historians and biographers have tended to gloss over Dee's occult practices in an attempt to avoid tainting Dee's reputation as a great scholar with the stain of superstition. Much the same was true for the memory of Sir Isaac Newton, who at one period of his life was an ardent alchemist, and who studied biblical prophecy and astrology. In recent decades, Dee's role as a magician has come forth in biographies that no longer attempt to conceal his communications with spirits or his practice of alchemy.

Although it is almost certain that Dee would have possessed a copy of the *Necronomicon*, had it existed on the material plane, it is unlikely that he would have made an English translation. Dee had no need to translate Latin texts into English for his own use. Latin was the universal language of European scholars of the period. Dee would have considered the *Necronomicon* far too dangerous a book to place into the hands of his untutored countrymen. If a copy of the work in Arabic or Greek had fallen into his hands, he would probably have made a Latin translation, not an English translation. Had he acquired a Latin copy, he would not have translated it at all.

Nonetheless, Lovecraft himself asserted in his fictional history of the *Necronomicon* that an English copy of the work, translated by John Dee, exists, and it has become a firm part of the lore of the mythos. No historical figure, with the possible exception of Johannes Trithemius, was better suited to make sense of the *Necronomicon* than John Dee. In the transcriptions of his communications with the Enochian angels, Dee produced a book that is almost as interesting as the *Necronomicon*, containing as it does an entire system of angel magic and an angelic language.

(*The Dunwich Horror*)

Delapore, Randolph

A descendant of the infamous de la Poer family of England, after his return to Carfax, Virginia, from the Mexican War in 1848, he went among the negroes and became a Voodoo priest. It is unlikely that he possessed any knowledge of the ancient curse that hung over his family.

(*The Rats in the Walls*)

Derby, Edward Pickman

A poetic genius and child prodigy, who at the age of seven was composing poems that astounded his tutors, both for their technical skill and their morbid subject matter. His juvenilia was published when he was eighteen under the title *Azathoth and Other Horrors*. His weak constitution caused his parents to keep him segregated from other children, but constantly watched over by nurses and servants, fostering a love of the fantastic and bizarre as an avenue of refuge. The wealth of his family removed any necessity for him to seek practical employment as an adult. He became a keen student of the occult while attending Miskatonic University, an institution of higher learning noted for its library of arcane and prohibited books on magic.

His mother died when he was thirty-four. He began to associate with occult groups in Europe and to perform rituals of black magic. When he was thirty-eight he married Asenath Waite, of the Innsmouth Waites, who shared his obsession with the occult. Lovecraft intimated that Asenath was a hybrid of a union between a human father and a mother who was a Deep One. The initial happiness of the union turned to horror for Derby when he became convinced that his wife was attempting to psychically displace his consciousness and occupy his body, to make it her own. Even more horrifying, it was not his wife seeking to accomplish this psychic rape, but the consciousness of her father, the wizard Ephraim Waite, who had previously stolen the youthful body of his daughter to serve as the vessel for his mind.

Derby found himself unable to resist the power of Ephraim's will. The old Innsmouth wizard forced his consciousness into the body of Derby, and simultaneously forced the consciousness of Derby into the body of Asenath. Then he killed Asenath's body. The soul of Derby, bound to the corpse of Asenath, was able through the use of his acquired necromantic knowledge to animate the putrefying flesh and use it to pass a message to his childhood friend, Daniel Upton, begging Upton to kill Ephraim and thereby stop Ephraim's evil practices. Upton shot Ephraim, in Derby's body, six times in the head. So ended, for the second time, the unfortunate life of Edward Pickman Derby.

(*The Thing on the Doorstep*)

Dorieb

The divine, or semi-divine, monarch of the dreamland city of Cathuria, which is noteworthy for its unusual architecture. The palace of Dorieb has marble turrets and a roof of pure gold supported by ten pillars. The floor is of glass, allowing the fish swimming in the river Narg that flows beneath the palace to be viewed by its inhabitants.

(*The White Ship*)

Dudley, Jervas

This twenty-one year old man from a wealthy Bostonian family does not attend university or hold a job, but spends his days wandering through the woods and fields near his home, particularly a wooden hollow that contains the ancestral tomb of the Hydes, to whom he is distantly related on his mother's side. He conceives an obsession for the tomb, and for the dead who lie within, with whom he begins to nightly frolic and mingle. As he puts it, "I tasted to the full joys of that charnel conviviality which I must not describe."

He gradually takes on the mannerisms and speech affectations of a rake of the late eighteenth century, specifically those of his ancestor Jervas Hyde, whose empty coffin lies within the tomb, but whose bones were burned to ashes and scattered in a house fire. The implication is that he becomes possessed with the spirit of Jervas Hyde, which longs to lie at rest within the family tomb. When his parents grow concerned about his outlandish behavior and have him watched, they discover that he goes each night and stretches out on the ground outside the stone door of the padlocked tomb, staring at the crack in the doorway with half-opened eyes in a kind of trance that resembles sleep. The young man swears he enters the tomb each night and converses and interacts with the shades of the dead. Ultimately, his parents have him committed to a mental institution.

It is obvious that Jervas Dudley is yet another fictionalized version of Lovecraft, who fancied himself an English gentleman with no need to work for a living, who affected the speech mannerisms of the eighteenth century, who had difficulty fitting into a school routine, who spent his youth wandering by himself, and who always feared the spectre of madness that took both his parents. Lovecraft was obsessed with genealogy, heredity, and the past. He was a dreamer who regarded his dreams as more attractive and in some ways more real than waking life. It is interesting to note that Dudley finds a key in a box in the attic, a family relic that opens the lock on the door of the tomb, but it turns out to exist only in his dreams; another of Lovecraft's alter egos, Randolph Carter, also finds a key in the attic, a family relic that for the dreamer Carter opens the gates beyond time and space.

There is a strong sexual innuendo in Dudley's pleasures within the tomb. After the first night he "staggers from the vault" and drags himself home in the "grey light of dawn [. . .] no longer a young man." Those who saw him pass in the street "marveled at the signs of ribald revelry." Lovecraft was not explicit about what the "full joys" of "charnel conviviality" might have been, but we may speculate that they included the loss of sexual innocence, since the virtuous Jervas Dudley becomes the dissipated rake Jervas Hyde—the name having been chosen by Lovecraft as a literary nod to *The Strange Case of Dr. Jekyll and Mr. Hyde* by Robert Louis Stevenson. It may be added that it is perfectly possible to have a full sexual experience with an astral being, so this erotic intimation of Lovecraft's is not without foundation in occult practices.

Those who might assume that the suggestion of sexual relations with the dead was too risqué for Lovecraft's era should examine the story *The Loved Dead*, co-written with C. M. Eddy, where the narrator takes work in a funeral home in order to have the freedom to, as he puts it, "devise new and unspeakable ways of lavishing my affections upon the dead that I loved." He is discovered in the early morning by the director of the funeral home, lying asleep on a slab with his arms wrapped around the "stark, stiff, naked body of a fetid corpse."

(*The Tomb*)

Eagle, John

A "swarthy, simian-faced, Indian-like" resident of the village of Chorazin, near Attica, New York. In 1935 he found the diary of Alonzo Typer in the collapsed ruins of the van der Heyl house, that had formerly stood near the center of the village.

(*The Diary of Alonzo Typer*)

Elton, Basil

The keeper of the North Point lighthouse at the mouth of Kingsport harbor, who boarded the White Ship that sailed out of the south, and was carried on a voyage past some of the fabled cities of the dreamlands. He stopped and lived in the land of Sona-Nyl, where there is neither time nor space, for "many aeons" before foolishly setting forth once more in the White Ship to seek the land of Cathuria, beyond the twin Basalt Pillars of the West. His dream galley was carried over the great cataract that forever falls off the edge of the world, and he regained awareness standing on the platform of his lighthouse, to find that no time had passed. In *The Dream-Quest of Unknown Kadath*, it is mentioned that Randolph Carter talked to Elton about his dreamland experiences, although Elton is not named.

(*The White Ship; The Dream-Quest of Unknown Kadath*)

Fowler, Goody

A female witch who once lived in a farm cottage near Arkham, and whose name has become a part of local legend. She was noted for her potions.

(*The Silver Key; Through the Gates of the Silver Key*)

Gilman, Walter

This native of Haverhill, Massachusetts, came to Arkham to attend Miskatonic University, where he studied higher mathematics and folklore, a curious combination of disciplines that perhaps would only make sense at this institution, with its world famous library of occult books. Gilman rebelled against the attempts by the witch, Keziah Mason, to dominate him. His heart was eaten out of his body by her familiar, Brown Jenkin.

(*The Dreams in the Witch House*)

Hermes Trismegistus *

In *The Case of Charles Dexter Ward* mention is made of "Hermes Trismegistus in Mesnard's edition," which is in the library of Joseph Curwen. In the story *The Tree on the Hill*, which Lovecraft co-wrote with Duane W. Rimel, Hermes Trismegistus is characterized as "the ancient Egyptian sorcerer." The German mystic Rudolf Yergler, author of the apocryphal text the *Chronicle of Nath*, is supposed in this story to have borrowed some of his lore from Hermes Trismegistus.

Hermes is a Greek god, but Hermes Trismegistus is Egyptian, and has been reckoned variously as a great sage, a demi-god born of a divine father and a mortal mother, and a full god, by those who place credence in his supposed existence. There is no proof that such a man ever lived. The Greek god Hermes was identified by the Greeks who ruled Egypt during the reign of the Ptolemies (305 BC–30 BC) with the Egyptian god Thoth. The two names are sometimes combined in the form Thoth-Hermes. "Trismegistus" means "thrice great" in Greek, and is a title of honor.

Many books of religion and philosophy were attributed to Hermes Trismegistus, but even more numerous books of ritual magic. Those that survive have been conjecturally dated to the second or third century, and hence are later than Hermes Trismegistus himself, the earliest surviving mention of whom may be 172 BC. Most of these Hermetic books have been lost to the past. The surviving books that concern philosophical matters are sometimes referred to as the *Corpus Hermetica*. Hermes Trismegistus was especially associated with the art of alchemy, which is Egyptian in its origins. Indeed, he was credited with its invention.

(*The Case of Charles Dexter Ward; The Tree on the Hill*)

Holm, Axel

This seventeenth-century glass and mirror maker, born in 1612, a native of Copenhagen, was also a Luciferian and a witch. Using an existing "ancient glass" with extraordinary properties which he fused into a much larger glass, he devised a chiffonier mirror that had the power to absorb and trap human beings in the fourth dimension, where they did not age or die. The small ancient mirror had spiral whorls or ripples on its surface that could only be viewed at certain angles, but which were part of its function as a dimensional portal. Holm entered the mirror in 1687, hoping to achieve eternal life, and, from time to time over the course of the following two centuries, drew others into his curiously inverted mirror world as companions. His shadow existence was ended when a private school tutor in Connecticut named Canevin used a glass-cutting tool to remove the small, ancient, oval piece of glass from the larger sheet to which it had been bonded by Holm.

(*The Trap*)

Houdini, Harry [*]

The stage magician and escape artist Harry Houdini (1874–1926), born Ehrich Weiss in Budapest, Hungary, of Jewish parents, immigrated with his family to the United States at age four years. From early childhood he was fascinated with stage magic. He took the name Harry Houdini, basing it on the name of the famous French magician Jean Eugène Robert-Houdin, and began to perform escapes along with his stage illusions in the 1890s, first with the help of his brother Dash, and later with his new wife, Bess, whom he married in 1893. When he realized the escapes were impressing the audiences more than his magic tricks, he dropped the magic and became an escape artist, and his legend was born.

Houdini commissioned Lovecraft to ghostwrite several works for him as a way of publicizing his name. The most important of these is the story *Imprisoned With the Pharaohs*, published in the May-June-July 1924 issue of *Weird Tales*, and featured on the cover of that magazine. Naturally an escape from bonds figures prominently in the story, which is quite readable, and very much a part of Lovecraft's mythos. Lovecraft put Houdini into the story as its hero, in an adventure in Egypt that takes Houdini under the Pyramids, where he witnesses unspeakable rites of sacrifice by ghouls in adoration of an enormous and deathless monster that in ancient times was the living model for the original Sphinx, before the head of the giant statue was recarved into the image of the pharaoh Khephren. So vast is the monster that at first Houdini is able to see only its great hairy paw as it reaches through an opening for its charnel sacrifices, although at the end of the story he intimates that he has seen its face as well.

Houdini died due to miscommunication. While about to give a performance in Montreal, Canada, a McGill University student in the crowd asked him if it was true that Houdini could withstand any punch to his abdomen, and if so, could he try hitting the performer? Houdini had not been paying attention to the fan, and agreed absently. The repeated forceful blows the student rained down before Houdini could prepare himself ruptured his appendix. Instead of having it attended to immediately, Houdini went on with his performance that night, and continued to travel and perform. The delay in treatment resulted in his death more than a week later, on the afternoon of Halloween.

At the time of his death, Houdini had been corresponding with Lovecraft regarding a book on which they intended to collaborate, along with the writer C. M. Eddy Jr., which was to be entitled *The Cancer of Superstition*. Lovecraft prepared a detailed outline of the work, which is extant, and Barlow actually began the writing and completed three chapters, but Houdini's widow cancelled the project—perhaps because she was herself more inclined to believe in the reality of spiritualist phenomena than her skeptical late husband.

(*Imprisoned with the Pharaohs*)

Imash-Mo

High priest of the hundred priests of the cult of the demon-god Ghatanothoa, in the kingdom of K'naa on the continent of Mu. According to the *Unspeakable Cults* of Von Junzt, he flourished in 173,148 BC.

(*Out of the Aeons*)

Jermyn, Arthur

He doused himself with oil and set himself on fire out on the moor on August 3, 1913, after learning the truth about his family bloodline—his great-great-great grandfather, Sir Wade Jermyn, had taken as his wife the princess of a race of hybrid white apes inhabiting the ruins of a great stone city in the Congo. Arthur Jermyn could not bear the thought of his tainted blood.

(*Facts Concerning the Late Arthur Jermyn and His Family*)

Jermyn, Sir Wade

English explorer of Africa and great-great-great grandfather to Arthur Jermyn, he was one of the earliest Europeans to see the Congo, and wrote a book about its tribes, animals, and antiquities. He often spoke of the stone ruins of a forgotten city in the jungle, with treasure vaults and catacombs beneath. The lost city was said by the Onga tribe to be inhabited by strange hybrid creatures resembling white apes. On his second African expedition he brought back with him to England a wife, who was never seen by others, not even the house servants, but was always kept in seclusion. She bore him one son. On his third and last African expedition he returned her to the Congo and left her there. In 1765 he was placed into a madhouse at Huntingdon, where he died three years later.

(*Facts Concerning the Late Arthur Jermyn and His Family*)

Kaman-Thah

Bearded priest of the earthly gods. In company with his fellow bearded priest, Nasht, he presides in a cavern temple with a pillar of flame that lies in the dreamlands, not far from the gates of the waking world. Randolph Carter invoked the gods by means of a sacrifice within this temple, when he was about to set forth on his epic quest to find Kadath, but they failed to respond to his invocation. The priests attempted to dissuade Carter from his purpose, pointing out that the gods had already indicated their disapproval of his intention, but he ignored their warning. The cavern of flame is reached by a descent down a stone stair of seventy steps while in a state of light slumber.

(*The Dream-Quest of Unknown Kadath*)

Ka-Nefer

The high-priest of Nath, remembered in the *Chronicle of Nath* by the German mystic Rudolf Yergler. He kept safe in the temple the amber gem that alone could show the true form of the Shadow that comes in the Year of the Black Goat to feed on the souls of men. Yergler wrote that the Gem was lost when a hero of Nath, Phrenes, attempted to use it to drive away the Shadow and was never heard from again.

(*The Tree on the Hill*)

Khephren *

This pharaoh of Egypt was associated with the renovation of the Sphinx. He had a dream about the Sphinx in which it was revealed to him that if he cleared away the sand from around the statue, and repaired the damage that had occurred to it over time, he would have a prosperous reign. He was said to have remodeled the face of the Sphinx to resemble his own face. Khephren's pyramid is the second in size of the three large pyramids on the Giza Plateau. It is easily recognizable, because it is the only pyramid to have retained part of its original outer covering of white stone, which can be seen around its apex.

In *Imprisoned with the Pharaohs*, ghostwritten for the escape artist Harry Houdini in 1924, Lovecraft wrote: "The whispers of Arabs are very wild, and cannot be relied upon. They even hint that old Khephren—he of the Sphinx, the Second Pyramid and the yawning gateway temple—lives far underground wedded to the ghoul-queen Nitokris and ruling over the mummies that are neither of man nor of beast."

(*Imprisoned with the Pharaohs*)

Klarkash-Ton

A high priest of Atlantis. The name is derived from the name of Lovecraft's friend, fellow fantasy writer Clark Ashton Smith.

(*The Whisperer in Darkness*)

Khephnes

An Egyptian of the 14th Dynasty who knew the "hideous secret of Nyarlathotep," which Lovecraft does not reveal to his readers. It may be surmised that Khephnes was either a priest or a magician of Egypt. The secret may have involved the Egyptian Sphinx.

(*The Shadow Out of Time*)

Kuranes

The king of the dreamland seaport of Celephaïs, which lies in the valley of Ooth-Nargai beyond the Tanarian Hills, on the shores of the Cerenerian Sea. In waking life Kuranes had been a native of Cornwall and a pauper living in a garret in London. He dreamed the city of Celephaïs into existence in the dreamlands. Randolph Carter had known this king in waking life. Kuranes had once ventured out beyond the stars into the ultimate void, and was said to be the only person who had ever returned sane from this perilous journey. For six months of the year Kuranes rules Celephaïs, and for the other half of the year he rules the sky city of Serannian, which is built of pink marble on the low-hanging clouds "where the west wind flows into the sky." The trading galleys from Celephaïs sail off the edge of the Cerenerian Sea and into the clouds that touch the western horizon, and in this way reach Serannian.

(*Celephaïs; The Dream-Quest of Unknown Kadath*)

Le Sorcier, Charles

An alchemist of the thirteenth century, who with the help of his father, the alchemist and sorcerer Michel Mauvais, succeeded in discovering the elixir of eternal life. When his father was unjustly killed by Henri, the Count de C———, Charles pronounced a terrible curse against all of the count's male descendants, that they should live no longer than the Count de C——— himself, and then he killed the count with a thrown vial of poison, and vanished before he could be apprehended. Over the following six centuries he continued to carry out his curse against the descendants of the count, who met with mysterious deaths at age thirty-two, until he was killed with fire by Antoine, last of the Counts de C———, in the early nineteenth century.

His body after six centuries was still vigorous, his hair and wild beard jet black in color. The cheeks beneath his high forehead were sunken and lined with wrinkles, and his black eyes glared forth as though from two dark pits. He spoke with a rumbling but hollow voice in a debased Latin of the Middle Ages, and wore a skullcap and dark medieval tunic.

Only the stoop in his back, and his claw-like, gnarled hands, so unnaturally bloodless and white, betrayed his centuries of age.

The quest for the elixir of eternal life that cured all diseases and banished death was one of two preoccupations of medieval alchemists, the other being the search for the philosopher's stone that would transform base metals into gold. Sometimes the stone was held to possess both occult virtues—touching it to lead or iron would transform the thing touched into pure gold, and dropping the stone into a glass of water and drinking the water cured disease and prolonged life.

(*The Alchemist*)

Lévi, Eliphas *

The French writer and occultist Alphonse Louis Constant (1810–75) is widely regarded as the foremost exponent of the modern revival of ceremonial magic in Europe. He wrote numerous influential books on the practice of magic, gave private lessons in magic for large sums of money, and had a great influence on the teachings of French occultists of his century, as well as on the system of magic formulated by S. L. MacGregor Mathers and W. Wynn Westcott for the English occult society known as the Hermetic Order of the Golden Dawn. Aleister Crowley, a member of the Golden Dawn in his youth, proclaimed himself to be a reincarnation of Lévi, such was his admiration for the occultist.

Lovecraft mentioned Lévi in connection with a ritual invocation in Latin beginning with the words "Per Adonai Eloim" that is incanted by Charles Dexter Ward for necromantic purposes, stating through his narrator, "its very close analogue can be found in the mystic writings of Eliphas Lévi, that cryptic soul who crept through a crack in the forbidden door and glimpsed the frightful vistas of the void beyond." For more on this incantation, refer to the Thirteenth Gate of this book.

(*The Case of Charles Dexter Ward*)

Marsh, Obed

Captain Obed Marsh was a Yankee trader in the South Seas who made his homeport in the New England coastal fishing town of Innsmouth. He flourished in the early decades of the nineteenth century, and was a leading figure in Innsmouth. With three trading ships, he must have been the most prosperous resident of the town, which had fallen on hard times following the War of 1812. His time spent among the savage tribes on the islands of the Pacific made him contemptuous of Christian piety. He told his fellow townsfolk that the gods of the islanders were superior to the Christian God, because they came when they were called, answered prayers, and gave good fishing in return for sacrifices.

On an island east of Othaheite, Marsh found a tribe of Kanaky natives that possessed a hoard of strange gold jewelry carved with monstrous figures described by Zadok Allen, a character in *The Shadow Over Innsmouth*, as "fish-like frogs or frog-like fishes." The tribe always had an abundance of fish in their nets, even when the natives on neighboring islands were starving. The chief of the tribe revealed to the Yankee trader the secret of the tribe's success—a pact they had formed with a race of aquatic humanoids known as the Deep Ones. Lovecraft intimated through Zadok Allen that these beings were the origin for all the legends about mermaids that are encountered throughout history.

The Deep Ones have their own cities on the floor of the ocean. When some of their dwellings were heaved up to the surface on an emerging island, carrying the Deeps Ones along with them, the Kanakys came into communication with the aquatic race and began to sacrifice to them and trade with them. The sacrifices consisted of children given over to the Deep Ones twice a year, on May-Eve and Halloween. Obed Marsh was not overly concerned about what became of the sacrifices after they were given to the Deep Ones. He was more occupied with the gifts of gold and fish offered to the islanders as payment.

The Deep Ones enjoyed mating with human beings, being at root of similar genetic structure. The hybrids born of such couplings were completely human in appearance when young, but as they matured and grew old, they became similar to the frog-like Deep Ones, and developed gills in their necks that allowed them to live under the sea. They were also eternal, and would never die unless by some physical accident causing great injury to their bodies. At about age seventy, the transformation progressed to such an extent that the hybrids left life on the land entirely and took up residence beneath the waves.

Here we see one of Lovecraft's most prevalent themes, the transformation of human beings from an outwardly normal condition into something strange and monstrous as a result of some taint in their blood. It may have arisen out of Lovecraft's own fear of insanity. Both his father and mother were committed to an insane asylum, and Lovecraft could never shake off the suspicion that he himself was not wholly sound of mind, not truly normal beneath the skin.

Marsh, being an enterprising Yankee who feared neither God nor the Devil, decided to bring the religion of the Deep Ones to Innsmouth, as a way of revitalizing the commerce and industry of the town, and making himself rich. From the chief of the tribe Marsh received a device made of lead that, when let down into the water accompanied by certain prayers, would summon the Deep Ones anywhere in the oceans of the world that they had one of their underwater cities. He held off from using it until 1838, when the entire tribe of islanders was wiped out by a neighboring tribe. This cut off his access to gold for trade, and he was forced to summon the Deep Ones himself and begin dealing with them directly.

He was able to establish contact off of Devil Reef, not far outside Innsmouth harbor, where there was a deep rift in the sea floor. He created a new religion, the Esoteric Order of Dagon. The priests of the new religion were drawn from the ranks of his own crew. Marsh began to offer in sacrifice the young people of Innsmouth to the Deep Ones off Devil Reef. In return, the town began to prosper. Marsh set up a refinery to smelt down the gold articles he bartered with the Deep Ones, since they could not be sold in their original state without arousing unwanted attention in the outer world. His three daughters decked themselves in this strange and sometimes ill-fitting gold jewelry, which had not been designed to be worn on the human body. Overnight, the fishing off Devil Reef became abundant.

Most of the town remained unaware of this hellish commerce. March and his cult abducted their sacrifices in secret, and kept silent about where they obtained the strange gold pieces they wore. Eventually, suspicions were raised, and in 1846 a group of townsfolk not in Marsh's circle rowed out to Devil Reef while a ritual was in progress, and arrested Marsh and thirty-two others, placing them in the town jail. For a period of two weeks nothing happened. Then one night the Deeps Ones emerged from the sea to liberate their human worshippers. There was a general massacre. The only ones allowed to live were those in the new church and those other townsfolk who swore not to interfere with the sacrifices and rituals. The loss of life due to the massacre was explained away in the outer world as a plague.

The Deep Ones demanded the freedom to visit with the townspeople and have social and sexual intercourse with them. Marsh did not even try to refuse. Perhaps he recognized that to oppose the amphibians would be futile, or he may have decided it was the best way to bind the townspeople in loyalty to the Deep Ones. Some of the Deep Ones began to stay as guests in certain houses in the town. Everyone was compelled to take the first Oath of Dagon as a display of solidarity. Those who were more closely involved in the affairs of the Deep Ones took a second or even a third oath that bound them to more serious consequences, which Lovecraft did not specify. Zadok Allen asserted that he took the first and second oath from Marsh himself, but would rather have died than to have taken the third oath.

In 1846, following the massacre, Marsh took a second wife from among the Deep Ones, and she gave birth to three children. Allen stated that two of them vanished in childhood, presumably beneath the waves, but that a daughter was educated in Europe and was married to an unwitting husband from Arkham. In 1927 when the story takes place, the Marsh refinery was being managed by Obed's grandson, Barnabas, who was half human and half Deep One. Barnabas was the son of Obed's eldest son Onesiphorus, who was wholly human, being from Obed's first marriage, but Barnabas had a Deep One for a mother, and was almost changed enough to retire from the land and take up his life beneath the sea.

The Old Ones planned a general attack against humanity using as weapons some of the creatures from the deepest depths, among them shoggoths, but this was disrupted, temporarily at least, by a government raid that took place early in 1928. Torpedoes were sent into the rift beyond Devil Reef, where the Deep Ones had their city. This did enough damage to at least delay their plans, but it did not destroy them. Obed Marsh died in 1878, but his legacy and his bloodline live on in Innsmouth. His hybrid children engendered on his second wife may never die, baring accidents. Those with the "Innsmouth look"—signs of the transformation from human to amphibian—turn up in odd places in Lovecraft's fiction, always connected with dark doings and evil magic.

(*The Shadow Over Innsmouth*)

Mason, Keziah

The witch Keziah Mason was convicted of witchcraft in the town of Salem in the year 1692, but before her execution could occur, she drew occult curves and angled lines on the solid stone walls of her jail cell using a sticky red liquid, and vanished into thin air. At her trial she had informed Judge John Hathorne of certain lines and curves that could point the way through the walls of space to other spaces beyond. By means of this alien geometry, Keziah was able to travel to distant worlds and through strange dimensions of space. The corner of the room in an old house in Arkham in which she had once lived was constructed in such a manner that the very angles of the walls served as a dimensional gateway.

She is hag-like in appearance, with a bent back, long nose, and shriveled chin, and her voice is an unpleasant croaking. She dresses in shapeless brown clothing. Keziah has the disturbing habit of appearing and disappearing at will. Never far from her is her familiar, a rat-like creature named Brown Jenkin with a bearded human face and paws that are like the tiny hands of a man. Keziah suckles it with her own blood. In return, the unnatural beast carries messages between the old witch and the Black Man of the sabbat, who is one of the guises adopted by Nyarlathotep when he has dealings with humanity. The Black Man gave Keziah a secret name, Nahab, by which she is known at the other-dimensional gatherings of witches. The old crone sacrifices infants in his honor, and to renew her own occult powers.

(*The Dreams in the Witch House*)

Mather, Cotton *

Cotton Mather (1663–1728), a religious fanatic and witch-hunter of New England, was mentioned in several of Lovecraft's stories, both for his *Magnalia Christi Americana* and for his *Wonders of the Invisible World*, where he examines the practices and nature of witches. The artist Richard Pickman of the story *Pickman's Model* reviled Mather because Mather witnessed the hanging of his "four-times-great-grandmother" for witchcraft on Gallows Hill at Salem. Pickman expressed the wish that someone had "laid a spell on him or sucked his blood in the night." Joseph Curwen wrote in *The Case of Charles Dexter Ward* "you are Sensible what Mr. Mather writ in ye *Magnalia* of ———, and can judge how truely that Horrendous thing is reported."

(*The Unnamable; Pickman's Model; The Case of Charles Dexter Ward*)

Morris, Daniel "Mad Dan"

A descendant of the Van Kauran clan of wizards, and native of Mountain Top, New York, he worked a spell from the *Book of Ebon* to turn the sculptor Arthur Wheeler to stone, because he believed that Wheeler was having an affair with his wife.

(*The Man of Stone*)

Nasht

Bearded priest of the temple to the earthly gods in the cavern of flame, near the gates to the dreamlands. He presides there with his fellow priest, Kaman-Thah.

(*The Dream-Quest of Unknown Kadath*)

Nephren-Ka

A pharaoh of ancient Egypt who erected a temple with a windowless crypt in which was placed the Shining Trapezohedron, a great, faceted black jewel with enormous occult power. In some way that is not recorded, but was regarded as an abomination by the priests of Egypt, Nephren-Ka made use of the jewel, and for that transgression, his name was erased from all monuments and scrolls, and the temple of the Trapezohedron pulled down on top of the jewel, which rested beneath the rubble until it was unearthed by Professor Enoch Bowen in 1844.

Nephren-Ka is mentioned in Lovecraft's story *The Outsider*—reference is made to the "catacombs of Nephren-Ka in the sealed and unknown valley of Hadoth by the Nile." They may be the same catacombs which Alhazred, author of the *Necronomicon*, explored near Memphis, as mentioned by Lovecraft in a letter to Clark Ashton Smith dated November 27, 1927. It may be that the temple of the Trapezohedron was located near the catacombs in the lost valley.

(*The Haunter of the Dark; The Outsider*)

Nitocris *

This queen of Egypt, and last pharaoh of the Sixth Dynasty, was mentioned by the Greek historian Herodotus in his *History* (bk. 2, ch. 100), and also by the Egyptian historian Manetho, whose Egyptian history, written in Greek, survives only in fragments. Herodotus related the story that Nitocris murdered a group of conspirators who had assassinated her brother (unnamed by Herodotus), the pharaoh, to whom she was married by the royal customs of Egypt, by luring the conspirators into a subterranean room for a banquet, and flooding it with water from the Nile. After achieving her revenge, she then killed herself by throwing herself into a chamber filled with ashes (Herodotus, pp. 113–4). Manetho claimed that she had built the third pyramid at Giza, and described her as beautiful. Modern historians question whether she ever existed, and tend to regard the account of Herodotus as a fable.

In the story *Imprisoned with the Pharaohs* she is characterized as the "ghoul-queen" who rules with her husband, the Egyptian pharaoh Khephren, over mummies who are neither animal nor human, deep underground in secret chambers and passages beneath the Sphinx and the Pyramids. The narrator of the story, Houdini, comments about the Pyramids, "Even the smallest of them held a hint of the ghastly—for was it not in this that they had buried Queen Nitocris alive in the Sixth Dynasty; subtle Queen Nitocris, who once invited all her enemies to a feast in a temple below the Nile, and drowned them by opening the water-gates? I recalled that the Arabs whisper things about Nitocris, and shun the Third Pyramid at certain phases of the moon." In *The Outsider*, mention is made of "the unnamed feasts of Nitocris beneath the Great Pyramid." Note the variation in the spelling of the name, which is probably just an error on Lovecraft's part.

(*Imprisoned With the Pharaohs; The Outsider*)

Nug-Soth

A magician of the "dark conquerors" of 16,000 AD whose mind had been displaced by the time-spanning mind of a Yithian, and trapped in the Yithian's cone-shaped body more than fifty million years in the past.

(*The Shadow Out of Time*)

Orne, Granny

This very old woman of Kingsport lives in Ship Street. Along with the Terrible One Man, who dwells in Water Street, she is the unofficial historian of Kingsport.

(*The Strange High House in the Mist*)

Peaslee, Nathaniel Wingate

A native of Crane Street, in the town of Arkham, he was born and raised in the town of Haverhill. In 1895 he became a teacher of political economics at Miskatonic University. Three years later he rose to the rank of associate professor, and in 1902 attained the title of full professor at this prestigious institution of higher learning. Peaslee's mind was forcibly displaced from 1908 to 1913 by the projected mind of a member of the Great Race of Yith, and he abruptly found himself within the ten-foot tall, cone-shaped body of the Yithian, a prisoner of an alien species in a distant time. During the duration of this captivity, the Yithian in his human body embarked on an intensive study of occult subjects, and participated in secret cultic activities. The alien mind sought out and read such forbidden works as *Cultes des Goules* by the Comte d'Erlette, *De Vermis Mysteriis* by Ludvig Prinn, the *Unaussprechlichen Kulten* of von Junzt, the surviving fragments of the enigmatic *Book of Eibon*, and the most infamous book of them all, the *Necronomicon* of Abdul Alhazred, a Latin copy of which is kept in the Miskatonic University Library.

After the mind of the Yithian learned all it considered useful, it constructed a machine of mirrors and lenses and used it to return to its own body. The mind of Peaslee was thrust back into his human shell, and he awoke with no memory of the time that had passed. He discovered that his wife had divorced him in horror at his changed manner. He regained custody of his second son, Wingate, who later became a professor of psychology at Miskatonic University. The Yithians had inserted a mental barrier that prevented him from remembering what had transpired while he inhabited the body of the alien. Gradually, Peaslee regained his memories, and recalled being in a great library with other alien prisoners whose minds had been displaced from their original bodies by the time-traveling minds of the Yithians. The Yithians took good care of their captive minds, and allowed them to study and converse amongst themselves.

Peaslee discovered that a secret cult existed among humanity that worshipped the Yithians and aided the time travelers from Yith when they made their presence known to its members. It was with this cult that the Yithian in Peaslee's body had trafficked, and it was a member of this cult that removed from Peaslee's room the machine by which the Yithian had effected a return to its own flesh. The existence of this cult is hinted at in the *Necronomicon*.

(*The Shadow Out of Time*)

Philetas, Theodorus

A scholar and occultist at Constantinople who translated the *Necronomicon* from its original Arabic into Greek in the year 950. It was Philetas who gave the book its Greek name—prior to his translation it had been known as *Al Azif*, which is said to signify the "howling of demons."

(*History of the Necronomicon*)

Phillips, Ward

Lovecraft inserted himself into his own stories a number of times, the most obvious example being the character of Randolph Carter, the dream adventurer. However, his identity was never more thinly veiled than in the person of Ward Phillips, who appears in *Through the Gates of the Silver Key*. "Ward" is the latter half of Lovecraft's first name, and "Phillips" is Lovecraft's middle name. He is a friend of Carter's, and the only one who is convinced that Carter is not dead, but has merely vanished into the dreamlands. He is described as an "elderly eccentric of Providence, Rhode Island"; Providence was Lovecraft's home town. Although Lovecraft was not an old man, he had the curious affectation that he believed himself much older than his years, on some mental or spiritual level, and would often refer to himself as an old man when speaking of himself to his friends.

The character Ward Phillips was a writer of fiction who had written about Carter's disappearance, even as Lovecraft had done. Phillips was convinced that Carter now "reigned as king on the opal throne of Ilek-Vad," a city of the dreamlands. Phillips described himself as a dreamer, meaning a dream traveler, and it seems beyond question that Lovecraft thought of himself in these terms. Phillips is said to be "lean, gray, long-nosed, clean-shaven, and stoop-shouldered," a description that very well suited Lovecraft himself.

(*Through the Gates of the Silver Key*)

Pickman, Richard Upton

In the story *Pickman's Model*, Pickman is an avant-garde painter of Boston who specializes in horrific portraits. Many critics are repelled by his work, particularly his masterpiece titled *Ghoul Feeding*. No art institution in Boston will exhibit it or accept it, no art patron will buy it, so horrible is its subject. Pickman keeps a studio in the rundown section of Boston known as the North End. The artist informs the narrator of the tale, a man named Eliot Thurber, that half the streets of the North End were laid out by 1650, and that the entire region was once interconnected by an intricate set of tunnels leading from the cellars of the houses to Copp's Hill burying ground and to the sea. Pickman asserts that north of Prince Street there are thirty or forty alleys, the existence of which is not even suspected by more than ten English Bostonians.

Pickman is not only abhorred by Boston art society for the subjects of his paintings, but because of his increasingly repellent appearance and manner, which the narrator hints may have something to do with his choice of diet. One of Pickman's former friends named Reid declares that Pickman's "features and expression were slowly developing in a way he didn't like; in a way that wasn't human." He believes that Pickman is "a sort of monster bound down the toboggan of reverse evolution," or so Pickman himself phrases it. Thurber mentions that Pickman came from old Salem stock and had an ancestor hanged for witchcraft in 1692.

One night, Pickman offers to show Thurber his studio in the North End. This studio was based on an actual building Lovecraft had seen while passing through this area of Boston. When Lovecraft returned in 1927 to view the structure, he found that it had been torn down, along with an irregular line of similar old buildings. It is described in the story as a dilapidated house with the windows boarded up, with a strange old brick well in its cellar. It is in the cellar that Pickman prefers to do his painting.

The location of this studio is not specified, but it is not far beyond Constitution Wharf on the waterfront. The building dates back to the period of the witch trials. On the walls of the studio are arrayed the portraits that Pickman could not exhibit or sell in polite Bostonian society. Indeed, they are so shocking, Pickman could not even allow them to be seen in the art circles he frequented. The subjects are creatures only partly human in appearance, their bodies possessed of an unpleasant rubberiness and forward-slumping posture, with a canine cast to the faces and pointed ears.

In a painting titled *The Lesson*, which Thurber finds particularly disgusting, these semi-humanoid creatures teach a young human child how to feed on human flesh in a graveyard. Thurber speculates that the child must represent an infant exchanged for a changeling—a human baby stolen from its crib, in which was left an inhuman infant of the race that committed the theft. The usual superstitious assumption is that such infant abductions are carried out by fairies, but Lovecraft intimated through his narrator that they have a darker source, and are performed by ghouls, who then raise the human child as their own, teaching it to feed on the flesh of human corpses. Indeed, it is suggested in the story that ghouls are not a completely separate race, but have their origin in a degenerate strain of humanity.

Pickman has depicted in another painting a young changeling child being raised as a human in a Puritan family. Thurber notes with growing horror that the face of the boy resembles very closely Pickman's own features. The implication is obvious, although unstated. Pickman is a ghoul who in infancy was left in exchange for a human baby, to be raised as a human being by his unwitting foster parents. That is the explanation for his degenerate facial features, noted by Reid. It must be presumed that when very young, ghouls look similar to human infants, but that as they mature they take on the more canine aspect of their own kind.

This was the reason Pickman aroused increasing revulsion among his acquaintances. As the artist aged, he took on more of the characteristics of his own kind, and found it more difficult to masquerade as a human being. In this tendency to change with maturity, we find an echo of Lovecraft's Deep Ones, who when interbred with human women appear completely human in youth, but gradually become inhuman in appearance as they grow older. The same evolution is described in the case of Wilbur Whateley, a hybrid of a human mother and a father who was one of the Old Ones. Wilbur became increasingly monstrous as he aged.

The canvases of Pickman depict an entire shadow world of Boston that is inhabited by ghouls who arise out of cracks and wells and wait in dark places to feed on the bodies of the dead, or if occasion arises, to slay the unwary living. In the cellar in which Pickman does his actual painting there is a circular well of brick, its rim raised some six inches above the floor, its mouth closed by a wooden cover. While the artist and Thurber are talking in an adjoining room, the cover clatters off the well, and Pickman rushes out with a revolver. The shots from the pistol frighten off whatever thing arises from the well. Mercifully for his sanity, Thurber does not see it.

This private showing of Pickman's work is enough for Thurber, who resolves never to have anything more to do with the artist. While in the studio, Thurber happens to place in his pocket one of the photographs from which Pickman worked, and later sees that his semi-human subjects were not imaginary, as Thurber had assumed, but were painted from life. This is how Pickman has been able to achieve such realism in his paintings—they are indeed portraits. Pickman disappears shortly thereafter.

It in an interesting choice made by Lovecraft as a writer, that he never used the term "ghoul" in this story, and never stated clearly what it is that the awful subjects of Pickman's art may be eating. We are left to form our conclusions from a series of allusions and intimations. Yet there is only one conclusion to draw—either Pickman is himself a ghoul, or he is a human being who has so greatly degenerated by constant close association with ghouls that he can scarcely be distinguished from them.

We have no way of knowing what became of him in 1926, following the end of the story *Pickman's Model*, but he reappears in *The Dream-Quest of Unknown Kadath*, where he plays a small but important role in Randolph Carter's quest. Carter encounters a group of ghouls, and is informed that his old friend Richard Pickman is not far away. The ghouls escort Carter to a dreamworld cemetery. Seated on a tombstone from the Granary Burying Ground in Boston that bears the year 1768 is Pickman, who has wholly assumed the appearance of a ghoul. Lovecraft wrote: "It was naked and rubbery, and had acquired so much of the ghoulish physiognomy that its human origin was already obscure."

Pickman agrees to help Carter forward his quest, and advises Carter to remove his clothing and disguise himself as a ghoul to escape notice. He gives Carter a password in the gibbering ghoul language that allows Carter safe passage among the night-gaunts, which have treaties with the ghouls of the dreamlands. Pickman remains Carter's friend and comrade in later adventures of the dream quest, leading with Carter a combined military force of ghouls and night-gaunts against the moon-beasts. It is mentioned that Pickman has had a civilizing influence on the ghouls, "for Pickman always discouraged the old ghoulish custom of killing and eating one's own wounded." This shows that Pickman's Boston education had not completely gone to waste.

In gratitude for his aid in their battle against the moon-beasts, the ghouls become Carter's companions in his quest for Kadath, along with their allies the night-gaunts, going so far as to accompany Carter into the great throne room of the gods of Earth as his personal escort. It is only the friendship of the ghoul who had once been known as Richard Pickman that allows Carter to find his way to Kadath and fulfill his dream-quest.

Lovecraft wrote in his brief publishing history of the *Necronomicon* that the Salem family of Pickman was rumored to own a sixteenth-century Greek translation of the text, but that if this rumor was true, the book disappeared when the artist Richard Pickman vanished in 1928. The presumption must be that Pickman took the *Necronomicon* with him when he left the habitations of men and went to live in the subterranean world of the ghouls in the tunnels beneath Boston.

(*Pickman's Model; The Dream-Quest of Unknown Kadath; History of the Necronomicon*)

Rogers, George

An artist in wax of the city of London who had been dismissed from the employ of Madame Tussaud's Wax Museum for mental instability, Rogers is a tall, lean man with dark eyes that stare wildly from a pallid and customarily unshaven face. He is a student of occult lore, and has a fascination that amounts to an obsession for the grotesque, which he creates in wax in his own private wax museum.

Some of the creatures on display in Rogers' Museum are not made of wax, but were gathered from the far corners of the world. In northern Alaska he acquired the mummified body of the god Rhan-Tegoth, an amphibious creature from the warm seas of the planetoid Yuggoth (which we call Pluto). Declaring himself Rhan-Tegoth's priest, Rogers sets about reviving the god with blood sacrifices and the long ritual from the eighth Pnakotic fragment. He makes the assertion that were Rhan-Tegoth to perish, it would be impossible for the Old Ones to return. He is killed by Rhan-Tegoth, who is in turn killed—or at least rendered dormant—by Rogers' strangely knowing servant, Orabona.

(*The Horror in the Museum*)

Sansu

The only man before Barzai the Wise ever to climb to the summit of the mountain Hatheg-Kla. It is written in the Pnakotic Manuscripts that he found nothing but "wordless ice and rock."

(*The Other Gods*)

Schacabao, Ibn

An Arab scholar quoted by Alhazred in the *Necronomicon*. In the short story *The Festival*, Alhazred is said to have written of him, "Wisely did Ibn Schacabao say, that happy is the tomb where no wizard hath lain, and happy the town at night whose wizards are all ashes." In *The Case of Charles Dexter Ward*, the necromancer Joseph Curwen writes to a fellow wizard, "I laste Night strucke on ye Wordes that bringe up YOGGE-SOTHOTHE, and sawe for ye first Time that Face spoke of by Ibn Schacabao in ye ———." The unnamed work represented by the line is probably the *Necronomicon*.

(*The Festival; The Case of Charles Dexter Ward*)

Shaddad *

The builder of thousand-pillared Irem, called Ubar by the Arabs, a city lost in the desert of the southern part of the Arabian peninsula that was once known as the Empty Space. According to the Koran, King Shaddad ignored a prophet, and for this transgression Irem was crushed beneath the sands by Allah.

(*Through the Gates of the Silver Key*)

S'gg'ha

One of the crinoid Elder Things dwelling in Antarctica who in the distant past was psychically abducted by a mind of the time-spanning Great Race of Yith, and held captive in an alien body in a tower of the Yithian city the ruins of which lie beneath the wastes of western Australia. S'gg'ha occupied his captivity by chiseling pictures on the walls of his prison.

(*The Shadow Out of Time*)

S'ngac

A being composed of violet gas who dwells in a distant region of space that is without form. He once warned the priest of Celephaïs, Kuranes, never to approach the central void that contains Azathoth, and Kuranes in his turn passed this warning on to Randolph Carter.

(*The Dream-Quest of Unknown Kadath*)

Snireth-Ko

A master dreamer in the class of Randolph Carter. He is fabled to have been the only completely human individual to have visited the far side of the Moon prior to Carter.

(*The Dream-Quest of Unknown Kadath*)

Solomon *

King of Israel, who built the first Temple at Jerusalem using the labor of demons, which he controlled through his magic. He is mentioned by the occultist Alonzo Typer in connection with the Dread Ones, "giant black beings whose number is legion and whose tread doth shake the earth."

(*The Diary of Alonzo Typer*)

Surama

An ancient wizard who accompanies the biologist Alfred Clarendon from North Africa to California, inciting him to kill animals and human beings by infecting them with the black fever, a plague that Surama has brought to the Earth from the spaces beyond the stars. He is associated with Nyarlathotep, but the nature of this association is not explicitly stated. In appearance, Surama is tall, lean, and bald. He is Caucasian, but of no recognizable existing race. There is the suggestion that he was a native of lost Atlantis, resurrected from the dead by Clarendon through the use of a ritual of necromancy with the aid of the Tuareg priests in Africa. Clarendon states that only fire can kill Surama, or a wooden stake driven through his heart while he sleeps.

(*The Last Test*)

Suydam, Robert

A recluse of Flatbush, New York, some sixty years of age, with unkempt white hair and a stubbly beard, he is a world-renowned expert on medieval superstitions, the author of a pamphlet on the Kabbalah and the legend of Faust. The descendent of an ancient Dutch family, he lives without family or servants in a dilapidated mansion on Martense Street behind a front yard densely wooded with ancient trees. He is considered to be a harmless eccentric by his neighbors, who glimpse his black-clad, corpulent figure striding down the streets at rare intervals. For a period of eight years in his middle life, he had lived in Europe. All of his meager funds are expended on the acquisition of rare occult books from London and Paris.

His relatives grow concerned when rumors begin to spread than he spends most of his nights in the disreputable Red Hook district, consorting with unsavory immigrants, and conducted strange rituals behind closed doors in a basement flat he maintains there. He has been overheard bragging that he is on the brink of obtaining limitless power, and uttering strange occult names. He was able to deflect attempts to have him declared mentally incompetent in court by claiming that he was merely conducting folklore research among the immigrant groups living in Red Hook.

A change occurs in his appearance. He seems to grow younger and thinner. By the use of some alchemical secret he becomes wealthy. He turns his back on Red Hook and its dark rituals, and opens his newly renovated house to society, eventually marrying a young woman of good social standing. While departing from New York aboard an ocean liner for his honeymoon, he and his bride are both killed by some phosphorescent, tittering thing that comes in through the open porthole of their stateroom, as Lilith is not a goddess to be spurned by her lovers. She expects fidelity from those she gifts with her alchemical secrets. Yazidi cultists carry the body of Suydam to an underground cavern beneath his mansion, where Lilith reanimates his corpse, seeking consummation, but by a trick the corpse of Suydam is able to cheat her of her payment.

(*The Horror at Red Hook*)

Taran-Ish

The high-priest of the doomed city of Sarnath, who is found one morning lying dead in his temple with an expression of terror frozen on his face. The day prior to his discovery, the looted statue of the lizard-god Bokrug, carried from the city of Ib across the lake from Sarnath, had been set up in the temple at Sarnath to commemorate the complete destruction of Ib and the massacre of all its population. Just before his death Taran-Ish managed to scratch on the chrysolite altar of his temple a single word: "Doom."

(*The Doom That Came to Sarnath*)

Terrible Old Man

This title is given to an elderly sea-faring man with a long white beard and strange yellow eyes who dwells in an ancient and dilapidated cottage on Water Street in Kingsport. Lovecraft has little to reveal about his early history, but he is an object of dread to the townsfolk, who regard him as a wizard. He is not fond of strangers, and it is only with difficulty that he can be induced to converse. He walks with the aid of a knotted cane, is tall and lean, and sometimes smiles horribly. He is renowned for paying his bills with ancient Spanish gold and silver coins two centuries out of date.

The Old Man figures prominently in two of Lovecraft's stories, *The Terrible Old Man* and *The Strange High House in the Mist*. The townsfolk believe that in his youth he was the captain of East India clipper ships, but there is some indirect suggestion that he may have come by his gold through piracy. Like Obed Marsh, he picked up various strange customs in distant lands. Amid the gnarled trees that grow in his front yard he keeps a curious collection of painted stones, perhaps gathered on his sea voyages, which are arranged to give the suggestion of a pagan temple.

The most curious practice of the Terrible Old Man is a kind of spirit divination, conducted with the aid of a number of empty bottles in which dangle small pieces of lead from strings. He keeps these vessels in a vacant downstairs room of his cottage, and can sometimes be overheard talking to them, and addressing each by a different name—such names as "Jack, Scar-Face, Long Tom, Spanish Joe, Peters, and Mate Ellis." Lovecraft is never explicit about these bottles, but it is evident that each contains the soul of a man. Perhaps they are the souls of the old man's friends, or perhaps the souls of his enemies, but he holds power over them, and they fulfill his commands and also protect him from harm.

When three thieves named Angelo Ricci, Joe Czanek, and Manuel Silva enter his cottage, intending to torture the old man into revealing the hiding place of his gold coins, their corpses are discovered the following day, washed in on the tide, disfigured by the marks of boot heels and the slashes of cutlasses. The spirits that dwell in the bottles evidently have the power to take on tangible form and commit violence on those who threaten their master. It is the piratical nature of some of their names, coupled with their use of cutlasses to exact their vengeance on the thieves, that leads me to assume that the Terrible Old Man may once have been a pirate, or at least have had commerce with pirates.

Lovecraft's specific and repeated use of the full names of the thieves is not accidental. He described them as "new and heterogeneous alien stock which lies outside the charmed circle of New England life and traditions." He wished to convey that these were not natives of his world, but immigrants from non-English nations who, in Lovecraft's view, did not belong in Kingsport. The terrible punishment meted out to the three thieves by the bottle spirits of the Terrible Old Man was for Lovecraft a fitting rebuke for their insolence.

Lovecraft's hostility toward foreigners, as he regarded all immigrants not of English blood, has a bearing on his mythos. The foreign immigrants who dwell in the more rundown sections of such places as Boston, Kingsport, and New York were for Lovecraft a kind of alien plague, no less destructive than the inhuman and unearthly things that in his mythos burrow in tunnels deep beneath the ground. They were regarded by Lovecraft as harmful to the continuing harmony and prosperity of polite New England society. This xenophobia, which rears its ugly head in some of Lovecraft's tales, is no more virulent than is usual in the popular fiction of his period, but it helped shape his belief in the dangers of intermingling the familiar and mundane with the alien and strange.

Lovecraft did not merely detest immigrants and their customs, he loathed them with an instinctive revulsion that made him physically ill. The brief period he lived in New York City almost killed him, so strong was his nausea at being compelled to interact with recent immigrants to the United States. That was the phase in his life during which he acquired a vial of poison, and carried it around with him everywhere he went, in case he suddenly came to the decision to end his own suffering. He alludes to this unhappy time in *The Silver Key*, where it is his alter ego Randolph Carter who carries the poison, not Lovecraft.

The mechanics of the bottle divination described by Lovecraft are not complex. A lead weight is suspended on a thread or fine string in a bottle with vertical sides, in such a way that the lead weight is very near the side of the bottle. The slightest movement or vibration sets the weight swinging on its string like a little pendulum, and it taps against the side of the glass vessel, raising a tinkling noise. This form of divination is based on a practice used by spiritualists in Lovecraft's period. A medium would suspend a small weight on the end of a piece of string inside an empty glass, her elbow resting on the table, holding the weight near the side of the glass, and then would ask questions of spirits, who would respond in a yes or no way by making the weight tink against the glass or not tink. It works in much the same way the Ouija board works, by involuntary movements of the muscles.

The Terrible Old Man of Kingsport used the bottles as host bodies for the spirits or souls of dead pirates. This practice is also common in magic, although the spirit may be contained in many objects, not only bottles. The responses of the pendulum of a particular bottle to his spoken communications would be from only the spirit contained within that bottle. It may be assumed that the old man used magic to bind the spirits to the bottles, but he also had the power to loose them from their prisons when necessary, and control their actions while they were outside.

The practice of trapping souls in bottles also makes an appearance in the story *Two Black Bottles*, co-authored with Wilfred Blanch Talman. In this story the souls are not made into familiar serving spirits or guardians, and do not communicate with their captor, but are kept in the bottles while their bodies continue to live. Without their souls, they naturally incline to evil thoughts and actions. Lovecraft did not indicate what replaced the souls in the bodies. In the story it appears that the soul represents the good nature of a man, and once removed, the evil nature has free rein to do as it pleases without restraint. Evidently removal of the soul extends the life of the body, since the soul of Abel Foster, sexton of the church at Daalbergen, had been removed and placed in a bottle two hundred years prior to the events of the story. Once Foster's soul is released from the bottle, his body falls to dust.

(*The Terrible Old Man; The Strange High House in the Mist*)

T'yog

High priest of the cult of Shub-Niggurath in the kingdom of K'naa, on the continent of Mu. He presided over the rites of the Mother Goddess in a copper temple. In the year 173,148 BC he attempted to destroy the demon-god Ghatanothoa, an ancient entity worshipped on Earth by the Mi-Go. He was betrayed by the high priest of the cult of Ghatanothoa, and when he looked upon Ghatanothoa he was outwardly turned to stone and leather, but remained inwardly conscious and aware.

(*Out of the Aeons*)

'Umr at-Tawil

The Most Ancient One, who instructs Randolph Carter in how to use his silver key to open the ultimate gate. In the *Necronomicon*, Alhazred referred to this mysterious being as one who is sometimes accepted as a guide by those who seek to glimpse beyond the veil, but cautioned that they would be well advised not to have dealings with the one he described as, "HE WHO guardeth the Gateway: HE WHO will guide the rash one beyond all the worlds into the Abyss of unnamable devourers." Alhazred made two references to the Most Ancient One from an older authority, the *Book of Thoth*. The scribe

of this book translated the name "'Umr at-Tawil" as "the Prolonged of Life," and wrote that there is a terrible price to be paid for even one glimpse beyond the veil.
(*Beyond the Gates of the Silver Key*)

Van der Heyl, Claes

Wizard who wrote two occult diaries between the years 1560 and 1580 that concern the Nameless One. The occult investigator Alonzo Typer found both diaries in the old van der Heyl house in the New England village of Chorazin in the year 1935.
(*The Diary of Alonzo Typer*)

Van der Heyl, Dirck

In 1746 he fled Albany with his Salem-born wife, a daughter of the notorious sorcerer Abaddon Corey, after they were accused of witchcraft. He built a farmhouse in the wilderness near what is now Attica, New York, over the hidden gateway to other worlds that is guarded by the creature known as the Nameless One.
(*The Diary of Alonzo Typer*)

Van der Heyl, Hendrik

Member of the van der Heyl family who came to New-Netherland from Europe in 1638 in search of occult information concerning the Nameless One, who is the Guardian of the Gate.
(*Diary of Alonzo Typer*)

Van Kauran, Bareut Picterse

Great-grandfather of Daniel Morris and one of the Van Kauran family of wizards. He disappeared from New Paltz in 1839.
(*The Man of Stone*)

Van Kauran, Hendrik

Uncle of Daniel Morris, and descendant of the wizard Nicholas van Kauran, he kept his family's copy of the infamous grimoire known as the *Book of Ebon* safe throughout his life, even when he was run out of town for practicing black magic.
(*The Man of Stone*)

Van Kauran, Nicholas

A wizard hanged in Wijtgaart in 1587 for black magic, who was widely known along the bank of the Hudson River in New York to have made "the bargain with the Black Man." The Black Man was the lord of the witches' sabbat, usually assumed by Christians to be the Devil or his proxy, but revealed by Lovecraft to have been Nyarlathotep. The bargain referred to was the infamous black pact.

(*The Man of Stone*)

Van Kauran, William

Grandson of the wizard Nicholas van Kauran, he carried the copy of the *Book of Ebon* owned by his grandfather from Europe to New England.

(*The Man of Stone*)

Waite, Asenath

The daughter of the wizard Ephraim Waite, one of the Innsmouth Waites. Her mother was an unknown woman who always went veiled in public. Lovecraft hints that she was one of the Deep Ones, an amphibious race that had contracted a hellish bargain with the folk of Innsmouth, and had intermarried with them to produce hybrid children. Asenath was such a hybrid, as her unnaturally protuberant eyes showed. She had what is known as the "Innsmouth look," a disfigurement that is characteristic of the hybrids. Early in life it is almost unnoticeable, but later in life the deformities of both face and body become so pronounced that the hybrids must conceal themselves from view.

(*The Thing on the Doorstep*)

Waite, Ephraim

A resident of Washington Street, Innsmouth, he was known to be a practitioner of black magic. Late in his life he married a mysterious young woman who always went veiled, and had by her a daughter, Asenath. It is intimated by Lovecraft that his wife was a Deep One, one of the amphibious race that dwell in cities deep beneath the oceans of the world and worship Dagon. Ephraim developed a technique for exchanging minds with another person based upon a ritual he discovered in the *Necronomicon*, and used it to remove his mind from his aging body and insert it into the youthful body of his daughter. He may have chosen her because, as a child of a Deep One, she was virtually immortal. Her consciousness was displaced into his old body, and she promptly was declared insane and locked away in a padded attic room. When the decrepit body died, there were rumors of poison found in its stomach, but nothing came of it.

To Ephraim's great dismay, he discovers that her brain is not equipped to handle some of the mental work of magic he attempts. It was inherently unsuited to the task both by virtue of its gender and its inhuman side. As a consequence, Ephraim is forced to find another male, fully human brain equal to the occult work he desires to accomplish. He finds his vessel in Edward Pickman Derby, a child prodigy of "fine-wrought brain and weak will," who is easily manipulated. Before Ephraim can force his mind permanently into Derby's body, Derby murders his wife and buried her corpse in the cellar.

Ephraim's will is too strong to be defeated by death—he completes the transfer, entering Derby's body at last, and relegates the mind of poor Derby to the decaying shell in the cellar. Derby has studied the same spell in the *Necronomicon* by which Ephraim worked his mind transfers, and manages to animate the corpse through magic long enough to convey a message to his childhood friend, Daniel Upton, revealing the mind transfer and its horrible implications. Upton shoots Ephraim, in Derby's body, six times through the head.

The ability of a magician to project his mind into the body of another human being, displacing the mind of that person and claiming the body for his own, was believed to be real among the shamanic Bon priests of Tibet. It is a natural elaboration of the concept of reincarnation, in which personalities are asserted to enter new bodies after the death of the old bodies. If consciousness can enter a new body after death, then why should it not be possible for it to shift from one body to another before death occurs? Students were said to sometimes offer their bodies as vessels for the consciousness of their dying masters.

(*The Thing on the Doorstep*)

Walakea, Chief

Old chief of the Kanaky islanders of the South Pacific who had dealings with the Deep Ones. He taught the Yankee clipper captain Obed Marsh how to contact them and trade with them. The group of Kanaky islands is known as New Caledonia today. The word "Kanaky" is from the Hawaiian word *kanaka*, meaning "people." Polynesians used it to refer to themselves, and it was applied by the French to all the islanders in the South Pacific, both Melanesian and Polynesian. It is likely that Lovecraft had this larger usage in mind when he wrote of the Kanakys.

(*The Shadow Over Innsmouth*)

Ward, Charles Dexter

The character of Charles Dexter Ward elicits both our pity and our revulsion—pity because he was the puppet of forces beyond his comprehension, and revulsion because he knowingly called forth horrors from beyond the grave. Born in 1902, he grew up in a privileged family environment in a Georgian mansion on Prospect Street, in Providence, Rhode Island. He was fascinated from early childhood by history and by ancient things. This was no accident. Late in the eighteenth century his ancestor Joseph Curwen had worked occult rituals taught to him by Yog-Sothoth to ensure that one of his descendants would turn his attentions backward in time.

In 1918 Ward confirms through his researches into old town records that he has an unacknowledged ancestor named Joseph Curwen, who had been buried in the year 1771 under a dark cloud of infamy. There were rumors that Curwen was a necromancer. His irresistible passion to learn about Curwen becomes the fanatical center of his existence, just as Curwen had planned it to be, so many years before. In August of 1919 he discovers some papers belonging to his black-sheep ancestor behind the paneling of a house in Olney Court, on Stampers' Hill, that had once been owned by Curwen. This discovery transforms his obsession for genealogy into a mania for the occult.

He begins a dogged search for Curwen's grave that does not attain its end for another eight years. During that time he studies anything he can acquire about necromancy. After using the information left by Curwen in his old house to resurrect Curwen from his essential salts, Ward aids the necromancer in continuing his dark researches, until at last his better nature rebels at some of the things Curwen requires him to do, things that are too horrible even for him to stomach. Curwen cannot risk exposure, so he murders poor Ward and assumes his identity. By the rituals of magic worked by Curwen during his first life, Ward had been born almost the twin image of Curwen, which made this impersonation possible.

However, the parents of young Ward are not entirely deceived, nor is the family doctor, Marinus Bicknell Willett. They assume that Charles has lost his mind, based on his strange manner of expression and his failure to remember recent events. Curwen is locked into an asylum for the insane. Willett investigates the catacombs beneath the old Curwen property where the two necromancers had worked, discovers the horrors hidden there, and learns enough necromancy to reduce Curwen once again to his essential salts by using the same magic formula of Yog-Sothoth that Ward had used to raise him, but in its reverse order.

(*The Case of Charles Dexter Ward*)

Warren, Harley

A native of South Carolina, student of the occult, and an expert on the lost Naacal language, with whom Randolph Carter lived and studied for a period of years, until Warren descended down a flight of stone steps beneath a tomb in an unnamed graveyard in Big Cypress Swamp, Florida, where he was killed by a legion of inhuman creatures. He obtained a book from India in 1919 written in unknown letters similar to those on the parchment that Carter would later discover in an old oak box containing the silver key of his ancestor Edmund Carter. It is intimated that this book may have been responsible for Warren's death. He had it with him when he descended into the sepulchre. Warren would not speak of the book to his friends Carter and Phillips, saying only that it was better they knew nothing about it, and hinting that it might have come from somewhere other than the Earth.

There is a discrepancy in the period of time Lovecraft says Carter studied with Warren. In the *Silver Key* he states that it was seven years, but in the opening of the *Statement of Randolph Carter*, the narrator Carter claims that it was five years. There may be a plausible explanation for this discrepancy. The seven-year period with Warren occurred during Carter's first life, which was lived before he used the silver key to travel back in time to his boyhood, from which he relived his life a second time. It may be that the five-year period with Warren occurred during Carter's second life.

(*The Statement of Randolph Carter; The Silver Key; Through the Gates of the Silver Key*)

West, Herbert

A brilliant medical student studying at the Miskatonic University Medical School, West has the obsession of finding a way to bring the dead back to life. His experiments, in which a reanimating fluid is injected into the veins of the corpse, have the unfortunate consequences of transforming the recently dead into homicidal maniacs. West is described as small and slender, with eyeglasses, blond hair, pale blue eyes, and a soft voice.

(*Herbert West—Reanimator*)

Whateley, Lavinia

Daughter of Old Whateley, the wizard. Her mother died violently when she was twelve, probably murdered by her father. She was an albino, and twisted in a way that made her appearance unattractive. At age thirty-five she participated in a ritual on top of Sentinel Hill conducted by her father, and was impregnated by one of the Old Ones with the twin brothers Wilbur and the invisible nameless one who resembled his alien father. She was murdered by her son, Wilbur, on Halloween night in 1926—probably by being fed to his monstrous brother. The whippoorwills carried her soul off to Hell.

(*The Dunwich Horror*)

Whateley, Wilbur

Born on Candlemass (February 2), 1913, nine months after his conception on May-Eve (Walpurgis Night), 1912. On the night he was born, noises came from the hills, all the dogs in the region began to bark, and a hideous screaming was heard. Wilbur was the son of Lavinia Whateley, of the decayed Whateleys of Dunwich, a thirty-five year old albino with a twisted body, the daughter of Old Whateley the wizard. His father was the Old One invoked by Old Whateley, Yog-Sothoth. Wilbur had a twin brother who is never named in the story, who took after his father's line. The brother was invisible to normal sight and grew rapidly from consuming the blood of live cows, and sometimes the blood of Lavinia Whateley and Old Whateley, until he filled the gutted Whateley farmhouse. Wilbur Whateley was a planned hybrid who was intended to be the primary mover in a plot to bring the Old Ones back to the Earth.

In the mythology of the ancient Greeks there are many stories about children born of women impregnated by god-like beings from the sky. The sky-god Zeus is rumored to have fathered numerous sons from mortal women, and these sons went on to become heroes of Greek myth, such as Herakles. In the Hebrew *Book of Enoch*, a class of angels known as the Watchers is said to have looked down upon the Earth and lusted after the daughters of men because of their beauty. Against the orders of God, the Watchers descended to the Earth and engendered a race of great heroes on the mortal women they married. It was this race with the blood of the Watchers in its veins that learned the secret arts and sciences of heaven. God ultimately punished the Watchers by casting them down into an abyss, and he destroyed their unnatural descendants with the Great Flood, washing the Earth clean of the stain of this mingling of angels and mortals.

It would not be unreasonable to speculate that these persistent tales of hybrid offspring that result from the coupling of mortal women and sky beings who are regarded as divine or semi-divine had its origin in the actual sexual unions between mortals and aliens from elsewhere, whether beyond the stars or beyond our dimensions of space. The myth has not ended, but persists into modern times. Over the past few decades, many individuals have reported being abducted, taken on board UFOs, and raped by aliens. At times the sex is consensual. Some of these abductees claim that they have been shown hybrid babies that resulted from sexual couplings between aliens and humans.

We may laugh at the alien abduction stories, but they are the same in their essential details to what Greek women were reporting three thousand years ago had happened to them while they were out walking in the meadows. Clearly there is something very basic going on here that cuts across historical and cultural barriers. Whether it is unfolding solely in the depths of the human psyche, as most people would probably wish to assume for the sake of their own sanity, or whether it has an elusive physical component that remains on the very edges of our known experience, can only be conjectured. If proof has ever been offered for the material existence of human-alien hybrids, modern research has rejected it, and it has never become an accepted part of the scientific record.

Wilbur Whateley was a member of the decayed Whateleys of Dunwich and surrounding farmlands. We are not informed by Lovecraft why they are described in this manner, but there is an intimation of incest and inbreeding that Lovecraft is never indelicate enough to state openly. Clans that have lived for many generations in relative isolation often fall prey to inbreeding. In the case of the Whateleys, there is something more at play—the use of wizardry of the blackest kind. Their decay is at least in part occult, as well as genetic. The decayed Whateleys had allied themselves with the demonic beings who move in the shadows of our reality.

Wilbur's very existence, as well as that of his invisible brother, were part of a great plan by his maternal grandfather, Wizard Whateley, to bring the Old Ones back to the surface of the Earth, so that they could consummate their ultimate purpose—wiping the world clean of all living things, and returning our lifeless planet back through a great dimensional doorway to the higher space from which it fell untold aeons ago. We may guess that the sterilization of the Earth is necessary because living things of ordinary flesh and blood cannot make this dimensional transition, and would prevent it from taking place.

Wilbur was taught from a very early age, both by Old Whateley and by things less natural, what his destiny would be, and he embraced it without a qualm. He was an evil child, by all the usual measures. It is intimated that he murdered his own mother. There is a dark suggestion that Lavinia Whateley was abused physically, and perhaps sexually, by Wizard Whateley, and that Wilbur was imitating his grandfather's treatment of her. His physical deformities and unnatural composition caused him to be ostracized by his peers, shunned by the townsfolk of Dunwich, and instantly attacked by any passing dog. Why dogs hated Wilbur with such a passion was never stated, but it may be observed that in *At the Mountains of Madness* the dogs transported to Antarctica by the Miskatonic University Expedition reacted in very much the same way when they smelled the alien scent of the crinoid race. They attacked the Elder Things savagely with no regard for their own safety.

In keeping with the fables concerning changelings—fairy infants substituted for human infants in their cradles—Wilbur not only grew much more rapidly than normal, but matured more rapidly. He acquired a sly knowingness both unnatural and repulsive in a young child. Although his education was spotty and unconventional, it is obvious from what he wrote in his diary that his latent intellect was superior to that of the average human being.

Lovecraft's changelings, to use the word in a general sense, are not static but evolve fluidly from a condition almost human to a condition horrifyingly alien. Pickman went from what was, in outward appearance at least, a normal human infant to what was in maturity indistinguishable from a ghoul. Wilbur Whateley underwent a similar transition from a baby quite normal in appearance to a giant who only vaguely resembled a human being above the waist, and bore no resemblance to humanity below the waist. The waist symbolically defines a plane that cuts Wilbur Whateley in half. What is above, in the light, is sane and close to normal, but what lies below concealed in the darkness is the stuff of nightmare. The upper part is the human side of the hybrid, the lower part the alien side.

Wilbur was nearly nine feet tall at the time of his death. His voice was so deep, it could not have been produced by a human voice box. He carried with him a foul odor that is characteristic of the Old Ones. His blood had become a greenish-yellow ichor. No doubt when he was younger, it more closely resembled human blood. His face, at the time of his death by the teeth of the watchdog in the library of Miskatonic University, was described as goatish and chinless. In spite of his young age he was bearded. The skin on his chest was leathery and reticulated, like the hide of an alligator; the skin on his back was piebald yellow and black, and said by Lovecraft to resemble the "squamous covering of certain snakes." By this, Lovecraft meant scaled.

The term "piebald" may be noted. It was a popular myth that when a Negro and Caucasian mated, their offspring might be piebald or spotted, like a painted pony, with patches of dark skin and light skin. This does not occur. Inter-racial marriages produce children of an intermediate and uniform skin shade. The appearance of birthmarks—irregular and often large patches of miscolored skin—in interracial children may possibly have given rise to this fable. Birthmarks are common, and occur in children of all racial backgrounds. Lovecraft deliberately used the term "piebald" to conjure up this interracial myth in the minds of his readers.

Below the waist Wilbur was described as covered in coarse black fur. From his lower belly hung a score of gray-green tentacles with red sucking mouths. On each hip in a pinkish socket surrounded by hairs was an undeveloped eye. At the base of his spine hung a kind of tail with purple rings that had a mouth on its end. His legs were like those of a dinosaur and terminated in feet in the shape of "ridgy-veined pads that were neither hooves nor claws." The color below the skin of Wilbur's body changed in rhythm with his breathing, as he heart pumped the yellowish ichor through his veins.

Wilbur's lower body resembles in a general way the lower bodies of some demons depicted in medieval and Renaissance woodcuts and manuscript paintings, which show such features as hairy legs, hoofs or claws in place of feet, and eyes or faces on the buttocks, groin, or knees. These demons are sometimes scaled, and often have tails. For example, the demon Belial in the illustrations to the 1473 German work *Das Buch Belial* has the beaked face of a bird on his buttocks, and paws or cloven hooves for feet (Lehner, p. 4). The devil in a woodcut from *Le purgatoire Sainct Patrice*, published at Paris in 1530, shows a figure with a face on its lower belly, a long tail, hawk-like talons for feet, spines on its knees, and serrated ridges down the backs of its legs (Lehner, p.14). It is obvious that Lovecraft took his inspiration for Wilbur's lower body from traditional depictions of demons.

Wilbur Whateley was born February 2, 1913, at 5:00 AM. He was killed by the guard dog as Miskatonic University in the "small hours" of August 3, 1928. He lived a few months more than fifteen years, but his hybrid body possessed a maturity much in advance of his age. He was able to contemplate without horror what he would look like when the final change in his physiology occurred, and observed in his diary with a calm and almost analytical interest that there would be little that was human left. A creature he called up from the depths of the earth using the Aklo formula told him that he might be transfigured, "there being much of outside to work on." This was a matter of prime concern for Wilbur, since the entire planet was to be purged of all living things of normal substance. He had reason to be assured that when that time came, his nature would be so radically transformed, he would escape destruction.

Wilbur differed from his invisible brother, who was of so strange a substance that his image would not register in the human brain without occult aids. In the *Necronomicon* Alhazred wrote that the hybrid offspring of the Old Ones engendered on mortal women range greatly in appearance, from the near-human to the totally alien. Both extremes are expressed in the Whateley brothers.

Wilbur was not quite human even at his birth—his legs were probably always alien in shape, and were kept covered to conceal them. We may assume this to be the case because, as early as one year of age, he was observed at a distance by Silas Bishop running naked up Sentinel Hill, and his upper legs were then covered with the rough and hairy pelt that he thereafter took great pains to conceal from human sight. Only two people saw Wilbur as an infant, Zechariah Whateley and Mamie Bishop, and neither one commented on any strangeness in Wilbur's appearance, so it may be guessed that his mother had him wrapped in a blanket and was careful that his legs were not uncovered.

The unnamed invisible brother matured even more quickly than Wilbur, and bore a much nearer resemblance to the Old Ones, even as his physical substance was much closer in its composition to theirs. He was fed on the blood of cattle, and at times on the blood of his mother. It formed a substitute for breast milk in the days and weeks immediately following his birth. In his diary Wilbur wrote that those from outside could not take body without human blood. It may have been necessary that the invisible thing that was Lavinia Whateley's child consume a portion of her blood merely to become tangible and stable enough to endure. Shortly after his death, Wilbur's body evaporated into the air, so alien was its substance, and the body of his brother was made of even stranger stuff.

Why Wizard Whateley conducted the ritual that brought forth Wilbur and his brother from the womb of his daughter Lavinia is not explained in the story. Did he hate humanity so much that he was eager for the Old Ones to wipe the human race utterly from the face of the Earth? Or was it something that happened without his full consent, something that both frightened him and filled him with pride? A week after the brothers were born, Wizard Whateley drove his sleigh into Dunwich to buy provisions at the general store, and the old man was observed to be strangely changed in manner, both furtive and fearful. Even so, he boasted of the unrevealed paternity of his grandson. In his sly, mocking way he asserted, "I calc'late her man is as good a husban' as ye kin find this side of Aylesbury." In later years, neither Wizard Whateley nor Wilbur showed the slightest doubt or qualm about the plan to open the gate for the Old Ones. Wizard Whateley may have foreseen that the destruction would take place only after he was dead.

(*The Dunwich Horror*)

Whateley, Wizard

Also known as Old Whateley. We learn from the poem "The Familiars" in Lovecraft's sonnet cycle *Fungi from Yuggoth* that his first name was John. He wished to open the gate of Yog-Sothoth so that the Old Ones could return to Earth and strip its surface of all life, before transporting the entire planet out of normal space and back to the alien dimension from which the planet had fallen uncountable aeons ago. This he meant to accomplish by causing his albino daughter, Lavinia, to breed with one of the Old Ones, Yog-Sothoth, and produce hybrid children who were capable of performing the necessary ritual for the opening of the gate. The Old Ones would then multiply her more unnatural child into an army of invisible monsters that would destroy all life on Earth. He had inherited two centuries worth of arcane occult books from his forefathers, including a damaged copy of the John Dee English translation of the *Necronomicon*. The incantation to open the gate was on the missing page 751 of that edition. His library eventually found its way to Miskatonic University.

(*The Dunwich Horror; Fungi from Yuggoth*)

Wormius, Olaus *

In Lovecraft's mythos, he was a Dominican priest of the thirteenth century who translated the *Necronomicon* in the year 1228 from Greek into Latin. Lovecraft referred to it in his story *The Festival* as the "forbidden Latin translation" about which "monstrous things" were whispered.

There was an actual historical figure of the same name, but he was a Danish physician and antiquarian of the seventeenth century. He studied first at the University of Marburg, and went on to receive a Doctorate in Medicine from the University of Basel in 1611, and a Master's degree in Arts from the University of Copenhagen in 1617. In addition to teaching medicine and languages at Copenhagen, he collected ancient rune texts and wrote several books on the runes.

(*The Festival; History of the Necronomicon*)

Yergler, Rudolf

A German mystic and alchemist, author of the *Chronicle of Nath*. He borrowed some of his lore from the books of Hermes Trismegistus, the mythical father of alchemy.

(*The Tree on the Hill*)

Zann, Erich

An elderly German mute who earns his living by playing viol in the evenings in a theater orchestra of an unnamed French city. He is a musical genius who sits alone in his high attic room and improvises wild alien harmonies. However, he does this not from a love of music, but out of dread that should he cease to play, something in the dark void beyond his shuttered window will force its way into his room.

(*The Music of Erich Zann*)

Zkauba

An inhuman wizard of the planet Yaddith, whose primary occupation is the weaving of spells to keep the bleached and viscous bholes (or Dholes) in their burrows beneath the surface of his world. When Randolph Carter passed through the Ultimate Gate, he asked Yog-Sothoth to send him into the body of Zkauba, which he subsequently inhabited. It is rugose and partly squamous, somewhat insect-like in the articulation of its limbs, but bears a faint resemblance to the human form.

(*Through the Gates of the Silver Key*)

The Key to the Second Gate

2nd Astral Gate: Capricornus—The Sea-Goat

Sun passes through Capricornus: January 20–February 17

Constellation is represented by a goat with the hindquarters of a fish.

Right Pillar: Dabih (Arabic: *Al Sa'd al Dhabih*—The Lucky One of the Slaughterers). Astronomical designation: Beta Capricorni. Astrological nature: Saturn-Venus. Influence: success in business, politics, dealings with people; but it may indicate suspicion, mistrust, frustration, and criticism. Magnitude: 3.1. Color: white. Sun crosses: January 23. Location: left eye of the goat. Comments: This star, second-brightest in Capricorn, can be either beneficial or harmful depending on circumstances.

Left Pillar: Deneb Algedi (Arabic: *danab al-jady*—The Tail of the Goat). Astronomical designation: Delta Capricorni. Astrological nature: Saturn-Jupiter. Influence: integrity, a sense of justice; but when ill-dignified it can indicate corruption. Magnitude: 2.9—multiple star system. Color: yellow. Sun crosses: February 13. Location: tail of the goat. Comments: The brightest star in Capricorn, which is the second darkest of the zodiacal constellations, after Cancer.

The astral gate of Capricornus lies between the star of its right pillar, located at the left eye of the sea-goat, and the star of its left pillar, on the fishy tail of the goat. The sun enters the gate by crossing the longitude of Dabih, the star of the right pillar, around January 23. The solar transition of this wide gate takes twenty-one days. The sun exits the gate around February 13, when it crosses the celestial longitude of the star of the left pillar, Deneb Algedi.

The key to the Second Gate opens Capricornus, allowing entry into that part of the walled city of the *Necronomicon* that contains the unique personalities dreamed by Lovecraft. Use it for divining information or receiving dreams about the named individuals of the mythos, or for communicating with a specific individual whose public or common name is known to you.

Seal of the Second Key on the Second Gate

Ritual of Opening Capricornus

Face the direction of the compass ruled by the Second Gate, which is east by north—that is, slightly to the left of due east. Visualize the closed gate in the eastern wall of the city in front of you so that it is more than large enough for you to walk through without bending your head. Take the time to create on the astral level its structure and shape in great detail, so that it appears in your imagination as a real gate. This is done by imagining each detail successively and impressing it on the mind, then shifting to other details, but returning the attention to each imagined part of the gate as it begins to fade in the imagination.

With the image of the gate clear in your mind and projected upon the astral level to the east by north, speak the following invocation to Yog-Sothoth, which is the invocation for all the gates:

> Guardian of the Gate! Defender of the Door! Watcher of the Way! Who art the stout Lock, the slender Key, and the turning Hinge! Lord of All Transition, without whom there is no coming in or going out, I call thee! Keeper of the Threshold, whose dwelling place is between worlds, I summon thee! Yog-Sothoth, wise and mighty lord of the Old Ones, I invoke thee!
>
> By the authority of the dreaded name, Azathoth, that few dare speak, I charge thee, open to me the gateway of Capricornus the Sea-Goat that lies between the blazing pillar Dabih on the right hand and the blazing pillar Deneb Algedi on the left hand. As the solar chariot [or, lunar chariot] crosses between these pillars, I enter the city of the *Necronomicon* through its Second Gate. Selah!

Visualize the key of the Second Gate in your right hand some six inches long and made of cast iron. Feel its weight, texture, and shape as you hold it. Extend your right arm and use the key to draw upon the surface of the gate the seal of the key, which should be visualized to burn on the gate in a line of white spiritual fire. Point with the astral key at the center of the gate and speak the words:

> In the name of Azathoth, Ruler of Chaos, by the power of Yog-Sothoth, Lord of Portals, the Second Gate is opened!

Visualize the gate unlocking and opening inward of its own accord upon a shadowed space beyond. On the astral level, walk through the gateway and stand in the dark space beyond. Focus your mind upon the individual person or being named in the mythos whom you wish to communicate with or understand. Open your mind to impressions concerning the human and alien persons scried by Lovecraft during his dreams. In a more general sense, this ritual and this gate may be used to scry or communicate with individual persons or spirits the names of whom are known.

After fulfilling the purpose for which this gate was opened, conclude the ritual by astrally passing out through the gate and visualizing it to close. Draw the seal of the Second Key on the surface of the gate with the astral key you hold in your hand, and mentally cause it to lock itself shut, as it was at the beginning of the ritual. Speak the words:

> By the power of Yog-Sothoth, and authority of the supreme name Azathoth, I close and seal the Second Gate. This ritual is well and truly ended.

Allow the image of the gate to grow pale in your imagination and fade to nothingness before you turn away from the ritual direction.

The Third Gate

Third Gate
Gods and Devils

It may at first glance seem strange to class gods and devils under the same gateway, but anthropologists and folklorists have long observed that the gods of a religion become the devils of the religion that supplants it. This occurred when Christianity replaced the pagan religions of ancient Rome—the pagan deities were given places in Hell and relabeled as demons. God and devil are the two faces of the same Janus-like spiritual presence, which is characterized by the possession of knowledge and power. Spiritual entities are classed as either gods or devils based on what they are believed to be capable of teaching, and on the harm they are thought to be able to work against humanity. A god without the power to do harm is a god without authority, and not much of a god at all.

Lovecraft created a hierarchy of gods that have their origins, not in the supernatural, but in the extraterrestrial and extradimensional. The various classes of Old Ones and their great lords are not native to this planet, but came to the Earth from other worlds or other realities in the distant past, before the human species differentiated itself from the apes. They came here for their own purposes, which did not involve mankind, and for those who remain today on the edges and in the shadows of our world, humanity is of little or no consequence. At best we can fulfill for them the role of minor servants. They look upon us in the way we regard insects—some are useful to us, and others are pests to be eradicated. But there can never be bonds of friendship or respect or affection between the Old Ones and humanity. They are simply too alien.

It is not to be wondered that when humanity became dimly aware of the presence of these various alien species, on the edges and in the dark places of our reality, that secret cults formed in which their great leaders were worshipped as gods. The lords of the Old Ones encouraged this worship, since it served their purposes. Cults arose to Cthulhu, Yog-Sothoth, Shub-Niggurath, and others the origins of which are lost in pre-history. In Lovecraft's Necronomicon mythos, witchcraft is a form of worship of Nyarlathotep, in his guise as the Black Man of the sabbat. It may be that magic itself appeared as a byproduct of this cultic adoration of the Old Ones, for magic is at times indistinguishable from the alien sciences of these beings. The creation of dimensional portals by the Salem witch, Keziah Mason, using certain angles and curves is nothing more than applied alien geometry.

The traditional pagan gods were not forgotten by Lovecraft, but he relegated them to the dreamlands, and accorded them a limited authority in comparison with that of the Other Gods under Nyarlathotep and Azathoth. They respond to the prayers of humanity in a capricious and unpredictable way, and are never to be relied upon in time of need. The gods of Earth reside in a great palace on the summit of the mountain Kadath, in the Cold Waste of the dreamlands. Whether this great mountain has a correspondence with an actual mountain is not clear, although Lovecraft hints that this may be so in his story *At the Mountains of Madness,* where it is intimated that Kadath may be located in Antarctica. Kadath serves as a kind of prison for the gods of Earth, which are at times let out to play by Nyarlathotep, but only under a strict supervision. These lesser gods sometimes dance atop the higher peaks of the mountain ranges in the dreamlands, where they are far enough removed from towns and villages to remain unobserved by men.

About the God of the Christians, Lovecraft has virtually nothing to say. Christ is not invoked to battle the evil of the Old Ones, because it is assumed that such invocation would be useless. In general it may be observed that Lovecraft treats the Christian God as though he does not exist. There are minor exceptions to this rule. In *The Dreams in the Witch House*, Walter Gilman uses a crucifix to startle the witch Keziah Mason into releasing her grip on his throat. Lovecraft wrote that she seemed "struck with panic" at the sight of the cross, but it may have been the faith Gilman unconsciously placed in it that startles the witch, rather than the crucifix itself, for there is no evidence of supernatural power emanating from the cross. Gilman uses its chain to strangle old Keziah, but he could have used any similar chain for the same purpose. The prayers recited nightly by his fellow boarder at the Witch House, the devout Catholic Joe Mazurewicz, seem in themselves to be without authority.

Lovecraft declared himself to be a man without religious faith in his 1922 essay, *A Confession of Unbelief.* He wrote that at age four, when told that Santa Claus was a myth, he asked the reasonable question, why isn't God also a myth? The dreariness of Sunday school drove from him any belief in Christianity. He progressed from an early fascination with the folklore of the Arab world to a love of Greek mythology at age six, to an interest in science at age nine that drove all religious belief from him. He wrote of this period in his essay, "Naturally, having an open and unemotional mind, I was soon a complete skeptic and materialist."

From age twelve to age seventeen Lovecraft studied astronomy intensively, collecting a library of sixty-one books on the subject. The effect of astronomy on his philosophy was to confirm in him a conviction that the place of mankind in the universe is vanishingly small, and that human needs, aspirations, and intentions are of no importance in the cosmic scheme of things. Always alienated from the rest of humankind, he began to look upon the human race dispassionately as just one more inconsequential species the fate of which was foredoomed. He summed up his philosophy at the time of writing the essay, when he was thirty-two years old, as "a cynicism tempered with immeasurable pity for man's eternal tragedy of aspirations beyond the possibility of fulfillment."

We can only imagine the immense battle being waged in Lovecraft's psyche, a battle of which he himself may have remained largely unaware. By his inherent nature he was a dreamer, a visionary, a storyteller, and myth-maker, drawn to the fantastic and the magical, taking delight in the imagination, seeking escape from the mundane. Yet his clear and uncompromising analytical mind informed him in terms that could not be refuted that all this was unreal, that there was no place for myths in the bleak universe revealed by astronomical observation.

Lovecraft responded in the only way he could respond, by casting his own myths into patterns that were in harmony with the frigid, godless universe he perceived through his telescope. He made his gods and devils into alien species from other worlds and higher dimensions of space. Religion was transformed into the worship by human cults of more advanced intelligent species, and magic became an alien science capable of manipulation by humans who knew the correct angles and spoke the necessary words of power.

The beloved Hellenic gods of his childhood he did not discard outright, but he relegated them to the dreamlands, and placed them into a kind of sanitarium atop Mount Kadath, with the Other Gods as their warders. Some of the older pagan gods do appear in Lovecraft's stories, but they are usually transformed and adapted to his new cosmic mythology. For example, the Black Man of European witch lore is revealed to be Nyarlathotep, one of the Great Old Ones, in *The Dreams in the Witch House*. The gorgon Medusa of the Greeks, and Lilith of the Hebrews, make appearances in his stories *Medusa's Coil*, and *The Horror at Red Hook*, reshaped as material creatures of alien and monstrous origins around whom mythologies evolved during ancient times.

It is not quite correct to say that Lovecraft was an atheist. He rejected the faith of Christianity with disgust, and that of the ancient Greeks with infinite sorrow, but in their places he built a new pantheon of gods and devils of his own design that he could reconcile with his bleak cosmic view. He always maintained that he did not himself believe in the mythic figures of his imagination, yet he took the trouble to integrate them with his understanding of the universe. If they were not gods Lovecraft presumed to exist, they were gods he suspected could exist, or at least were not so absurdly impossible as the gods of ancient Greece, or the gods of Rome. Lovecraft thus became the first high priest of a new religion for the scientific age, his place before its altar all the more secure by virtue of his skeptical disbelief in its deities.

All-In-One and One-In-All

The "All-In-One and One-In-All" is another title for Yog-Sothoth, the keeper of the gateways of time and space. This expression is used in modern Western occultism to describe the highest conception of God, and can be found in the mystical writings of Buddhists, Christians, and Islamics.

(*Through the Gates of the Silver Key*)

Atys *

Atys (also spelled Attis) was the consort of the goddess Cybele (also spelled Kybele). He was compelled by the goddess to castrate himself as a punishment for his infidelity. The priests of Cybele castrated themselves in imitation of his example. Atys was originally a god of vegetation of the Phrygians. This god is mentioned in the midst of a wild invocation to various Greek deities.

(*The Electric Executioner*)

Azathoth

There is not a huge amount to be written about this god of chaos, who can scarcely be examined apart from his messenger, Nyarlathotep. Perhaps the most important understanding is that he is really no more than an archetype of formless chaos itself. He is an attempt to embody that which cannot be embodied, and to describe that which defies description. In *The Dreams in the Witch House*, the ancient witch Keziah Mason tells Walter Gilman that Azathoth sits on a throne at the center of ultimate chaos. She also tells him that Azathoth has a book for recording in blood the names of new witches, which appears absurd until it is realized that the throne and the book are merely Keziah's way of interpreting aspects of Azathoth that she can comprehend. To even consider that which lies beyond all understanding, it must be given a form that the mind is able to hold.

Gilman remembers the name "Azathoth" in the *Necronomicon* "for a primal evil too horrible for description." Nonetheless, some description must appear in that dread book, since Gilman later considers the reference, which concerns the mindless being Azathoth, who rules all time and space from a black throne. The *Necronomicon* also alludes to the music that is heard in this chaotic center, the monotonous piping of a flute.

The flute of Azathoth is a symbol that represents the engine of creation by which the formless substance of chaos is transformed into cosmos, and by which its diversity of forms is sustained from moment to moment. The music of Azathoth's flute is the very lifeblood of the universe. Lovecraft does not actually place the flute into the hands of Azathoth, but its music is his constant accompaniment.

Elsewhere, Gilman characterizes the place of Azathoth as "spiral black vortices." It is central to the creation myth of the Kabbalah that the universe emanated within a chaotic primal swirling or vortex that is the highest conceivable expression of God. This swirling occurs in Kether (The Crown), the first emanation, which is literally the crown of creation. The place of Azathoth seems to be a kind of dark reflection of the primal swirling of bright sparks that gave rise to the universe. Perhaps it is the end of things, as Kether is their beginning. Yet on that level of reality, the timeless serpent of infinity bites its own tail, and the end and beginning are one. Lovecraft explicitly states that Azathoth exists "beyond time."

In a more tangible sense, the chaos of Azathoth resembles a black hole, which is a super-dense object that distorts time and space to such a degree that not even light can escape from it. It is theorized that stars can under the right conditions collapse into a black hole. At the center of our spiral galaxy there is believed to be a massive black hole composed of the conglutination of millions of collapsed stars. Perhaps at the center of the universe there is an even larger black hole that is made up of millions of collapsed galaxies. This would be the physical corollary to the spiral chaos of Azathoth. Scientists have theorized that the universe sprang forth from an exploding black hole in what is known as the Big Bang. In *The Whisperer in Darkness* Azathoth is described as that "monstrous nuclear chaos beyond angled space." This is a good description of a black hole. Many times in *The Dream-Quest of Unknown Kadath* Azathoth is characterized as "gnawing" and "ravenous"—apt descriptions for a black hole, which consumes everything around it, yet is never filled.

Dancing to the notes of Azathoth's ceaseless flute are the Other Gods, called this to distinguish them from our earthly gods of classical mythology. They are strange beings described by Lovecraft as slow, awkward, gigantic, blind, voiceless, black, and mindless. They represent potential forms, potential essences and qualities. That is why they are mindless, dark, blind, and voiceless. They do not exist in actuality, but only in potentiality. From their potential substance, the actual universe is spun forth. They are in a sense the angels of Azathoth. The ultimate blasphemy, which Lovecraft never dared to utter, is that Azathoth and God are one. Azathoth is God's dark mirror reflection, a role that is in part fulfilled in Christian myth by the figure of Satan. However, Azathoth is a much greater being than the fallen angel Satan. He is the chaotic shadow-twin of God, or to put it another way, God's alter ego.

It is significant in this respect that Lovecraft frequently asserts that the name Azathoth is never to be spoken aloud. For example, in *The Dream-Quest of Unknown Kadath* he is referred to as "the boundless daemon sultan Azathoth, whose name no lips dare speak aloud." In a Jewish religious practice that began not long before the fall of the Temple at Jerusalem in 70 AD, Jews were, and still are, forbidden to say the ultimate name of God aloud. Instead, a title of God such as "Lord" or "Almighty" must be substituted for it. This alone would suggest that Azathoth and Yahweh are at root one and the same, but viewed through opposite ends of the telescope, one the Alpha and the other the Omega. A title of Azathoth is "Lord of All Things."

Nyarlathotep is the messenger of Azathoth. The word "angel" means "messenger." He serves as the active and manifest agent for Azathoth, who exists outside of time and space. He is Azathoth's chief or archangel, who manifests the thoughts of Azathoth, which could not have any existence without this medium of manifestation. He serves as the eyes, ears, and voice of Azathoth. Yet since the blind idiot god does not have a mind, in the manifest sense, Nyarlathotep believes these thoughts to be his own, and resents his dependence on Azathoth—in the poem "Azathoth" of Lovecraft's sonnet cycle *Fungi from Yuggoth* he contemptuously strikes Azathoth in the head. The truth is that without Azathoth, Nyarlathotep would have no purpose, and would be merely a hollow vessel, assuming that he had any existence at all. Nyarlathotep is a puppet who believes himself to be pulling the strings of the cosmos, which lead outside time and space.

(*The Haunter of the Dark; The Dreams in the Witch House; The Whisperer in Darkness; The Dream-Quest of Unknown Kadath; Fungi from Yuggoth*)

Beyond-One

The name under which the Mi-Go of Yuggoth worship Yog-Sothoth.

(*Through the Gates of the Silver Key*)

Black Man *

An avatar of Nyarlathotep, used when he presides over the sabbats of European witches. The Black Man was a common feature of European witchcraft lore. Margaret A. Murray quoted one of the Lancashire witches, Margaret Johnson, concerning the Black Man, who said in her trial testimony of 1633 that he was "a spirit or divell in the similitude and proportion of a man, apparelled in a suite of black, tyed about with silke pointes." In the same place Murray quoted Joan Wallis, the Huntingdonshire witch, who reported in 1646 that "the Devill came to her in the likenesse of a man in blackish cloathing, but had cloven feet." By another account of her testimony, Wallis confessed that the Devil came to her "like a man something ancient, in blackish cloathes, but he had ugly feet uncovered" (Murray, *Witch-Cult*, pp. 33–4).

(*The Man of Stone*; *The Dreams in the Witch House*; *The Case of Charles Dexter Ward*)

Bokrug

The water-lizard god of the inhuman green-skinned people of the gray city of Ib, which was built beside a nameless lake in the land of Mnar. The statue of the god is carved from a sea-green stone. It was stolen by the men of Sarnath, another city on the same lakeshore, when they killed the people of Ib and cast their corpses and all their idols into the lake. Only the statue of Bokrug did they preserve to set up in their temple, as a tangible sign of their victory over Ib. The night after it was erected in the temple at Sarnath, it mysteriously vanished, and the high priest of Sarnath, Taran-Ish, was found dead from fright, after having scrawled on the chrysolite altar of the temple the sign of doom.

(*The Doom That Came to Sarnath*)

Buddai *

Lovecraft described this god of the Australian Aborigines as a "gigantic old man who lies asleep for ages underground with his head on his arm, and who will some day awake and eat up the world." He indicated that this sleeping god was connected with "great stones with marks on them."

In his 1899 study of the Aborigines, John Mathew quoted the folklorist Andrew Lang as having written: "There are certain traditions among the aborigines that appear to me to have somewhat of an Asiatic character and aspect. Buddai, or, as it is pronounced by the aborigines towards the mountains in the Moreton Bay district, Budjah (Buddah), they regard as a common ancestor of their race, and describe as an old man of great stature, who has been asleep for ages" (Mathew, p. 147). Lang probably had in mind the giant statues of reclining Buddha, common in Thailand, that depict him with his head cradled on his hand, propped up by his arm. The reclining Buddha at Wat Pho, Thailand, is fifty yards long. "Buddai" is an alternative form of the term "Buddha." However, Mathew disputed Lang's conjecture.

Various hills and mountains around the world are said by local peoples to be the bodies or bones of reclining gods, which at times come to wakefulness and arise from their earthy beds. For example, Sleeping Giant, also known as Mount Carmel, is a mountain in south-central Connecticut, so-called due to its resemblance to a reclining humanoid form. There are many such formations in North America alone, such as the Old Man of the Mountain in Bridgeport, California; Sleeping Ute in the San Juan Basin of Colorado; Sleeping Beauty Mountain in Columbia Gorge, Oregon; Sleeping Princess at Mount Timpanogos, Utah; Sleeping Chief in Squamish, British Columbia; and Sleeping Giant on the Sibley Peninsula of Ontario—to name only a few.

(*The Shadow Out of Time*)

Chaugnar Faugn *

An alien being who descended to Earth ages ago from another dimension. He is humanoid, with physical characteristics that resemble features of the octopus and the elephant. The god is able to move with astonishing quickness, and uses his elephant-like trunk to drain blood from living creatures. From amphibians native to this planet he created the race of Miri Nigri to be his servants. These things later bred with primitive human beings to produce the repellent Tcho-Tcho people. Chaugner Faugn is a creation of the writer Frank Belknap Long and appeared first in Long's 1931 novel *The Horror From the Hills*. He was mentioned by Lovecraft in his story *The Horror in the Museum*, and in this way found himself a part of the Necronomicon mythos.

(*The Horror in the Museum*)

Children of the Fire Mist *

In *Through the Gates of the Silver Key*, Lovecraft referred to the Children of the Fire Mist, who "came to Earth to teach the Elder Lore to man." These ancient beings appear to be derived from *The Secret Doctrine* of Madame H. P. Blavatsky, published in 1888, where reference is made (vol. 1, p. 86) to the "Sons of the Fire-Mist" in connection with the apocryphal *Book of Dzyan*. These Sons of the Fire-Mist, or Sons of the Fire are, according to Blavatsky, the first beings evolved from primordial fire. In the fourth stanza of the *Book of Dzyan*, they are called the "instructors" of the Sons of Earth. The *Book of Dzyan* is their teachings.

The Theosophist W. Scott-Elliot, while making reference to the *Book of Dzyan* in his own 1904 work *Lost Lemuria* (p. 35), wrote that these teachers came from the more advanced world Venus in spiritual form to inhabit the bodies of the Lemurian race. They naturally became "rulers, instructors in religion, and teachers of the arts" (p. 36) in Lemuria due to their superior intellects.

There is a parallel here with the myth in the *Book of Enoch* of the angels known as the Watchers, who lusted after the daughters of men, and who descended to Earth to take them as wives and to engender a race of hybrid demi-gods or heroes, called in

Genesis 6:4 "mighty men which were of old, men of renown," whom they instructed in the forbidden arts and sciences of heaven.

Lovecraft chose not to use in this context the concept that the minds of the Children of the Fire Mist were projected across space from Venus, but rather in his story *The Diary of Alonzo Typer*, he wrote that the *Book of Dzyan* "was old when the lords of Venus came through space in their ships to civilize our planet." Elsewhere in his fiction, Lovecraft does describe beings who project their minds through space while their bodies remain behind. For example, in *Through the Gates of the Silver Key*, the mind of Randolph Carter is projected into the body of the alien wizard Zkauba, and in *The Shadow Out of Time*, the mind of Nathaniel Wingate Peaslee is forcibly displaced from its body for several years by the projected mind of a Yithian.

(*Through the Gates of the Silver Key*; *The Diary of Alonzo Typer*)

Cthulhu

Whether Cthulhu qualifies for god status is open to debate, but he was worshipped as a god by human beings. He is an alien creature of immense power from beyond the stars, who crossed space to reach our planet. Who is to say that all the gods of our mythologies are not based on alien beings that originated in distant star systems or in other dimensions of reality? When we humans become aware of the power and presence of these beings, we worship them, and so they become gods to us. What they are in their essence is probably beyond our limited comprehension.

In *At the Mountains of Madness* Lovecraft wrote that a land-dwelling race of beings shaped like octopi filtered down to our planet from cosmic infinity long before the evolution of humanity. These beings came to be known as the spawn of Cthulhu. They immediately fought a war with the Elder Things (which Lovecraft called "the Old Ones" in this story), the crinoid race that had the center of their civilization in their great stone city in Antarctica. For a time the spawn were able to drive the Elder Things completely off the land and into the sea, but eventually the tide of war shifted, and the Elder Things secured a treaty of peace that ceded the new lands arising from the floor of the ocean to the spawn of Cthulhu, while retaining all the old land masses for their own habitations.

Lovecraft mentioned in this story that both the spawn of Cthulhu and the Mi-Go are composed of radically different matter from that of the Elder Things, whose bodies are made of more or less normal substances. From this Lovecraft deduced that the spawn of Cthulhu had originated from "even remoter gulfs of the cosmic space" than had given rise to the Elder Things.

The center of the civilization of the octopi of the Cthulhu spawn was the island of R'lyeh, in the Pacific Ocean, where they constructed their great capital city of the same name. Lovecraft provided its exact location, which is "S. Latitude 47° 9', W. Longitude 123° 43'." Like the Antarctic city of the crinoid race with which the spawn shared the Earth, it was built of cyclopean blocks of stone, using a strange geometry that defies human understanding. The stone was said to be greenish in color. On R'lyeh was a mountain, and on the top of this mountain Cthulhu built his mighty house, surrounded by the houses of his spawn. His house was crowned with a great monolith covered with strange hieroglyphics. For ages he dwelled here, sending out his thoughts to control those earthly creatures who worshipped him. Eventually his servants included the primitive race of man.

Then a great catastrophe occurred. The rays of the stars in the heavens became poisonous to Cthulhu and his spawn. It seems likely that it also became poisonous to a number of other cosmic beings of a similar nature, forcing them to withdraw from the Earth. The alien substance that composed their bodies could not tolerate the shifting alignment of the constellations, or perhaps it was the arrangement of the planets—the histories that tell of the event are not clear on exactly how the stars or planets (which in ancient times were known as wandering stars) went wrong, only that a transformation in the pattern of the night sky forced Cthulhu to place his spawn into a state of suspended animation from which only he had the power to awaken them.

He retired inside the protective walls of his great house and placed himself in a similar hibernation that was indistinguishable from death, except that he remained aware and dreamed strange dreams, sending his thoughts across the surface of the world to command his worshippers as before. The death-like sleep protected him. Even as the rays of the malign stars destroyed his substance, his dreaming mind rebuilt it and renewed it, so that his body was perpetually reborn. Cthulhu became dependent on his worshippers to open the door of his house from the outside and liberate him, once the stars again came right in their turnings.

Cthulhu could not foresee that a geological event would occur that would sink the island of R'lyeh to the bottom of the Pacific. The miles of seawater between him and his worshippers acted as a barrier to his projected telepathic commands, severing the control he held over them. He could no longer summon them at will to R'lyeh to open the door of his great house, which in any case was unreachable beneath the crushing weight of the ocean. He remained aware of what transpired on the Earth, but was trapped and helpless. It is perhaps to this condition that the enigmatic couplet in the *Necronomicon*, written by the mad Arab, Abdul Alhazred, alludes:

> That is not dead which can eternal lie,
> And with strange aeons even death may die.

A sentence written in the ancient language of the Great Old Ones describes Cthulhu's frustrating suspension between being and nonbeing: *Ph'nglui mglw'nafh Cthulhu R'lyeh wgah'nagl fhtagn*. It may be translated, "In his house at R'lyeh dead Cthulhu waits dreaming." These words were chanted by the members of the Cthulhu cult in their rituals, for his cult survived even though his mental control over its members was cut off by the miles of intervening ocean water. A shorter form of chant used by the cult was *Cthulhu fhtagn*, which was not translated by Lovecraft, but which may mean "Cthulhu waits dreaming."

The members of the Cthulhu cult assert that they worship the Great Old Ones who came from the sky before there were human beings. They do not know if Cthulhu resembles these Old Ones, because no man has ever seen them. All of this race has vanished, either beneath the ground or beneath the waves, but in the first dawn of humanity their dead bodies revealed their secrets in dreams to their human worshippers.

In *The Call of Cthulhu*, the sleeping alien is described by his cult as a "great priest," but whether he is considered to be the great priest of the cultists, or of the dreaming Old Ones, or of the Cthulhu spawn, is not completely clear. The obvious assumption is that Cthulhu is the priest of the Cthulhu spawn that lie dreaming in their stone houses around his mountain on sunken R'lyeh. Perhaps a better description of his role to the spawn would be magician or even scientist. He cast the suspended animation over his spawn that protects them from the malign stars, and only he has the power to lift it. Whether it was done by prayers, magic, or alien science, who can say? These are human distinctions and do not apply to the Old Ones.

The Cthulhu spawn are probably not the same as the Old Ones, because the spawn are described in *At the Mountains of Madness* as octopi, but the Cthulhu cult asserts in *The Call of Cthulhu* that no man has ever seen the Old Ones, or can say what they may look like. It is possible that the cult remained unaware that the spawn were octopoidal, and that the spawn are indeed the same as the Old Ones they worship, but I believe the Old Ones are not the same as the spawn. Lovecraft does not make clear whether the spawn are octopoidal only in the general shape of their heads, as is Cthulhu himself, or if their entire bodies resemble octopi. It may be that they are smaller versions of Cthulhu who have in some manner budded off him or been generated asexually by him.

The cult has a very good idea of what Cthulhu himself looks like, because they possess his image in the form of statues, or plaques carved in bas-relief. The image on one such bas-relief was said to resemble at once "an octopus, a dragon, and a human caricature." A statue taken from a Cthulhu cult in the swamps of Louisiana was around eight inches tall, done in a type of stone completely unknown to geologists. Lovecraft described this stone as a "soapy, greenish-black stone" with "golden or iridescent flecks and striations." The artistic style of the carving resembled no human artistic style, inviting speculation that the small statue predated the human race. It may even have originated from another planet. One of the leaders of the Cthulhu cult at New Orleans, a man named Old Castro, asserted that when the Great Old Ones came down from the stars, they brought their images with them.

These statues or carvings allowed a very precise description of Cthulhu, even before he emerged briefly from the waves during the temporary rising of R'lyeh from the ocean. Lovecraft described his body as scaly, rubbery-looking, and "vaguely anthropoid" in outline. This does not mean a human body, and depictions of Cthulhu with a human-like body are probably incorrect. His body is vaguely ape-like in its overall outline, that is all. It has two arms and two legs. His head is said to be "octopus-like" and again, this is not the same as asserting that it looks like an octopus. His face is a "mass of feelers." Feelers are not the same as tentacles. On the ends of his arms and legs are prodigious claws that may be somewhat similar to those of a bird of prey. It was these claws that caused his image to be characterized as dragon-like, along with a set of narrow leathery wings on his back.

Cthulhu is depicted squatting on a rectangular block. The curved tips of his folded wings touch the edge of the block in the back. In front, the claws of his feet curl over the edge of the block and extend down a quarter of its height. His clawed hands clasp his elevated knees, and the feelers hanging from his face brush the backs of his hands. It seems obvious that Lovecraft based this description on stone images of gargoyles. Or, if we were inclined to be more fanciful in our speculations, that the images of medieval gargoyles reflect in their posture the dim racial memory of the stone idols of Cthulhu.

The pedestal of greenish stone taken from the New Orleans cult is carved on its sides with unreadable symbols that resemble writing. The posture of Cthulhu is threatening and malignant in some way that is difficult to define. Lovecraft described his body as a "bloated corpulence." This indicates a heavy torso and thick limbs. Nothing is mentioned concerning Cthulhu's eyes, but in one of his letters Lovecraft drew a small image of the squatting Cthulhu, on the head of which he placed a triangular cluster of three eyes. It is not clear in the crude sketch whether Lovecraft intended Cthulhu to have three eyes in total, or three on each side of his head. My own interpretation of the sketch is that there are three eyes on each side of the head, or a total of six eyes. Cthulhu is often depicted in popular art with two eyes, and this is definitely incorrect.

The cult of Cthulhu in the swamps near New Orleans did not worship alone, but were aided by inhuman creatures—a race of black-winged flying devils that came out of caverns under the earth, and "a huge, formless white polypous thing with luminous eyes" that rose from the depths of a deep lake. The identity of these beings can only be speculated about, but the winged devils resemble night-gaunts, and the formless white thing may have been a shoggoth. Lovecraft gave no definite information that would confirm their natures. The black-winged creatures were the ones who carried out the ten human sacrifices of the ritual described, not the human members of the cult, and it appears that a kind of esoteric symbiosis existed between the human worshippers of Cthulhu and these winged things, which the cultists called the Black Winged Ones. Arguing against the identification of these creatures with the night-gaunts is the explicit statement in *The Dream-Quest of Unknown Kadath* that the night-gaunts owe their allegiance only to the god Nodens, not to the Old Ones.

In *The Call of Cthulhu*, an upheaval on the floor of the Pacific Ocean thrusts up the sunken island of R'lyeh so that the monolith and the citadel of Cthulhu that crown the central mountain project above the surface of the waves. This is enough to allow dreaming Cthulhu to send his thoughts outward over the surface of the world to summon his worshippers to release him. His powerful telepathic messages affect not only the minds of his committed followers, but the mind of anyone with a sufficient degree of psychic perception, giving them disturbing and frightening dreams in which they perceive the city with its monolith, and even the form of Cthulhu himself.

Before a faction of the cult of Cthulhu made up of "Kanakas and half-castes" can reach the newly risen island in their pirated steam yacht the *Alert* to liberate their great priest from his tomb, their ship is captured and taken over by the crew of the schooner *Emma*. In the battle, the *Emma* is sunk, requiring the eight surviving members of her crew to transfer to the *Alert*, where they kill all of the cultists. They steam on to encounter R'lyeh and explore it, inadvertently opening the door to Cthulhu's house and setting him free. Evidently the stars are right at this moment, for Cthulhu is able to venture forth into the open air. It may be speculated that it was the temporary coming right of the stars in their turnings that caused R'lyeh to rise from the ocean depths.

The door to Cthulhu's house is like a great barn door in size, but whether set flat in the ground beside the base of the monolith like a trap door, or angled like a cellar door, the alien geometries of the city make it impossible to determine. It is carved with an image described as a "squid-dragon bas-relief" that the crew of the sunken *Emma* also observe elsewhere in the citadel, and its frame is intricate and ornate. When one of the crew climbs onto the stone slab of the door, it begins to open inward from the top under the pressure of his scant weight, indicating that it is delicately balanced. A tangible black smoke issues forth, followed by Cthulhu himself.

The small statues and carvings of the god can reveal everything about his appearance except the nature of the substance of which his body is composed, and his size. The sole surviving member of the crew of the captured yacht, Second Mate Gustaf Johansen, later reported that the body of Cthulhu was green and gelatinous. The term "sticky" was also used. This indicates that his body is transparent or translucent. Cthulhu's size was never given precisely. He was compared to a walking mountain. One of those who received his telepathic communications when R'lyeh first arose from the waves asserted that he was a mile high, but this appears to have been an exaggeration.

When Cthulhu enters the water to pursue the fleeing steam yacht, his head comes "nearly up to the bowsprit." This indicates that almost all of his body is below the water. We have no way to know how deep the water just off R'lyeh may have been, but since Cthulhu's house was on the top of a mountain, the ground of the island probably sloped away steeply. Cthulhu's size may be roughly estimated from the size of the doorway to his house, which was compared to a barn door. But it is possible that his gelatinous body was able to squeeze itself through a small opening, relative to its dimensions, so the size of the door is no certain measure of the size of Cthulhu. It may be guessed that he stands at least a hundred feet tall, and his height may well be double that estimate.

Second Mate Johansen has the presence of mind and the courage to send the steam yacht racing toward Cthulhu rather than away from him. It strikes his great rounded head, described in the story as "like the stern of a daemon galleon." The gelatinous head explodes like a burst bladder into a noxious and acrid green cloud of gas, but almost immediately after the ship has passed, it begins to draw together and reform itself. The ship is able to escape before Cthulhu has time to repair his body. Since the island of R'lyeh soon after the encounter sank beneath the ocean, and since the thought emanations of Cthulhu ceased, it was presumed by the narrator of Lovecraft's story that Cthulhu had returned into his house, and was within it when R'lyeh once more plummeted to the depths of the Pacific Ocean.

Whether the stars are presently right, and the rule of Cthulhu over the Earth awaits only another rising of R'lyeh, or whether it was the brief coming right of the stars that caused R'lyeh to rise, and their going wrong again that made it descend, Lovecraft did not speculate. He only asserted that Cthulhu lives, and observed, "What has risen may sink, and what has sunk may rise."

In the story *The Mound*, Cthulhu figures prominently as one of the primary gods worshipped by the people of blue-litten K'n-yan, who dwell in an enormous self-illuminated cavern somewhere deep beneath the plains of Oklahoma. The twin ruling gods of the copper-skinned people of K'n-yan, who somewhat resemble American Plains Indians, are Cthulhu and the serpent-god Yig. The reason for the reverence paid to Cthulhu, who in K'n-yan is known as Tulu, is the teaching that it was Cthulhu who, long ages ago, carried the race of the cavern-dwellers across the gulf of space to the Earth, along with ritual objects made of a dark and lustrous metal, magnetic to itself, that is not to be found on this planet.

The writer August Derleth, when attempting to classify Lovecraft's elder gods into four elemental categories, placed Cthulhu under the heading of water, because of his resting place on sunken R'lyeh. This is clearly an error. Lovecraft states in *At the Mountains of Madness* that the Cthulhu spawn are a land-dwelling race. An additional consideration is that the waters of the ocean block the projection of Cthulhu's telepathic commands. If he were watery in his nature, it seems unlikely that he would be frustrated by water.

The division by Derleth of the elder gods into four elemental categories was a mistake in general, because they do not lend themselves to a fourfold elemental division. In my version of the *Necronomicon* I have placed the chiefs among the Old Ones under the seven planets of traditional astrology, and this seems to serve much better than an elemental division. The Old Ones are sky gods, having come from the stars, so they do not belong to the elements, but to the heavenly spheres. I have set Cthulhu under Mars because he is the most war-like of the lords of the Old Ones. It may be disputed whether Cthulhu can even be classed among the Old Ones, but he is clearly related to them. The *Necronomicon* states that Cthulhu is their cousin, an attempt by Alhazred to indicate some close blood connection.

(*The Call of Cthulhu; At the Mountains of Madness; The Mound*)

Dagon [*]

The fish-god made his first appearance in the Lovecraft mythos story *Dagon*, written in 1919. As is true of so much of Lovecraft's seminal work, this story was little more than a description of one of Lovecraft's dreams. An escaped American officer of the merchant marine during the First World War, fleeing the German navy across the Pacific Ocean in a small boat, finds himself beached on a vast island that rises up beneath his boat. He explores the new landmass under moonlight and discovers a deep chasm with a band of water that resembles a river flowing along its bottom. He descends into the chasm and looks across the watery fissure, which not long before had lain submerged under miles of ocean. On the opposite side of the water is an enormous block of white stone, covered with pictographs, and also with images of amphibious creatures that seem disproportionately large, almost the size of whales. From the water arises one of these creatures. It clasps the monolith in its great arms and began to make "certain measured sounds" that are not specified.

Lovecraft is vague in his description of the monster, but we can assume that the images carved on the monolith depict its form. The images show a man-like being with webbed feet and hands, scaly skin, and a hideous head with wide, flabby lips and glassy, bulging eyes. Upon seeing the monster, the escaped American officer immediately goes mad, flees back to his boat, is vaguely aware of a great storm, and recovers his senses in a hospital in San Francisco. The experience continues to prey upon his mind, and he becomes a drug addict, then decides that the only way to escape its memory and the fears it evokes is to end his own life.

The images on the monolith are obviously prototypes for the Deep Ones who appear later in Lovecraft's fiction. They closely resemble the Deep Ones apart from their size. In the story *Dagon*, the American officer associated them with the Philistine fish-god Dagon, and in *The Shadow Over Innsmouth*, the people of Innsmouth under the leadership of Obed Marsh instituted the Esoteric Order of Dagon as their new religion. The monolith that the monster embraces, with its pictoglyphs, foreshadows the monolith that in a later story surmounts the house of Cthulhu on the submerged Pacific island of R'lyeh, which also rises from the sea floor during some great but temporary geological upheaval.

The story *Dagon* raises more questions than it answers. Is the amphibious monster that clings to the monolith only one of many such gigantic creatures in the ocean depths, or is it the last of its kind? Does it hug the carved stone block in worship, or in fear, or in sorrow? Are the noises it makes prayers, the sounds of weeping, or is it calling others of its kind up from the depths? Why are the Deep Ones of the later tale *The Shadow Over Innsmouth* so much smaller than this great being?

The clue to this mystery may lie in the nature of some living creatures to continue to grow larger throughout their entire lifespan. Their growth is only ended by their deaths. If Dagon is ancient beyond reckoning, it may be that all the others of his race, apart from his mate, are much smaller, those of Dagon's own age having been killed in the past. We know he has a mate because mention is made in *The Shadow Over Innsmouth* of "Father Dagon and Mother Hydra." Assuming that this mated pair of aliens decided to breed, their offspring would be relatively diminutive in size, having not had the vast span of ages to reach the dimensions of their progenitor.

Or it may be that, like the termite, the breeder of the colony is much larger in size than its workers. The queen termite is enormous relative to the others of its species. We do not know what Mother Hydra looks like, because Lovecraft never even hinted at her appearance, but perhaps she is radically different in shape, and also much larger, than Father Dagon. Human myths about the hydra suggest that this monster does not look like a Deep One. Perhaps in the race of the Deep Ones, both the female and male of the breeding pair are larger than their progeny. It may even be that Dagon and Hydra traveled through space to this planet for the specific purpose of breeding a new race beneath our seas, just as a queen bee sets out from an existing hive to found a new hive at a distant location. We are not told by Lovecraft that Dagon and his mate are alien to this planet, but it seems likely to me.

Even though it is obvious that *The Call of Cthulhu* was in large measure inspired by the earlier story *Dagon*, Cthulhu and Dagon are not the same and should not be confused. Cthulhu and his octopoidal spawn are a land-dwelling race that was trapped beneath the waves when R'lyeh unexpectedly sank under them while they lay in suspended animation in their stone houses to avoid the poisonous rays from the stars. The race to which Dagon belongs is water-dwelling. The substance of which the body of Cthulhu is composed is wholly alien to normal Earth matter, but the body of Dagon appears to be of physical flesh. It closely resembles in its shape and substance the bodies of the Deep Ones. For these reasons it is clear that the people of Innsmouth do not worship Cthulhu under a more familiar name, but worship a completely different being.

The Deep Ones live in stone cities with many pillars in the deepest rifts in the floors of the world's oceans. Lovecraft named only one of their cities, Y'ha-nthlei, which is located in the ocean chasm that lies off Devil Reef, just outside Innsmouth harbor in the Atlantic. They are said to have the resources to rise up from the depths in the millions and destroy the entire race of humanity, but refrain from doing so in part because they prefer to interact and interbreed with human beings. Children born from a union between a Deep One and a human resemble humans in their childhood and youth, but become more like Deep Ones as they age. At around age seventy years they take to the ocean for good, and cease to dwell on the land, but sometimes return to it for brief visits.

Dagon is either the god or the patriarch of this vast undersea race. It may be that he is both. Ancestor worship is common among human cultures. It is not difficult to imagine that a single living ancestor, grown both ancient beyond measure and gigantic in dimension, would be worshipped by his distant descendants as a god. The people of Innsmouth swore loyalty to Dagon with three oaths of increasingly serious significance. Lovecraft did not provide the text of these oaths, but old Zadok Allen, who refused to take the third oath, said that he would rather die than take it.

(*Dagon; The Shadow Over Innsmouth*)

Dionysos *

The Greek god of wine and vegetation, son of the god Zeus and the woman Semele of Thebes. While still a child he was kidnapped by the Titans, who slit his throat with a sacrificial knife while he gazed enraptured at his own image in a mirror. They cut up his corpse, boiled the pieces, then roasted them. Zeus was attracted by the odor. He killed the Titans and resurrected Dionysos. This god is mentioned by Lovecraft in a list of Greek boy-gods.

(*The Electric Executioner*)

Forgotten One

An alien creature who is the Guardian of the Ancient Gateway.

(*The Diary of Alonzo Typer*)

Ghatanothoa

God or patron demon of the Mi-Go of Yuggoth, a deathless being who resided in the crypts below a great stone fortress built long before the evolution of humanity by the Mi-Go upon Mount Yaddith-Gho, in the ancient kingdom of K'naa on the lost continent of Mu. Long after the Mi-Go returned to Yuggoth, their god continued to burrow beneath the fortress. Any who might look upon the Dark God, as it was known in K'naa, instantly turned to stone and leather on the outside, but remain alive and conscious within. To prevent its descent down the mountain from the crypts of Yaddith-Gho, a cult ruled by a hundred wealthy priests performed a yearly sacrifice of twelve young warriors and twelve maidens in a marble temple at the base of the mountain.

The deathless demon was also worshipped by this "hidden and detested" cult in Atlantis and on the plateau of Leng. The writer of *Nameless Cults*, von Junzt, asserted that the cult of Ghatanothoa had existed in subterranean blue-litten K'n-yan. It was rumored to have survived in "Egypt, Chaldaea, Persia, China, the forgotten Semite empires of Africa, and Mexico and Peru in the New World." Lovecraft called the demon a behemothic monstrosity and described it in the following terms: "gigantic—tentacled—proboscidian—octopus-eyed—semi-amorphous—plastic—partly squamous and partly rugose."

(*Out of the Aeons*)

Great Messenger

A title applied to Nyarlathotep by the Mi-Go and their secretive human cult in the hills of Vermont. The Great Messenger is characterized as the "bringer of strange joy to Yuggoth through the void" and the "Father of the Million Favoured Ones"—presumably a reference to the race of the Mi-Go that dwells on Yuggoth, who seem to worship Nyarlathotep.

(*The Whisperer in Darkness*)

Hastur *

Hastur first appeared as a pastoral god in *Haïta the Shepherd*, an 1893 short story by Ambrose Bierce. The name was adopted by Robert W. Chambers for use in his series of stories collected under the 1895 anthology title *The King In Yellow*. It is probably the work of Chambers that inspired Lovecraft to use the name of this god. In *The Whisperer in Darkness*, Hastur is a god worshipped by a human cult that serves the purposes of "monstrous powers from other dimensions" that seek to track down and do injury to the Mi-Go dwelling in secrecy on our planet. Lovecraft does not reveal why these powers should seek to harm the Mi-Go.

(*The Whisperer in Darkness*)

Haunter of the Dark

Thought to be an avatar of Nyarlathotep, this strange god shuns the light. It may be called by means of the irregularly faceted black crystal known as the Shining Trapezohedron. This god knows all occult secrets, but demands of his worshippers sacrifice in human blood. He was called through the crystal and adored in Providence, Rhode Island, by the occult sect known as the Church of Starry Wisdom. This sect was driven out of the town in 1877 by enraged Irish locals when attention was drawn to the mysterious and recurring disappearance of children in the vicinity of the gothic-revival stone church on Federal Hill used by the sect. However, the Haunter remained hidden in the complete dark of the steeple, above the tower room where it had been evoked. In 1935 the writer Robert Blake stirred it to awareness by gazing into the Trapezohedron in the tower room of the church. It was prevented from leaving the abandoned church by the electric lighting of the city, but when the city power failed, it was freed.

(*The Haunter of the Dark*)

Huitzilopotchli *

Literally, "Hummingbird of the South," a war god and sun god of the Aztecs, and a great wizard. According to legend, his mother was impregnated with a ball of feathers. His sister tried to end his life in the womb by killing his mother, but he sprang forth fully formed and killed his sister, then cut off her head and cast it into the sky, where it became the Moon. He also slew many of his four hundred siblings, and threw them into the heavens, where they became stars. Every morning he uses the serpent of fire (the first ray of the rising Sun), as a weapon to conquer his hostile siblings, allowing the dawn to come and turn night into day. His Aztec worshippers sustained his strength for this daily battle by giving him human hearts in sacrifice. He was also a god of death and guide to the underworld.

(*The Electric Executioner*)

Hylas *

A handsome youth, the companion of Hercules. He was dragged down into a spring by water nymphs, who could not resist his beauty, and his corpse was never found. One in a list of Greek boy-gods mentioned by Lovecraft.

(*The Electric Executioner*)

Iacchus *

Greek demigod in the form of a youth who served as attendant for the goddess Demeter. He was a manifestation of the Phrygian Bacchus, and was sometimes called the son of Bacchus. He led the ceremonies of the Eleusinian Mysteries. Iacchus (also spelled Iakchos) is said to have received his name from the ecstatic cry *iakkhe!* that the worshippers of Demeter shouted during their processions.

(*The Electric Executioner*)

Ialemus *

Greek god of sad songs, who took the form of a youth. The muse Calliope is sometimes said to be his mother.

(*The Electric Executioner*)

Lathi

God of the dream city Thalarion, known as the City of a Thousand Wonders. He is represented by an eidolon, or carven image, that is nowhere described, but he must be a terrible god, since the streets of the city are littered with the bones of those who have dared to look upon his image. They are driven mad and doomed to walk the streets, haunted by daemons, for eternity. Those who enter the carven gate Akarial never leave the city or are heard from again.

(*The White Ship*)

Lilith *

A demoness who has her origin in ancient Sumer. She was associated with crib death, the mysterious death of infants in their cribs for no obvious physical reason. Sometimes young babies simply stop breathing and die. This was attributed to Lilith. In the folklore of the Jews she became the bride of Samael, the Jewish equivalent to Satan, and the queen of Hell. In some Jewish tales she is the first wife of Adam, before Eve.

Lovecraft made her the goddess worshipped by a cult of Kurdish devil worshippers known as the Yazidi who lived in Red Hook, a neighborhood of Brooklyn, New York. She was worshipped with the sacrifice of kidnapped children. Her worshippers bathed her feet in their blood. Lovecraft described her as a "phosphorent thing," and wrote, "in the blood of stainless childhood the leprous limbs of phosphorescent Lilith were laved." She has for her throne a golden pillar within a large cavern that opens to the sea, and in Lovecraft's story she is adept at swimming.

(*The Horror at Red Hook*)

Linos *

Greek god of flax, the fibers of which are used to make linen.
(*The Electric Executioner*)

Lobon

One of the three bearded gods worshipped at the lakeside city of Sarnath before its destruction. Along with Zo-Kalar and Tamash, Lobon sat on an ivory throne, his statue so cunningly fashioned that it had the appearance of life. The seated statues of the three gods of Sarnath were located within long halls forever filled with the scent and smoke of burning incense. These halls were all on the ground level the largest of the seventeen religious temples at Sarnath, which possessed a tower a thousand cubits tall. The temples were built from "a bright multi-colored stone not known elsewhere" but what the statues of the gods were made from is not stated. Each god probably had his own hall, since the text speaks of the "halls" of the gods. The statues of the gods were probably of human dimensions, since they could be so easily mistaken for living men.

(*The Doom That Came to Sarnath*)

Lord of the Woods

An obscure deity worshipped in the rituals of the Mi-Go and their cult of human followers in Lee's Swamp, at the base of the western slope of Dark Mountain. From his title the god would seem to be male. He is mentioned along with the Black Goat of the Woods with a Thousand Young, which seems to be a title for Shub-Niggurath. This has led to the assumption that the Lord of the Woods is a male form of Shub-Niggurath, perhaps the same as the Black Goat of the Woods. However, it is quite possible that a different deity is intended, the consort of the Black Goat rather than the Black Goat herself. It has even been speculated that the Black Goat is a different deity from Shub-Niggurath, or, at least, a different avatar or embodiment.

(*The Whisperer in Darkness*)

Magnum Innominandum

The title is Latin for "the Great Unnamable," and is mentioned among a list of names and terms with the "most hideous of connections" in Lovecraft's story *The Whisperer in Darkness*. It is possible that Azathoth, whose true name must never be spoken aloud, is intended. In *The Dream-Quest of Unknown Kadath* Azathoth is referred to as the "boundless daemon sultan Azathoth, whose name no lips dare speak aloud." It is less likely that this title applies to the god Hastur, even though the writer August Derleth linked the two in his stories.

(*The Whisperer in Darkness*)

Mother Hydra *

The mate of Dagon, who gave birth to the race of amphibian man-like creatures known as the Deep Ones. In the Order of Dagon, a religious cult that grew up in the New England town of Innsmouth, Mother Hydra was worshipped along with Father Dagon. In Greek mythology, the Hydra was a monster with many heads and poisonous breath that dwelt in the Lake of Lerna in Argolis, a district of Greece. The Hydra was killed by Hercules as one of his twelve labors. The lake no longer exists, but according to the ancient Greek historian, Pausanius, it was too deep to be measured, and anyone who tried to swim across it was sucked under and never seen again. It was considered one of the entrances to the Underworld. How closely Mother Hydra corresponds to the description of the Greek Hydra is impossible to guess, since Mother Hydra was never described by Lovecraft.

(*The Shadow Over Innsmouth*)

Nath-Horthath

The chief god worshipped in the city of Celephaïs, which lies in the dreamlands.

(*The Dream-Quest of Unknown Kadath*)

Nodens *

The Lord of the Great Abyss, this ancient god is described as "hoary and immemorial Nodens" in *The Dream-Quest of Unknown Kadath*, where he is mentioned most frequently by Lovecraft. The night-gaunts are his servants, and under his protection they have no need to fear the Old Ones, but defy even the will of Nyarlathotep. It is evident from the delight expressed by Nodens when Randolph Carter escapes the treachery of Nyarlathotep that no love is lost between these two deities. Lovecraft characterizes him as "potent and archaic." He is mentioned in company with Neptune in *The Strange High House in the Mist*, and the abyss in which he dwells must be a watery abyss, since he comes to the house riding on a giant seashell.

Nodens is an actual Celtic god worshipped in Britain in pre-Roman and Roman times. He was known as Nodens the Catcher, and was a hunter deity. All his power was supposed to reside in his grasping hand. Arthur Machen mentioned Nodens in his work *The Great God Pan*, which Lovecraft knew well. In Machen's story, the god's name occurs on a Latin inscription, where he is described as "Nodens (the god of the Great Deep or abyss)." He was also worshipped in Ireland under the name "Nuada," and was associated with water, sunlight, youth and healing. The name of this god has been linked with the Welsh word *nudd* (fog), which may in part explain Lovecraft's characterization of him as "hoary."

(*The Dream-Quest of Unknown Kadath; The Strange High House in the Mist*)

Not-To-Be-Named One

A god worshipped in the subterranean land of blue-litten K'n-yan. He is the husband of Shub-Niggurath. A slightly different form of the title of this god is used by the cult of the Mi-Go that gathered in Lee's Swamp, at the base of the western slope of Dark Mountain in Vermont. There the god is titled "Him Who is not to be Named." The title *Magnum Innominandum* (Latin for "the Great Not-To-Be Named") may be yet a third title for this mysterious god. The cultists of the Mi-Go called the goddess Shub-Niggurath "the Black Goat of the Woods," and also invoked a being known as the Lord of the Woods, who may be the same as Him Who is not to be Named.

A descriptive title is not the same as a true name, in an occult sense. A descriptive title refers to one aspect of a god, but its true name embodies its essential identity. The god of the Hebrews had one true name, which in Roman times everyone but the priests at the Temple in Jerusalem were forbidden to utter, but many descriptive titles such as "the Wrathful," "the Mighty One," "the Ancient of Days," and so on, which could be freely spoken. To know the true name of a god, or of anything else for that matter, is to possess power over it.

Thanks to the writings of August Derleth, who identified Him Who is not to be Named with the god Hastur, the general opinion is that the Not-To-Be-Named One is Hastur. There is no reason to suppose that Hastur is the Not-To-Be-Named One, or Him Who is not to be Named, other than Derleth's unfounded assumption.

(*The Mound; The Whisperer in Darkness*)

Nug and Yeb

Twin monstrosities of blue-litten K'n-yan, the ceremonies of which were found by the sixteenth-century Spaniard Zamacona in the story *The Mound* to be too sickening to be described. They are mentioned in *Out of the Aeons* in connection with Shub-Niggurath, along with the serpent-god Yig, and may be her twin children. The high priest of Shub-Niggurath in Mu is said to have "the power of Shub-Niggurath and her sons on his side." In *The Last Test*, reference is made to the underground shrines of Nug and Yeb in connection with Irem, the City of Pillars, in the Crimson Desert.

(*The Mound; The Last Test; Out of the Aeons*)

Nyarlathotep

Of all the alien deities who descended to this planet in the distant past from beyond the stars, Nyarlathotep is the most personable, if we may use this term to describe a being who invariably inspires terror in the human heart. He sometimes walks the surface of the Earth in the form of a man, and talks directly to individual human beings in their own languages. He involves himself in human affairs and enjoys causing suffering. He has many forms, and may be described as faceless since his true face, if indeed he has such a thing, is unknown. He appears as the mysterious Black Man of the witch cult of Western Europe.

Nyarlathotep began as an enigmatic Egyptian sage in one of Lovecraft's dreams. Lovecraft described this dream, which he had been having repeatedly since the age of ten, in a December 21, 1921, letter to Rheinhart Kleiner. In the dream, a stage performer is touring New England giving shows that astound audiences. Lovecraft's close friend Samuel Loveman, who took so active a role in Lovecraft's other dream that became *The Statement of Randolph Carter*, wrote to Lovecraft in this dream urging him not to miss the stage show of Nyarlathotep, should this extraordinary performer come to Providence. "He is horrible—horrible beyond anything you can imagine—but wonderful," Loveman wrote. "He haunts one for hours afterward. I am still shuddering at what he showed."

In the dream, Nyarlathotep gives a show in Providence, and although Lovecraft is warned by others not to go near him, he attends. Nyarlathotep is not so much a stage magician as a kind of esoteric prophet who combines a cinema show with a practical exhibition of the strange and marvelous. His performance is divided into two parts, a silent film presentation during which he narrates an explanation of what is appearing on the screen, followed by a demonstration that involves electrical devices and is presumably connected in some way with the things shown in the film. Lovecraft characterized the cinematic part of the performance as "horrible—possibly prophetic."

This enigmatic being first appeared in Lovecraft's fiction in the brief story *Nyarlathotep*, written in 1920. It presents him very much as he had appeared in Lovecraft's repeating dream, as an Egyptian showman who claims or hints at an ancient past:

> And it was then that Nyarlathotep came out of Egypt. Who he was, none could tell, but he was of the old native blood and looked like a Pharaoh. The fellahin knelt when they saw him, yet could not say why. He said he had risen up out of the blackness of twenty-seven centuries, and that he had heard messages from places not on this planet. Into the lands of civilization came Nyarlathotep, swarthy, slender, and sinister, always buying strange instruments of glass and metal and combining them into instruments yet stranger. He spoke much of the sciences of electricity and psychology and gave exhibitions of power which sent his spectators away speechless, yet which swelled his fame to exceeding magnitude. Men advised one another to see Nyarlathotep, and shuddered. And where Nyarlathotep went, rest vanished, for the small hours were rent with the screams of nightmare.

Again, we see how closely Lovecraft's fiction follows his dream vision, which may well have been a glimpse of some astral reality. The instruments of glass and metal suggest that Nyarlathotep is engaged in some alchemical or perhaps necromantic work that will have dire consequences for the human race. Lovecraft wrote in his story, "everyone felt that the world and perhaps the universe had passed from the control of known gods or forces to that of gods or forces which were unknown."

In the story, while the audience is mesmerized by the strange images of his cinema show, Nyarlathotep works his static-electrical devices and causes shadow creatures to materialize above them and squat on their heads, stealing some essence of free will or humanity. They all become slaves to Nyarlathotep, and are in some inexplicable way transported into a bleak future, or perhaps into an alternative dimension of reality in which their familiar world has decayed. They march against their will into a gulf containing "ghastly midnights of rotting creation, corpses of dead worlds with sores that were cities" in which the narrator, who we know from his dream is Lovecraft himself, catches a glimpse of the ultimate abyss where dance the blind gods of creation to the "maddening beating of drums, and thin, monotonous whine of blasphemous flutes." Nyarlathotep is said to be the soul of these grotesque gargoyle gods.

Although this brief story has very little in the way of plot, it is important to an understanding of Nyarlathotep because it presents the Crawling Chaos in his purest form, as Lovecraft perceived him in his persistent repeating dream. We see foreshadowed at the end of the tale the blind Azathoth, who sits at the center of the universe and unrolls worlds with the shrill music he sends streaming forth from his cracked flute. In later work Nyarlathotep became not only the soul of the blind gods, but the messenger or agent of Azathoth. It is almost as though in his dream Lovecraft glimpsed an astral reality in a partial way, that in later years he was able to fill in more completely.

When he came to write *The Dream-Quest of Unknown Kadath* six years later, Lovecraft used almost an identical description of the central chaos of the universe that is the cauldron of creation, but he added more detail and included its name, Azathoth, a being who does not merely reside there, but is himself the chaotic maelstrom, just as Yog-Sothoth is not merely the gatekeeper but the gate itself. Lovecraft referred to Azathoth as "that last amorphous blight of nethermost confusion which blasphemes and bubbles at the centre of all infinity—the boundless daemon sultan Azathoth, whose name no lips dare speak aloud, and who gnaws hungrily in inconceivable, unlighted chambers beyond time amidst the muffled, maddening beating of vile drums and the thin, monotonous whine of accursed flutes; to which detestable pounding and piping dance slowly, awkwardly, and absurdly the gigantic Ultimate gods, the blind, voiceless, tenebrous, mindless Other gods whose soul and messenger is the crawling chaos Nyarlathotep."

As can be gathered from this description, Nyarlathotep is the active agent of the blind Other Gods who with their tortured dance spin the cosmos out of the raw fabric of chaos. Because he is so close to the chaotic source, there is madness and danger in his very nature. The orderly laws that govern our universe cannot contain him. The forms by which he is perceived by human beings cannot begin to express his true nature, but are vessels through which he works his various purposes. They are sometimes called his avatars. This is a Hindu term much used in Theosophy, and stands for a human being who is filled with divine essence—a god in human form, who has descended to our level of reality and put on human flesh for the purpose of teaching the human race. Nyarlathotep's avatars, such as the Egyptian showman, have some dark ultimate purpose that is never fully revealed.

In *The Haunter of the Dark*, Lovecraft indicated that the ageless Egyptian showman who steals the souls of his audience in the story *Nyarlathotep* was indeed an avatar of the messenger at the central chaos. A character in the later tale, Robert Harrison Blake, asks himself, "What am I afraid of? Is it not an avatar of Nyarlathotep, who in antique and shadowy Khem even took the form of man?" "Khem" is an ancient name for Egypt. The implication is that the Egyptian showman of the earlier story is the same deathless avatar from Khem, who has descended to modern times.

Nyarlathotep's avatar is described as "swarthy, slender, and sinister," and is a manifestation of Lovecraft's lifelong phobia for foreign cultures. He regarded the familiar customs of New England as sane and correct, and those of the various immigrant types with which he came into contact as in some indefinable way distorted and unwholesome, a kind of cultural plague that was spreading across the world. Since this dream began at age ten, it may be assumed that his aversion to foreign culture was deeply rooted in his childhood, and was not something he developed when he later went to live in New York City, although it found its worst fears realized there, and so much tormented his mind that he almost committed suicide by poison.

One of the most important of Nyarlathotep's various avatars is the Black Man of European witches. This fascinating figure who straddles myth and reality was incorporated by Lovecraft into some of his stories, particularly *The Dreams in the Witch House*. In her profoundly influential but often disparaged 1921 book *The Witch-Cult In Western Europe*, Margaret A. Murray offered the opinion that the Black Man was not mythical but was a kind of theatrical role played by a real man who appeared at the witches' sabbat with his identity veiled and who enacted the part of the god of the witches. The demonologists of the Christian Church identified the Black Man with Satan himself, leading later historians to assume that he was mythical, but Murray was convinced that he was a leader of the witches, perhaps a nobleman, who impersonated an older pagan deity. Lovecraft was familiar with Murray's book, and undoubtedly drew upon it for his own interpretation of the Black Man as an avatar of Nyarlathotep.

Walter Gilman, the protagonist of the story, who was a student both of mathematics and the occult, takes a room in an ancient house in the "legend-haunted city of Arkham." The house is known as the Witch House because it had once been the residence of the notorious witch Keziah Mason. Indeed, the room he rents is the very eastern attic room in which Keziah had practiced her spells more than two centuries earlier. Once within its oddly distorted walls, Gilman begins to suffer from horrible nightmares. In the dreams, he sees repeatedly an old woman who tells him that he must meet with the Black Man and travel with them to the throne of Azathoth at the center of ultimate chaos. Once there, Gilman must sign the book of Azathoth in his blood and take a new secret name to symbolize his initiation into the witch cult.

These details are more or less correct, insofar as the records of the witch trails are concerned. Witches were reputed to gather for great celebrations known as sabbats that took place, not at the center of chaos, but on top of high places far from cities or towns. Here a new witch met with the Black Man who presided over the sabbat, was marked by him, and took a secret witch name. The new witch pledged allegiance to the Black Man and signed his or her name in blood in a book to seal the oath. These were the beliefs of the Christian demonologists of the Renaissance period, who wrote about the doings at the witches' sabbat.

Why a deathless being as potent as Nyarlathotep would participate in such human theatricals can only be conjectured. Nyarlathotep seems to enjoy interacting with human beings, or why else would he walk among them in human form? Perhaps the worship of our race for the Old Ones provides some kind of occult energy that can be used for their higher purposes. Or perhaps Nyarlathotep merely enjoys being worshipped, and inspiring fear and awe in humans.

One of the avatars of Nyarlathotep is a youthful-looking Egyptian pharaoh with an erect posture and a regal bearing, who is dressed in "prismatic robes" and crowned with a golden pshent. He has the manner of a fallen archangel. Capricious humor sparkles in his eyes. His voice is melodic. This outwardly attractive being is there to meet Randolph Carter when he reaches the end of his dream-quest for Kadath. He orders Carter to return the gods of Earth to Kadath where they belong—the gods were so attracted to Carter's dream city of Boston that they left their mountain fortress and went to live and play in Carter's dream city. Nyarlathotep gives Carter the final warning at their parting, "Send back earth's gods to their haunts on unknown Kadath, and pray to all space that you may never meet me in my thousand other forms." Nyarlathotep, even in this smiling and attractive human form, is not to be trusted, since he attempts to trick Carter into the chaos of Azathoth. It is only with great difficulty that Carter eludes the trap and manages to awaken in his bed.

Nyarlathotep is also worshipped by the Mi-Go. In *The Whisperer in Darkness*, they invoke his name and praise him during their joint rituals with their human cultists. They are instructed by the litany of the ritual to go among men in the outer world and learn all that they can learn, in order that Nyarlathotep may inform Azathoth, who is called "He in the Gulf." For this purpose of acquiring knowledge, the Mi-Go put on wax masks and the clothing of human beings, so that they can pass unnoticed by human observers. Nyarlathotep is called in the ritual "the Great Messenger," "bringer of strange joy to Yuggoth through the void" and is also characterized as Father of the Million Favored Ones—presumably the favored ones of Yuggoth.

(*Nyarlathotep; The Dream-Quest of Unknown Kadath; The Haunter of the Dark; The Dreams in the Witch House; The Whisperer in Darkness*)

Quetzalcoatl *

Quetzalcoatl is a word in the Nahuatl language that literally means "bird-serpent" but is more usually rendered "feathered serpent." In the religion of the Aztec of Mexico he was linked with the planet Venus. The protagonist of Lovecraft's story *The Curse of Yig*, co-written with Zealia Bishop, refers to Quetzalcoatl as the great, benign snake-god of the Mexicans, by which he means the natives of Mexico, the Aztec. He hints darkly that this god "had an older and darker prototype." That prototype is the serpent god Yig, worshipped by the Central Plains tribes of the United States. Lovecraft seems to equate Quetzalcoatl with Kukulcan, the feathered serpent god worshipped by the Maya.

(*The Curse of Yig*)

Rhan-Tegoth

This mummified god was discovered seated on a carved ivory throne in the northern part of Alaska by George Rogers, the proprietor of a private wax museum in London. It is a ten-foot tall amphibious being from the warm seas of Yuggoth that came to Earth three million years ago. The six sinuous limbs on its globular torso terminate in crab-like claws. Its head is globular as well, with three staring, lidless eyes arranged in a triangular pattern and a foot-long proboscis. Its entire body is covered with slender tentacles that are almost hair-like, each terminating in a sucking mouth. Those on its head and below the proboscis are larger and resemble the serpent-hair of Medusa. The god was revived with sacrifices of blood, coupled with the long ritual on the eighth Pnakotic Fragment, and sustained in a deep tank of water in the basement of the museum. Rogers, who had made himself the priest of this ancient god, asserted that if Rhan-Tegoth died, the Old Ones could never come back to the Earth, but what he meant by this cryptic remark remains unclear.

(*The Horror in the Museum*)

Shub-Niggurath

This female deity is first mentioned in *The Last Test*, where she is named but not described. To human beings Shub-Niggurath is a Mother Goddess. One of her titles is "the Goat With a Thousand Young." Her worship is ecstatic, similar in this regard to the ancient Greek worship of Bacchus. Her rites are punctuated by the cries "Iä! Shub-Niggurath!" In *The Mound* she is described as the All-Mother and the wife of the Not-To-Be-Named One. Lovecraft compared her to "a kind of sophisticated Astarte." In *The Whisperer in Darkness* she is called "the Black Goat of the Woods with a Thousand

Young." Mentioned in the same incantation is a deity called "the Lord of the Woods," who may be a masculinized form of this goddess—or it is possible that the Lord of the Woods is a separate deity, perhaps even the Not-To-Be-Named One.

Esoterically, Shub-Niggurath is similar to the Kabbalistic concept of Binah, the bitter salt-sea of creation from which all life arose. Binah is anthropomorphized into a mother goddess, and is the creative womb from which arises all manifest forms. These forms are engendered within her by the divine sparks of the father god, Chokmah, who is a seminal expression of the primal swirlings of creation in Kether. In the system of Jewish mysticism known as the Kabbalah, these are the three highest emanations of the ten-fold process by which the universe came into being out of nothingness. Collectively they are known as the Supernals.

Kether is the first and highest of all the ten emanations, so exalted that it can scarcely be said to exist, having no form or quality of its own. In Lovecraft's mythos, it corresponds with the mindless, blind Azathoth. Chokmah is the second emanation, the masculine spark that engenders creation, the divine seed that impregnated the womb of Binah. Chokmah is described as the mirror reflection of Kether, alike to it in all respects, save only that it is one stage lower on the process of emanation, and therefore slightly more manifest than Kether. It corresponds with Nyarlathotep, god of a thousand faces, who is the messenger of the Blind God and carries out his will. Azathoth is too exalted to act directly, so he must act through the intermediary Nyarlathotep. Binah is the third emanation, the feminine womb in which all forms and qualities are shaped. These forms of things cannot grow of themselves but must be engendered by the sparks from Chokmah.

Nyarlathotep, the god of a thousand faces, acting as the messenger of Azathoth, who is Shub-Niggurath's true husband, impregnates the mother goddess and engenders her thousand young—a thousand is a number which in ancient times signified too many to count. Shub-Niggurath is the mother of a multitude of monsters. Her fertile womb is a chaotic ground from which may arise any abomination. She is the dark side, or dark reflection, of Binah. The things that grow in her womb flourish like cancers, ungoverned and unchecked, and take the forms of nightmares.

Nowhere in his stories did Lovecraft describe Shub-Niggurath. Her association with the proverbially prolific goat links her with the Greek god Pan, and also with the Christian Devil, who is supposed to have the legs and feet of a goat. The form of Baphomet, oracular god of the Knights Templars, that was drawn by the French occultist Eliphas Lévi, depicts him as a torso with prominent female breasts, the horned head and hairy hind legs of a goat, but the arms of a man. Lovecraft was familiar with some of Lévi's writings. He may have had Lévi's version of Baphomet in mind when he created Shub-

Niggurath. However, in one of his private letters to Willis Conover, he described Shub-Niggurath as an evil cloud-like entity. This is about as vague as a description can get.

It may be fair to assume that Shub-Niggurath acquired different forms during different periods of her worship. As is the case with Nyarlathotep, a multiplicity of forms would have had the effect of making her formless, since no single form could be said to be the goddess. At the very least, she must have had a higher and a lower form, represented respectively by the evil cloud and the black goat. The evil cloud would correspond with the shadow side of Binah, the third emanation, the endlessly fecund womb from which all monsters arose. The black goat would correspond with the lower aspect of this goddess, a fertility deity presiding over the growth of crops, the health of domestic cattle, and the birth of babies.

(*The Last Test; The Mound; The Whisperer in Darkness*)

Tamash

One of the three chief bearded gods of the doomed city of Sarnath, the other two being Zo-Kalar and Lobon.

(*The Doom That Came to Sarnath*)

thousand-faced moon *

A title for the goddess of witches, Hecate. An alternative translation is "moon of a thousand forms." Lovecraft applied this title to the demoness Lilith in an incantation that is chanted by a cult of Yazidi devil worshippers at Red Hook in New York: "Gorgo, Mormo, thousand-faced moon, look favourably on our sacrifices!"

(*The Horror at Red Hook*)

Tiráwa *

The creator god of the Pawnee Indians, credited by them with teaching their ancestors religious rites and sacrifices, language, hunting, farming, and the making of fire. In *The Mound*, this deity is mentioned by Chief Gray Eagle of the Wichita Indians of Oklahoma, who were a neighboring people to the Pawnee, in connection with the mound-covered entrance to blue-litten K'n-yan. Gray Eagle describes Tiráwa as the father of men. He is described along with Yig, the father of snakes.

(*The Mound*)

Tsathoggua *

This dark god of unilluminated N'kai was not invented by Lovecraft, but by his close friend, the writer Clark Ashton Smith. His nature differs somewhat between Lovecraft and Smith, but it is primarily Lovecraft's conception of the god that we will examine. Tsathoggua is a part of Lovecraft's mythos because Lovecraft chose to incorporate the god into it. It is perhaps the most sinister and evil of all the Old Ones or their related alien races who came to this planet in the dim beginnings of its formation.

This god is described by Lovecraft as "black, formless" in one place in *The Horror in the Museum* and as "black amorphous Tsathoggua" in *Out of the Aeons*. In *Through the Gates of the Silver Key* it is called "black, plastic Tsathoggua." Lovecraft used these vague descriptions because the servants or spawn of the god who inhabit dark N'kai are without form, their bodies a shapeless black liquid similar to black oil or ooze that can take on any form it chooses. Lovecraft associated this amorphous spawn with the god's own primal nature, and regarded Tsathoggua's statues, which have the shape of a seated humanoid figure with the head of a toad, as only a kind of symbolic representation.

In *The Mound*, Lovecraft characterized the image of Tsathoggua as a "very terrible black toad-idol" but he was describing the idol, not the god itself, and it is evident from how he described the god in other stories that he believed it to be in its essence formless, as are its ebon flowing servants, who sometimes occupy bowls or basins in its temples, ever ready to take on shape to do the god's bidding. In a later place in *The Horror In the Museum*, Tsathoggua is observed to have "molded itself from a toad-like gargoyle to a long, sinuous line with hundreds of rudimentary feet," indicating that Lovecraft believed the toad-god form to be merely one of its many shapes.

By contrast, Clark Ashton Smith was much more material in his concept of this god. He described Tsathoggua as squat and corpulent, with a toad-like head, sleepy globular eyes, a fat mouth from which the tip of an oddly shaped tongue projects, and a body covered in short hair that resembles bat fur. In his story *The Whisperer in Darkness*, Lovecraft split the difference, so to speak, and described the god as both "amorphous" and "toad-like" in the same sentence.

Tsathoggua was the ruling deity of lightless N'kai, an unilluminated cavern-world beneath the red-litten cavern-world of Yoth, which in its turn lies beneath the blue-litten cavern-world of K'n-yan. For a period of time the alien but humanoid inhabitants of K'n-yan worshipped the stone idols of Tsathoggua and erected temples to the god. The temples were built from black basalt blocks following an architectural plan that existed in the archives of the Vaults of Zin. They are squat structures unadorned by a single carving, and contain only an onyx pedestal for the idol of the god.

The people of K'n-yan got these idols of Tsathoggua from red-litten Yoth. When they descended to the cavern of Yoth to explore it, they found its civilization destroyed, and took the numerous idols of Tsathoggua up to their own realm to worship. They even renamed what was to later become their capital city Tsath, in honor of this god. By studying the histories of Yoth, they discovered that the god was named Tsathoggua in the Yothian language, and that the reptilian quadrupeds of Yoth had not created the images of the god themselves, but had looted the idols from an unlighted realm below their own, which they named in their language N'kai. This lower realm had supported a great civilization with mighty gods long before the race of Yothians had even come into existence, but at the time the Yothians entered it they found it deserted.

The explorers of K'n-yan finally got around to making an entrance passage from Yoth down to N'kai and descended to these stygian depths with powerful radioactive light emitters that turned the darkness to day. What they discovered horrified them. The historical records of Yoth had reported that N'kai was deserted and lifeless. The men of K'n-yan found a form of life that Lovecraft characterized as "amorphous lumps of viscous black slime that took temporary shapes." These black-slime beings flowed along stone channels that served them as pathways—channels that had existed when the Yothians first entered N'kai, but for which the Yothians had not been able to conceive any purpose. The slime beings worshipped the remaining onyx and basalt idols of Tsathoggua.

The terrible suspicion began to dawn on the men of K'n-yan that some chance geological upheaval had released these strange beings of black ooze from whatever crypts or tunnels had for long ages imprisoned them, and that their release coincided with the destruction of the civilization of Yoth. The amorphous beings attacked and tried to kill the members of the exploratory expedition. In fear and revulsion, the men of K'n-yan withdrew from N'kai, sealed up the passage between the dark world and red-litten Yoth, and, upon returning to their own blue-litten world, persuaded their leaders to have all the statues of Tsathoggua destroyed. They did not want the fate that had arisen into Yoth to also ascend to K'n-yan. The existing temples of the toad-god were given over to the worship of other gods such as Shub-Niggurath, or were abandoned.

Before the destruction of the cult of Tsathoggua in K'n-yan, it made its way to the surface of our world and found its devotees among human beings. One small black image of the toad-god was worshipped in a shrine at Olathoë, in the prehistoric kingdom of Lomar near the North Pole. The cult survived the destruction of Lomar by the hairy Gnophkehs and the great ice sheet that covered the land. So it was rumored in K'n-yan, at any rate. In the ancient land of Hyperborea, this god was adored by a race of furry pre-human creatures that Lovecraft did not name. Tsathoggua was also worshipped in Leng by its horned and semi-human inhabitants, and in *The Whisperer in Darkness*, the name of the god is included in the litany of the Vermont cult of the Mi-Go in connection with the almost-men of Leng. Tsathoggua is mentioned in the *Necronomicon*, in the Pnakotic Fragments, and also in the *Commoriom Myth-cycle* of Atlantis.

(*The Horror in the Museum*; *Out of the Aeons*; *Through the Gates of the Silver Key*; *The Mound*; *The Whisperer in Darkness*)

Yig

Most of the lore concerning this snake god comes from *The Curse of Yig*. He appears either as half-human and half-serpent, or wholly serpentine. The killing of snakes angers him and calls down his vengeance. He was associated explicitly with the gods Kukulcan and Quetzalcoatl by Lovecraft, who called Yig an "older and darker prototype" of Quetzalcoatl, and may be regarded as representative of all great primal serpent deities. Yig, the Father of Serpents, is a god of the Plains Indians, and his cult is particularly strong in Oklahoma, beneath which lies the great cavern of blue-litten K'n-yan, where Yig is the primary deity along with Cthulhu.

Lovecraft wrote that Yig is not wholly evil in his nature, and shows no hostility toward those who respect serpents, but in the autumn of the year he becomes ravenous and wild, and must be driven away with Indian rites that involve the ceaseless sounding of drums, rattles, and whistles throughout the months of August, September, and October. Yig never forgets injuries done to his children. The Indians so fear his wrath that they hesitate to even defend themselves from the bites of rattlesnakes. It is the usual punishment of Yig to turn those humans who offend him into spotted snakes. To placate Yig, the Pawnee, Wichita, and Caddo Indians make sacrifices of corn to him, and dance to the sound of his ritual music. They also call upon the aid of the god Tiráwa, whom the Indians believe to be the father of men.

In *The Curse of Yig*, a white woman named Audrey Davis who came from Arkansas to settle in Oklahoma with her husband, Walker, in the spring of 1889, angers the serpent god by killing a nest of baby rattlesnakes. She is later driven mad, loses her hair, and her skin becomes scaly and white. She can no longer speak, but only hisses. Worst of all, the god impregnates her in a dream, and nine months later she gives birth to four hybrid babies, half-snake and half-human, only one of which survives to adulthood. It is kept locked in the basement room of an insane asylum in the town of Guthrie. It is almost human in size, with a scaly back speckled and brown near the shoulders, a flat head, and small beady black eyes. It wriggles naked on the straw strewn over the floor of its cell, and does not speak but only hisses.

In this story we have the familiar theme of the human-alien hybrid that so obsessed Lovecraft. There is an element of reality in his description of the mad Audrey Davis, who writhed on the ground on her belly and hissed wordlessly, and the similar behavior of Audrey's half-serpent offspring. When the great serpent god of Voodoo, Dambala, possesses or "mounts" his worshippers, they fall to their bellies on the ground and cease to speak. They communicate only by means of hissing sounds. Dambala is the only *loa* (god) of Voodoo who deprives worshippers of speech when they are possessed. All other *loa* talk through the human hosts they mount, but Dambala only hisses.

In the story *The Mound*, the alien but humanoid race that inhabits the cavern of blue-litten K'n-yan regard Yig as the principle of life, represented for them by the symbol of the serpent, which was widely regarded in human cultures around the world as deathless and capable of renewing itself with the periodic shedding of its skin. The temples of Yig are common in K'n-yan, almost as common as those of Cthulhu. The passage of time is marked in sunless K'n-yan by the tail-beats of Yig, corresponding roughly with the cycle of day and night, and waking and sleeping, each a span of around twenty-four hours. The time of Yig's shedding marks a period similar in function to a year, although it is around eighteen months in length.

(*The Curse of Yig; The Mound*)

Yog-Sothoth

There seems little question that Yog-Sothoth is one of the Old Ones referred to in *The Dunwich Horror*. He is their leader, and he controls the gates by which they move between dimensions of reality and across space. Although they can fly through the air by a kind of levitation, they rely on these gates for more significant journeys. The name of this great being was given to one of the two historical cycles hinted at in the *Necronomicon* during which the Old Ones dominated the Earth. It was called the Yog-Sothoth Cycle. It was ended by the coming to our planet of the time-traveling Great Race of Yith, which with its vast knowledge was easily able to defeat the Old Ones. The Great Race found it impossible to reason or coexist with the Old Ones, so they drove the Old Ones into tunnels and caverns deep beneath the surface of the ground, and built their cities on the ruins of the cities of the Old Ones.

It is noteworthy that Yog-Sothoth is a being who can be invoked by human beings using ritual methods. In *The Dunwich Horror*, Wizard Whateley invoked him on the festival of May-Eve in 1912, when Yog-Sothoth impregnated his daughter Lavinia with hybrid twins, one of whom was Wilbur Whateley, and the other the nameless invisible thing that was fed on fresh blood and kept locked away while it matured. In *The Case of Charles Dexter Ward*, where Yog-Sothoth receives his first mention by Lovecraft, Joseph Curwen noted in his diary "Rais'd Yog-Sothoth thrice and was ye nexte Day deliver'd."

It is not usual for gods to come at the beck and call of humans, so it must be speculated that Yog-Sothoth has his own good reasons for doing so. In the matter of the Whateley family it was to bring about the return of the Old Ones to the surface of the Earth, so that they could wipe it clean of all life and wrest it from its orbit, passing the sterilized planet through a dimensional gateway that would return it to the higher space from which it fell untold aeons ago. This plan failed due to Wilbur Whateley's inability to learn for the ritual the necessary long chant that appears on page 751 of the complete John Dee translation of the *Necronomicon*. In the matter of Joseph Curwen and his necromantic experiments with the essential salts of human corpses, it is not at all clear why Yog-Sothoth should have involved himself, unless by his very nature, he is compelled and constrained in limited ways by the symbols and words of power used in necromantic rituals.

The invocation of the name "Yog-Sothoth" is part of a chant that raises the dead up from their essential salts, or returns them once again to dust. It occurs in a pair of occult formulae linked with the astrological symbols of the Head of the Dragon (*Caput Draconis*) and Tail of the Dragon (*Cauda Draconis*):

☊	☋
Y'AI 'NG'NGAH,	OGTHROD AI'F
YOG-SOTHOTH	GEB'L-EE'H
H'EE-L'GEB	YOG-SOTHOTH
F'AI THRODOG	'NGAH'NG AI'Y
UAAAH	ZHRO

The first formula is similar to the second, but reversed, except for the name of Yog-Sothoth, which has the same form in both, and the final exclamations.

The Head of the Dragon is an appropriate symbol for raising the dead, because it represents the point in the heavens at which the Moon, as viewed from the surface of the Earth, crosses the apparent path of the Sun, known as the ecliptic, in a rising direction, moving from below to above the Sun's path. The Sun is the symbol of life, since it is the source of all vitality and warmth. What lies below the ecliptic may in this sense be regarded as the zone of death. The Tail of the Dragon represents the point in the heavens at which the Moon appears to cross the path of the Sun in a downward direction, moving from above the Sun's path to below it. For this reason, it is a good symbol to represent the return to death of what was raised up by necromancy from its essential salts.

It is easy to understand why this activity falls under the power of Yog-Sothoth. He is the keeper of all the gates, including the gateway between life and death. As I have indicated, it is more mysterious why Yog-Sothoth should trouble himself for the benefit of human necromancers, who are working for their own selfish, personal purposes. It may be that Yog-Sothoth cannot always control the use of his gates—that when they are called upon in the correct ritual manner, he has no choice but to open them, being himself governed by higher laws. On this perplexing matter Lovecraft had nothing to write.

In one of the passages from the *Necronomicon*, which is quoted by Lovecraft in the story *The Dunwich Horror*, is written: "Yog-Sothoth knows the gate. Yog-Sothoth is the gate. Yog-Sothoth is the key and guardian of the gate. Past, present, future, all are one in Yog-Sothoth. He knows where the Old Ones broke through of old, and where They shall break through again. He knows where They had trod earth's fields, and where They still tread them, and why no one can behold Them as They tread." It is their mastery of time that earned the Great Race its title. It seems that Yog-Sothoth has a portion of their ability to span time, at least with his awareness.

Alhazred went on to write in the *Necronomicon* that Yog-Sothoth is "the key to the gate, whereby the spheres meet." This enigmatic statement may have given rise to the common description of the face of Yog-Sothoth as a conjunction of spheres or circles. Lovecraft himself in the story *The Horror in the Museum* described Yog-Sothoth as "a congeries of iridescent globes." This may be only his higher-dimensional appearance. Since he is one of the Old Ones, he probably resembles them in a general way. His body would be gigantic, invisible to human eyes, capable of levitation through the air, and characterized by a tight mass of writhing tentacles. He would be blind, like the rest of the Old Ones, but possessed of higher senses that transcend ordinary vision.

The Mi-Go of Yuggoth worship Yog-Sothoth under the title "the Beyond-One." A race of intelligent gases in the spiral nebulae know this Old One only as an untranslatable symbol, the shape of which Lovecraft did not reveal. In the story *Through the Gates of the Silver Key*, Randolph Carter called him the "All-in-One and One-in-All," and came to the realization that Yog-Sothoth is not limited to only one time-space continuum, but is associated with the "ultimate animating essence of existence's whole unbounded sweep." It is this transcendence that allows Yog-Sothoth to know both past and future, as well as the present.

(*The Case of Charles Dexter Ward*; *The Dunwich Horror*; *The Horror in the Museum*; *Through the Gates of the Silver Key*)

Zagreus *

Greek god, son of Zeus and Persephone, who took the form of a youth. The Titans tore him to pieces, but Apollo rescued his heart and enabled his regeneration.

(*The Electric Executioner*)

Zo-Kalar

One of the three chief, bearded gods of the doomed city of Sarnath, the other two being Lobon and Tamash.

(*The Doom That Came to Sarnath*)

The Key to the Third Gate

3rd Astral Gate: Aquarius—The Water-Bearer

Sun passes through Aquarius: February 17—March 12

Constellation is represented by a water-carrier who empties water from his inverted clay pot.

Right Pillar: Sadalmelik (Arabic: *al sa'd al malik*—The Lucky One of the King). Astronomical designation: Alpha Aquarii. Astrological nature: Saturn-Mercury. Influence: success in ventures concerning the sea. Magnitude: 3. Color: pale yellow. Sun crosses: February 18. Location: right shoulder of the Water-Bearer. Comments: A strongly favorable star.

Left Pillar: Skat (Arabic: *al shi'at*—A Wish). Astronomical designation: Delta Aquarii. Astrological nature: Saturn-Jupiter. Influence: luck in achieving desired purposes. Magnitude: 3.2. Color: blue. Sun crosses: March 3. Location: the right shin of the Water-Bearer. Comments: As it true of all stars in this constellation, it has watery associations.

The astral gate of Aquarius lies between the star of its right pillar, which is located on the right shoulder of the figure of the Water-Bearer, and the star of its left pillar, which is found on the right shin of the figure, just below the knee. The Sun enters the gate around February 18 when it crosses the longitude of Sadalmelik, the star of the right pillar, and leaves the gate around March 3, when it crossed the star of the left pillar, Skat. The transition of the gate takes around thirteen days.

The key to the Third Gate opens the constellation Aquarius, allowing entry into the section of the walled city of the *Necronomicon* that contains gods and devils. Use it for divining information, receiving dreams about, or communicating with, deities both good and evil mentioned in the *Necronomicon* mythos.

Seal of the Third Key on the Third Gate

Ritual of Opening Aquarius

Face the direction of the compass ruled by the Third Gate, which is east by south—that is, slightly to the right of due east. Visualize the closed gate of the walled city before you just as though it were a real gate in an ancient walled city, and make sure that it is large enough for you to walk through. Take the time to create it on the astral level in precise detail.

With the image of the gate clear in your mind and projected upon the astral level to the direction east by south, speak the following invocation to Yog-Sothoth, taking care to insert those references that are specific to the Third Gate:

> Guardian of the Gate! Defender of the Door! Watcher of the Way! Who art the stout Lock, the slender Key, and the turning Hinge! Lord of All Transition, without whom there is no coming in or going out, I call thee! Keeper of the Threshold, whose dwelling place is between worlds, I summon thee! Yog-Sothoth, wise and great lord of the Old Ones, I invoke thee!
>
> By the authority of the dreaded name, Azathoth, that few dare speak, I charge thee, open to me the gateway of Aquarius the Water-Bearer that lies between the blazing pillar Sadalmelik on the right hand and the blazing pillar Skat on the left hand. As the solar chariot [or, lunar chariot] crosses between these pillars, I enter the city of the *Necronomicon* through its Third Gate. Selah!

Visualize the key of the Third Gate in your right hand some six inches long and made of cast bronze. Feel its weight, texture and shape as you hold it. Extend your right arm and use the key as a pointer to project upon the surface of the gate the seal of the key, which should be visualized to burn on the gate in a line of white spiritual fire. Point with the astral key at the center of the gate and speak the words:

> In the name of Azathoth, Ruler of Chaos, by the power of Yog-Sothoth, Lord of Portals, the Third Gate is opened!

Visualize the gate unlocking and opening inward of its own accord upon a shadowed space beyond. On the astral level, walk through the gateway and stand in the dark space beyond. Focus your mind upon the particular god or devil of the mythos that you wish to investigate and open yourself to receive communications or impressions from this deity—for the devils are merely deities that work hate and destruction. In a more general sense, the ritual of the Third Gate may be used to scry or communicate with any deity or ruling power, whether good or evil by nature.

After fulfilling the purpose for which this gate was opened, conclude the ritual by astrally passing out through the gate and visualizing it to close. Draw the seal of the Third Key on the surface of the gate with the astral key in your hand, and mentally cause it to lock itself shut, as it was at the beginning of the ritual. Speak the words:

> By the power of Yog-Sothoth, and authority of the supreme name Azathoth, I close and seal the Third Gate. This ritual is well and truly ended.

Allow the image of the gate to grow pale in your imagination and fade to nothingness before you turn away from the ritual direction.

The Fourth Gate

Fourth Gate
Monsters

Lovecraft was a firm believer that the universe is not only stranger than we imagine, but stranger than we can imagine. He was infuriated when writers of weird fiction made their alien races humanoid, and gave the members of those races human emotions and motivations. In 1927 he commented in a note that accompanied a story submission to the magazine *Weird Tales*: "To me there is nothing but puerility in a tale in which the human form—and the local human passions and conditions and standards—are depicted as native to other worlds or other universes."

A consequence of Lovecraft's philosophy that alien races and creatures should be truly alien is the large number of bizarre and shocking monsters that populate his stories. Lovecraft was able to draw upon his background studies in astronomy, geology, and biology to invest his monsters with unique shapes and unearthly purposes. An example is the alien beings that inhabit the unilluminated cavern world of N'kai, deep beneath the plains of Oklahoma. They are composed of a viscose black fluid that moves by flowing along channels cut in the stone floors of their chambers, but are capable of rearing up and taking on other shapes. This same concept was used to good advantage in the episode of the television series *Star Trek: The Next Generation* that is titled "Skin of Evil," illustrating that even in the present generation it has not lost its power to shock.

An unusual aspect of Lovecraft's monsters is that they seldom care about human motivations or intentions. Either they are indifferent to our race, or they look upon us as something to be eaten, or manipulated for their own purposes. They are seldom evil in the usual sense of the term, and have nothing to do with Christian morality. By the same token, they are seldom good in the Christian sense, and show no interest in helping human beings. They do not tempt us, unless it is with the temptation to learn about things utterly alien to the usual human sphere. Some of the more intelligent monsters may be induced to barter knowledge at a price, but only when it is to their own advantage.

All of Lovecraft's alien races might be classed as monstrous, since all of them are bizarrely inhuman. Beyond this gate are gathered lesser species with degenerate or malicious tendencies and grotesque individual creatures, as well as things uncanny and uncouth that make up the varied living detritus of the mythos. A scattering of them are based on examples from the classic Greek mythology that Lovecraft studied in his boyhood, such as the Medusa and the Sphinx. A few were inspired by the creations of other writers of horror fiction, such as the living black slime, which was conceived first by Clark Ashton Smith, the Dholes (or bholes) that derive from a word used in a story by Arthur Machen, and the Hounds of Tindalos, which are the invention of Frank Belknap Long.

Black Slime *

The worshippers of onyx and basalt images of the toad-god Tsathoggua in the lightless cavern realm of N'kai were alien creatures with bodies of viscose black slime that flowed from place to place along channels cut into the stone floors. They were able to assume different shapes at will. When the men of blue-litten K'n-yan descended through red-litten Yoth to the depths of black N'kai to explore this unknown land with powerful atomic searchlights, they were attacked by the creatures of black slime, and many of them were killed before they could seal the entrance to N'kai.

The viscose black slime was first described by Clark Ashton Smith in his story *The Tale of Satampra Zeiros*, in which the living black slime is not presented as a species of beings, but as a solitary guardian in a jungle temple of the toad-god Tsathoggua, who pursues two thieves that enter the temple. Smith sent his manuscript for Lovecraft to read in 1929, shortly after writing the story. Lovecraft responded with delight to Smith that the story came "close to being your high point in prose fiction to date." He incorporated the concept of a conscious, living black liquid into his own story *The Mound*, co-authored with Zealia Bishop, the writing of which was begun in December of 1929, and finished in the spring of the following year.

(*The Mound*)

Black Winged Ones

Creatures who came out of the depths of a Louisiana swamp south of New Orleans to assist in the sacrifices of the cult of Cthulhu. It was these things that did the actual killing of the sacrificial victims. There is no clear description of their appearance.

(*The Call of Cthulhu*)

Bog-Wraiths

These creatures dance across the bog to the sound of reedy flutes and beating drums beneath the moonlight, luring men to their doom in the dark waters. They are "strange airy beings in white" said to resemble pale, wistful naiads.

(*The Moon-Bog*)

Dholes

The term or one very like it originated in the 1904 story *The White People* by Arthur Machen, where the sentence appears, "And I must not say who the Nymphs are, or the Dôls, or Jeelo, or what voolas mean." Machen gave no indication elsewhere of what the Dôls may have been.

In Lovecraft's fiction, the Dholes (or bholes, as originally spelled by Lovecraft) are monstrous creatures several hundred feet long, with bodies bleached and viscous, who inhabit tunnels that honeycomb the distant planet Yaddith. In the past, they were in unceasing battle with the ruling race of that planet, who were powerful wizards, and forever strove to make their way to the surface. The great wizard Zkauba worked spells to keep them in their burrows. Eventually they prevailed, and in our present time the world is theirs.

In the dreamlands of our Earth, they are said to crawl and burrow in the Vale of Pnath, which lies amid the Peaks of Throk. No human being has ever seen a Dhole because they crawl about only in absolute darkness. Their touch as they wriggle past those who find themselves in their presence is slimy. They can be heard by the rustling they make amid the piles of bones of their prey.

In *The Whisperer in Darkness*, the detached brain of Henry Wentworth Akeley of Vermont reveals in conversation with Albert Wilmarth the true nature of the Dhols. What that nature may be is not specified in the story. "Dhol" is probably only a variation in spelling of "Dhole," so it seems doubtful that a different alien species is intended.

(*Through the Gates of the Silver Key*; *The Dream-Quest of Unknown Kadath*; *The Whisperer in Darkness*)

Five-Headed Monster

A monster the size of a hippopotamus with five hairy heads is observed by Houdini after he is cast into a pit beneath the "gateway temple of Khephren beside the Sphinx" by a band of Arab thieves. He watches by torchlight as the undead Egyptian pharaoh Khephren and his decaying queen Nitokris make offerings of mummified corpses to the monster, amid a host of the undead. Suddenly the awareness dawns on him that it is merely the forepaw of a much vaster monster—the very creature upon which the original Sphinx had been modeled.

(*Imprisoned with the Pharaohs*)

ghasts

Lovecraft described them as "repulsive beings" who die in the light, and who leap about on long legs like kangaroos. They dwell in the Vaults of Zin. The hairy and gigantic gugs use the ghasts for food.

(*The Dream-Quest of Unknown Kadath*)

ghouls *

Lovecraft's ghouls first appear in his 1923 story *The Lurking Fear*. In this early story they have not reached their final form, but are the members of the degenerate and isolated Martense clan, the inbred and prolific remnants of which dwell in a network of tunnels beneath the cellar of the deserted Martense mansion on Tempest Mountain, in the Catskills. These ghouls, who resemble and were probably inspired by the ghouls of the legendary Sawney Bean Clan of Scotland, venture out of their burrows at night during the frequent thunder storms that plague the mountain, seeking human victims for food.

The Sawney Bean legend was popular in Scotland and England, although it is not known with certainty whether it was based on historical fact or wholly fabulous. According to the legend, Alexander Bean and his wife lived in a cave on the seacoast of West Ayrshire during the sixteenth century. Over a span of twenty-five years they produced through incestuous interbreeding children and grandchildren that numbered forty-six. They avoided human contact and remained unknown to the people of the region, in part because their deep cave was treacherous to access, the entrance being blocked by high tides. They survived by murdering travelers, stealing their possessions, and using the corpses for meat, the excess of which they pickled for later consumption. When an attempt to murder a man and his wife on the road went awry and they were discovered, King James the VI of Scotland ordered the matter investigated. The entire Bean clan was captured and executed.

The protagonist in *The Lurking Fear* described one of the Martense clan as "a filthy whitish gorilla thing with sharp yellow fangs and matted fur. It was the ultimate product of mammalian degeneration; the frightful outcome of isolated spawning, multiplication, and cannibal nutrition." Nowhere in this story did he actually refer to these creatures as ghouls, although he called the Martense mansion "ghoulishly haunted." The ape-like creatures he described as "cannibal devils."

Parallels between the Bean legend and Lovecraft's tale are obvious. Both the Bean and the Martense clans lived beneath the ground and only ventured forth at night. The existence of both clans remained unknown to the local populations. Both were the product of incestuous inbreeding. Both produced a numerous and degenerate brood, although Lovecraft's ghouls are more outwardly devolutionary, having the matted fur and fangs of apes. Both clans lived on the flesh of human beings they hunted.

The theme of human beings who have degenerated into subhuman monsters is common in the mythos. It appears in one of Lovecraft's earliest stories, *The Beast In the Cave*, written in 1905 when he was only fifteen years old, in which an explorer of the labyrinthine Mammoth Cave encounters and kills in the darkness a horrible semi-human creature who turns out to be a man lost in the bowels of the cave years before who had been unable to find his way to the surface. The unfortunate was described by the explorer as "an anthropoid ape of large proportions" with long, snow-white hair, and long rat-like claws extending from the atrophied hands and feet. The implication is that this creature has been surviving on the flesh of human beings he has murdered in the darkness.

The Rats in the Walls presents the reader with a multigenerational clan of decadent English aristocrats named de la Poer that in past centuries interbred with semi-human subterranean creatures and feasted on the flesh of degenerate human beings raised as livestock in a grotto below the foundations of their estate house of Exham Priory, near the village of Anchester. An American descendant of the family buys the ruins and restores them, but upon investigating what lies below, he goes mad, murders one of his friends, and half-devours his corpse before this American is found and placed into a madhouse. The similarity with the Martense clan is obvious, but the de la Poer ghouls have all expired and are no more than gnawed bones. It is the protagonist's horror at realizing that he has descended from such monsters that drives him insane.

The source of Lovecraft's lifelong fascination with human degeneration may have been the ordeal in early childhood of watching his father descend into madness. He father was probably the victim of syphilis, although this diagnosis, if it was ever made, does not appear to have been revealed to the Lovecraft family. Not many years after his father's death, Lovecraft's mother began to exhibit signs of mental instability. She was committed to the Butler Hospital for the Insane, where her mad husband had died, and she lived there the remainder of her life.

Whatever the reason, Lovecraft developed a deep fascination for ghouls. In *Pickman's Model* they are a separate race that dwell in tunnels beneath the streets of old Boston, unsuspected by the human population of the city, coming to the surface only at night to hunt for their human prey. These Bostonian ghouls have the custom of exchanging their infants for human infants, which they raise as their own children, teaching the toddlers how to consume human flesh. Lovecraft asserted a close genetic link between ghouls and humans, writing, "The dog-things were developed from mortals!" The ghoul babies left in the cribs of Boston families are raised as human beings, but they eventually revert to their ghoulish natures. The artist Pickman, who is one of these changelings, leaves human society behind him altogether and goes to dwell permanently beneath the ground in the darkness.

A practical reason for the exchange of ghoul infants for human infants is to refresh the ghoul bloodlines, which otherwise might decline irrevocably through excessive inbreeding. It must be assumed that human babies raised as ghouls go on to breed with ghoul females. The same theme of hybridization between human and nonhuman races figures prominently in *The Shadow Over Innsmouth*, where the Deep Ones are eager to interbreed with human beings, perhaps for the revitalization of their bloodlines.

In *Pickman's Model* the ghouls are described as dog-faced, with a flat nose, bloodshot eyes, pointed ears, and drooling lips. On the hands are "scaly claws"—thickened and elongated fingernails with ridges. The feet he described as "half-hooved" in order to evoke the cloven feet of the Devil, and perhaps to suggest that the fables about the Devil's cloven hooves had their origin in the feet of ghouls. Lovecraft often did this—in *The Shadow Over Innsmouth* he made the suggestion that the myths about mermaids had their origin in past sightings by mariners of the Deep Ones. In this manner he interwove his own mythos with the classic mythology of ancient Greece, as a way of lending his mythos greater authority.

The ghouls reach their fullest development in *The Dream-Quest of Unknown Kadath*. Randolph Carter encounters them while exploring their part of the dreamlands in his sleep. They dwell on a plain high above the Vale of Pnath, beyond the Peaks of Throk. The Vale of Pnath, home to the burrowing Dholes (or bholes), contains a mountain made of bones from humans and other beings such as the enormous, hairy gugs that ghouls use as food. The ghouls ceaselessly drop these bones over the edge of a high crag at the limit of their plain, which is barren and empty apart from randomly strewn boulders and the entrances to underground ghoul burrows.

They are ruled by none other than the former artist Richard Pickman, who has cast off the trappings of his polite Bostonian upbringing and reverted to his ghoul nature. Even so, he has exerted a moderating influence on ghoul society. Of olden times it had been the custom of the ghouls to kill and eat their own comrades wounded in warfare, but Pickman discouraged this custom.

Pickman advises his friend Carter to disguise himself as a ghoul. Carter shaves off his beard because, as Lovecraft stated, ghouls have no beards. He rolls himself naked in grave mold to give his skin the proper shade and texture, and imitates the slumping lope of the ghouls. That Carter is able so easily to imitate ghouls indicates that they are not too dissimilar from men in appearance, apart from their canine faces, although the naked Pickman was described by Lovecraft as "rubbery." They have their own language, which consists of meeping and glibbering noises. Carter is able to speak a few words of it, having been taught by Pickman. This indicates that the intelligence of ghouls is not greatly less than that of human beings.

The ghouls acknowledge no masters, not even the Old Ones. For this reason they are willing to defy the wrath of Nyarlathotep by helping Carter in his quest to reach Kadath. They are presented in *The Dream-Quest of Unknown Kadath* as sociable, self-controlled, and well organized. They are bound by solemn treaties of mutual assistance with the night-gaunts, who have no lord but hoary Nodens. Both are hostile toward the moon-beasts and the horned inhabitants of Leng. Pickman characterizes the night-gaunts as "the advance guard and battle steeds of the ghouls." The night-gaunts carry ghoul warriors through the air into battle. The leaders of the ghouls are called chiefs.

(*The Lurking Fear; The Rats in the Walls; Pickman's Model; The Dream-Quest of Unknown Kadath*)

Gnophkehs

Hairy, long-armed monsters that destroyed the ancient human civilization of Lomar, which existed in a past age near the North Pole. When the great ice sheet crushed the land of Zobna beneath its advancing edge, the people of Zobna fled south and seized control of Lomar from the cannibal Gnophkehs, establishing there a new kingdom. It appears that their victory was not permanent, for the Gnophkehs eventually took back the land that had been taken from them.

(*The Mound; Polaris; The Dream-Quest of Unknown Kadath*)

Gnorri

An aquatic race of beings described as "bearded and finny" who dwell in labyrinths they build in the dark sea below the hollow glass cliffs that support the town of Ilek-Vad, in the dreamlands.

(*The Silver Key; Through the Gates of the Silver Key*)

gugs

Hairy gigantic creatures who erected stone circles and made sacrifice to the Other Gods and Nyarlathotep. For this outrage, the gods of Earth, who rule in the dreamlands at the sufferance of the Other Gods, banished them to a cavern beneath the ground. They have a great city composed of "cyclopean round towers," and their doorways are thirty feet high. In the center of the city is a great tower bearing the sign of Koth with a stair that leads upwards to the upper dreamland and the enchanted wood.

A single gug corpse will feed a ghoul community for almost a year. The ghouls sometimes toss stripped gug bones over the edge of the high plain on which the ghouls have their burrows, and the bones fall into the Vale of Pnath. Gugs have black fur over their bodies, paws that are two and a half feet across with long talons, a head the size of a barrel from which jut out to the sides bony ridges containing pink eyes, and a mouth filled with yellow fangs that opens vertically rather than horizontally. Each of their hairy arms has two forearms with a paw upon each end. They are voiceless, but communicate with each other by means of facial expressions.

(*The Dream-Quest of Unknown Kadath*)

gyaa-yothn

Partly human, the gyaa-yothn are genetically engineered creatures used by the people of blue-litten K'n-yan in place of horses for transportation. They are carnivorous and feed on the flesh of genetically bred human slaves used by the people of K'n-yan as cattle. Lovecraft described them as floundering white things with black fur growing along their backs, and a single rudimentary horn in the center of their foreheads. Their faces are vaguely humanoid, but with flat noses and bulging lips. Their intelligence is less than that of a man, but more than that of a beast.

(*The Mound*)

High-Priest Not To Be Described

In *The Dream-Quest of Unknown Kadath*, this enigmatic and inhuman resident of the dreamlands dwells on the plateau of Leng alone in a squat and windowless stone monastery surrounded by a circle of stone monoliths, where it prays to the Other Gods and to Nyarlathotep. The walls of the monastery are frescoed with "frightful scenes older than history." Randolph Carter is led captive into the monastery by the servant of the high-priest, a horned man of Leng, for an audience with the high-priest.

Deep within the monastery is a domed chamber, its walls decorated with bas-relief carvings, in the midst of which sits a "lumpish figure" on a throne of gold atop a stone dais, robed in yellow silk figured with red silk threads, wearing over its face a mask also of yellow silk. The same silk covers its hands. It uses a flute of carved ivory to make sounds by which it communicates with its servant, raising the bottom edge of the silk mask to blow into the flute. The domed chamber is unilluminated by any window or lamp, other than the lamp carried by the servant, and "evil-smelling." In front of the five steps that lead up to the dais of the high-priest's throne is a well that is rumored to extend down to the underworld of the dreamlands, even to the fabled Vaults of Zin. A ring of six blood-stained altars surrounds the mouth of the well.

Randolph Carter glimpses one of the "greyish-white paws" of the priest when its silk covering slips, and he recognizes the identity of the creature. In a sudden outburst of acute terror, he pushes his captor into the open well and flees from the vaulted chamber. By thus escaping the high-priest, he joins a select company. In the story *Celephaïs*, Kuranes, who is a dreamer of London, is said to have barely escaped from this same inhuman priest.

Its identity is never revealed in either story. Lovecraft always referred to the high-priest as "it" rather than "he." It seems to be related to the moon-beasts that conquered the inhabitants of Leng, and who use ivory flutes to communicate. Some have speculated that it is Nyarlathotep or one of his avatars, but Lovecraft explicitly stated that the high-priest prays to the Other Gods "and their crawling chaos Nyarlathotep," and it seems unlikely that Nyarlathotep would pray to himself. By its use of the flute for communication, we may assume that the high-priest is incapable of normal speech, presumably because its inhuman body does not possess the required vocal apparatus.

(*The Dream-Quest of Unknown Kadath; Celephaïs*)

Hounds of Tindalos *

In his long conversation with Albert Wilmarth in *The Whisperer in Darkness*, what remains of Henry Wentworth Akeley conveys the essence of the Hounds of Tindalos, though he does not reveal their origin. These demonic creatures come across the dimension of time through angles to punish those who transgress the distant past in which they dwell. There is something in the basic nature of humanity that awakens in them a cosmic hunger, and they will pursue tirelessly and ceaselessly those who attract their notice. They can manifest into our reality through any corner more acute than 120 degrees, but not through flat surfaces or curves. The deathless Hounds inhabit the angles of time, whereas normal living things inhabit the curves of time.

The Hounds originated in the 1931 short story of Frank Belknap Long, *The Hounds of Tindalos*, where their shape is never clearly described, but since they are mentioned in passing by Lovecraft, they have earned their place in his Necronomicon mythos.

(*The Whisperer in Darkness*)

Inutos

A race of warriors described by Lovecraft as "squat, hellish yellow fiends" who came out of the west to attack the ancient northern kingdom of Lomar. The tall and gray-eyed men of Lomar detested the invaders as being without honor. There is no indication that the Inutos succeeded in conquering Lomar, which was weakened by an advancing glacier and eventually fell to the predations of the cannibal Gnophkehs. It is suggested by Lovecraft that the Inutos are the ancestors of the modern Inuit.

(*Polaris*)

Kallikanzarai *

The Kallikanzarai, more properly *Kallikantzaroi* (singular form: *Kallikantzaros*), are monsters half-human and half-animal, that dwell beneath the ground, but emerge to wander the Greek countryside on the twelve nights between Christmas and Epiphany, which are known as the Twelve Nights of Christmas, or Twelve-tide. The period begins the night of December 25 which runs past midnight into the early morning hours of December 26, and ends on the night of January 5, which runs past midnight into the early morning hours of January 6.

Any man or domestic beast they find they tear apart, and any house in their path they assault and destroy unless its doors and windows are protected by the sign of the cross, and a propitiatory offering of food or other items is left outside the front door. Fires were kept burning in the fireplace to prevent them coming down the chimney. Sometimes a colander was put outside the door on the step, because these foolish creatures cannot resist counting the drain holes. Since three is a sacred number, they can only count up to two, and then must begin again. In this way they are kept occupied all night, and the security of the house is preserved.

Throughout the year they remain hidden beneath the ground, sawing at the roots of the world tree with the intention of causing it to collapse, so that it will destroy the world, but at Christmas they forget this occupation and come forth to terrorize human beings. When they return at the Epiphany, they discover that the world tree has healed its wounds, and they must begin their forever-futile task all over again.

They are generally said to have hairy bodies, horse legs, and boar-like tusks, but descriptions of them vary from region to region. Children born during the week of the Saturnalia (Dec. 17–23) are at risk of turning into *Kallikantzaroi* when they reach adulthood. To prevent this horrible fate, their mothers bind the babies in straw or garlic stalks, and singe their toenails with fire.

(*The Whisperer in Darkness*)

Larvae of the Other Gods

In the dreamlands described in *The Dream-Quest of Unknown Kadath*, when the black galleys of the moon-beasts sail beyond the Basalt Pillars of the West, and pass over the ultimate cataract at the edge of the world to rise into the void between worlds enroute to the far side of the Moon, they are surrounded by shapeless black things that "lurk and caper and flounder all through the aether, leering and grinning at such voyagers as may pass." Sometimes they fumble those on the passing ships with "slimy paws" but they do no injury. They are the nameless larvae of the Other Gods, as sightless and as mindless as the Other Gods themselves, who dance around the black throne of Azathoth at the center of chaos, but they are said to possess "singular hungers and thirsts."

The concept of larvae comes from the tradition of Western occultism. A larva is a spirit of the astral realm that has been created unintentionally by strong thoughts and emotions. Larvae can be generated by individuals, or by groups of people all thinking or feeling the same things. Their emotionally energized thoughts, charged by fear or desire or rage, impress themselves on the plastic matrix of the astral realm and shape it into whatever may be the subject of those thoughts. The created things are mindless, and drift about the lower astral plane like jellyfish in the sea, but they are not completely lacking in basic urges and desires. They will seek to interact with and feed upon the energies of those who venture into the astral realm, and even those in the waking everyday world, who remain oblivious to their presence because to ordinary waking sight they are invisible.

A person who broods with great intensity on any of the lower impulses or desires will create these larvae, and they will remain clustered around him in his daily life, in the place where he does his brooding, and will draw energy from his constantly repeated and reinforced emotion-laden thoughts. Others who enter such an environment, and possess even a small degree of psychic ability, will be oppressed and sickened by the thickly clustered presence of these larvae, even though they cannot see them.

Most Western occult traditions accept the reality of larvae with various minor distinctions. This includes the traditions of the Golden Dawn, Thelema, the OTO, witchcraft ,and Theosophy.

(*The Dream-Quest of Unknown Kadath*)

Man-Lizards of Venus

The race native to Venus, who worship small crystal energy eggs. They have flat heads with snouts like those of a tapir, green and slimy frog-like skin, and walk on thick stumps with suction-disks on the ends. They stand seven or eight feet tall and have four tentacles on their chests that they wave around for communication with others of their species, which is neither related to men nor to lizards, in spite of the chance resemblances. Lovecraft's protagonist in his story *Within the Walls of Eryx*, co-written with Kenneth Starling, speculates that this race was not the oldest intelligent species on Venus, but that an unknown much more ancient and more advanced species once inhabited our sister planet.

The Venus of Lovecraft's story, which the man-lizards dominate, has a climate that is almost suitable for human life, so it is obvious that the story cannot describe a time period close to our own. This was a common error for science-fiction writers who wrote about Venus in the 1920s and 1930s, and even as late as the 1950s—they portrayed Venus as a tropical jungle world, warm and wet. The conception of Venus as a mist-shrouded jungle world in popular literature was complimented by the persistent conception of Mars as a dry, cold desert world.

Most authorities on the mythos of Lovecraft would probably not classify this story as a part of the mythos at all, but I believe it deserves inclusion because it suggests that Venus was inhabited by an older, more advanced lost race that left traces of its existence in the form of ruins and artifacts. This is very much a mythos theme. This story may be considered a part of the mythos if we assume that it is set in a distant future time period when the climate of Venus is very different from its present climate.

(*Within the Walls of Eryx*)

Medusa *

The three gorgons (Medusa, Stheno, and Euryale) were sisters. Ancient Greek myths made them daughters of a sea monster, although the identity of their father varies. Sometimes they were said to be the daughters of Typhon with Echidna. In their earliest form, the gorgons were monstrous, with wings, talons, fangs, and serpents for hair. They had the power of turning to stone anyone who looked upon their faces. This may have originally been intended in a metaphorical sense, since in the earliest legends the gorgon is solitary, and inspires intense, paralyzing terror. For this reason her severed head was affixed to the aegis of Zeus, to terrify his foes. In Ovid's *Metamorphosis*, Medusa was romanticized into a beautiful priestess of Athena who had sex with Poseidon in the temple of the goddess, thereby incurring her fury. Athena changed Medusa's hair to snakes and made her so hideous to look upon, the sight turned men to stone.

Lovecraft mentioned Medusa in connection with tentacles on the head of a six-limbed monster from Yuggoth in the story *The Horror in the Museum*, co-written with Hazel Heald—but the description of the monster is pure Lovecraft: "On the head and below the proboscis the tentacles tended to be longer and thicker, marked with spiral stripes—suggesting the traditional serpent-locks of Medusa." Earlier in the same story he referred to images of gorgons. In *Medusa's Coil*, co-written with Zealia Bishop, a living incarnation of the being who served as the source for the myth of Medusa marries Denis de Russy, the son of a southern plantation owner, and leads him to madness and death. Her long coil of hair has an unnatural life of its own, and when cut from her corpse continues to move about like a giant serpent. Her father-in-law commented that "she was the thing from which the first dim legends of Medusa and the Gorgons had sprung."

(*The Horror in the Museum; Medusa's Coil*)

moon-beasts

Fungous beings from an ancient port city on the far side of the Moon who sail across space in black galleys, capturing slaves and conveying sacrifices. The moon-beasts, who are sometimes called toad-things or moon-things, worship and serve Nyarlathotep. They conquered the horned, semi-human race of Leng and enslaved them. In their dealings with the inhabitants of the dreamlands at the port of Dylath-Leen, they employ the humanoid men of Leng as intermediaries to trade rubies for gold and slaves, while they conceal their hideous forms below the decks of their galleys.

The moon-beasts maintain an outpost on an island of Earth's dreamlands in the Cerenerian Sea that is known only as the Nameless Rock. To this place they take unfortunate slaves. The screams of the slaves are heard by the mariners of ships that sail incautiously close to the island. The moon-beasts feed upon the flesh of these human and semi-human slaves, but what else they do to them on the Nameless Rock is unknown. They are in league with the giant cats of Saturn, who war against the cats of Earth on the far side of the Moon.

Lovecraft described them as "polypous and amorphous blasphemies that hopped and floundered and wriggled," and also wrote that they were "great greyish-white slippery things which could expand and contract at will, and whose principal shape—though it often changed—was that of a sort of toad without any eyes, but with a curious vibrating mass of short pink tentacles on the end of its blunt, vague snout." It should be noted that white is one of the colors of the Moon, and that the toad is a lunar creature. Things soft, pale, and fungous occultly express the nature of the Moon. The dark, high-walled city of the blind moon-beasts has no windows, since none are needed. Although they have no voices, they play a weird sort of music on carven ivory flutes.

(*The Dream-Quest of Unknown Kadath*)

Mormo *

A kind of ghoul named in a Greek incantation to the goddess of witches, Hecate, that was recorded by the third-century Greek writer Hippolytus in his *Refutation of All Heresies* (bk. 4, ch. 35). Lovecraft used the incantation in his story *The Horror at Red Hook*, but omitted the name "Hecate" because he wished the incantation to apply to the demoness queen of Hell, Lilith.

(*The Horror at Red Hook*).

Nemesis of Flame *

In the story *The Last Test*, Doctor Alfred Clarendon threatens his servant Surama with the Nemesis of Flame, should the servant, who is a necromantically resurrected priest of Atlantis, ever follow through on his threat to end Clarendon's life. The *Nemesis of Fire* is the name of a short story by Algernon Blackwood, published in 1908 in the anthology collection *John Silence, Physician Extraordinary*. It concerns a salamander, or fire elemental, a being composed of pure flame. Lovecraft mentioned this story in his essay, *Supernatural Horror in Literature*, remarking "a hideous elemental is evoked by new-spilt blood." Lovecraft finished his essay in 1927, the same year *The Last Test* was written, so it seems clear that Blackwood's elemental spirit was what he had in mind.

(The Last Test)

night-gaunts

Black creatures with rubbery bodies, bat-like wings, curved horns, barbed tails, and no faces. They dwell high in caves in the gray mountain range that separates the plateau of Leng from the land of Inquanok, and worship hoary Nodens as their god. They give no allegiance to Nyarlathotep. The Great Ones fear them. Even the monstrous shantak-birds who make their nests midway up the slopes of these mountains shun the night-gaunts. They fly unceasingly between the Vale of Pnath and the passes to the outer world.

The night-gaunts have a special place in the Lovecraft mythos. They are the product of Lovecraft's dreams at a very early age. In 1915 he wrote in a letter to M. W. Moe, "When I was 6 or 7 I used to be tormented constantly with a peculiar type of recurrent nightmare in which a monstrous race of entities (called by me "Night-Gaunts"—I don't know where I got hold of the name) used to snatch me up by the stomach & carry me off through infinite leagues of black air over the towers of dead & horrible cities. They would finally get me into a grey void where I could see the needle-like pinnacles of enormous mountains miles below. Then they would let me drop—& as I gained momentum in my Icarus-like plunge, I would start awake in such a panic that I hated to think of sleeping again."

He described these beings in this letter as "black, lean rubbery things" with bat-like wings, horns on their heads, a barbed tail, and no faces at all. They never spoke, but before snatching him into the air by the stomach they tickled him unmercifully. They came in his dreams in flocks of twenty-five or fifty members, and as they carried him through the night sky would toss him back and forth for sport. They were voiceless. In his dreams Lovecraft knew that they lived in burrows honeycombing the peak of a some unnamed high mountain.

In his poem "Night-gaunts," which is part of the sonnet cycle *Fungi From Yuggoth*, he added the detail that the barbed tails of the creatures are forked. Bifurcation is symbolically associated with evil because it suggests lies or deceptions—the forked tongue of the snake, for example, or the cloven hoof of the Devil. The facelessness of the creatures suggests that they may have represented for Lovecraft some horror he did not wish to confront or recognize consciously. In the poem he names the needle-like mountains over which the night-gaunts drop him the "jagged peaks of Thok."

In *The Dream-Quest of Unknown Kadath* Lovecraft's alter ego, Randolph Carter, enlists the aid of the ghouls through their leader, the former avant garde artist of Boston, Richard Pickman, who has reverted to his ghoulish origins. The ghouls, in turn, call upon their allies the night-gaunts, with whom they share strong treaty obligations. The night-gaunts serve the ghouls of the dreamlands as flying steeds and carry the ghoul warriors into battle.

Early on in his quest, Carter received the information that the night-gaunts have their caves near the mountain Ngranek. In trying to find out about these creatures, Carter asked some rather curious questions concerning them of lava-gatherers working on the lower slopes of Ngranek—he inquired if the night-gaunts "sucked blood and liked shiny things and left webbed footprints." The frightened lava-gatherers denied these specific matters. So specific are the questions that it is tempting to believe that Carter had heard other rumors of the night-gaunts and their nature. These three characteristics are not denied elsewhere, so I believe they are accurate, in spite of the denials of the lava-gatherers, who did not wish to invoke the night-gaunts by talking about them.

While sleeping on a ledge high on the face of the mountain, Carter was seized by the night-gaunts, who first stripped him of his sword, then bore him up into the air, one holding his neck and another his feet while the rest of the flock clustered around. When Carter struggled, the night-gaunts tickled him until he stopped. They were completely silent, even the beating of their wings. Carter characterized the touch of their paws as "cold and damp and slippery." There is little doubt that Lovecraft in this passage was merely describing his recurring dream of childhood. He added the detail to their description that the horns on their heads "curved inward toward each other."

They are described as "mindless guardians of the Great Abyss whom even the Great Ones fear." They fly ceaselessly between the Vale of Pnath and the passes to the outer world. The night-gaunts are wholly of the dream world. It does not appear that they ever leave it, unless they are the winged creatures who serve the cult of Cthulhu in the swamps near New Orleans—but this is doubtful. Many of the other inhabitants and places in the dreamlands have their representations in waking reality. Pickman, for example, exists both in the dreamlands and also in the waking world. So do the ghouls. The plateau of Leng is a place in the dreamlands, but also a place on the surface of the waking world, although precisely where it is located, Lovecraft never definitely states, suggesting in one place in his fiction that it is in Asia and in another place that it is in Antarctica.

The night-gaunts carried Carter over the Peaks of Throk that had so terrorized Lovecraft as a child, and deposited him safely on the pile of bones at the base of the cliff that led to the barren, boulder-strewn plain on which the ghouls had their burrows. Eventually Carter was able to enlist the aid of the ghouls through the mediation of Pickman, and after many adventures, including a war between the ghouls and the moon-beasts, was carried through the air to Kadath, the end of his quest, by the night-gaunts, who have allegiance with the ghouls and with the god Nodens, but not with the other gods of Earth or with Nyarlathotep and his alien kind.

The night-gaunts that tormented Lovecraft's childhood dreams become in *The Dream-Quest of Unknown Kadath* the means of Carter's salvation. Lovecraft transmutes their power to useful purposes, and in this way mitigates its terror. Lovecraft came to terms with the night-gaunts on a personal level, and achieved a kind of truce with them. It might be argued that much of Lovecraft's fiction is an attempt to exorcise his own personal demons. This is certainly the case with the night-gaunts.

(*Fungi from Yuggoth; The Dream-Quest of Unknown Kadath*)

old people

The Wichita Indians of Oklahoma call the apparitions seen from a distance atop ancient Indian mounds on the plains the "old people" or "they who dwell below." They do not recognize the tribe of these spectres, who wear strange costumes and carry strange weapons, and do not claim them as kin, but are afraid of the ghosts and avoid them. The "old people" are the psychic projections of the subterranean race of K'n-yan, a race not originally native to this planet. Their reddish or copper-colored skin leads to the mistaken initial impression that they are Native American. They have the power to project their images when they dream, and it is these images that are sometimes seen on the Indian mounds. They are also able to physically walk through solid objects, and sometimes set up sentries at the entrance to their tunnels that are located beneath these mounds, to ward off human beings.

(*The Mound*)

shoggoths

The creatures known shoggoths were created by the Elder Things to serve as their slaves. The crinoid race controlled them by hypnotic commands that were projected telepathically. Alhazred mentioned them briefly in the *Necronomicon*, writing that they were unknown on this planet except in the dreams of those who chewed "a certain alkaloidal herb." He was mistaken. In the Lovecraft mythos, shoggoths were created on Earth by the genetic sciences of the Elder Things before they created, for their amusement, the forms of life that presently flourish across our world. The shoggoths have never died off. Some still survive beneath the ground and deep in the seas.

The bodies of shoggoths resemble giant amoebas, and like the amoeba they reproduce by fission. They move by expanding and contracting their viscose substance, and eat by surrounding and engulfing their prey. They possess the ability to extrude sensory organs such as eyes and ears, and manipulatory limbs such as arms, as these are required. When the limbs or organs are no longer needed, they are reabsorbed into the amorphous body. By expanding their bodies, they can lift and move enormous blocks of stone. The Elder Things employed them as workers to build their great undersea cities. Their strength is almost beyond limit—they may well be the strongest things that have ever lived on the Earth.

Lovecraft described shoggoths in *At the Mountains of Madness* as "a viscous jelly which looked like an agglutination of bubbles." When contracted into a spherical shape, the bodies of the early shoggoths measured approximately fifteen feet in diameter. Later in their history the Elder Things evolved shoggoths that were even larger. The explorers of the Miskatonic Expedition to Antarctica encountered one of the later shoggoths, which was said to be "vaster than any subway train," black in color, and faintly self-luminous. It was characterized as a "plastic column of fetid black iridescence." It formed eyes that glowed with greenish light on its forward surface as it rolled its body along a tunnel, which its bulk completely filled, in pursuit of the fleeing explorers. Shoggoths have no fixed shape of their own, but are able to stretch and mold their masses into any shape that is necessary for their immediate purposes.

Over the passage of ages shoggoths began to develop their own independent intelligence. This allowed them to at times defy the hypnotic commands of the Elder Things, which made them increasingly treacherous slaves. Around a hundred and fifty million years ago they rose up in rebellion against their masters, killing the crinoids by decapitating them. They were only subjugated after much trouble through the use of atomic disintegrators. Even so, they never again became the docile and mindless slaves they once had been. The Elder Things were forced to watch and control them with constant vigilance. Though shoggoths can live quite well on land, and are highly resistant to cold and other extremes of weather, the crinoid race for a long period discouraged them from emerging from the seas when they themselves established their land cities, so as to avoid the considerable burden of controlling them. Eventually, however, they were forced to breed giant land shoggoths to aid in their survival in an increasingly hostile climate.

Shoggoths possess the power to extrude vocal organs. They use these to communicate with each other in the piping language of the Elder Things, which they remember from ancient times, for they are virtually deathless. Like human beings, they learn through imitation. They are superb natural mimics. The Miskatonic scientists exploring the passage leading to the underground sea from beneath the crinoid city heard one shoggoth issue the eerie cry "Tekeli-li! Tekeli-li!" What this means is unknown, but the shoggoths must have learned it from their masters, in the same way that parrots imitate human speech. It may be a cry of alarm, or warning. On the walls of this passage the shoggoths had inscribed works of art in imitation of the style of the Elder Things.

Lovecraft hinted darkly that it was the unruly shoggoths who were responsible for the final abandonment of the great land city of the crinoids in Antarctica. Those bred to live and work on the land simply became too dangerous to control, and the Elder Things retreated to the warm depths of the subterranean sea in a great cavern far below the frozen surface. The shoggoths held the surface alone, apart from the giant blind, albino penguins that move through the tunnels under the deserted city. These penguins swim in the waters of the subterranean sea, and provide food for the shoggoths. Eventually the shoggoths triumphed completely over the crinoids and came to rule the underwater city in the deep cavern, just as they possessed unopposed except for the penguins the remains of the last land city of their former masters.

In *The Thing on the Doorstep* Lovecraft alluded to the "pit of the shoggoths," which is located at the bottom of a flight of six thousand steps. This may perhaps be the "black pit" mentioned in connection with "proto-shoggoths" during the insane ravings of the explorer Danforth after his escape from the deserted city of the Elder Things in *At the Mountains of Madness*.

(*At the Mountains of Madness*; *The Thing on the Doorstep*; *The Shadow Over Innsmouth*)

Sphinx *

In his short story *Imprisoned With the Pharaohs*, ghostwritten for Harry Houdini, Lovecraft asked the question, "What huge and loathsome abnormality was the Sphinx originally carven to represent?" The answer he gave to this question in his story was a gigantic monster that dwells in the vast subterranean chambers beneath the Pyramids, and is never seen in its entirety, "the unknown God of the Dead, which licks its colossal chops in the unsuspected abyss, fed hideous morsels by soulless absurdities that should not exist." According to Egyptian legend, the face of the Sphinx is that of the pharaoh Khephren, who was buried beneath the Second Pyramid on the Giza Plateau, close to this mammoth sculpture. However, Khephren did not build the Sphinx; he merely uncovered it from beneath the sand of centuries and repaired the damage it had suffered from erosion. In the process of this renovation, he had the worn face recarved to match his own features.

The famous stage magician and escape artist Harry Houdini encounters this monster when he becomes trapped beneath the Pyramids. It is of such vast dimensions that at first he only sees its paw as it reaches for its sacrifice of corpses through a great cavern mouth. When its head appears and he realizes what he is looking at, the shock is so strong that he flees and falls into unconsciousness. When he wakes in the dawn on the open sands of Giza beneath the face of the Sphinx, he firmly tells himself that what he saw was only a dream.

(*Imprisoned with the Pharaohs*)

Vegetable entities

An intelligent race of vegetable entities will inhabit the planet Mercury in the distant future. They are described by Lovecraft only as "bulbous." The time-spanning Great Race of Yith will project their minds into the bodies of these beings as the surface of the Earth becomes uninhabitable.

(*The Shadow Out of Time*)

Wamps, Web-footed

A species of ghoul spawned in the dead cities of the upper dreamland.

(*The Dream Quest of Unknown Kadath*)

Zoogs

A small, brown race of the dreamlands, furtive and secretive. They live in burrows for the most part, but a few dwell in the hollow trunks of great trees. Fungi is their nourishment, along with an occasional meal of meat. There are rumors that men have disappeared near where the zoogs lurk, both in the waking world and in the dreamlands. They cannot travel far outside the dreamlands, but move freely through its parts that are nearest the waking world. They delight in gathering stories, which they tell around their forest campfires. The cats of Ulthar arch their backs in challenge when zoogs approach. The zoogs gave Randolph Carter a bottle of moon-wine when he stopped to converse with them.

(*The Dream-Quest of Unknown Kadath*)

The Key to the Fourth Gate

4th Astral Gate: Pisces—The Fishes

Sun passes through Pisces: March 12—April 18

Constellation is represented by two kinds of fish tied together at their tails by the two ends of a loose cord, which is attached to a fixed point at its midlength.

Right Pillar: Alpherg (The Pouring Point of Water). Astronomical designation: Eta Piscium. Astrological nature: Saturn-Jupiter. Influence: Magnitude: 3.8. Color: yellow. Sun crosses: April 15. Location: northern end of the cord that links the fishes. Comments: This star marks the beginning of the sidereal zodiac.

Left Pillar: Al Rischa (The Cord). Astronomical designation: Alpha Piscium. Astrological nature: Mars-Mercury. Influence: Magnitude: 4. Color: green-blue. Sun crosses: April 22. Location: knot or fixed point in the middle of the cord linking the fishes. Comments: In ancient times this star was brighter, but it has dimmed.

The astral gate of Pisces lies between the star of its right pillar, located on the northern section of the cord linking the fishes, and the star of its left pillar, which occupies the fixed midpoint of the cord. The sun enters the gate around April 15 when it crosses the longitude of Alpherg, the star of the right pillar, and leaves the gate around April 20, when it crossed the star of the left pillar, Al Rischa. The transition of this narrow gate takes seven days.

The key to the Fourth Gate opens the constellation Pisces, allowing entry into the section of the walled city of the Necronomicon that contains the monsters of the mythos. Use it for divining information or receiving dreams about monstrous creatures and outrages to nature mentioned in Lovecraft's writings.

Seal of the Fourth Key on the Fourth Gate

Ritual of Opening Pisces

Face the direction of the compass ruled by the Fourth Gate, which is southeast by east—that is, slightly to the left of the southeast point. Visualize the closed gate of the walled city before you just as though it were a real gate in an ancient walled city, and make sure that it is large enough for you to walk through. Take the time to create it on the astral level in precise detail.

With the image of the gate clear in your mind and projected upon the astral level to the direction southeast by east, speak the following invocation to Yog-Sothoth, taking care to insert those references that are specific to the Fourth Gate:

Guardian of the Gate! Defender of the Door! Watcher of the Way! Who art the stout Lock, the slender Key, and the turning Hinge! Lord of All Transition, without whom there is no coming in or going out, I call thee! Keeper of the Threshold, whose dwelling place is between worlds, I summon thee! Yog-Sothoth, wise and great lord of the Old Ones, I invoke thee!

By the authority of the dreaded name, Azathoth, that few dare speak, I charge thee, open to me the gateway of Pisces the Fishes that lies between the blazing pillar Alpherg on the right hand and the blazing pillar Al Rischa on the left hand. As the solar chariot [or, lunar chariot] crosses between these pillars, I enter the city of the *Necronomicon* through its Fourth Gate. Selah!

Visualize the key of the Fourth Gate in your right hand some six inches long and made of cast silver. Feel its weight, texture, and shape as you hold it. Extend your right arm and use the key as a pointer to project upon the surface of the gate the seal of the key, which should be visualized to burn on the gate in a line of white spiritual fire. Point with the astral key at the center of the gate and speak the words:

In the name of Azathoth, Ruler of Chaos, by the power of Yog-Sothoth, Lord of Portals, the Fourth Gate is opened!

Visualize the gate unlocking and opening inward of its own accord upon a shadowed space beyond. On the astral level, walk through the gateway and stand in the dark space beyond. Focus your mind upon the particular monster of the mythos that you wish to investigate and open yourself to receive communications or impressions from this horrifying being. In a more general sense, the ritual of the Fourth Gate may be used to scry or communicate with any monstrous spirit or alien being that is grossly deformed or misshapen in mind or body.

After fulfilling the purpose for which this gate was opened, conclude the ritual by astrally passing out through the gate and visualizing it to close. Draw the seal of the Fourth Key on the surface of the gate with the astral key in your hand, and mentally cause it to lock itself shut, as it was at the beginning of the ritual. Speak the words:

By the power of Yog Sothoth, and authority of the supreme name Azathoth, I close and seal the Fourth Gate. This ritual is well and truly ended.

Allow the image of the gate to grow pale in your imagination and fade to nothingness before you turn away from the ritual direction.

The Fifth Gate

Fifth Gate
Human Habitations

A great deal of the charm and sense of place in Lovecraft's fiction stems from his determination to locate most of his stories in his native New England. He broke this rule on rare occasions, but for the most part his own tales are set in the countryside with which he had been intimately familiar from boyhood, and which he loved with a passion. His tombstone, erected by admiring fans long after his death, bears the motto, "I am Providence." The words are derived from one of Lovecraft's letters in which he makes this proclamation. So potent was his sense of time and place that he could scarcely separate his own being from the townscapes and countryside in which it had developed.

When he married Sonja Greene and went to live with his new wife in New York City, the shock of removal from his familiar Providence haunts and the disruption it caused to his thoughts and emotions nearly killed him. He contemplated suicide with such seriousness that he took to walking around the crowded, noisy streets of New York with a small bottle of deadly poison in his pocket, so that he could at any time he felt the impulse end his own life. It was perhaps more a blessing to Lovecraft than a burden when his wife was forced to leave New York and seek employment in Cleveland. The forced separation gave Lovecraft the excuse to return to Providence alone—a move that saved him from suicide, even though it ended his brief marriage.

Lovecraft was bound to Providence, and in a larger scope to New England, not only by a sense of place but by a sense of time—past time, as expressed in the architecture and relics of New England history, which, although it would be considered brief from a European perspective, was long and ancient by American standards. Lovecraft lived in the past by studying the old buildings of New England, and by surrounding himself with objects and books from previous centuries. Like several of his characters, he studied the history and genealogy of New England.

He even adopted as a young man the strange affectation of speaking and writing in the manner of an Englishman of the eighteenth century. After a few years, he broke himself of this studied pose, but even to the day of his death his manner of speaking and writing retained an archaic quality. He liked to use obsolete expressions and words that had fallen out of fashion. He never did embrace the use of the typewriter, but composed his stories and essays in longhand with a fountain pen. Though he loved New England, it was the New England of a bygone day, not the New England of his present, which he observed with sorrow to be changing in unfortunate ways.

As it true of other aspects of the Necronomicon mythos, Lovecraft seamlessly blended real locations with fictional locations. He did this with such skill that it is sometimes difficult to determine whether a place mentioned exists on the map of New England, or was drawn from Lovecraft's own rich geography of the mind. Often Lovecraft will describe a fictional town or location, and set it into a real region, or beside a genuine geographical feature. This mixing of the real with the fictional, coupled with the reuse of fictional locations across numerous stories, helps to give Lovecraft's scenes a startling presence.

Books have been written that place Lovecraft's fictional New England upon the real New England of today. The matches between real and fictional locations are surprisingly apt. Lovecraft usually had a real place in mind when he invented a fictional place for one of his stories. There are even bus tours to Lovecraft's imaginary New England—or at least to the existing towns, hills, and houses that are supposed to correspond with his imagination.

Arkham is the center of Lovecraft's imaginary world. It is a thriving city in the Miskatonic River Valley in Massachusetts, located on the river, with a prestigious institution of higher learning, Miskatonic University. On the coast is the quaint old town of Kingsport, its ancient houses climbing steeply up the hillside from the harbor, overlooked by a high sea cliff not far in the distance. Although both these communities have their strange folklore and histories of unnatural events, neither is as unsettling as the decayed town of Innsmouth, with most of its dockside idle and most of its houses shuttered. Even more forbidding is the little village of Dunwich, whose clustered and sagging colonial cottages conceal dark secrets of the past that its inbred inhabitants for the most part keep to themselves.

Lovecraft's landscape is littered with ancient Indian monoliths, curious hills, caves, haunted farmhouses and deserted cottages, cursed islands and reefs. It extends as far north as the wooded hills of northern Maine, but is mostly gathered around Massachusetts, the state in which the Salem Witch Trials were held. Salem figures prominently in several of Lovecraft's stories, notably *The Dreams in the Witch House* and *The Case of Charles Dexter Ward*. The supernatural influences on this landscape are twofold—the history of witchcraft in Salem and surrounding towns, and the occult practices of the Indian tribes of New England, who have left traces of their practices in the form of stone circles and altars.

So detailed in Lovecraft's imaginary Miskatonic River Valley that it is possible to draw complete maps of Arkham, Innsmouth, and other places, as fans of the mythos have done. Readers of Lovecraft find themselves entering a unique world of steep, cobblestone streets overhung with gambrel-roofed cottages under the brooding shadows of old stone churches. These scenes are drawn from Lovecraft's dreams of Providence, not only as it existed in his time but as he imagined it to have existed in centuries past. It is possible to become lost in these streets and step from this world to another that exists on the astral level, slightly out of phase with our reality, a world where the *Necronomicon* is real.

Ai

A river in the ancient land of Mnar that winds past the cities of Thraa, Ilarnek, and Kadatheron.

(*The Doom That Came to Sarnath; The Quest of Iranon*)

Arkham

A decaying yet still vibrant town in New England on the Miskatonic River that is noted for dark sorceries. It and the surrounding region had been settled in 1692 by those fleeing the witch persecutions at Salem. Edmund Carter, the ancestor of Randolph Carter, was one of those who fled to Arkham to avoid execution. "The hills beyond Arkham are full of a strange magic—something, perhaps, which the old wizard Edmund Carter called down from the stars and up from the crypts of nether earth," wrote Lovecraft in *Through the Gates of the Silver Key*. Elsewhere, he referred to it as "witch-accursed Arkham" and "legend-haunted Arkham," and wrote of its "hoary willows and tottering gambrel roofs." In *The Colour Out of Space* is it called "a very old town full of witch legends." It is the home of Miskatonic University, renowned as a center of arcane studies and for both its excellent library and museum. St. Mary's Hospital in Arkham is noted in the region for its high quality of care.

(*The Festival; The Dreams in the Witch House; Through the Gates of the Silver Key; The Colour Out of Space*)

Arkham Sanitarium

Edward Pickman Derby was committed to the Arkham Sanitarium after he began to rave that his former wife was trying to steal his body. His friend, Daniel Upton, was made his guardian and visited Derby twice weekly. When Upton became aware that

Derby's body had been usurped by the mind, not of his former wife, but of his wife's father, the wizard Ephraim Waite, he shot Derby six times in the head in his cell at the sanitarium.

(*The Thing on the Doorstep*)

Atlaanat

Called by Randolph Carter "hoary Atlaanat, of which few even dare speak," in this place Carter witnessed a circle of adepts transform a thought into tangible substance.

(*Through the Gates of the Silver Key*)

Atlantis *

This island continent in the Atlantic Ocean was ruled by a city-state empire of traders and warriors who conquered much of the ancient world. According to the scraps of myth related by Plato in his dialogues *Timaeus* and *Critias*, Atlanteans enjoyed a civilization more sophisticated than any other until the island abruptly sank beneath the waves around the year 3000 BC. The myth of Atlantis is the keystone in the esoteric theorizing that civilizations more advanced even than that of the modern West existed on the Earth prior the beginnings of recorded human history. The Theosophists believed that our present race is in part descended from the people of Atlantis. These ideas were popularized in 1882 by Ignatius Donnelly in his book *Atlantis: The Antediluvian World*. Donnelly was probably influenced by the views of H. P. Blavatsky, whose *Isis Unveiled* had come forth from the press five years earlier.

Lovecraft referred to Donnelly's book in his story *The Descendant*, calling it "Donnelly's chimerical account." In his story *The Last Test* Lovecraft spoke of "the mysterious Saharan Tuaregs, whose descent from the primal race of lost Atlantis is an old archaeological rumour." The Tuaregs are a nomadic people of the Sahara Desert of North Africa. A character of the story named Surama is a priest of Atlantis who has been resurrected through necromancy. Elsewhere in the story, the character Alfred Clarendon says of Atlantis, "There were cults, you know—bands of evil priests in lands now buried under the sea. Atlantis was the hotbed. That was a terrible place. If heaven is merciful, no one will ever drag up that horror from the deep."

In *The Strange High House in the Mist* mention is made of how "the kings of Atlantis fought with the slippery blasphemies that wriggled out of rifts in ocean's floor." The undersea ruins of a great city into which the German submarine U-29 sinks in the story the *Temple* are assumed by the commander of the submarine to be the ruins of Atlantis. Among the ruins is an immense temple carved from a solid cliff of rock, from the windows of which lights emanate, suggesting that the sunken city is not entirely uninhabited.

(*The Descent; The Last Test; The Strange High House in the Mist; The Temple*)

Aylesbury

The nearest city to the village of Dunwich.

(*The Dunwich Horror*)

Banof

A distant, mist-shrouded valley visible east of the city of Olathoë, in the land of Lomar.

(*Polaris*)

Bethmoora *

A "white and beautiful city" with copper gates beyond the Hills of Hap, described in the 1908 fantasy story *Bethmoora* by Lord Dunsany. It has been strangely deserted and left to the desert, and Dunsany's narrator speculates as to why this may be, but does not reach any firm conclusion. Lovecraft merely mentions it in a list of names and places intended to be vaguely evocative.

(*The Whisperer in Darkness*)

Binger

A town in Caddo County, Oklahoma, near an earthen mound that marks the entrance to a passage that leads into the bowels of the earth to the land of blue-litten K'n-yan.

(*The Mound*)

Bnazic desert

A desert region in Mnar.

(*The Doom That Came to Sarnath*)

Catskills *

The Catskills, or the Catskill Mountains, figure in several of Lovecraft stories. In *The Man of Stone*, it was on Sugar-Loaf in the Catskills that the wizard Bareut Picterse Van Kauran, great-grandfather of the wizard "Mad Dan" Morris, was supposed to have participated in the Great Sabbat, and received a spell for turning men to stone. In *The Lurking Fear*, the deserted but evil-omened Martense mansion, home of the inbred Martense clan, was located atop Tempest Mountain in the Catskills. Joe Slater, who became possessed by an alien intelligence in *Beyond the Wall of Sleep*, was a native of the Catskills.

(*The Man of Stone; The Lurking Fear; Beyond the Wall of Sleep*)

Chesuncook

A fictional town in northern Maine Lovecraft characterized as close to the "wildest, deepest, and least explored forest belt" in the state, that has near it a circle of ancient standing stones, beneath which is a passage leading down six thousand steps to the pit of the shoggoths, where Ephraim Waite and other witches of his coven were wont to hold their sabbats in company with shoggoths. It is in this pit where "the black realm begins and the watcher guards the gate." There is an actual lake of this name in Maine, which may have given Lovecraft the idea for the name of his town.

(*The Thing on the Doorstep*)

Chorazin

The name of a village that sprang up around an old country house near present-day Attica, New York. The house was built about the year 1760, and served as the homestead of the Dirck van der Heyl family, which had fled Albany in 1746 after being accused of practicing witchcraft. His wife was a native of Salem, a daughter of the "unmentionable" Abaddon Corey. The house attracted a small community of Iroquois Indians, which formed the germ of Chorazin, and later this group was supplemented by "renegades" of white European blood who intermarried with the Indians, producing a mixed population in the village. Alonzo Typer described these inhabitants of the village as "no better than idiots," so considerable inbreeding among the villagers must be presumed to have taken place.

Behind the village, but in clear sight from the house, is a hill topped by a circle of ancient standing stones that were regarded with "fear and loathing" by the Iroquois. Typer wrote of the stones in connection with "the N——— estbat." An estbat, or as it is more common spelled today, an esbat, is a minor rite conducted by witches, having less importance than a sabbat. The initial *N* may refer to Nyarlathotep. In 1872 the entire van der Heyl family and all their servants suddenly vanished from the house. Thereafter, the house remained deserted. Attempts to inhabit it met with death, disappearance, or insanity.

The origin of the name "Chorazin" is not stated by Lovecraft, but it is strikingly similar to the name of the arch-demon of Enochian magic, Coronzon, recorded in the transcripts of the conversations conducted with the Enochian angels by the Elizabethan magician John Dee and his crystal gazer Edward Kelley. Aleister Crowley chose to misspell the name "Choronzon" for numerological reasons. Crowley considered Choronzon to be the ultimate negation of all life, and the death of the soul. Lovecraft had some passing knowledge of Crowley, so it is not beyond the bounds of possibility that he derived the name from Crowley's writings. In the Enochian language recorded by Dee, Coronzon is called *teloc vovim* (Laycock, p. 267), the Death Dragon, or "Him-that-is-Fallen."

(*The Diary of Alonzo Typer*)

Christchurch Cemetery

A cemetery in Arkham, much frequented by Herbert West in search of raw material for his experiments in reanimation. It is also mentioned in an unsigned letter from Philadelphia received by the necromancer Joseph Curwen, where it appears along with the names of other burial places.

(*Herbert West—Reanimator*; *The Case of Charles Dexter Ward*)

church, old stone

The old stone Catholic church at Red Hook, New York, had fallen into decay and been abandoned. It was used by the ill-visaged immigrant residents as a dance hall. The walls were decorated with painted panels showing religious figures with knowing and sardonic expressions on their faces, and indecorous poses out of keeping with religious art. One wall bore an ominous Greek inscription that translated as:

> O friend and companion of night, thou who rejoicest in the baying of dogs and spilt blood, who wanderest in the midst of shades among the tombs, who longest for blood and bringest terror to mortals, Gorgo, Mormo, thousand-faced moon, look favourably on our sacrifices!

The church was used by a cult of Yazidi devil worshippers for rituals honoring Lilith, queen of Hell, to whom children were sacrificed. The Greek quotation given by

Lovecraft has nothing directly to do with the Yazidi. It is directed at the Greek goddess of the Moon, Hecate, the goddess of witches. The Greek writer of the third century, Hippolytus, in his *Philosphumena*, quoted substantially the same words. The incantation was used by worshippers of Hecate at crossroads when they offered sacrifices to her. Lovecraft omitted the name of Hecate, because he wished the incantation to be applied to Lilith. Gorgo and Mormo were names applied to Hecate, but they were also the names of other separate hellish spirits.

(*The Horror at Red Hook*)

Cold Spring Glen

A wooded ravine near Dunwich that was the place of refuge for the invisible monstrous child of Lavinia Whateley after it broke free from its farmhouse prison. The glen has a bad reputation for unhealthiness, and it is said that the whippoorwills and fireflies that live there do not behave in a natural way. Those who stand near the entrance to a cave in the glen that is known as the Bear's Den can hear rushing sounds and a kind of talking in the air.

(*The Dunwich Horror*)

Commoriom

A fabled city of spires built of marble and granite, at one time the capital of Hyperborea (present-day Greenland). The city was founded by a prehuman race from the south. It is the invention of Lovecraft's friend and fellow writer, Clark Ashton Smith. In Smith's fiction, the people abandoned Commoriom and moved to the city of Uzuldaroum, a day's travel from the capital. Eventually, both cities were covered by the advancing glacier. Lovecraft mentioned Commoriom along with Atlantis, Lemuria, Uzuldaroum, and Olathoc in Lomar. The high priest of Atlantis, Klarkash-Ton, is remember for having preserved the myth-cycle of Commoriom.

(*At the Mountains of Madness; The Whisperer in Darkness*)

Congregational Hospital

A hospital built at Kingsport on Central Hill in place of the old Congregational Church with its distinctive tall steeple. It is next to the ancient graveyard, and it is rumored that strange caves or burrows hollow the ground beneath its foundations.

(*The Strange High House in the Mist; The Silver Key*)

Damascus *

Presently the capital city of Syria, Damascus is the most ancient continuously inhabited city on earth. Human traces have been found that are twelve thousand years old. It is the place the mad poet of Yemen, Abdul Alhazred, chose to settle after his many years of wandering the deserts and tombs of the ancient world. In Damascus he wrote his infamous *Al Azif*, later translated into Greek as the *Necronomicon*, and in this city he vanished from a public square at the hands of an invisible demon in the year 738. During Alhazred's residence the city was the capital of the Umayyad Empire, and the political center of the Muslim world.

(*History of the Necronomicon*)

Dark Mountain

A mountain in Vermont associated with the secretive cave-dwelling race known as the Mi-Go.

(*The Whisper in Darkness*)

Devil Reef

A black reef about a mile off the mouth of the harbor of the New England fishing port of Innsmouth. It is above the surface of the waves only at low tide, and it was rumored to contain the hidden openings to caves in its uneven surface, from which monsters would sometimes emerge and wander over the rocks. At Devil Reef the Yankee trading captain Obed Marsh called the Deep Ones up from the depths of the ocean and offered sacrifices to them on May-Eve and Halloween, in order to seal a bargain with this amphibious race that was to the profit of the folk of Innsmouth. Just beyond the reef the ocean drops to a depth that cannot be sounded. Somewhere at the bottom of this fathomless sea trench lies Y'ha-nthlei, the submerged city of the Deep Ones.

(*The Shadow Over Innsmouth*)

Devil's Hop Yard

A hill near Dunwich upon which nothing will grow, not even a blade of grass. It was used in the worship of the Old Ones. To this hill the invisible brother of Wilbur Whateley made its way after its escape from the Whateley farmhouse.

(*The Dunwich Horror*)

Devil's Woods

This dark stretch of woods in Maine, between the towns of Mayfair and Glendale, has the reputation for being haunted by the ghost of the Russian immigrant Vasili Oukranikov, who was killed for being a werewolf.

(*The Ghost-Eater*)

Dunwich

A small town to the northwest of Arkham, in the Miskatonic Valley, in northern Massachusetts, that lies just off the Aylesbury pike road beyond Dean's Corners. It is a bleak countryside of dense undergrowth and marshlands. The farming is poor there. The town of Dunwich, which is more properly characterized as a village, is in an advanced state of neglect, with many of its ancient gambrel-roofed houses falling to ruin. The steeple of the old church has collapsed in on itself, and the church has been turned into a general store. Dunwich is nestled in close to the almost vertical side of Round Mountain. The sole access to the town from the main road is had over a moldered covered bridge crossing the upper stream of the Miskatonic River, which runs past the town, hemming it in against the side of the mountain. Residents are furtive and few, and are noted for their unfriendly manner. The place breathes an atmosphere of decay.

(*The Dunwich Horror*)

Easter Island *

The writer Robert Harrison Blake, protagonist of *The Haunter of the Dark*, discovered in the Church of Starry Wisdom at Providence, Rhode Island, seven brooding, black-painted plaster images that resembled the statues on Easter Island. They surrounded the altar on which rested the Shining Trapezohedron. In *Medusa's Coil* the unnatural woman that Denis de Russy married in Paris, who called herself the priestess "Tanit-Isis" reincarnated into the body of Marceline Bedard, was revealed to be no true woman at all: "It was the old, hideous shadow that philosophers never dared mention—the thing hinted at in the *Necronomicon* and symbolized in the Easter Island colossi."

The statues of Easter Island are linked in an unspecific way with the cult of Cthulhu and the Old Ones. In *Out of the Aeons*, mention is made of the speculation by scholars that the great stone figures on Easter Island may be a remnant of an ancient civilization that occupied a Pacific continent that has since sunk beneath the waves, leaving only its highest mountain peaks to form the scattered islands of Melanesia and Polynesia. The continent that sank beneath the Pacific, leaving only scattered islands, may be the same continent of newly formed volcanic upheavals occupied in the distant past by Cthulhu and his spawn after their war against the Elder Things, but prior to the sinking of the city of R'lyeh.

(*The Haunter of the Dark; Medusa's Coil; Out of the Aeons*)

Egypt *

Egypt figures prominently in several of Lovecraft's stories. At the time he was writing, Egyptology was all the rage. The tomb of King Tutankhamen had been unearthed by the English archaeologist Howard Carter in 1922, and all things ancient Egyptian were in the news. Egyptian styles were displayed in films and in women's fashions. Even before the actual discovery of the tomb, there had been considerable anticipation. Carter had been searching for the tomb since 1914. The books of E. A. Wallis Budge had made Egyptian history accessible to the masses.

To take advantage of this Egyptian craze, the escape artist Harry Houdini hired Lovecraft to write a story in which Houdini was the protagonist. *Imprisoned with the Pharaohs*, written in 1924, managed to embroil Houdini in an adventure beneath the Second Pyramid, and indicated that the great monster after which the original likeness of the Sphinx had been carved was still alive deep underground, nourished on ancient mummies by a cult of the undead that was led by the pharaoh Khephren and his ghoul-queen Nitokris.

Nyarlathotep, written in 1920, was based entirely on a dream in which the Crawling Chaos came out of Egypt to tour America as a stage performer. "He said he had risen up out of the blackness of twenty-seven centuries, and that he had heard messages from places not on this planet." Part of his stage show consisted of displays of alchemical wonders. His face resembled that of an ancient Egyptian pharaoh. It transpired in the story that Nyarlathotep's real purpose was the harvesting of human beings, which he led in an entranced state back with him to the vortex of ultimate chaos.

In *The Case of Charles Dexter Ward*, the necromancer Simon Orne wrote to his fellow searcher of occult secrets, Joseph Curwen, "I gott such a Thing in Aegypt 75 yeares gone, from the which came that Scar ye Boy saw on me here in 1924. As I told you longe ago, do not calle up That which you can not put downe; either from dead Saltes or out of ye Spheres beyond." What Orne meant was that he had revived by necromancy a sorcerer of ancient Egypt who was so powerful in magic that he had very nearly escaped Orne's control and killed him. The magicians of ancient Egypt have for thousands of years been considered the most skilled in all the world—as appears in the book of Genesis, where they contested with the God-given power of Moses, and very nearly matched it.

In was in Egypt where the Shining Trapezohedron was found by professor Enoch Bowen, during the excavation of the tomb of the forgotten pharaoh Nephren-Ka, in Lovecraft's *The Haunter of the Dark*. Nephren-Ka had committed the indiscretion of building a temple for the black stone and attempting to draw upon its power. For this hubris his name and image was stricken from all records and monuments of Egypt. The black stone sat buried in the wreckage of the temple until 1844, when Bowen found it and carried it back to Providence.

(*Imprisoned with the Pharaohs; Nyarlathotep; The Case of Charles Dexter Ward; The Haunter of the Dark*)

empire of Tsan-Chan

A cruel empire that will flourish on the Earth around the year 5000 AD.

(*Beyond the Wall of Sleep*)

Exham Priory

An ancient structure built by the Saxons on the crest of a high cliff near Anchester, a village in the hills to the north of Exeter, in southwestern England. Around 1000 AD it was the home for a "strange and powerful monastic order," surrounded by extensive gardens, but unwalled—no walls were needed to keep away the local peasants, who held the place in dread. Before its occupation by the Saxons, a more ancient Roman temple to the goddess Cybele, the Great Mother, had stood on the site, built by the Third Augustan Legion and presided over by a Phrygian priest. Prior to that, a druidic or pre-druidic temple dated to about the same antiquity as Stonehenge had occupied the ground. Each subsequent structure had been erected on the ruins of the preceding one, incorporating the earlier building's foundation stones into its own, so that the priory was a mixture of architectural styles, the pre-druidic blocks at its very base sitting directly on the primal limestone of the cliff, and its Saxon walls surmounted with gothic towers.

In the year 1261 King Henry III gave the priory and the surrounding land to Gilbert de la Poer, First Baron Exham, who transformed it into his family estate. It remained in the de la Poer family until 1610, when Walter de la Poer, Eleventh Baron Exham, slaughtered his father, his five siblings, and a number of servants, after learning some terrible family secret, then fled for his life to Virginia. Within a century his descendants had changed their family name to Delapore. Exham Priory reverted to the crown, and was eventually transferred into the hands of the Norrys family of Anchester, who chose not to occupy it due to the odium in which it was held. The Delapores prospered in the New World but never forgot their English roots. A distant descendant of Walter de la Poer, a wealthy retired manufacturer of New England whose first name does not appear in the story, bought the Priory from the Norrys family in 1918, had it renovated, and on July 16, 1923, came to England to live in it.

Troubled by the persistent sound of scurrying rats in the walls, the new American owner investigated with the help of Edward Norrys and five other men, and discovered under an ancient altar in a crypt beneath the building a passage leading downward via a flight of worn stone steps. From the marks of the chisels on the stone, it was evident that the tunnel had been cut from below, upwards. In the mammoth cavern beneath the priory they found countless human bones, and pens of ancient construction designed to keep degenerate, inbred human beings captive, who were fed on vegetables grown in the extensive priory gardens. It was evident that the pens had been maintained right up to the time of the departure of Walter de la Poer for the American colonies. The new owner of the priory realized the horrible truth—that his revered family had engaged in pagan worship and cannibalism. It was to end this plague that Walter de la Poer had killed his father, siblings, and their servants.

It was the common practice in Europe to build Christian churches and monasteries on top of the foundations of pagan temples. A priory is a sort of lesser monastery, a prior being somewhat lower in rank than an abbot. Much is left unsaid in Lovecraft's story *The Rats in the Walls*, or is left only implied, but it may be gathered that some race of inhuman or semi-human ghouls dwelling in the earth tunneled their way up to the pre-druidic temple on its top and confirmed an unholy pact with the priests who inhabited it. Their rites must have involved human sacrifice and ritual cannibalism. Over the centuries the pact was maintained by subsequent owners of the holy structures on the cliff, until the priory fell into private hands, and then the pact devolved on to the not-unwilling de la Poer family. Perhaps the promise of forbidden secrets and occult power was too tempting to resist.

It cannot have been Gilbert de la Poer who bound his bloodline to such an unholy purpose, for the family curse is said to have begun in the year 1307. It was probably his son, who is not named in Lovecraft's story, who discovered the tunnel beneath the ancient pagan altar, and who descended to have dealings with whatever maintained the pens and their horrifying cattle in the great cavern. After Walter de la Poer slaughtered his family and servants in 1610, the food supply for the pens was cut off, the subhuman things inside them starved, rats ate their flesh and bred unchecked, and then three months after the date of the murders, burst forth from the cavern and ravaged the village of Anchester.

It is probable that the rats also destroyed whatever deep dwellers in the caverns had consorted with the de la Poer family in their cannibal rituals. In his madness, brought on by the horrible discovery and his realization of what it meant concerning his ancestry, the modern owner of the Priory raved about "those grinning caverns of earth's centre where Nyarlathotep, the mad faceless god, howls blindly in the darkness to the piping of two amorphous idiot flute-players."

(The Rats in the Walls)

Gallows Hill *

A low hill in Salem, Massachusetts, where witches were hanged. In *Pickman's Model*, one of the canvases painted by Richard Upton Pickman shows a ring of ghouls baying like animals around a hanged witch, whose face resembles their own.

(Pickman's Model)

gardens of Zokkar

Gardens in Sarnath from which roses were plucked to crown the heads of dancers and lutanists who mocked and derided the elder gods of the city of Ib, destroyed by the men of Sarnath in an unprovoked sneak attack. This took place yearly at the feast of the destruction of Ib, the most important annual celebration in Sarnath.

(The Doom That Came to Sarnath)

Greenland *

A tribe or cult of "degenerate Esquimaux" living on the northern coast of West Greenland was found in 1860 by the anthropologist William Channing Webb, of Princeton University, to be composed of worshippers of Cthulhu. The other native tribes of Greenland wanted nothing to do with them, saying that the religious practices of the devil-worshippers had come down from ancient aeons before the world was made. Those practices included human sacrifice. Webb was able to verify that the cultic stone image of their god depicted Cthulhu. Their ritual chants included the phrase *Ph'nglui mglw'nafh Cthulhu R'lyeh wgah'nagl fhtagn*, which may be translated, "In his house at R'lyeh dead Cthulhu waits dreaming."

(The Call of Cthulhu)

Hadoth

A sealed and unknown valley beside the Nile in Egypt that holds the catacombs of Nephren-Ka, a pharaoh accursed by his own people for the abominations he worked with the Shining Trapezohedron. His catacombs were probably hidden, and all records of them erased, by the outraged priests of Memphis after his death.

(*The Outsider*)

House in the Mist

This cottage in the late seventeenth-century style of architecture was built on the very edge of the sheer, mile-high sea cliff that faces east and lies alongside the mouth of the Miskatonic River. The cliff and its cottage are visible from the town of Kingsport. When the sea mists lie around the base of the cliff, the cottage seems to float on the air. It is a single room with windows on all four sides that contain leaded panes of bull's-eye glass, and a door to the east. So near is the cottage to the edge of the cliff that it is impossible for a normal human being to enter through the door. It is inhabited by a black-bearded hermit who has some strange commerce with the gods of Earth, particularly with the god Nodens. According to the Terrible Old Man of Kingsport, the cottage has remained unchanged from the boyhood of his grandfather. No one in Kingsport will visit the cottage. Natives do not even like to look upon it for very long. It is an uncanny place, a gateway between worlds.

A summer visitor to Kingsport, Thomas Olney, becomes interested in the legends told about the house by the Terrible Old Man of Water Street, and Granny Orne of Ship Street. He decides to climb to the top of the cliff to investigate. Starting in the morning, he works his way past Hooper's Pond and the old brick powder-house on the western side, the only side of the jutting cliff that is accessible, but finds no road or path leading eastward through the tangled brush to the cliff edge and the house, even though lights in the windows of the house at twilight show that it is inhabited. A natural rift some ten feet deep cuts across the thrust of the cliff, dividing the land occupied by the house from the rest of the prominence. This suggests that the end of the cliff is gradually separating from the main portion, and that at some future time it will drop into the estuary of the Miskatonic far below, taking the house with it.

Olney discovers that the house itself is gray in color, with worm-eaten wooden shingles on its walls and a brick chimney. The bearded owner helps him climb into the house through the western window, which he unlocks for the purpose. The interior is furnished in the Tudor style, indicating the immense age of the house. During Olney's visit, something comes and knocks on the door for entry, which Olney later describes to the Terrible Old Man as a shape "black and inquisitive," but the tenant of the house refuses to open the door. It can only have been some unwelcome creature from the abyss of gray mist beyond that was known to the bearded owner. When the god Nodens,

Lord of the Great Abyss, comes to call, Olney passes out the door with his host and into the giant seashell of the god, which floats on the mist like a ship on the water.

The next day Olney comes down from the house and returns to Kingsport. He cannot remember what transpired after he passed through the eastern door into the shell of Nodens. He leaves Kingsport soon afterward and settles at Bristol Highlands. Outwardly he seems unchanged, but his interest in strange tales and far wanderings in strange places has vanished. The Terrible Old Man is certain that he has left a portion of his soul behind him in the high house, that part which had been filled with wonder and mystery.

Dimensional gateways figure prominently in Lovecraft's fiction. Either they are opened by magic or alien science, or they are already in existence but hidden from casual access. The eastern doorway of the house in the mist is one such gateway, which leads to the dreamlands, where Nodens rules in the Great Abyss. Like the door, the house itself and its bearded tenant exist between worlds, half real and half imaginary. Lights can be seen in the windows of the house from Kingsport, yet the bearded owner has no way to travel to town to buy food, and seems never to leave his house. His needs are supplied from out of the mist, through the eastern door, by the entities of the dreamlands—which would be impossible were he not half a creature of dreams himself.

(*The Strange High House in the Mist*)

Hyperborea *

This ancient land was not invented by Lovecraft, but was a part of ancient Greek mythology and history. It is a land to the far north of the world. The name "Hyperborea" means "beyond the north wind." The Greeks described it as a land of perpetual sunshine, a happy place of music and dancing, where disease and the infirmities of old age were unknown, whose inhabitants never suffered warfare or were forced to endure hard labor.

In Lovecraft's mythos, Hyperborea was the source of the *Book of Ebon*. The toad-god, Tsathoggua, was worshipped in Hyperborea 200,000 years ago by its "furry, pre-human" inhabitants. These creatures were not natives of this planet, but had descended from "Kythamil, the double planet that once revolved around Arcturus." From this statement given by Randolph Carter in *Through the Gates of the Silver Key*, we must assume that Kythamil no longer exists. Perhaps it was the imminent destruction of Kythamil that drove the furry creatures to the Earth, where they established themselves in the northern land of Hyperborea. The silver key that Carter used to travel through space and time was a product of Hyperborea, and had power "over the personal consciousness-angles of human beings alone."

(*Out of the Aeons; The Shadow Out of Time; Through the Gates of the Silver Key*)

Ilarnek

One of the first three cities of men built in the land of Mnar, on the river Ai. The other two are Thraa and Kadatheron. These early cities were established by dark-skinned shepherds. They were astonished by the shining domes on the buildings of Sarnath, a lavish city that was subsequently founded by more aggressive wandering tribes deeper into the land of Mnar. After the destruction of Sarnath, the green stone idol of the water-lizard god Bokrug, which the warriors of Sarnath had looted from the city of Ib, was taken from the ruins of Sarnath and carried back to Ilarnek to be worshipped.

(*The Doom That Came to Sarnath; The Quest of Iranon*)

Innsmouth

Of all the somber and ensorcelled towns in Lovecraft's fiction, none is more accursed than Innsmouth. The men of the Massachusetts fishing community of Innsmouth, led by Obed Marsh, formed a pact with a race of sea-dwelling amphibious creatures known as the Deep Ones, whereby they would be insured an abundance of fish in their nets and an equal abundance of gold, in return for the sacrifice of their very humanity. At the time Marsh proposed this bargain to his fellow townsmen, their families were living in poverty and starving. He had an easy time turning them away from the worship of Christ and toward the worship of Dagon, god of the Deep Ones.

Obed Marsh was a Yankee trader in the South Seas who prospered for many years. While among the Kanaky islanders he learned of a tribe on one island that always had fish, no matter how difficult the fishing was on nearby islands. The tribe was shunned by the other islanders. Marsh approached them and learned their secret—they traded with the Deep Ones, who inhabit the deep places of the oceans all around the globe. They were ensured prosperity by the occasional sacrifice of young men and women, and by an agreement to intermarry with Deep Ones and have children by them. Marsh learned how to summon the Deep Ones, and what they demanded of their human confederates.

Years later, when hard times fell upon the New England town of Innsmouth, Marsh put his knowledge to use, persuading the townspeople to give their worship and their children to Dagon. In 1840 he founded a new religion, the Esoteric Order of Dagon. He rowed out to Devil Reef at the mouth of the harbor of Innsmouth and called the

Deep Ones up from the depths of an abyss that lay just off the reef. Arrangements were finalized, and sacrifices offered. The transformation in Innsmouth was immediate. The fishermen of the town could not haul their nets up, so heavy were they with the fish driven into them by the Deep Ones. The woman of the town appeared wearing strange but beautifully wrought gold jewelry not made to fit the shape of the human form.

It was only later that the unfortunate aspects of the pact made with the Deep Ones began to reveal themselves to the inhabitants of surrounding towns. Strange foreign women who always went veiled appeared in Innsmouth, and their children by their husbands in the town, although normal in appearance at birth, began to change as they grew older, acquiring what came to be known as the "Innsmouth look"—a strange form of degenerate appearance unlike any other that afflicted the isolated, inbred communities of New England. The hybrid offspring of human and Deep One marriages began to acquire the physical attributes of amphibians. Their eyes bulged, their mouths became broad and their noses flat, their skin took on a bluish cast and grew perpetually moist, their fingers and toes acquired webbing, and eventually gills developed in their necks.

But these were only the early signs of the transformation. At it progressed, they were forced to hide themselves away from view in the attics of the houses of the town. Visitors to Innsmouth who happened to glimpse their faces at attic windows recoiled in horror and swore never to set foot in Innsmouth again. As a result, in spite of its wealth the town of Innsmouth began to decay. At a certain point in their transformation, the hybrids stripped off their clothing, entered the sea, and spent most of their time beneath the waves. The population of the town declined, leading to more boarded-up and neglected houses and businesses.

This was the state of affairs when Lovecraft wrote about Innsmouth. The name itself first appears in his story *Celephaïs* in reference to a fictional town in England, but there is no direct connection between the English town and the one in Massachusetts, founded in 1643. As was often the case, the people of Lovecraft's New England took the name of the English town for one of their own villages. By so doing, they made it a name that would forever be associated with human degradation and horror. Lovecraft would later claim that Innsmouth was a "twisted version of Newburyport." Innsmouth is located in Essex County, Massachusetts, not far from Ipswich and Rowley.

The protagonist of *The Shadow Over Innsmouth* describes the town as an extensive and densely packed expanse of buildings, but almost devoid of visible inhabitants. The population was estimated for him by a railway ticket agent at Newburyport as being around three to four hundred, and most maps do not even show the town. There is a branch railway line to Rowley, but it has been unused for decades. The only public transportation in or out of the town is by means of an old bus, operated by an Innsmouth native, that runs to Arkham and Newburyport. Those foolish enough to take this bus can, if they wish, spend the night as the single remaining operational hotel in Innsmouth, the Gilman House.

A few lonely wisps of smoke trail up from the countless chimney pots on the sagging gambrel roofs. There are three tall steeples in the town, but all show advanced decay, their clocks ripped out to leave gaping holes. The rot and neglect is worse near the silted-up harbor, which is sheltered by an ancient stone breakwater. A few of the Georgian houses further back from the water seem in somewhat better repair, suggesting that they are still tenanted. The town sprawls on both sides of the Manuxet River, and several bridges cross the river inside the town. The sole active industry is the Marsh Refinery, where the gold of the Deep Ones is smelted down to shapes that are apt to attract less attention when offered for sale.

Innsmouth is mentioned in connection with Asenath Waite, one of the Innsmouth Waites, who married Edward Derby in the *Thing on the Doorstep*. In the story is it said that "dark legends have clustered for generations about crumbling, half-deserted Innsmouth and its people." There is a "strange element 'not quite human' in the ancient families of the run-down fishing port," an inhuman element that Asenath exhibited in her features.

(Celephaïs; The Shadow Over Innsmouth; The Thing on the Doorstep)

Irem *

Termed by Lovecraft the "City of Pillars" because of its many columns and towers, it is an ancient lost city in the depths of the Empty Space, the great desert on the Arabian Peninsula more commonly known in modern times as the Crimson Desert. The legend of Irem is part of the Arab story cycle, *The Thousand-and-One Nights*. The city was built by jinni at the command of Shaddad, lord of the tribe of Ad. Legend states that it was thrust down into the sand by wrathful God to punish the arrogance of Shaddad, who ignored the warnings of a prophet. Ruins recently found at Shisha have been identified as lost Irem. Lovecraft did not know about the existence of these ruins. The actual city upon which the legends are based is conjectured by archaeologists to have been founded around 3000 BC, and to have disappeared around 300 AD.

In *The Last Test*, Doctor Alfred Clarendon claimed to have spoken while in Yemen with an old man who had seen Irem, and had worshipped at the underground shrines of Nug and Yeb. The implication of the text is that these shrines were located beneath Irem. In *Through the Gates of the Silver Key*, reference is made to the sultan Shaddad, who "with his terrific genius built and concealed in the sands of Arabia Pettraea the prodigious domes and uncounted minarets of thousand-pillared Irem."

(The Last Test; The Nameless City; Through the Gates of the Silver Key)

Island in the Miskatonic River

In the midst of the Miskatonic River there is an unpopulated island that is associated with strange happenings. In *The Dreams in the Witch House*, the witch Keziah Mason told Judge Hathorne at her Salem trial for witchcraft about gatherings of witches on this island, which has rows of moss-covered, gray standing stones arranged in strange angles. The island is distantly visible when standing on the bridge on Garrison Street, in Arkham, and gazing upriver. In *The Colour Out of Space* mention is made of this island where "the devil held court beside a curious 'lone altar older than the Indians." It does not appear to have ever received a name from Lovecraft, but it is undoubtedly one of those places that acts as a gateway between this world and other worlds. It is reasonable to assume that it is connected by ley lines to other significant occult locations in New England.

(*The Dreams in the Witch House; The Colour Out of Space*)

Jaren

An onyx-walled city on the river Xari. Soldiers are stationed there.

(*The Quest of Iranon*)

Kadatheron

A city on the river Ai, in the land of Mnar, that is noted for its ancient historical records, which are inscribed on brick cylinders. It was originally founded by shepherds, along with its sister cities Thraa and Ilarnek.

(*The Doom That Came to Sarnath; The Quest of Iranon*)

Kingsport

A town in New England created by Lovecraft to serve as a background for some of his stories. He based it on Marblehead, Massachusetts. Like his fictional Arkham, it is an ancient place of narrow streets and decaying architecture. Both the Terrible Old Man and Granny Orne live in Kingsport, he on Water Street and she on Ship Street, close to the docks. Granny Orne is regarded as the unofficial historian of the community. Not far north of the town is the towering cliff atop which sits the strange high house in the mist. The town itself is dominated by Central Hill, which used to be the location for the old Congregational Church, since torn down to make way for Congregational

Hospital. Beside the hospital is the ancient church graveyard, which according to town rumor has beneath it a series of caves or burrows.

In *The Thing on the Doorstep*, Asenath Waite of the Innsmouth Waites attended the Hall School for girls in Kingsport. In *The Case of Charles Dexter Ward*, John Merrett, an English resident of Kingsport during the eighteenth century, had heard rumors of "monstrous things" involving "nameless rites" conducted at Kingsport, which in his day was no more than an odd little fishing village. Nyarlathotep mentioned Kingsport with appreciation while speaking to Randolph Carter in *The Dream-Quest of Unknown Kadath*, describing it as "antediluvian Kingsport hoary with stacked chimneys and deserted quays and overhanging gables." In the same work, the lighthouse-keeper of Kingsport is said to be an accomplished dream traveler who had spoken to Randolph Carter about the wondrous cities of the dreamlands.

(*The Terrible Old Man; The Strange High House in the Mist; The Festival; The Silver Key; The Case of Charles Dexter Ward; The Thing on the Doorstep; The Dream-Quest of Unknown Kadath*)

K'naa

A "kingdom or province" in the ancient land of Mu where early humans discovered ruins left by a race of beings who had dwelt there in the distant past. Lovecraft indicated that they were the ruins of more than one alien race, because he wrote of "vague waves of unknown entities." In the midst of K'naa was a great mountain called Yaddith-Gho that was surmounted by a stone fortress older than mankind built by the race from Yuggoth, the Mi-Go. In the crypt beneath this fortress dwelt the deathless demon Ghatanothoa, left behind after the passing away of the race from Yuggoth in this land. A cult of human beings worshipped the unseen Ghatanothoa, each year sacrificing to it twelve young warriors and twelve young maidens, who were offered to the god in a temple at the base of Yaddith-Gho.

(*Out of the Aeons*)

Lee's Swamp

A swamp in Vermont at the base of the wooded western slope of Dark Mountain. The swamp has an evil reputation due to strange voices that rise out of it, particularly on May-Eve. These voices are connected with the elusive Mi-Go, who meet there with a human cult that worships them.

(*The Whisperer in Darkness*)

Lefferts Corners

Nearest village to Tempest Mountain, in the Catskills. In August, 1921, its hotel became the base of operations for those state troopers searching for the missing inhabitants of a small squatter village destroyed during a lightning storm, and for the reporters who covered the story. Of the seventy-five inhabitants of the village, which is never named, fifty were slaughtered and torn apart by what was assumed to be an animal or animals, and the other twenty-five simply vanished without a trace.

(*The Lurking Fear*)

Lemuria *

A lost continent in the South Pacific Ocean that is supposed to have sunk beneath the waves aeons ago. By some accounts it is said to be the same as Mu, but others call it the motherland of Mu. In *The Diary of Alonzo Typer*, the manuscript book of the wizard Claes van der Heyl mentions the city of Shamballah, which was built by the Lemurians fifty million years ago, and is still in existence behind a "wall of psychic force" in the eastern desert. In *The Haunter of the Dark*, the diary of Robert Blake refers to Lemuria as one of the places in the distant past where the Shining Trapezohedron was kept and studied. "Myth-whispered Lemuria" is mentioned in passing in *Medusa's Coil* along with Babylon and Atlantis.

(*The Diary of Alonzo Typer; The Haunter of the Dark; Medusa's Coil*)

Implan

A hill district in Mnar.

(*The Doom That Came to Sarnath*)

Lomar

An ancient land that lay near the north pole, in which was located the many-templed marble city of Olathoë, "on the plateau of Sarkia, betwixt the peaks of Noton and Kadiphonek." Lomar was settled by men from Zobna, a land further north, when they were forced to move southward to escape the spread of the glacial ice sheet. They drove out of Lomar a race of hairy, long-armed cannibal humanoids known as Gnophkehs. Around twenty-six thousand years ago a yellow-skinned people called Inutos (which we know today as the Inuit) devastated Lomar. Eventually the Gnophkehs returned to claim the land once again. Within Lomar was kept the Pnakotic Manuscripts, and other texts known collectively as the wisdom of the Zobnarian Fathers.

(At the Mountains of Madness; Polaris; The Horror in the Museum; Through the Gates of the Silver Key)

Martense mansion

Home of the generations of the Martense family, it was built in the year 1670 by the New Amsterdam merchant Gerrit Martense on the summit of a rounded, wooded hill in the Catskills known locally as Tempest Mountain, due to the prevalence of thunderstorms above it. Other, smaller rounded hills surrounded Tempest Mountain and seemed to radiate from it. His descendants remained isolated by the wilderness around their family home, and by their stubborn use of the Dutch language instead of English. All in the numerous bloodline were marked by the peculiarity of having one blue eye and one brown eye. They intermarried with their servants, and many descendents of these unions settled in small, squalid villages near Tempest Mountain, but a core of the family line remained in the Martense Mansion, refusing to mingle with the surrounding communities.

In 1754 one of the clan, Jan Martense, left to serve in the colonial army. When he returned six years later, he found himself disgusted by the insularity and degeneration of his relatives. In 1763 his own family murdered him by smashing in his skull. When one of his former friends discovered the murder, official charges were laid in Albany, New York, and the Martense clan became ostracized, even though no conviction in a court of law was made due to a lack of evidence. The isolated clan degenerated. The last occupancy of the Martense mansion was observed around the year 1810, after which the house was believed abandoned. When an investigation was made in 1816 it was found to be empty and partially in ruins.

The presumption that the mansion had been deserted was not entirely correct. The degenerate but prolific remnants of the Martense clan had simply left its rooms to dwell beneath it, creating a network of tunnels that radiated from its cellar. They had regressed to the level of animals, losing the use of language, and sustaining themselves on human flesh. Under cover of darkness and storm they made forays into the surrounding countryside in search of pray, a clan of naked, silent, humanoid ghouls numbering in the thousands.

(The Lurking Fear)

Meadow Hill

A hill outside of Arkham. Beyond it lies a dark and barren valley, sometimes called a ravine, that contains a white stone. The valley was said by Keziah Mason in *The Dreams in the Witch House* to have been used for witch gatherings, where certain lines and curves were drawn "leading through the walls of space to other spaces beyond." The same was said by Mason of the unnamed island in the Miskatonic River near Arkham.

Herbert West and his accomplice set themselves up in the deserted Chapman farmhouse beyond Meadow Hill for their experiments in reanimating corpses. It must have been very near Meadow Hill because in one place Lovecraft described it as on Meadow Hill.

In *The Unnamable*, a "frightful loping, nameless thing" was seen on Meadow Hill sometime around 1710, being pursued by an old man. The thing may have been his grandson, the product of a union between his daughter and a creature from beyond. When the narrator of the story and his friend are knocked unconscious by a flying fiend while sitting and talking in the old burying-ground of Arkham, they are discovered a mile away, in a field beyond Meadow Hill.

(*The Dreams in the Witch House; Herbert West—Reanimator; The Unnamable; The Color Out of Space*)

Miskatonic River

A rapidly flowing river that passes through the Miskatonic Valley in Massachusetts. Towns on the river include Arkham, which is built on both banks, and Dunwich near its headwaters, which is hemmed in by the lively stream against the shoulder of Round Mountain. Of the beginnings of the Miskatonic in the upper Miskatonic Valley, Lovecraft wrote in *The Dunwich Horror*, "The thin, shining line of the Miskatonic's upper reaches has an oddly serpent-like suggestion as it winds close to the feet of the domed hills among which it rises." Further downstream, in the midst of the river is a small island that is visible from Arkham. The island has the reputation as a haunt for witches, and boasts an ancient stone altar of uncertain origins. The island served the same function for witch gatherings as the ravine beyond Meadow Hill, outside Arkham. The mouth of the river lies two miles down the Atlantic coast from Kingsport.

(*The Colour Out of Space; The Silver Key; The Dunwich Horror*)

Miskatonic University

Nestled in the heart of Arkham, Massachusetts, a town on the banks of the beautiful Miskatonic River, this institute of higher learning is typical of the small Ivy League universities in New England during Lovecraft's period: conservative, quiet, its student body mostly male, although some women were accepted as students—Asenath Waite, of the Innsmouth Waites, was one such woman, and she majored in medieval metaphysics. Edward Pickman Derby attended the university, majoring in English and French, as did Walter Gilman, who studied mathematics and folklore. Herbert West attended the Miskatonic University Medical School.

The university is noted for its extensive library of rare occult books and manuscripts. In *The Thing on the Doorstep*, the library is said to be famous for its "subterranean magical lore." Prized among the books is a copy of the dread *Necronomicon* in the Latin translation of Olaus Wormius, printed in Spain in the seventeenth century. Under the watchful eye of chief-librarian Henry Armitage, the staff is cautious about who is permitted access to this book.

The university specializes in exploring the mysteries of the past, as might be expected from the general nature of its library. Lovecraft mentioned a surprising number of faculty members in his various stories.

In *The Dunwich Horror*, we learn the names of Henry Armitage, already referred to above, as well as those of Francis Morgan, professor of archaeology, and Warren Rice, professor of languages.

In *The Shadow Out of Time*, we have the history professor Ferdinand C. Ashley, along with Tyler M. Freeborn, professor of anthropology, Nathaniel Wingate Peaslee, professor of political economy, his son Wingate Peaslee of the department of psychology, and William Dyer, professor of geology.

The Whisperer in Darkness names a Professor Dexter of the zoology department, and Albert N. Wilmarth of the English department.

Wilmarth's name occurs again in *At the Mountains of Madness*, as does that of William Dyer, along with the names of Lake, professor of biology, Atwood, professor of physics, and Frank H. Pabodie of the engineering department.

From *The Dreams in the Witch House* we learn of Professor Ellery of the chemistry department, and in mathematics Professor Upham. Old Waldron, the university doctor, is also mentioned.

The name of the dean of the medical school at Miskatonic University, Dr. Allen Halsey, occurs in *Herbert West—Reanimator*, when Halsey prohibits West from experimenting with human cadavers. After his death, Halsey becomes West's first really successful experimental subject.

(*The Thing on the Doorstep; The Dunwich Horror; The Shadow Out of Time; The Whisperer in Darkness; At the Mountains of Madness; The Dreams in the Witch House; Herbert West—Reanimator*)

Mnar

A land first settled by human beings when wandering tribes of shepherds built the cities of Kadatheron, Thraa, and Ilarnek along the river Ai. Later, more aggressive tribes pushed further into Mnar and built the city of Sarnath beside an unnamed lake. The spot was chosen because it was rich in precious metals that could be easily mined. On the other side of this lake was the city of Ib, populated by a race of humanoid amphibians who were said to have descended from the Moon in the distant past with their city and the lake. The land of Mnar is said to be remote from other lands "both of waking and of dream." It appears to be an actual place, not a dream place, but one that existed in the distant past. In *The Nameless City* mention is made of "the land of Mnar when mankind was young."

(*At the Mountains of Madness; The Doom That Came to Sarnath; The Nameless City*)

mounds *

Raised mounds of earth in the western part of Oklahoma have an artificial appearance, and mark the entrances to the subterranean blue-litten land of K'n-yan. The flat-topped mound near the town of Binger rises thirty to forty feet above the level plain and extends three hundred feet in its longest diameter by fifty feet across, being elliptical in circumference. Although the particular mounds described by Lovecraft do not exist, there are Indian mounds at Spiro, Oklahoma.

(*The Mound*)

Mtal

A port city of Mnar noted for its pearl-diving industry.

(*The Doom That Came to Sarnath*)

Mu *

A "vanished continent" that Lovecraft asserted in his story *Out of the Aeons* had flourished 200,000 years ago, according to tablets inscribed in the Naacal tongue. The concept of the Naacal civilization of Mu comes from the fanciful writings of James

Churchward (1851–1936), who wrote three books on the subject of Mu. Lovecraft further indicated that Mu had been inhabited by the Mi-Go from Yuggoth before the coming of mankind to its shores. The Mi-Go built an enormous stone fortress on the top of Mount Yaddith-Gho to hold their god Ghatanothoa.

(*Out of the Aeons*)

Narthos

A valley through which flows the frigid river Xari. On its southern slope is the town of Sinara, through which pass dromedary men.

(*The Quest of Iranon*)

Nath

An ancient land scried by the mystic writer Rudolf Yergler, the history of which he detailed in his book the *Chronicle of Nath*. We know this land was not in the dreamlands because an amber gem once guarded by the high-priest of Nath has come down to modern times and is presently in the keeping of an unnamed museum.

(*The Tree on the Hill*)

Northam Keep

An ancient castle built by Lunaeus Gabinius Capito, military tribune in the Third Augustan Legion, which was stationed in Britain at Lindum. Gabinius was cast out of the Roman army for participating in certain forbidden rites in a cliff-side cavern on the shore of the North Sea with a strange tribe feared by the native Britains, that was rumored to have descended from the inhabitants of lost Atlantis. He constructed his keep on the cliff above the cavern.

(*The Descendant*)

Olathoë

City in the land of Lomar, near the North Pole, which was destroyed by the coming of an Ice Age and the attacks of the hairy Gnophkehs. It was located "on the plateau of Sarkia, between the peaks of Noton and Kadiphonek," and was constructed largely of marble. It had a great public square that contained numerous statues, and several smaller squares where the inhabitants met to socialize. The gray-eyed men of the city are said to have been the bravest of all the Lomarians. The smallest of the images of the toad-god Tsathoggua that was found in the red-litten underground cavern world of Yoth by the men of the blue-litten cavern world of K'n-yan eventually found its way to the city of Olathoë in Lomar, where it was worshipped.

(*Polaris; The Mound; The Quest of Iranon*)

old burying-ground

An ancient graveyard at Arkham, unused for over a century prior to the events related in the story *The Unnamable*, which was written by Lovecraft in 1923. That would date the last interment to around 1800. A great willow tree grows in the midst of the tombs, the expanding trunk of which has nearly engulfed one of the tilted headstones. Beside this graveyard stands a deserted house that dates from the seventeenth century.

(*The Unnamable*)

Oonai

A "city of lutes and dancing" that lies beyond the Karthian Hills from the granite city of Teloth. The men of Teloth say that Oonai is both lovely and terrible, and camel-drivers sometimes whisper leeringly about it.

(*The Quest of Iranon*)

Osborne's General Store

The main commercial center in the village of Dunwich. It was here, a week after the birth of Wilbur Whateley, that Old Whateley the wizard made the prophetic statement that the people of the place would one day hear his daughter's child call out his unknown father's name on the top of Sentinel Hill. The child cried the name "Yog-Sothoth."

(*The Dunwich Horror*)

Pnath

A land conquered by the city state of Sarnath, which ruled the land of Mnar ten thousand years ago. Pnath was noted for the excellence of its wine.

(*The Doom That Came to Sarnath*)

Red Hook

An area in the city of New York described by Lovecraft as "a maze of hybrid squalor near the ancient waterfront opposite Governor's Island, with dirty highways climbing the hill from the wharves to that higher ground where the decayed lengths of Clinton and Court Streets lead off toward the Borough Hall. Its houses are mostly of brick, dating from the first quarter to the middle of the nineteenth century, and some of the obscurer alleys and byways have that alluring antique flavour which conventional reading leads us to call 'Dickensian.'"

Having lived in this part of New York in 1924, Lovecraft was able to describe it from first-hand observation. He was appalled at the racially and culturally mingled population, and used it as the location for a fictional secret cult of Yazidi devil worshippers. He characterized it as "a babel of sound and filth" that "sends out strange cries to answer the lapping oily waves at its grimy piers and the monstrous organ litanies of the harbour whistles."

(*The Horror at Red Hook*)

Riverside

A southern plantation house built in 1816 by a former plantation owner from Louisiana on low-lying land in southern Missouri. It was the scene of a macabre tragedy in 1916, one hundred years after its erection. Denis de Russy, son of the owner Antoine de Russy, murdered his French wife, Marceline Bedard, with a machete and hacked off her long black hair, under the conviction that she was a gorgon masquerading in the form of a beautiful woman, and that the hair was animated with an evil life of its own. The mansion burned to the ground, and afterwards its foundations were widely believed to be haunted.

(*Medusa's Coil*)

Roba el Khaliyeh *

The vast and forbidding desert of the southern Arabian Peninsula, which lies to the east of Yemen, was known in ancient times as the Empty Space, or Empty Quarter (*Roba el Khaliyeh*) but it is presently referred to as the Crimson Desert or simply as the Sands. At 225,000 square miles, it is the largest expanse of sand in the world. The Sahara in Africa may be fifteen times bigger, but the Sahara is made up mostly of rock and gravel. The Empty Space is almost all sand. Only the wandering tribes of the Bedouin have been able to live upon its edges, and even they seldom venture across its terrible burning expanse.

Deserts have always been regarded as the haunts of evil spirits and supernatural creatures that prey upon human beings. In the biblical book of Leviticus 16:20–2 it is written that the scapegoat was led out of Jerusalem into the desert wilderness and left as a sacrifice for the demon Azazel. The Empty Space is the land of the jinn, spirits malicious towards mankind who travel across its sands in the form of whirling dust columns. They haunt the night and forever try to tempt the unwary traveler away from his tent. Their voices howl on the wind.

The Empty Space is best known as a place where the mad poet and author of the *Necronomicon*, Abdul Alhazred of Yemen, wandered in search of occult knowledge. Hidden somewhere amid the endless sand dunes lies Irem, the City of Pillars, that is described in the Arabian text, *The Book of A Thousand Nights and a Night*, a favorite book of Lovecraft's as a young boy. Lovecraft wrote of Alhazred in his *History of the Necronomicon* that he had "spent ten years alone in the great southern desert of Arabia—the Roba el Khaliyeh or 'Empty Space' of the ancients—and 'Dahna' or 'Crimson' desert of the modern Arabs, which is held to be inhabited by protective evil spirits and monsters of death. Of this desert many strange and unbelievable marvels are told by those who pretend to have penetrated it. [. . .] He claimed to have seen fabulous Irem, or City of Pillars, and to have found beneath the ruins of a certain nameless desert town the shocking annals and secrets of a race older than mankind." Lovecraft asserted in a latter to Clark Ashton Smith dated November 27, 1927, that Alhazred had learned the worship of Yog-Sothoth and Cthulhu in the Empty Space.

In *The Last Test*, the necromancer and physician Doctor Alfred Clarendon claimed to have spoken in Yemen with an old man who had come back alive from the Crimson Desert, and had seen Irem, City of Pillars, and had worshipped at the underground shrines of Nug and Yeb. These twin gods were worshipped in the subterranean empire of K'n-yan—however, the great blue-litten cavern of K'n-yan lies beneath Oklahoma, so the old man of Yemen cannot have reached K'n-yan from the Empty Space. He must have found another site of worship of Nug and Yeb.

(*History of the Necronomicon*; *The Last Test*)

Round Hill

A wooden hill in Vermont east of Dark Mountain, on which was found the black stone, a stone carved with unknown hieroglyphics that pertain to the Mi-Go.

(*The Whisperer in Darkness*)

Rue d'Auseil

An ancient street in an unnamed French city, probably Paris. It lies on the other side of a dark river from the more traveled part of the city, the banks of which are lined with soot-stained brick warehouses. A stone bridge spans the river. For a description of this river, see Lovecraft's poem "The Canal" in *Fungi from Yuggoth*. The hill which the street ascends is extremely steep, so much so that it has been closed to all except foot traffic, and some portions of it are flights of steps. Its narrow surface is composed of a mixture of paving stones, cobblestones, and bare earth, and on either side the old houses lean drunkenly, their upper stories almost touching above the street, or linked by elevated walkways. At the summit of the hill is a tall wall against which the Rue d'Auseil terminates. A decaying rooming house stands third from the end of the street, but at five stories is the tallest structure near the wall.

The silent, withdrawn inhabitants of the street are all very old, including the proprietor of the rooming house, the paralytic Blandot, and the tenant of its attic chamber, the mute German musician Erich Zann. A student of metaphysics takes a room in the house because the street lies less than half an hour's walk from the university. He looks out the attic window of Erich Zann, hoping for a view of what lies beyond the wall, since that attic window is the only window in the street high enough to see over the wall. He is horrified to discover that he sees only a black void alive with motion, unlike anything on Earth. The shock causes a nervous breakdown, and when he recovers, the student finds that he can no longer locate the Rue d'Auseil no matter how many maps of the city he studies, or how diligently he searches for it.

It was a theme of Lovecraft's work that certain sensitive individuals, at significant dates of the year or in states of mental abstraction, could wander through unknown city streets and unwittingly find themselves transported back in time. This theme is central to the story *He*, and there are echoes of it in *The Festival* and *The Haunter of the Dark*. The mind itself, when heightened to a pitch of alienation that is a kind of trance, becomes the gateway between dimensions of reality. In the case of *The Music of Erich Zann*, we are left in doubt whether the university student is unable to relocate the Rue d'Auseil because his shattered mind refuses to allow him to revisit the street, or because the street does not exist in this reality, but in view of the street's ancient appearance and the strangeness of its inhabitants, the latter assumption seem more likely.

(*The Music of Erich Zann*)

Salem-Village *

This town in Essex County, in the northeastern corner of Massachusetts, on the Danver River, was settled in 1636. It is now called Danvers. The famous Salem Witch Trials of 1692 were held here. According to Joshi (*A Dreamer and a Visionary*, p. 164), Lovecraft visited Salem-Village in April of 1923, and examined the farmhouse of Rebekah Nurse, one of those accused of witchcraft and hanged. Lovecraft was able to locate her grave. The massive red structure of Danvers State Hospital provided Lovecraft with inspiration for Arkham Sanitarium.

In *The Case of Charles Dexter Ward*, Jedediah Orne of Salem wrote to Joseph Curwen at Providence, Rhode Island, concerning the failed attempts at necromancy of one Edward Hutchinson, a native of Salem-Village: "Certainly, there was Noth'g but ye liveliest Awfulness in that which H. rais'd upp from What he cou'd gather onlie a part of." Curwen was himself a former native of Salem-Village, who had been forced to flee to Providence in advance of charges of necromancy. We learn in *The Silver Key* that the same course was taken by Edmund Carter, an ancestor of Randolph Carter, who was forced to flee from the witch trials at Salem-Village with his mysterious silver key, and who also came to Providence. In *The Dreams in the Witch House*, it was from the jail at Salem-Village that the witch Keziah Mason escaped by drawing strange curves and angles in the corner of her cell that opened a dimensional portal through time and space.

(*The Case of Charles Dexter Ward; The Silver Key; The Dreams in the Witch House*)

Sarnath

This ancient city of the land of Mnar was constructed beside a lake to take advantage of deposits of metals nearby that could be easily mined. Sarnath met its doom at the hands of the inhuman race that inhabited the city of Ib, on the other side of the lake. After the men of Sarnath sacked Ib, slaughtered its inhabitants, and stole the green stone statue of its lizard-god, Bokrug, a terrible fate was visited upon Sarnath, and it was utterly destroyed.

(*The Doom That Came to Sarnath; The Quest of Iranon; The Lost City; The Nameless City*)

Sentinel Hill

A rounded hill not far from Dunwich that has a table-like rock on its crest that served as an altar during rites of worship dedicated to the Old Ones. Deposits of human skulls and bones have been found around the rock.

(*The Dunwich Horror*)

Shamballah *

In the mythology of Tibetan Buddhism, Shamballah is supposed to be a perfect kingdom of peace and enlightenment ruled by a line of enlightened kings, that lies north of the Himalayas near or in the Gobi Desert. However, many Buddhists view it as not a physical place at all, but a state of mind that all can enter when they achieve enlightenment.

In *The Diary of Alonzo Typer* it is a city built by the Lemurians fifty million years ago, which continues to exist undecayed behind a wall of psychic force in the eastern desert. It is described in the notebook for the years 1560 to 1580 of the Dutch wizard, Claes van der Heyl, which Alonzo Typer found in the attic of the van der Heyl family farmhouse, in the village of Chorazin, near Attica, New York, in 1935.

(*The Diary of Alonzo Typer*)

Ship Street

A street in Kingsport that is in the older section of town, near the harbor. It runs parallel with the wharfs but is set somewhat further back from the water than Water Street. Granny Orne, one of the ancients who acts as informal historian for the town, lives there in a tiny gambrel-roofed house that is covered with moss and ivy. After three thieves tried to rob the house of the Terrible Old Man on Water Street, the car they used was later found abandoned on Ship Street, near the rear gate entrance to the back yard of the Terrible Old Man's house. This indicates that Ship Street is adjacent Water Street. It has a higher elevation than Water Street, being further from the wharfs.

(*The Strange High House in the Mist; The Terrible Old Man*)

Sinara

A town on the southern side of the Narthos valley, beside the river Xari. It is on a caravan route, and is the stopping place for dromedary men, who get drunk in the town.

(*The Quest of Iranon*)

Snake-Den

This cave not far from Arkham has an evil reputation. It lies behind the old Carter family farm, and is deeper than it appears to be. A small fissure in the rear opens upon a larger cavern. It is linked with the silver key that was the legacy to Randolph Carter from his ancestors. At age ten Randolph Carter entered it with the key and emerged strangely altered and able to foretell events in the future. It was rumored that the wizard Edmund Carter had used the Snake-Den for his dark rituals.

(*The Silver Key; Through the Gates of the Silver Key*)

Starry Wisdom, Church of

The Church of Starry Wisdom was a stone church on Federal Hill in Providence, Rhode Island, built in the style of the gothic revival around 1810 or 1815. It had a great tower with a tapering steeple, high stone buttresses, a sloped roof, three massive doors, and pointed gothic stained-glass windows. The earth upon which it was built was surrounded by a retaining wall that elevated the churchyard a full six feet above the level of the streets of the town. This retaining wall was surmounted by a wrought-iron fence. Within this enclosure, beside the church, were the remnants of an old graveyard.

Professor Enoch Bowen, an archaeologist and occultist, acquired the church in July of 1844 for the purpose of housing the Shining Trapezohedron, which he had unearthed in Egypt a year earlier while excavating the ruins of the temple of the unknown pharaoh Nephren-Ka. The church acted as the meeting place for the Starry Wisdom sect, an occult brotherhood of some two hundred members devoted to the worship of the Shining Trapezohedron and of the terrifying being it summoned from beyond, known as the Haunter of the Dark. Above the altar of the church, an Egyptian ankh replaced the Christian cross.

The Trapezohedron itself was housed in the steeple tower of the church, which was shuttered tightly with opaque screens to exclude all light. No bells occupied its fifteen-foot square tower chamber. In the center of the floor, a stone pillar of curiously angled sides covered in strange hieroglyphics supported the unsymmetrical metal box that contained the Trapezohedron. Seven high-backed chairs surrounded this pillar in a circle. Behind each chair stood the representation of a monstrous image similar to the statues of Easter Island, sculpted in black-painted plaster.

The church boasted an extensive library of rare esoteric texts. In 1877 the Starry Wisdom sect abandoned the church and fled from Providence to avoid mob persecution inflamed by rumors of blood sacrifices, and thereafter the church remained closed and unused, many of the occult book still on its shelves in a rear vestry. It was in a greatly decayed state when the writer and painter Robert Blake discovered it late in April of 1935.

(*The Haunter of the Dark*)

Stethelos

In *The Quest of Iranon* it is place, probably a city, that lies below the great cataract on the Xari river, but whether Stethelos is part of the dreamlands or of some distant world or time is not perfectly clear. In *The Green Meadow* is written, "beyond the deafening torrent lies the land of Stethelos, where young men are infinitely old." It seems to be part of the material universe in this latter story, since a book was sent by an ancient Greek from Stethelos "across the horrible immeasurable abyss" to modern Earth within a meteorite. The book probably took millennia to reach the Earth, but it may have traveled through dimensions rather than strictly across space.

The green meadow of Stethelos evokes thoughts of the Elysian Fields of the ancient Greeks, and also of the Summerland of European witches. The deathlessness of its inhabitants may refer to reincarnation.

(*The Quest of Iranon; The Green Meadow*)

Swamp Hollow

The location of the old burying-ground outside the decaying and repellent New England town of Stillwater, where Tom Sprague and Henry Thorndike were buried alive on June 17, 1886. Their ghosts haunt the shuttered house of Sophie Sprague, who knowingly allowed them to be interred while still living but unable to move or speak, and a curse emanating from Swamp Hollow lies over the entire town of Stillwater.

(*The Horror in the Burying-Ground*)

Sydathria

A land not far from the land of Mnar that was famed ten thousand years ago for the excellence of its spice groves.

(*The Doom That Came to Sarnath*)

Tanit, temples of *

Tanit, also sometimes spelled Tinith or Tinnit, is a Phoenician goddess of the moon who was worshipped at Carthage, a Phoenician colony founded in 814 BC in North Africa. This goddess was also worshipped on the Mediterranean islands of Malta and Sardinia, and in Spain. She is depicted wearing the crescent moon on her head, holding a flowing cornucopia in each hand. Her image was erected over the funeral urns containing the cremation dust of children sacrificed to her. A more stylized symbol of Tanit shows a triangle surmounted by a horizontal bar with a circle above it. This represents a woman with her arms outstretched. Sometimes this symbol was crowned with an inverted lunar crescent. In addition to being a goddess of fertility, she was the consort of Baal and a war goddess. By the fifth century BC her worship in Carthage had become more prominent than that of Baal. A shrine to Tanit was established by Carthaginian colonists on the Spanish island of Ibiza, in the cave at Es Culleram on the mountain of

Sant Vincent, after the Carthaginians settled on the island in 654 BC. Offerings are still given to the goddess there.

(*Medusa's Coil*)

Teloth

A rather severe city on the sluggish river Zuro, built of granite, where the men are dark and stern, live in square houses, and frown more often than they smile. There is no laughter or song in Teloth. Singing is viewed as a folly. The Tower of Mlin dominates the center of the city. Before it is a large and open public square. By the laws of the city, all men in Teloth must labor. This is enforced by archons—men appointed to enforce the city laws. The inhabitants of Teloth worship gods who say that toil is a good unto itself, and that beyond death is an illuminated haven of crystal coldness where there is rest eternal. (*The Quest of Iranon*)

Tempest Mountain

A mountain in the Catskills, occupied by the lonely and deserted Martense family mansion. The ground beneath and around the house is riddled with tunnels in which dwell in their thousands the degenerate and cannibalistic Martense clan, naked and hairy, resembling apes.

(*The Lurking Fear*)

Than

The river Than flows through the valley of Nis. Its waters are red, but the source of this coloration is unknown. The river rises from hidden springs, and flows into subterranean grottoes. Its slow-moving waters are slimy and filled with weeds. Beside the river are the ruins of an ancient stone city, inhabited by numerous monkeys.

(*Memory*)

Uganda *

In the jungle of this nation are cyclopean ruins that the natives avoid. The megaliths are said to be older than mankind, and an outpost for the Fishers from Outside, and of the evil gods "Tsadogwa and Clulu" (Tsathoggua and Cthulhu). The natives claim they are associated with soul-stealing "devil-flies" and have a harmful influence on those who venture close.

(*Winged Death*)

Washington Street

A street in Innsmouth, Massachusetts, on which is situated the half-decayed mansion of the Waite family. Ephraim Waite was a notorious magician. He took a Deep One for his wife and engendered a daughter named Asenath. The attic windows of the house were always boarded up, and strange sounds were heard to come from behind them.

(*The Thing on the Doorstep*)

Water Street

The street in Kingsport where the Terrible Old Man has his cottage. It is one of the oldest streets in the town and runs along the harbor behind the wharves. The more ancient houses, such as that of the Terrible Old Man, which is described as "antediluvian," are set back from the street by front yards in which trees grow. Behind Water Street runs Ship Street, where the cottage of Granny Orne is located.

(*The Terrible Old Man*)

Widener Library *

Library at Harvard University, in Cambridge, Massachusetts, that holds a seventeenth-century Latin edition of the *Necronomicon*. Wilbur Whateley went there in 1928 in an effort to gain access to the book, but was refused.

(*The Dunwich Horror; Out of the Aeons*)

Witch House

This large old rooming house at Arkham, Massachusetts, located at the corner of Pickman Street and Parsonage Street, was once the residence of the notorious witch, Keziah Mason, who vanished mysteriously from a Salem jail in the year 1692. It had a reputation for being haunted. The familiar of the witch, a rat-like thing with a human face named Brown Jenkin, was often seen running through the halls of the house at night, and its tittering could be heard through the walls.

In 1927 Walter Gilman, a student of mathematics and folklore at Miskatonic University at Arkham, took an upper room in the boarding house, which was rumored to have been Keziah Mason's room. He discovered one corner of the room to be strangely angled, and learned that it was a dimensional portal still in use by the witch and her familiar, who were not dead, but who had escaped through the spaces between worlds. The witch attempted to recruit Gilman into her coven, but Gilman resisted. One morning Gilman was found dead in his room with a hole chewed into his chest and his heart missing.

The tenants and the manager of the rooming house refused to stay in it any longer and vacated it. Years later, the abandoned house was demolished, revealing behind the strangely angled corner on the north side of the witch-room a secret chamber with a boarded-up window that was filled with the bones of children, and an ancient sacrificial knife.

(*The Dreams in the Witch House*)

Yemen *

An ancient Arab land that was the birthplace of the poet and necromancer Abdul Alhazred, author of the dread *Necronomicon*. It lies on the edge of the great desert once known as the Empty Space. The physician and biologist Alfred Clarendon referred to the country when speaking of an old man who had wandered alive out of the desert and made his way back to Yemen—"he had seen Irem, the City of Pillars, and had worshipped at the underground shrines of Nug and Yeb."

(*The Last Test*)

Yhe

Lovecraft referred to this place only once, as "vanished Yhe in the Pacific." He associated it with an arch-mage, so it must have been the dwelling place of magicians. We may infer that Yhe was probably an island that sank beneath the Pacific Ocean—perhaps it was one of the islands off the coast of the lost Pacific continent of Mu. Other writers elaborated on this cryptic hint after Lovecraft's death. Lin Carter wrote of the *Rituals of Yhe*, and in the Hay version of the *Necronomicon* there is something called the Talisman of Yhe which is supposed to control the "Black one" and the "thousand Horned Ones"—it consists of squiggles inside a double hexagon inside a circle (Hay, p. 137).

(*The Shadow Out of Time*)

Yian-Ho

Yian is a city described in the 1896 fantasy story *The Maker of Moons* by Robert W. Chambers. In the story, Yian is a city on a great river having a thousand bridges, where the flower-scented air is filled with the music of silver bells. It is obviously not a city in our dimension of reality, since it is said to be located across the seven seas and on a river longer than the distance from the Earth to the Moon. Lovecraft was a fan of Chambers' work and sometimes referred to characters and places in Chambers' stories. He named a "forbidden city" on the plateau of Leng in honor of Yian, calling it Yian-Ho. In *The*

Diary of Alonzo Typer Lovecraft described it as "that lost and forbidden city of countless eons whose place may not be told."

(*The Whisperer in Darkness; Through the Gates of the Silver Key; The Diary of Alonzo Typer*)

Xari

A frigid river that flows through the valley of Narthos, which has the town of Sinara on its southern slope. Further downstream is the onyx-walled city of Jaren, a barracks for soldiers. Barges carry trading goods up and down the river. Further down, below Jaren, is a great cataract, and below that, the city or land of Stethelos.

(*The Quest of Iranon*)

Zimbabwe *

This is not the nation that presently bears this name, but a lost African empire that was spoken about along with such places as Atlantis and Mu. In *Medusa's Coil* reference is made to "forgotten sources of hidden truth in lost African civilizations—the great Zimbabwe." Lovecraft also referred to this lost kingdom in the poem "The Outpost," in which a king of Zimbabwe dreams of an alien city far to the west populated by the Fishers from Outside, amorphous beings half solid and half aether. S. T. Joshi wrote that Lovecraft had probably heard about Zimbabwe from Edward Lloyd Sechrist, who had actually visited the ruins of Zimbabwe (Joshi, *A Dreamer and a Visionary*, p. 279). The ruins of Great Zimbabwe are located near Fort Victoria, which has been renamed Masvingo, in the African country of Zimbabwe, formerly Rhodesia. The ancient city of Great Zimbabwe was constructed of large stones between the years 1100 and 1500. There are many smaller ruins of stone constructions in the region that are simply referred to as Zimbabwes.

(*Medusa's Coil;* "The Outpost")

Zobna

Land to the north of Lomar that was crushed beneath the advance of the great ice sheet that drove its inhabitants southward. The Zobnarian Fathers were noted for their great wisdom.

(*Polaris*)

The Key to the Fifth Gate

5th Astral Gate: Aries—The Ram

Sun passes through Aries: April 18—May 14

Constellation is represented by a reclining ram.

Right Pillar: Sheratan (Arabic name: *Al Sharatain*—The Signs). Astronomical designation: Beta Ari. Astrological nature: Mars-Saturn. Influence: acts of violence. Magnitude: 2.6. Color: pearl-white. Sun crosses: April 20. Location: left horn of the ram. Comments: Considered by the ancients in unison with Mesarthim, a star of magnitude 5 further down the left horn—the pair was known to the Persians as The Protecting Pair.

Left Pillar: Hamal. (Arabic name: *ras al-hamal*—Head of the Ram. Also called: El Nath (Arabic: *an-nath*—The Butting Horn). Astronomical designation: Alpha Ari. Astronomical nature: Mars-Saturn. Influence: unfortunate, associated with danger, violence, and injuries to the head. Magnitude: 2—slightly variable. Color: yellow. Sun crosses: April 25. Location: forehead of the ram. Comments: Two thousand years before the birth of Jesus, this star was located near the vernal equinox, and was considered to mark the beginning of spring.

The astral gate of Aries lies between the star of its right pillar, located on the left horn of the ram, and the star of its left pillar, on the forehead. The sun enters the gate around April 20 when it crosses the longitude of Sheratan, the star of the right pillar, and leaves the gate around April 25, when it crossed the star of the left pillar, Hamal. The transition of this narrow gate takes five days.

The key to the Fifth Gate opens the constellation Aries, allowing entry into the section of the walled city of the *Necronomicon* that contains the dwelling spaces of humanity. Use it for divining information or receiving dreams about the houses, villages, cities, and other places where human beings live and travel that are mentioned in Lovecraft's writings.

Seal of the Fifth Key on the Fifth Gate

Ritual of Opening Aries

Face the direction of the compass ruled by the Fifth Gate, which is southeast by south—that is, slightly to the right of the southeast point. Visualize the closed gate of the walled city before you just as though it were a real gate in an ancient walled city, expanding it in your imagination and drawing it nearer so that it is large enough for you to walk through. Take the time to create it on the astral level in full detail, being aware of all its minor imperfections and marks.

With the image of the gate sustained clearly in your mind and projected astrally toward the compass point southeast by south, speak the following invocation to Yog-Sothoth, taking care to insert those references that are specific to the Fifth Gate:

> Guardian of the Gate! Defender of the Door! Watcher of the Way! Who art the stout Lock, the slender Key, and the turning Hinge! Lord of All Transition, without whom there is no coming in or going out, I call thee! Keeper of the Threshold, whose dwelling place is between worlds, I summon thee! Yog-Sothoth, wise and great lord of the Old Ones, I invoke thee!
>
> By the authority of the dreaded name, Azathoth, that few dare speak, I charge thee, open to me the gateway of Aries the Ram that lies between the blazing pillar Sheratan on the right hand and the blazing pillar Hamal on the left hand. As the solar chariot [or, lunar chariot] crosses between these pillars, I enter the city of the *Necronomicon* through its Fifth Gate. Selah!

Visualize the key of the Fifth Gate in your right hand some six inches long and made of cast silver. Feel its weight, texture, and shape as you hold it. Extend your right arm and use the key as a pointer to project upon the surface of the gate the seal of the key, which should be visualized to burn on the gate in a line of white spiritual fire. Point with the astral key at the center of the gate and speak the words:

> In the name of Azathoth, Ruler of Chaos, by the power of Yog-Sothoth, Lord of Portals, the Fifth Gate is opened!

Visualize the gate unlocking and opening inward of its own accord upon a shadowed space beyond. On the astral level, walk through the gateway and stand in the dark space beyond. Focus your mind upon the house, church, library, village, city, or other human place of habitation related to the mythos that you wish to investigate and open yourself to receive communications or impressions from within the place. In a more general sense, the ritual of the Fifth Gate may be used to scry the history or psychically read the atmosphere of any house, road, plaza, or ruin where men live, or once lived.

After fulfilling the purpose for which this gate was opened, conclude the ritual by astrally passing out through the gate and visualizing it to close. Draw the seal of the Fifth Key on the surface of the gate with the astral key in your hand, and mentally cause it to lock itself shut, as it was at the beginning of the ritual. Speak the words:

> By the power of Yog-Sothoth, and authority of the supreme name Azathoth, I close and seal the Fifth Gate. This ritual is well and truly ended.

Allow the image of the gate to grow pale in your imagination and fade to nothingness before you turn away from the ritual direction.

The Sixth Gate

Sixth Gate
Alien Dwellings

There is more to the world of the Necronomicon mythos than meets the eye. The Sixth Gate open on the secret and hidden places where dwell monstrous creatures and forgotten alien races. They are all around us, even though we usually pass through life without ever becoming aware of their existence. Lovecraft believed that what we consider to be the real world is nothing more than a comforting illusion, a mask on the face of reality that prevents us from seeing the horror that lies beneath. As he wrote at the beginning of his story, the *Call of Cthulhu*:

> The most merciful thing in the world, I think, is the inability of the human mind to correlate all its contents. We live on a placid island of ignorance in the midst of black seas of infinity, and it was not meant that we should voyage far. The sciences, each straining in its own direction, have hitherto harmed us little; but some day the piecing together of dissociated knowledge will open up such terrifying vistas of reality, and of our frightful position therein, that we shall either go mad from the revelation or flee from the light into the peace and safety of a new dark age.

The practical consequence of this philosophy for Lovecraft's fiction is that there is always something lurking just below the threshold of perception, and those unfortunate individuals who become aware of it are never quite the same afterward. Once opened, Pandora's box cannot be shut, nor can the jinni be forced back into the lamp. Lovecraft placed these off-stage horrors in various plausible locations that allowed them to be present in our world, but undetected by the greater mass of mankind.

Many of the great alien races he fixed in the Earth's distant past. The mythos contains an entire history of the various species that rose to prominence on this planet before the ascent of *Homo sapiens*. They are assigned various geographical regions of the world for their own territories. Cthulhu and his spawn occupied the newly formed volcanic landmasses of the Pacific Ocean. The Elder Things at various times inhabited all parts of the lands and seas, but eventually were concentrated in their great stone city in Antarctica. The primary city of the Yithians, Pnakotus, occupied what is presently the Great Sandy Desert of Australia. The Mi-Go were at one time concentrated on the lost continent of Mu. The race of K'n-yan occupied the Earth's surface before retreating into their blue-litten cavern land. Each of these and other alien species came to prominence at one period in the distant past, and then declined in power. They did not vanish completely, however, but merely retreated to places of security, where they wait the opportunity to emerge and dominate once more.

The horrors of the real world of the present time, beneath the mask of illusion we have placed upon it for our own peace of mind, are to be found under the ground, under the seas, and behind dimensional portals to other levels of reality. The remains of their cities lie in wastelands of ice or sand, or steaming jungles, or beneath the waves. Their catacombs and caverns and tunnels riddle the body of the Earth, sometimes stacked one atop the other like worm-tracks in an apple.

Perhaps the most horrifying of Lovecraft's realizations is that alien creatures are all around us, just slightly out of phase with our time and space, but forever waiting for their opportunity to pass over the boundary of the known and destroy us. In the story *The Beyond*, Crawford Tillinghast invents a machine that awakens dormant human senses by stimulating the pineal gland, allowing humans to see what has always been all around them, but had mercifully passed unnoticed. What is more chilling is that the rays of the machine allow these terrifying creatures to see us. Once aware of us, they are able to do us harm.

Lovecraft, speaking through his character Tillinghast, wrote: "Our means of receiving impressions are absurdly few, and our notions of surrounding objects infinitely narrow. We see things only as we are constructed to see them, and can gain no idea of their absolute nature. With five feeble senses we pretend to comprehend the boundlessly complex cosmos, yet other beings with wider, stronger, or different range of senses might not only see very differently the things we see, but might see and study whole worlds of matter, energy, and life which lie close at hand yet can never be detected with the senses we have."

This is the ultimate horror to contemplate—that malignant alien things intent on our destruction are not safely locked away beneath the earth or the oceans, but are with us this very instant, all around us, passing through our very flesh, and we can never truly escape from them because we share the same space and time. Something similar to this terrifying realization was achieved by Lovecraft's close friend, Frank Belknap Long, in his story *The Hounds of Tindalos*. Once the Hounds catch the scent of their human prey, they never cease to pursue, and can materialize anywhere at any time out of the angles of space itself.

The only refuge lies in blissful obliviousness. Those who refuse to look when given a chance to see, who close their eyes and resolutely turn their thoughts away from the harsher colors of reality, remain comparatively safe. Their materialistic worldview serves as an armor of ignorance. Danger threatens the few who cannot contain their curiosity, or slack their thirst for knowledge. They explore lost cities and buried tombs, they seek out and read forbidden books, or they simply become aware of things that were always there, waiting to be noticed.

Antarctica *

Among the mountains on a high plateau of Antarctica is located the last great city of the crinoid species known as the Elder Things. It was abandoned when the crinoids retreated from the intensifying cold to a warmer subterranean sea beneath the city. In his story *At the Mountains of Madness* Lovecraft located this plateau at the coordinates "Latitude 76° 15', Longitude 113° 10' E." He hinted that it might be the true location of the fabled plateau of Leng, which most mythologists placed in Central Asia. There is the intimation that beyond the deserted cyclopean city and the mountains, which are higher than those of the Himalaya range, lies something even vaster and more sinister that may be what is referred to in the *Pnakotic Fragments* as Kadath in the Cold Waste.

(*At the Mountains of Madness*)

Atlaanat

An ancient place referred to by Randolph Carter as, "hoary Atlaanat, of which few even dare speak." In this place thought was given tangible form and substance by adepts.

(*Through the Gates of the Silver Key*)

City of the Elder Things

The vast city of the crinoid race known as the Elder Things, their final citadel on the surface of this planet, is located in Antarctica on a high plateau amid the peaks of a mountain range. It is mostly buried under glacial ice, but its taller towers and walls are visible. They are of massive dimensions, and show an architecture like nothing else on earth. The city is constructed from "prodigious blocks of dark primordial slate, schist, and sandstone—blocks in many cases as large as 4 x 6 x 8 feet." Elsewhere, the walls are cut from the matrix of the rock of the mountains itself, so that the city seems to grow organically out of the mountains. It is a jumble of truncated cones, terraces, pyramids, cylinders, cubes, and needle-like spires grouped in clusters of five, all linked by arched bridges that once spanned the air, but which are now locked within the ice. Many of the blocks of stone lie scattered where they were pushed by the moving glacier, and all surfaces are weathered by millions of years of erosion. Once there were domes in the city, but these have fallen in upon themselves. The coming of the cold and the ice to Antarctica forced the crinoids to abandon their city and seek refuge in the waters of a warm subterranean sea that lies beneath the mountains.

The mathematics student of Miskatonic University, Walter Gilman, was transported through a dimensional portal by the witch Keziah Mason to a very similar city on a planet with three suns of different colors in the sky. This city of the Elder Things flourishes in another star system, but whether it exists in the present or the distant past is impossible to know. The climate is tropical, and is probably the climate the crinoids find most suited to their physiology, even though they can withstand prolonged periods of freezing.

(*At the Mountains of Madness; The Dreams in the Witch House*)

Grħ-yan

A range of low hills on the plain of Nath in blue-litten K'n-yan. They conceal the entrance to a forgotten tunnel leading from subterranean K'n-yan to the surface of the earth.

(*The Mound*)

Hell's Acres

A very rough region of deep canyons and sharp hills seven miles to the south of Hampden, Idaho, part of the Blue Mountain Forest Reserve. There is a local superstition that the area is haunted, but no one seems to know by what. The Nez Perce Indians have shunned it for countless generations. They say it is the playground for giant devils from the Outside. It is to a hill in Hell's Acres that the shadow from the starless gulf, the coming of which was foretold in the *Chronicle of Nath*, manifested in the form of a tree in the year 1938, which was the Year of the Black Goat.

(*The Tree on the Hill*)

Ib

A gray stone city in the land of Mnar that was located on the shore of a vast and misty green lake fed by no river or stream. The inhuman inhabitants of Ib are described on the brick cylinders of Kadatheron as having been green in color, with "bulging eyes, pouting, flabby lips, and curious ears." They were voiceless. It is also written that they descended in a mist from the moon one night along with their city and their lake. They worshipped an idol of sea-green stone carved in the likeness of Bokrug, the great water-lizard. The papyrus of Ilarnek records that when this inhuman race discovered the making of fire, they thereafter worshipped Bokrug by kindling sacred flames on ceremonial occasions. Within the city were strange sculptures on gray monoliths.

How long Ib endured alone in the land of Mnar is not known. Lovecraft wrote that it was "many eons." Around eleven thousand years ago, a nomadic race of human beings built the city of Sarnath not far from Ib on the lakeshore, to exploit rich deposits of minerals in the area. The proud men of Sarnath came to hate and despise the inhabitants of Ib. One day they attacked Ib, killed all its inhabitants and pushed their corpses into the lake, along with their gray sculpted monoliths, and then cast down the city. Sarnath prospered for a thousand years, but on the thousandth anniversary of the destruction of Ib, it was destroyed so that not a trace remained, not even the foundation stones.

(*The Doom That Came to Sarnath*)

K'n-yan

An inhabited land within a great cavern deep beneath the surface of Oklahoma. It is known as blue-litten K'n-yan because it is illuminated by a natural blue radiance. The name is also written as "Xinaián."

(*The Whisperer in Darkness; The Mound*)

Leng

The location of Leng is never specified with precision in Lovecraft's stories. It is a sinister desert plateau in Central Asia, or perhaps in Antarctica. It lies in the dreamlands, but may also exist in our world as well. It is a place not quite of this reality. In the dreamlands, Leng is on a plateau located near to the land of Inquanok, but on the other side of a range of high mountains that acts as a protective barrier against the hated plateau. In the story *The Hound*, "inaccessible Leng" is placed in Central Asia on the authority of the *Necronomicon*, wherein is said to be described a corpse-eating cult of Leng.

In *At the Mountains of Madness*, Leng is said to be described in the *Necronomicon*. It is characterized as "evilly fabled" and "evilly famed." The narrator of the story, geology professor of Miskatonic University, William Dyer, commented "Leng, wherever in space or time it might brood, was not a region I would care to be in or near." The story *Out of the Aeons* referred to the "abhorred plateau of Leng" as one ancient site for the worship of the god Ghatanothoa. Randolph Carter spoke in *The Dream-Quest of Unknown Kadath* of the "horrible stone villages on the icy desert plateau of Leng, which no healthy folk visit and whose evil fires are seen at night from afar."

In the dreamlands, Leng is the home of a race of squat, horned humanoids who were conquered by the moon-beasts, and who now serve them as slaves on their black galleys that ply the waters of the dreamland seas, and fly between the earth and the Moon. It is the location of a prehistoric stone monastery in which dwells in solitude the High-Priest Not to be Described, who wears a yellow silken mask to conceal his features. Somewhere on Leng is the forbidden city of Yian-Ho, of which a yogi known to Harley Warren once boasted that he was the only living human being ever to have visited it.

(*Celephaïs; The Hound; The Dream-Quest of Unknown Kadath; At the Mountains of Madness; Out of the Aeons; The Whisperer in Darkness; Through the Gates of the Silver Key; Fungi from Yuggoth*)

Nameless City

A lost and all but forgotten alien city in the great Arabian desert known as the Empty Space. In *The Descendant* the belief is expressed that no man has ever beheld it. This was an error. In *The Nameless City* a man enters the ruins of the city, which he describes as poking like parts of a corpse above the sands in a dry valley. It is immensely ancient and was buried beneath the sand before the first foundation stones of Babylon were laid. The Bedouin of the desert fear it as accursed and avoid the valley it is rumored to occupy. The mad Arab poet Abdul Alhazred, author of the *Necronomicon*, is said to have dreamed of this city the night he penned his enigmatic and most celebrated couplet:

> That is not dead which can eternal lie,
> And with strange aeons death may die.

The explorer compares the city to Sarnath, fabled to exist at the early awakening of the human race, as a habitation equally mysterious and ancient. When he crawls into an opening of the buried city, he finds that the roofs of the rooms are very low, and the furniture seems unsuited to the human body. Eventually he comes to realize that the inhabitants of the city were not human beings, but intelligent lizard-like creatures that predated the evolution of mankind. Countless aeons ago, before Africa arose from the ocean, the nameless city was a thriving seaport. Gradually the sea withdrew, and the desert sands came. Its inhabitants cut passages in the rock beneath its base, deeper and deeper into the earth, until they came to a great cavern, where, it is hinted they continue to dwell.

(*At the Mountains of Madness; The Descendant; The Nameless City*)

Nith

A gorse-grown plain in the blue-litten subterranean land of K'n-yan.

(*The Mound*)

N'kai

A land inside a cavern deep beneath the surface of the ground of Oklahoma that is known as black, lightless N'kai because it is unilluminated, in contrast with red-litten Yoth, a similar cavern world above it that is illuminated by a reddish glow, and blue-litten K'n-yan, a cavern world above Yoth that is illuminated by a bluish glow.

(*The Whisperer in Darkness; The Mound*)

Pnakotus

The chief city of the time-spanning Great Race of Yith, the immensely ancient ruins of which lie beneath the Great Sandy Desert of Australia.

(*The Shadow Out of Time*)

R'lyeh

The sunken city of Cthulhu and his spawn lies deep beneath the southern Pacific Ocean, at the map coordinates S. Latitude 47° 9', W. Longitude 123° 43'. It is built of massive blocks of greenish stone, the architecture a maddening mingling of non-Euclidian angles. Lovecraft wrote in *Medusa's Coil*, "The geometry of the whole thing is crazy—one gets the acute and obtuse angles all mixed up." The highest ground in the city, the summit of a mountain, is crowned by an enormous carved obelisk, much larger and thicker than any fashioned by the Egyptians. During the period when Cthulhu contested for dominance of the primordial Earth, the vast city of R'lyeh occupied a large volcanic island. When the pattern of the stars in the heavens became noxious to his kind, Cthulhu and his spawn sealed themselves into stone houses on this island to await the time when the stars should "come right" once again. The vault where great Cthulhu lies dreaming is on the mountaintop, at the base of the obelisk.

In his death-like sleep, Cthulhu was able to rule his worshippers around the globe by sending forth his thought commands, but an unforeseen disaster occurred—the island of R'lyeh sank beneath the waves of the ocean, and the miles of water above it cut off the dreaming mind of Cthulhu from his followers. At rare intervals, upheavals occur in the sea floor, R'lyeh rises just high enough so that the obelisk and the stone tomb at its base are above the waves, and Cthulhu once more reaches out with his mind to his faithful cults, but before they can voyage to his island to release him from his stone prison—for he cannot release himself—R'lyeh falls once more beneath the waves.

(*At the Mountains of Madness; The Call of Cthulhu; Medusa's Coil; The Man of Stone; The Shadow Over Innsmouth; The Whisperer in Darkness; Through the Gates of the Silver Key*)

Stygian sea

A subterranean sea deep beneath Antarctica to which the remnants of the crinoid Elder Things retreated to escape the increasing cold and ice that covered their great city.

(*At the Mountains of Madness*)

Tsath

Great city of blue-litten K'n-yan, it occupies an upland in a vast subterranean cavern and is the home of an alien race that resemble in facial features and skin pigmentation the Plains Indians. It is said to have a "million golden minarets" and to be overhung by a perpetual gray haze. The name derives from the cult of Tsathoggua, which for a time ruled in K'n-yan.

(*The Mound*)

Valusia

Ancient land inhabited by a reptile race.

(*The Shadow Out of Time*)

Vaults of Zin

Chambers below the largest ruined city of red-litten Yoth, a land contained in a great cavern beneath the equally vast cavern of blue-litten K'n-yan. The vaults contain manuscripts and carvings connected with the lost race of Yoth, which Lovecraft indicates was quadrupedal and reptilian. The strange half-human beasts ridden by the humanoid race dwelling in K'n-yan may be the descendants of the reptilian race of Yoth, after having been cross-bred with the human cattle of the race of K'n-yan. Within the Vaults of Zin are depictions of the temples that house the idols of the toad-god Tsathoggua.

The Vaults of Zin are also part of the dreamlands, where they are describes as an underground cavern that has its entrance through a large cave in the cemetery next to the Tower of Koth. The Vaults of Zin in the dreamlands are inhabited by the cannibal ghasts, repulsive creatures who die in strong light, although they can endure twilight for several hours at a time. They leap about on long hind legs like kangaroos. The ghasts sometimes emerge from the cave entrance to hunt the gugs and ghouls while they sleep.

There are a number of persons and places in Lovecraft's fiction that exist both in the real world and simultaneously in the dreamlands. Kadath is perhaps the most significant of these—it is both a mountain in Antarctica and a mountain in the dreamlands. There is no reason why a place cannot be in the real world, yet be echoed in a distorted and fantastic form in the dreamlands. Material things has astral shadows, and exist simultaneously both in the material world and the astral world.

(*The Mound; The Dream-Quest of Unknown Kadath*)

Yaddith-Gho

A great mountain situated in the middle of the kingdom of K'naa, on the ancient sunken continent of Mu. It is surmounted by a fortress of Cyclopean stones older than mankind that was erected prior to the beginnings of terrestrial life by the spawn of Yuggoth (Pluto) when they settled the Earth. This alien race was either the Mi-Go or the species that inhabited Yuggoth prior to the coming to the Mi-Go—Lovecraft does not actually name the race from Yuggoth that built the fortress, and Yuggoth had two intelligent races, the Mi-Go and an earlier race.

In the crypts beneath the fortress on Yaddith-Gho, a demonic being named Ghatanothoa continued to survive aeons after the alien spawn of Yuggoth had perished from the earth. He survives there still, beneath the waves.

(*Out of the Aeons*)

Y'ha-nthlei

The undersea city of the Deep Ones that lies in the floor of an ocean trench off Devil Reef, just outside of the harbor mouth of the New England port of Innsmouth. It is only one of many such undersea cities. Lovecraft described it as "Cyclopean and many-columned Y'ha-nthlei." In February of 1928 the United States Navy sent a deep-diving submarine into the waters of the abyss beyond the reef, where it discharged downward a spread of torpedoes and damaged the city, but failed to destroy it.

(*The Shadow Over Innsmouth*)

Yian-Ho

A city of Leng, described in *The Diary of Alonzo Typer* as "that lost and hidden city wherein brood eon-old secrets." The wizard Claes van der Heyl claimed in his manuscript book to have been the only man to have visited Yian-Ho in the flesh. From that forbidden city he brought back a padlock and a key, which were to be used to lock behind a specially constructed door the hellish thing that he and his future descendants had been commanded to find.

The strange coffin-shaped clock with four hands in the possession of Randolph Carter's executor, Etienne-Laurent de Marigny, was taken away from Yian-Ho by a yogi who was sometimes mentioned by the unfortunate Harley Warren. The yogi is said to have boasted that he and he alone "among living men" had been to Yian-Ho. Since Claes van der Heyl was long dead at the time the yogi lived, it is possible that both his boast and that of the yogi were accurate statements.

In *The Whisperer in Darkness* there is mention made of Yian amidst a list of other potent names, but it seems likely that Yian-Ho was intended, since Leng follows immediately after it in the list.

(*The Diary of Alonzo Typer; The Gates of the Silver Key; The Whisperer in Darkness*)

Yoth

An inhabited land deep beneath the surface of the Earth in a vast cavern. Called red-litten Yoth because it is illuminated by a natural red radiance.

(*The Whisperer in Darkness; The Mound*)

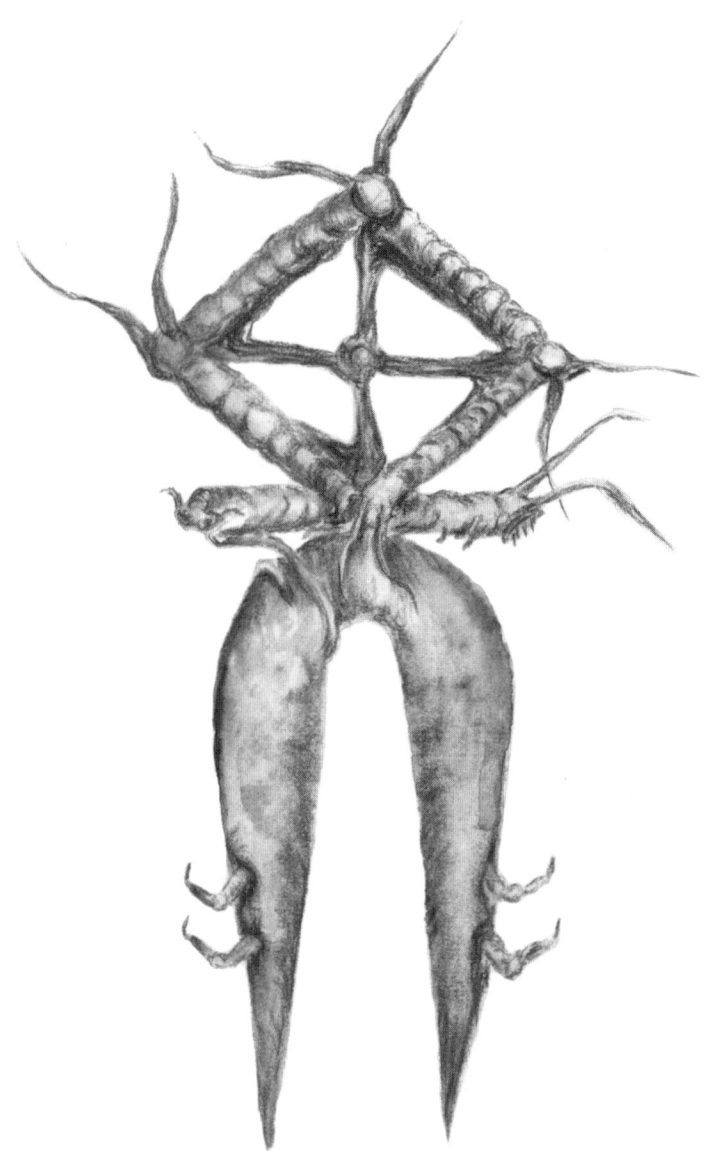

The Key to the Sixth Gate

6th Astral Gate: Taurus—The Bull

Sun passes through Taurus: May 14—June 21

Constellation is represented by the upper body of a bull emerging from the waves.

Right Pillar: Aldebaran (Arabic: *al-dabaran*—The Follower). Astronomical designation: Alpha Tauri. Astrological nature: Mars. Influence: good fortune, honor and wealth, but with danger of a fall from grace. Magnitude: .9—irregular variable. Color: rose-red. Sun crosses: June 1. Location: the southern eye of the bull. Comments: Associated by the ancient Persians with the vernal equinox, it is one of the four royal stars of the Persians.

Left Pillar: El Nath (Arabic: *al-natih*—The Butting One). Astronomical designation: Beta Tauri. Astrological nature: Mars. Influence: fortune and promotion through cleverness, but a danger of quarrels and the enmity of others. Magnitude: 1.7—a double star. Color: white. Sun crosses: June 13. Location: tip of the northern horn. Comments: Threat of violence is minor.

The astral gate of Taurus lies between the star of its right pillar, located on the southern eye of the bull, and the star of its left pillar, which occupies the tip of the northern horn. The sun enters the gate around June 1 when it crosses the longitude of Aldebaran, the star of the right pillar, and leaves the gate around June 13, when it crossed the star of the left pillar, El Nath. The transition of this gate takes twelve days.

The key to the Sixth Gate opens the constellation Taurus, allowing entry into the section of the walled city of the *Necronomicon* that contains the dwelling places on the planet Earth of the alien beings described in the mythos. Use it for divining information or receiving dreams about alien cities, caverns, tombs, and ruins mentioned in Lovecraft's writings that are hidden in this world.

Seal of the Sixth Key on the Sixth Gate

Ritual of Opening Taurus

Face the direction of the compass ruled by the Sixth Gate, which is south by east—that is, slightly to the left of due south. Visualize the closed gate of the walled city before you just as though it were a real gate in an ancient walled city, and make sure that it is large enough for you to walk through. Take the time to create it on the astral level in precise detail.

With the image of the gate clear in your mind and projected upon the astral level to the direction south by east, speak the following invocation to Yog-Sothoth, taking care to insert those references that are specific to the Sixth Gate:

Sixth Gate: Alien Dwellings

> Guardian of the Gate! Defender of the Door! Watcher of the Way! Who art the stout Lock, the slender Key, and the turning Hinge! Lord of All Transition, without whom there is no coming in or going out, I call thee! Keeper of the Threshold, whose dwelling place is between worlds, I summon thee! Yog-Sothoth, wise and great lord of the Old Ones, I invoke thee!
>
> By the authority of the dreaded name, Azathoth, that few dare speak, I charge thee, open to me the gateway of Taurus the Bull that lies between the blazing pillar Aldebaran on the right hand and the blazing pillar El Nath on the left hand. As the solar chariot [or, lunar chariot] crosses between these pillars, I enter the city of the *Necronomicon* through its Sixth Gate. Selah!

Visualize the key of the Sixth Gate in your right hand some six inches long and made of cast iron. Feel its weight, texture, and shape as you hold it. Extend your right arm and use the key as a pointer to project upon the surface of the gate the seal of the key, which should be visualized to burn on the gate in a line of white spiritual fire. Point with the astral key at the center of the gate and speak the words:

> In the name of Azathoth, Ruler of Chaos, by the power of Yog-Sothoth, Lord of Portals, the Sixth Gate is opened!

Visualize the gate unlocking and opening inward of its own accord upon a shadowed space beyond. On the astral level, walk through the gateway and stand in the dark space beyond. Focus your mind upon the hidden places on or within this planet where the alien creatures of the mythos dwell and open yourself to receive impressions of these realms. In a more general sense, the ritual of the Sixth Gate may be used to scry any alien habitation or residing place of spirits within the earthly physical realm and its astral reflection. For example, it would be the gate to scry the lands of fairies.

After fulfilling the purpose for which this gate was opened, conclude the ritual by astrally passing out through the gate and visualizing it to close. Draw the seal of the Sixth Key on the surface of the gate with the astral key in your hand, and mentally cause it to lock itself shut, as it was at the beginning of the ritual. Speak the words:

> By the power of Yog-Sothoth, and authority of the supreme name Azathoth, I close and seal the Sixth Gate. This ritual is well and truly ended.

Allow the image of the gate to grow pale in your imagination and fade to nothingness before you turn away from the ritual direction.

The Seventh Gate

Seventh Gate
The Dreamlands

Lovecraft's dreamlands are in many ways his greatest creation. Not only are they described with a richness of detail and verisimilitude unmatched by his descriptions of more mundane settings, but their very concept challenges our usual way of looking at reality. A significant part of Lovecraft's fiction is based on the notion that men lead two lives, one while they are awake, and another while they sleep and dream. Lovecraft proposed in his dream cycle of stories that dreams are not mere fantasies lacking permanence and tangibility, but are a real world that we enter during sleep. More than this, he advanced the daring speculation that the time we spend in the dreamlands is more important than the time we spend in the waking world.

This opinion that human beings lead double lives, one while awake and the other while asleep, was not unique to Lovecraft, but was also held to be true by Madame Blavatsky and her Theosophists, who believed that more developed souls assist the evolution of less evolved souls during dreams, most of them without ever knowing the nature of the work they perform during sleep. Similarly, those helped in their dreams awake with no conscious awareness of the lessons they have learned.

Lovecraft set forth his philosophy of the dreamlands at the beginning of his 1919 story, *Beyond the Wall of Sleep*. Who can doubt but that these reflections on dreams and dreaming are a true expression of Lovecraft's own thoughts?

> I have often wondered if the majority of mankind ever pause to reflect upon the occasionally titanic significance of dreams, and of the obscure world to which they belong. Whilst the greater number of our nocturnal visions are perhaps no more than faint and fantastic reflections of our waking experiences—Freud to the contrary with his puerile symbolism—there are still a certain remainder whose immundane and ethereal character permit of no ordinary interpretation, and whose vaguely exciting and disquieting effect suggests possible minute glimpses into a sphere of mental existence no less important than physical life, yet separated from that life by an all but

> impassable barrier. From my experience I cannot doubt but that man, when lost to terrestrial consciousness, is indeed sojourning in another and uncorporeal life of far different nature from the life we know, and of which only the slightest and most indistinct memories linger after waking. From those blurred and fragmentary memories we may infer much, yet prove little. We may guess that in dreams life, matter, and vitality, as the earth knows such things, are not necessarily constant; and that time and space do not exist as our waking selves comprehend them. Sometimes I believe that this less material life is our truer life, and that our vain presence on the terraqueous globe is itself the secondary or merely virtual phenomenon.

Lovecraft distinguished between chaotic, trivial dreams that are generated by the memories of random waking incidents, and more coherent dreams that carry with them a sense of significance and meaning. Most of us have experienced this firsthand. There are a small minority of our dreams that stand out with greater clarity and carry with them a sense of importance. They seem in some indefinable way more real than the usual dreams. Their settings and characters are so clear, and often so unlike anything we have experienced or would ever choose to invent, that the dreams leave us wondering about their source. Lovecraft dreamed such dreams more frequently than the average human being, and some of them he dreamed repeatedly.

These repeating dreams varied in their particular details, but the setting and main characters were the same from one dream to the next. One such repeating dream that left a life-long impression on his psyche was one he dreamed in early childhood, in which he found himself snatched out of his bed and carried high aloft by faceless black creatures with bat wings and barbed tails, who threatened to drop him onto a landscape far below that consisted of needle-sharp mountain peaks. Lovecraft called these things the night-gaunts. He succeeded in partially exorcising the terror they aroused in him when he made them allies to the dreamer Randolph Carter in his epic novel *The Dream-Quest of Unknown Kadath*, which tragically remained unpublished during Lovecraft's lifetime.

"Dreamer" was Lovecraft's term for a person who could enter specific dream landscapes and cityscapes at will, retain consciousness and a sense of self while exploring these dream places, and retain a memory of them after waking. Today we would call such a person a "lucid dreamer," but that term was not common in Lovecraft's period. Lucid dreaming is a form of astral projection that occurs during sleep. Randolph Carter, an idealized portrait of the way Lovecraft wished to see himself, and a vehicle by which Lovecraft was able to enter into and actively participate in the unfolding of his own stories, was such a dreamer whose skill in dreaming was unsurpassed by any other living human being.

Dreamers such as Carter are not only able to enter the dreamlands and explore them, but can create entire cities there through repeated dreams. For example, the dreamer Iranon dreamed the city of Aira, Kuranes dreamed Celephaïs into existence, and Carter dreamed a certain city that was based on his boyhood memories of New England. These cities persist in the dreamlands as they are discovered and experienced by other dreamers. The ability to create cities and such things as houses in the dreamlands is a strong indication that they astral. The mind has the power to create and shape astral substance.

The dreamlands of Earth are those surrounding our planet that are visited by human beings and other residents of our world during sleep, while their corporeal bodies remain in the physical world. Other planets in orbit around other stars also have their own dreamlands. The Moon, being quite near the Earth by astronomical measures, is a part of our dreamlands, or at least in contact with them. Black galleys sail between the dreamlands and the far side of the Moon, and the cats of Earth are able to leap from the rooftops of the dreamlands to the Moon. The dreamlands are a vast place, perhaps larger in total area than the physical surface of the Earth. They have more than one level, and they extend off the edge of the world, which is flat in the dreamlands.

Many ancient kingdoms with great cities, peopled with numerous races not all of whom are human, occupy the river valleys, deserts, and mountain ranges of the dreamlands. The plateau of Leng, which may have its correspondence in the physical world in a high mountain plateau in Antarctica, is represented in the dreamlands as is the mountain of the gods, Kadath in the Cold Waste. The seas of the dreamlands, are crossed by ships that carry goods from port to port, and from islands to the mainland. The edge of the western sea is marked by a great cataract that falls eternally into the gray void between the Basalt Pillars of the West, which correspond symbolically to the Pillars of Hercules of the waking world. The black galleys of the moon-beasts have the ability to sail between the Basalt Pillars and through the aether to the far side of the Moon, where the moon-beasts make their home.

The dreamlands lie beneath the level of common dreams that lack any important significance. To travel from common dreaming to the dreamlands, it is necessary to enter light sleep and descend a staircase of seventy steps, and then pass through the cavern of flame that is presided over by the bearded priests Nasht and Kaman-Thah. Within the depths of the cavern are 700 steps that lead down to the Gate of Deeper Slumber, beyond which lies the beginning of the dreamlands, a region known as the Enchanted Wood.

Below the surface of the dreamlands is a darker underworld filled with horrifying monsters and ever-present dangers, to be traversed only by the bravest of dreamers. It represented for Lovecraft the dark depths of his nightmares, which he could in his stories order, limit, and control. In *The Dream-Quest of Unknown Kadath*, Randolph Carter enters this dark zone of the dreamlands and emerges with allies in the form of the race of ghouls, who help him fulfill his quest for Kadath.

A recurring theme of Lovecraft's dreamland tales is the desire of his characters to leave the waking world and remain in the dreamlands permanently. Time passes at a different rate in the dreamlands, so that in a single night a dreamer can experience months or even years, without growing any older. However, to remain in the dreamlands forever it is necessary to either die in the flesh, or undergo a kind of physical transition to the astral plane in which the body vanishes from the waking world. The latter event seems to have happened to the artist Richard Upton Pickman, who disappeared from Boston and became the king of the ghouls in the dreamlands.

It might be argued that Lovecraft's stories of the dreamlands are not a part of his mythos, but the *Necronomicon* is mentioned in dream stories as well as the more commonly recognized mythos stories, and the dream stories contain figures and places from the mythos, such as Nyarlathotep and the plateau of Leng. Characters such as Randolph Carter appear in both stories of the dreamlands, and stories universally recognized as of the mythos. Indeed, there is such a cross-fertilization between the dream stories and the stories of the Old Ones and their kin, that it is impossible to separate them. Lovecraft presented both types of tales as belonging to a single unified reality. In my opinion the dreamland stories are a part of the Necronomicon mythos and should not be divided from it.

Aira

City of marble and beryl located beside the glassy and curving river Nithra, where the wandering poet Iranon asserted that his father had once ruled as king. The city contains palaces with golden domes and painted walls that are surrounded by gardens with flowing fountains in the midst of reflecting pools. Upon the crest of a central hill stands a citadel with an open observation terrace from which the entire city can be viewed. Beyond the walls of the city in the valley it occupies are groves and fertile fields. A brook called the Kra crosses the valley from the hills in a series of waterfalls. The sheltering hills are forested with brightly colored yath-trees. This city was dreamed by the beggar boy Iranon, who searched for it in vain for the remainder of his long life, at last committing suicide when he was told it was only a dream.

(*The Quest of Iranon*)

Aran

A snow-capped mountain in the land of Ooth-Nargai, not far from the city of Celephaïs. Its lower slopes are covered in gingko-trees.

(*The Dream-Quest of Unknown Kadath*)

Baharna

Mighty port city of the great island Oriab. Ships are guided into its harbor at night between the twin beacons Thon and Thal. The wharves of made of porphyry, and the city rises steeply from them in a series of stone terraces. The flights of steps that connect these terraces are over-arched by buildings and bridges. Beneath the city is a canal that leads to the lake of Yath. On the far shore of the lake are the ruins of an ancient and unremembered city that was built of clay bricks.

(*The Dream-Quest of Unknown Kadath*)

Basalt Pillars

The Basalt Pillars of the West are the dreamlands equivalent to the Pillars of Hercules. They mark the end of the known ocean. Beyond them the sea falls over a great cataract into a void—what is in the waking world only an ancient myth is in the dreamlands a reality. The black galleys sail between them and into the aether on their voyages to the far side of the Moon.

(*The Dream-Quest of Unknown Kadath*)

Camorin

A place of "fragrant groves" containing aloe and sandalwood, similar to what is said in legend of the forests of unknown Cathuria.

(*The White Ship*)

Cathuria

An unvisited land known only in legend that lies beyond the "Basalt Pillars of the West." It is said to be the Land of Hope, where reside all perfect ideals. In it are said to be many groves and cities with splendid palaces. Its forests contain aloe and sandalwood, and are filled with birds. On its flowering mountainsides stand temples of pink marble. The cities of Cathuria are enclosed in walls of gold, and are paved with gold. Within the gardens of the cities are strange orchids and perfumed lakes. The dwellings are all palaces roofed with gold. They are built over canals of the sacred river Narg, which flows out from within the depths of the earth.

In contrast to these bucolic legends surrounding Cathuria, "wise dreamers" such as Randolph Carter know that the twin Basalt Pillars of the West are really the gates of a monstrous cataract where the oceans of dreamland drop into empty space toward other worlds and other stars, and ultimately to the voids beyond the known universe that are ruled by the daemon sultan Azathoth, where dance the blind and mindless Other Gods, whose soul and messenger is Nyarlathotep.

(*The White Ship; The Dream-Quest of Unknown Kadath*)

Cavern of Flame

Located near the beginning of the dreamlands that surround the Earth, it is accessed from light slumber by descending a stair of seventy steps. The bearded priests Nasht and Kaman-Thah preside over the temple in the cavern, which has a pillar of flame. Randolph Carter offered sacrifice in the temple, and consulted the priests about his intention to seek unknown Kadath in the Cold Waste. They advised strongly against it.

(*The Dream-Quest of Unknown Kadath*)

Celephaïs

A thriving port city located on the river Naraxa, in the valley of Ooth-Nargai near the shore of the Cerenerian Sea. Snow-capped Mount Aran rises not far distant, its lower slopes covered with a forest of gingko-trees. A great stone bridge spans the river near the bronze city gates on the landside, eastern approach. The city has a white marble wall dotted with bronze statues, above which the glittering minarets of the port are visible to those approaching from the sea. Its streets are paved with onyx. Low hills extend behind the port to the east, dotted with groves, flower gardens, cottages, and shrines. Beyond these low hills, the purple ridge of the higher Tanarian Hills marks the horizon. Noteworthy features within the city of interest to tourists are the turquoise temple of Nath-Horthath, and the Street of Pillars that runs from the gate to the seaside wall. The galleys sailing from its port do considerable trade throughout the dreamlands that ensures its continuing prosperity. Many merchants live in the city.

The city appeared as a vision in one of Lovecraft's dreams. In the dream, Lovecraft found himself flying over its rooftops and minarets, gazing down upon it. This was the inspiration for his story *Celephaïs*. In that story, the city was dreamed into existence by a nameless wandering pauper, a native of Cornwall and former indigent resident of

London who, after his death, became King Kuranes of Celephaïs. Randolph Carter had known Kuranes in life, and later visited him in Celephaïs, seeking advice about the finding of Kadath. Within the bounds of the city there is no passage of time.

(*Celephaïs; The Dream-Quest of Unknown Kadath*)

Cerenerian Sea

Called the "billowy Cerenerian Sea that leads to the sky" due to the way the clouds massed along its distant horizon make it appear that the sea and sky merge together without division.

(*Celephaïs*)

Dreamlands

This is the name Lovecraft gave to all those places intelligent beings visit during their dreams. Each planet has its own dreamlands. The dreamer Randolph Carter spent most of his time in the dreamlands of Earth, which are divided into two zones, the upper and lower dreamlands. The upper dreamlands are divided into regions of the east, south, west, and north. The lower dreamlands are called the underworld and are inhabited by ghouls and other creatures of darkness. Earth's dreamlands extend to the Moon, which has its inhabited region on the far side that is never seen by astronomers on this planet. Sometimes Lovecraft refers to the dreamlands of Earth in the plural, and sometimes he talks about Earth's dreamland in the singular. The dreamlands of Earth are subdivided into many regions, each occupied by its own peoples or inhuman races, and having its own cities and towns.

In *The Dream-Quest of Unknown Kadath*, the bearded priests Nasht and Kaman-Thah in the cavern of flame near the entrance to the dreamlands of Earth tell Carter that only three human souls have crossed the black gulfs to the dreamlands of other worlds, and of the three, two came back insane. The dreamlands of Earth are ruled "feebly" by the gods of Earth, who have "no power or habitation elsewhere." The gods of Earth are all those gods conceived by men, such as the gods of the ancient Egyptians and Greeks.

(*The Dream-Quest of Unknown Kadath*)

Dylath-Leen

Costal city of the dreamlands built of basalt, with tall and angular black towers that are visible from far out at sea. Its streets are dark and uninviting, and the many taverns near the wharves throng with foreign seamen, some of whom may not be native to this planet. Among them are the turbaned and almost-human men of Leng who trade rubies from the black galleys on behalf of their masters, the moon-beasts, who are not human in the slightest degree.

(*The Dream-Quest of Unknown Kadath*)

Great Abyss

A vast emptiness in the lower dreamland that lies below the dreamland city of Sarkomand, which is located in a valley below the plateau of Leng. In the midst of the ruins of this city is a circular plaza with "cyclopean pedestals whose sides were chiseled in fearsome bas-reliefs" upon which crouch two enormous winged lions carved from diorite, their heads twenty feet above the plaza. They are the guardians of the entrance to the Great Abyss. Between the lions, in a tiled court, a patch of darkness marks the black well that is the opening to the "black nitrous stairway," which winds down into the Abyss. The steps are narrow and steep, slippery and worn with the tread of countless aeons.

The Lord of the Great Abyss is "hoary and immemorial Nodens," a god who is beyond the control of Nyarlathotep. His servants are the faceless night-gaunts, "mindless guardians of the Great Abyss whom even the Great Ones fear, and who own not Nyarlathotep but hoary Nodens as their lord." In *The Strange High House in the Mist*, Lovecraft observed, "there are strange objects in the great abyss, and the seeker of dreams must take care not to stir up or meet the wrong ones."

(*The Dream-Quest of Unknown Kadath; The Strange High House in the Mist*)

Hatheg-Kla

A peak in the dreamlands crowned with an "aureole of mournful mist," located thirteen days journey deep in the stony desert beyond the village of Hatheg, from which it takes its name. Other villages nearer the foot of the remote mountain are Ulthar and Nir. Barzai the Wise, companion of Atal the priest of Ulthar, climbed it in an effort to watch the gods of Earth dancing on its summit by moonlight. He was drawn up into the sky screaming and never again seen. When the men of Hatheg, Ulthar, and Nir climbed the mountain to search for him, they found only a strange symbol some fifty cubits wide blasted into the naked rock of the summit.

(*The Dream-Quest of Unknown Kadath; The Other Gods*)

Ilek-Vad

A town in the dreamlands, built on top of a hollow glass cliff that overlooks a dark sea in which dwell the aquatic Gnorri. The town is noted for its many turrets, magnificent domes, and for the opal throne from which its king rules. At the zenith of its alien sky shines a single red star. It was rumored by an elderly eccentric of Providence, Rhode Island, that Randolph Carter became the king of Ilek-Vad. This elderly eccentric was Ward Phillips, a character undoubtedly intended to represent Lovecraft himself.

(*Through the Gates of the Silver Key; The Dream-Quest of Unknown Kadath; The Silver Key*)

Inquanok

This thriving port city with its many squat domes is noted for its onyx trade and its beauty. Much of the city is built of polished onyx. The streets are paved with this semi-precious stone. They radiate like the spokes of a wheel from the great central Temple of the Elder Ones, which is a massive tower with sixteen sides surmounted by a flattened dome from which rises a pinnacled belfry. The temple is set within a walled garden of seven gates, in the center of an enormous round city plaza. The gates are never closed but provide entry for the residents of the city to the wonders of the temple garden, which is filled with tiled lanes, quaint shrines to ancient lesser gods, fountains, pools, and basins designed to reflect the fires that burn in tripods around the base of the high dome atop the tower.

The other great wonder of the city is the palace of the Veiled King, set upon the crest of a hill behind massive fortification walls and buttresses. A visitor must climb a series of steep flights of steps to reach the onyx terraces and colonnaded walks within its garden. The garden is filled with flowering trees, lifelike statues in veined black marble, bronze urns, tripods, blossoming vines, fountains containing luminous fish, and miniature temples of iridescent singing birds atop stone columns. No visitor is permitted to enter the palace itself, the central dome of which is said to contain the father of all shantak-birds.

The architecture of the city is quaint with "inlaid doors and figured house-fronts, carven balconies and crystal-paned oriels." Some of the older houses near the waterfront bear signs of gold above their arched doorways, in honor of the lesser gods that guard the houses. There are many small plazas decorated with statues that are scattered throughout the city, and that afford the visitor breathtaking vistas across the domes and spires of its rooftops.

(*The Dream-Quest of Unknown Kadath*)

Kadath

Kadath in the Cold Waste is a lofty mountain located in the dreamlands. Before Randolph Carter succeeded in reaching it, no man had ever visited Kadath or had even known in which part of space it stood, or whether it was in Earth's dreamlands or those of another star system. On its summit is a great fortress of onyx in which dwell the gods of Earth's dreamlands, known as the Great Ones. Ruling over them is Nyarlathotep, emissary of the Other Gods who are the protectors of the gods of Earth, but also their masters. The summit is described in *The Dream-Quest of Unknown Kadath*:

> There were towers on that titan mountaintop; horrible domed towers in noxious and incalculable tiers and clusters beyond any dreamable workmanship of man; battlements and terraces of wonder and menace, all limned tiny and black and distant against the starry pshent that glowed malevolently at the uppermost rim of sight. Capping that most measureless of mountains was a castle beyond all mortal thought, and in it glowed the daemon-light.

Kadath is mentioned in the portion of the *Necronomicon* that is quoted in *The Dunwich Horror* concerning the Old Ones: "*Kadath in the cold waste hath known Them, and what man knows Kadath?*" It may have a material correspondent in Antarctica, as does the plateau of Leng. This is suggested in the story *At the Mountains of Madness*, where mention is made of the whispers concerning Kadath in the Pnakotic Manuscripts. It is explicitly stated in *The Mound*, where reference is made to a civilization "at the South Pole near the mountain Kadath."

(*The Dunwich Horror*; *The Dream-Quest of Unknown Kadath*; *Medusa's Coil*; *The Mound*; *The Other Gods*; *The Strange High House in the Mist*)

Kled

Called "orchid-heavy" Kled, a land through which flows the golden river Oukranos. It is a land of forgotten cities that contain palaces of veined ivory columns, where elephant caravans tramp through the flower-scented jungles. One of its cities is named Thran, and is noted for its gilded spires.

(*Through the Gates of the Silver Key*)

Koth, Tower of

A large black tower glimpsed in the dreamlands at twilight by some dreamers. It has an occult symbol in bas-relief fixed above the archway of its "colossal doorway" that is called the sign of Koth. Lovecraft used the term "fixed" in two places rather than "carved," so the symbol is probably on some sort of separate stone plaque or metal plate. In *The Case of Charles Dexter Ward*, Doctor Marinus Bicknell Willett encounters the symbol chiseled above a small door in the chambers deep beneath the farmland of Joseph Curwen. The Tower is located not far from the cave in the dreamlands that is the entrance to the Vaults of Zin. Its doors stand open, so that its shadowed interior is visible from the outside. Within, a great flight of stone steps leads upward to the upper dreamland and the enchanted wood.

(*The Case of Charles Dexter Ward; The Dream-Quest of Unknown Kadath*)

Lerion

One of the mountains upon which the gods of Earth sometimes return to dance. Another such mountain is Thuria. These were once the homes of the gods, but the intrusion of human beings climbing the mountains caused them to depart to dwell in the fortress atop Kadath in the Cold Waste. Kadath is the tallest of Earth's mountains in the dreamlands, and has never been climbed.

(*The Other Gods*)

Naraxa

This river flows beneath a great stone bridge of the city of Celephaïs and into the sea.

(*The Dream-Quest of Unknown Kadath*)

Narg

A sacred river in unknown Cathuria that arises from a grotto. Its scented waters are said to flow beneath the glass floor in the palace of the king of Cathuria, the god or demigod Dorieb. In the cunningly lit waters swim gaudy fish unknown outside that land. All of the palatial houses of the cities of Cathuria are built over fragrant-scented canals that carry the waters of the sacred river, in imitation of the palace of the king, beneath which the river proper flows.

(*The White Ship*)

Nath-Horthath, Temple of

A turquoise temple in the port city of Celephaïs that is presided over by orchid-wreathed priests.

(*Celephaïs*)

Ngranek

Mountain of the dreamlands the side of which was long ago blasted by the wrath of the Other Gods, leaving only "sheer crags and a valley of sinister lava." On its peak is carved the stone face of a god of Earth. It is two-day zebra ride away from the port of Baharna.

(*The Dream-Quest of Unknown Kadath*)

Ooth-Nargai

This land lies beyond the Tanarian Hills. It holds a valley near the Cerenerian Sea that contains the city of Celephaïs.

(*The Dream-Quest of Unknown Kadath*)

Oukranos

A golden river that runs through the land of "orchid-heavy" Kled, with its forgotten ivory cities. There is a jasper temple on the bank of the river devoted to the river god. It was visited once a year by the king of Ilek-Vad prior to Randolph Carter's ascension to the throne of that city. The river god sang to the king while he was a youth living on the bank of the river, and for this reason the king came annually to offer the god his prayers. The temple to the god of Oukranos has seven towers with pinnacles. Its walls and courts cover a full acre of land. Part of the river flows through the inner shrine of the temple via hidden channels, producing a singing sound that may be heard in the stillness of the night. This is interpreted as the singing voice of the river god. The temple is tended by silent priests who make music to accompany the singing of the river. Only the priests of Oukranos and the king of Ilek-Vad are permitted to enter this temple.

(*The Dream-Quest of Unknown Kadath; Through the Gates of the Silver Key*)

Pnath, Vale of

This is a dark valley in which "crawl and burrow the enormous bholes." It is filled with "mountains of bones." The night-gaunts fly ceaselessly back and forth between the Vale of Pnath and the passes to the outer world.

(*The Dream-Quest of Unknown Kadath*)

primal city

The ruins of a clay-brick city lie on the far shore of Lake Yath, opposite the canal that runs under the port city of Baharna, on the island of Oriab. The name of this city is not remembered by the people of Oriab.

(*The Dream-Quest of Unknown Kadath*)

Sarkomand

A deserted port city of the dreamlands that fell to ruins a million years before the evolution of mankind. Presently it consists of basalt quays, crumbling walls and sphinx-crowned gates, broken black columns, and tufts of grass growing up from cracks between its paving stones. It was ruled by the nearly human inhabitants of the plateau of Leng, before these horned creatures were enslaved by the monstrous, white, amorphous moon-beasts, who descended from the Moon to the Earth in their black galleys. The basalt cliff supporting the edge of the plateau of Leng rears high above the city. In the side of this cliff, which is carved in bas-relief into repellent scenes, is an arched entranceway to a passage leading up to the monastery of the High-Priest Not To Be Described. Twin winged stone lions of titanic size untouched by time guard a flight of steps that extends down from Sarkomand to the Great Abyss.

(*The Dream-Quest of Unknown Kadath*)

Selarn

This city lies to the northwest of the port city of Inquanok. The great caravan road runs north from Inquanok to the small-domed village of Urg, then turns west to Selarn.

(*The Dream-Quest of Unknown Kadath*)

Serannian

Sky-city built of pink marble amid the low-lying clouds on the horizon of the Cerenerian Sea. It is possible to sail in galleys on the west wind from the port of Celephaïs off the edge of the sea and into the clouds. King Kuranes rules over Celephaïs for half the year and over Serannian for the other half.

(*Celephaïs; The Dream-Quest of Unknown Kadath*)

Skai

A river in the dreamlands. Not far beyond it, near a stony desert, lies the town of Ulthar. The river is crossed by a bridge at Nir.

(*The Dream-Quest of Unknown Kadath; The Cats of Ulthar*)

Sona-Nyl

The Land of Fancy, in which there is "neither time nor space, neither suffering nor death." It is a land with green pastures and groves, many flowers, musical streams, and clear fountains. Splendid golden-domed cities occupy the countryside, filled with happy people who do not experience pain or death.

(*The White Ship*)

sunken city

Three days sail from Dylath-Leen in the dreamlands, ships pass over a sunken city so ancient that its very name has been forgotten. The ruins can be seen through the clear water by moonlight on calm nights. Dolphins sport amongst the fallen pillars of a great domed temple at the end of an avenue of "unnatural sphinxes" that leads to a public square. Beyond the houses of the city, on the crown of a submerged hill, there is a basalt temple of a simpler and more ancient design, yet in better repair. It is square with towers at its corners and round windows. A strange phosphorescence emanates from within it. From an open courtyard in its center rises a great monolith. To the side of this stone block dead sailors from passing ships are sometimes glimpsed, tied in sacrifice to an unknown god with their heads downward and their eyes cut out.

(*The Dream-Quest of Unknown Kadath*)

Tanarian Hills

A range of purple hills that divides the familiar dreamlands from those that are wilder and less well-known. They lie beyond the foothills of the land of Ooth-Nargai, and can be seen against the horizon from the city of Celephaïs. Lovecraft called the Tanarians "potent and mystical, behind which lay forbidden ways into the waking world and toward other regions of dream."

(*The Dream-Quest of Unknown Kadath*)

Temple of the Elder Ones

This great tower temple with its sixteen sides covered in carvings, its flattened dome, and its lofty, pinnacled belfry rising from the center of the dome, looms above the rooftops of the onyx city of Inquanok. Around the perimeter of the high dome are arrayed tripods that are ignited into flame at regular ritual times each day. The temple is set in the center of a walled garden having seven arched gateways that are never closed. Above each gate is carved the head of a different god. Beside each gate within the garden is a priest lodge. This walled garden is at the center of an open round plaza from which radiate the main streets of the city like the spokes of a wheel. The garden is a popular haunt for the people of Inquanok, thanks to its tiled paths, quaint shrines to lesser gods, and various fountains and reflecting pools designed to catch the light from the ignited tripods.

When the bell in the belfry above the dome clangs at certain hours, the masked and hooded black-robed priests of the temple exit its seven doors and march in a stately goosestep in seven long single files toward the lodges beside the open gates of the garden, carrying golden bowls of steaming liquid, accompanied by the music of horns and viols and voices issuing in invitation from the lodges. The priests enter the lodges, but are never seen to emerge. It is presumed that they return to the temple by means of underground tunnels. No one but the Veiled King of Inquanok is permitted to enter the temple by any of its doors.

The rumor circulates among the people of the city that the masked priests are not quite human. They inspire a vague dread in curious onlookers who gather in the garden to watch the procession and view the lighting of the tripods when the hour of the bell arrives. The chanted rhythms of the formula used by the priests are said to be recorded in scrolls that are older than the Pnakotic Manuscripts.

(*The Dream-Quest of Unknown Kadath*)

Thalarion

Called "the City of a Thousand Wonders" and "the Demon City," it is protected by grim, gray walls. Above them rise the spires of its temples, which reach so far into the sky that their tops cannot be discerned. Lovecraft characterized it as "fascinating and repellent." Those who pass into it through its huge carven gate Akariel, and who gaze upon the idol of Lathi, its ruling god, never leave it again. They join the throngs of daemons and the mad things no longer men who shuffle along its white streets of unburied bones.

(*The White Ship*)

Thran

A city of gilded spires on the golden river Oukranos, in the jungle land of Kled.
(*The Dream-Quest of Unknown Kadath; Through the Gates of the Silver Key*)

Throk, Peaks of

A range of high mountains in the dreamlands, beyond which lies the Vale of Pnath. Lovecraft calls them awful and sinister. They guard terrible valleys where dwell the burrowing bholes (or Dholes).
(*The Dream-Quest of Unknown Kadath*)

Thurai

A snow-capped mountain, one of the high mountains upon which the gods of Earth are supposed to dance. The men of the dreamlands avoid the peak at night, for the gods do not like to be observed.
(*The Other Gods*)

Ulthar

Called the City of Cats, it is a city in the dreamlands beyond the river Skai where cats are revered. It is a crime punishable by death to kill a cat in Ulthar. Randolph Carter traveled there to consult the priest, Atal, concerning the whereabouts of Kadath in the Cold Waste. Barzai the Wise, who once dared to look upon the dancing gods of Earth, was a native of this city. It is said by the zoogs that within Ulthar is the last copy of the Pnakotic Manuscripts, which were made by waking men, but were carried into the dreamlands by the hairy cannibal Gnophkehs, who overcame many-templed Olathoë in the land of Lomar.
(*The Dream-Quest of Unknown Kadath; The Other Gods; The Cats of Ulthar*)

Urg

A small village of dome-shaped houses, on the caravan road from the south that turns sharply west at Urg and runs to the town of Selarn. The tavern at Urg is a favorite stopping place for traders and miners. If you continue onward in a northerly direction from Urg along the quarry road, you come to the place where onyx is mined.
(*The Dream-Quest of Unknown Kadath*)

Xura

In *The White Ship*, Xura is "the Land of Pleasures Unattained," which from a distance at sea appears to be a land of bright flowers and fertile arbors, from which can be heard snatches of music and song. Its shoreline is edged with lilies. As it is approached nearer, the breeze carries out from it the stench of rotting corpses. In *The Dream-Quest of Unknown Kadath*, Randolph Carter referred to the "charnel gardens of Xura."

(*The White Ship; The Dream-Quest of Unknown Kadath*)

Yath

A lake on the great isle of Oriab that lies some distance inland from the port city of Baharna. Lake Yath is connected to the sea by means of a canal with granite gates that runs under Baharna. On the shore of the lake opposite the canal are the ruins of a city of bricks that is so ancient even its name has been forgotten.

(*The Dream-Quest of Unknown Kadath*)

Zakarion

A city in the dreamlands that contains a yellowed papyrus written by the dream-sages of Zakarion, who are so exalted they have never known incarnation in waking bodies of flesh.

(*Ex Oblivione*)

Zar

A land of terraces that are covered with trees and greenery, from which rise white-roofed temples. It is a land of forgotten dreams and thoughts of beauty, and those who walk upon its terraces never return. This region of the dreamlands was described to Randolph Carter by Basil Elton, the lighthouse keeper of the North Point lighthouse, just off Kingsport, who had seen it in his dreams—the same lighthouse keeper who is the narrator of *The White Ship*. While in the dreamlands, Carter spoke to the men of a trading ship with violet sails, which was bound for the land of Zar with a cargo of "strange coloured lilies."

(*The White Ship; The Dream-Quest of Unknown Kadath*)

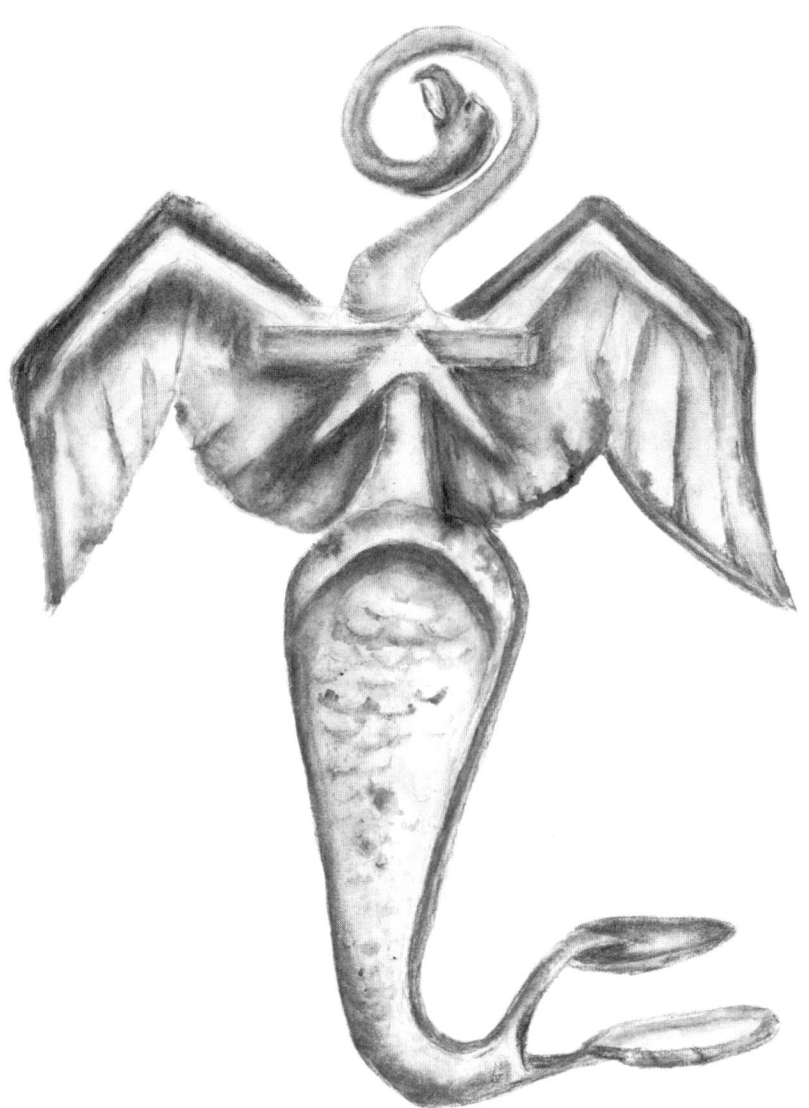

The Key to the Seventh Gate

7th Astral Gate: Gemini—The Twins

Sun passes through Gemini: June 21—July 20

Constellation is represented by the twin boys of Greek mythology, Castor and Pollux, who had the same mother but different fathers.

Right Pillar: Castor (Greek: Eques—The Horseman; Arabic name: *Al-Ras al-Tau'am al-Mukaddim*—Head of the Foremost Twin). Astronomical designation: Alpha Geminorum. Astrological nature: Mercury. Influence: skill with horses, wisdom, studies and intellectual pursuits. Magnitude: 1.9. Color: white. Sun crosses: July 13. Location: the head of the northern twin. Comments: Castor was the son of Tyndarus, the king of Sparta. At one time this star was the brightest in Gemini.

Left Pillar: Pollux (Greek: Polydeuces—the Immortal One; Arabic name: *Al-Ras al-Tau'am al-Mu'akhar*—Head of the Second Twin). Astronomical designation: Beta Geminorum. Astrological nature: Mars. Influence: strength, fierceness, violent actions. Magnitude: 1.2. Color: reddish. Sun crosses: July 16. Location: the head of the southern twin. Comments: Pollux was the son of the god Zeus. Presently the brightest star in Gemini.

The astral gate of Gemini lies between the star of its right pillar, located on the head of the northern twin, and the star of its left pillar, located on the head of the southern twin. The Sun enters the gate by crossing the longitude of Castor, the star of the right pillar, around July 13. The solar transition of this narrow gate takes only three days. The Sun exits the gate around July 16, when it crosses the longitude of the star of the left pillar, Pollux.

The key to the Seventh Gate opens the constellation Gemini, allowing entry into the corresponding part of the walled city of the *Necronomicon* that contains the landscape of the dreamlands. Use it for divining information about the dreamlands, or to obtain oracular dreams or visions concerning places in the dreamlands.

Seal of the Seventh Key on the Seventh Gate

Ritual of Opening Gemini

Face the direction of the compass ruled by the Seventh Gate, which is south by west—that is, slightly to the right of due south. Visualize the closed gate set in the southern wall of the city in front of you, making it more than large enough to enter without bending your head. Take the time to create on the astral level the details of the gate so that it so that it appears to be a real city gate in your mind's eye. Imagine each aspect in succession and impress it on your mind, periodically returning your attention to reinforce each part as it begins to fade in the imagination.

With the image of the gate held clearly in your mind and projected upon the astral level to the compass direction south by west, speak the following invocation to Yog-Sothoth, which is the invocation for all the gates, save only that the names of the pillars, the constellation, and the gate, change for each:

> Guardian of the Gate! Defender of the Door! Watcher of the Way! Who art the stout Lock, the slender Key, and the turning Hinge! Lord of All Transition, without whom there is no coming in or going out, I call thee! Keeper of the Threshold, whose dwelling place is between worlds, I summon thee! Yog-Sothoth, wise and mighty lord of the Old Ones, I invoke thee!
>
> By the authority of the dreaded name, Azathoth, that few dare speak, I charge thee, open to me the gateway of Gemini the Twins that lies between the blazing pillar Castor on the right hand and the blazing pillar Pollux on the left hand. As the solar chariot [or, lunar chariot] crosses between these pillars, I enter the city of the *Necronomicon* through its Seventh Gate. Selah!

Visualize the key of the Seventh Gate in your right hand some six inches long and made of cast bronze. Feel its weight, texture, and shape as you hold it. Extend your right arm and use the point of the key to trace upon the surface of the gate the seal of the key, which should be visualized to burn on the gate in lines of white spiritual fire. Point with the astral key at the center of the gate and speak the words of opening:

> In the name of Azathoth, Ruler of Chaos, by the power of Yog-Sothoth, Lord of Portals, the Seventh Gate is opened!

Visualize the gate unlocking and opening inward of its own accord upon a shadowed space beyond. On the astral level, walk through the gateway and stand in the dark space beyond. The key in your hand is your seal of authority. Focus your mind upon the place in the dreamlands you wish to scry remotely, or travel to in the astral body. In a more general sense, this ritual and this gate may be used to generate and to enter lucid dreams.

After fulfilling the purpose for which this gate was opened, conclude the ritual by astrally passing out through the gate and visualizing it to close. Draw the seal of the Seventh Key on the surface of the gate with the astral key you hold in your hand, and mentally cause it to lock itself shut, as it was at the beginning of the ritual. Speak the words:

> By the power of Yog-Sothoth, and authority of the supreme name Azathoth, I close and seal the Seventh Gate. This ritual is well and truly ended.

Allow the image of the gate to grow pale in your imagination and fade to nothingness before you turn away from the ritual direction.

The Eighth Gate

Eighth Gate
Other Worlds

Lovecraft's fascination with astronomy began in 1903 when his mother gave him an astronomical telescope. From his grandmother on his mother's side of the family, who died when he was six, Lovecraft had inherited a small library of books on astronomy. Most prized among them was the *Geography of the Heavens* by Elijah H. Burritt, first published in 1835. He began to haunt the Ladd Observatory of Brown University, which was about a mile north up Tin-top Hill from where he lived, taking every opportunity the tolerant director, Professor Winslow Upton (1853–1914), who was a family friend, allowed him to view the night sky through the observatory telescope, an instrument of much greater power than his own. He delighted in studying the surface of the Moon, and found it frustrating that half the Moon was forever turned away from the Earth. He complained in a 1916 letter to a friend that the long hours of observation gave him a permanent curve in his neck.

From 1906 to 1918 Lovecraft contributed monthly articles on astronomy to local Providence newspapers. He gave illustrated lectures on astronomy to clubs, using lantern slides made for him by one of the assistants at Ladd Observatory, and spent much time reading the books in the Observatory library. For years Lovecraft seriously considered becoming an astronomer, but he was never able to gain the necessary education in mathematics for this exacting profession, due to difficulties he had remaining in school. He was subject to periods of nervous collapse that compelled him to withdraw from school for long intervals. Although Lovecraft never wrote about such matters, it seems likely that he found social interaction with large groups of other young people an immense strain.

His interest in astronomy gave Lovecraft a scientific awareness of the vastness of the universe, not only its vastness in the dimensions of space, but in time as well, and it showed him the insignificance of our own planet in the greater scheme of things. Always inclined to rationalism, Lovecraft had rejected religion at a young age due to the inconsistencies in the lessons he received at Sunday school. His study of astronomy confirmed in him the atheistic philosophy to which he had already been inclined. It shows itself in his fiction in the form of the pitiless indifference with which the Great Old Ones regard humanity.

In religion, man is the center of the universe, the single most important creation of God, but in astronomy man is only one species among millions on a single tiny planet circling an ordinary star in a common spiral galaxy composed of billions of stars that is itself only one among countless billions of galaxies. The recognition of this truth so deeply impressed Lovecraft that he became something of a nihilist, unable to believe that anything any member of our tiny species might accomplish could truly matter in the cosmic scheme of things, either for good or for ill. He deliberately distanced himself emotionally from the human race, and thought of himself as an observer rather than a participant.

Part of the joy of amateur astronomy is the lore of star names. The more prominent visible stars were named by the Greeks, and after them by the Arabs and Persians, in the process acquiring an extensive mythology. Star names such as Aldebaran, Algol, and Betelgeuse are Arab. Other stars, such as Sirius and Polaris retain their Greek names. Lovecraft was familiar with the ancient lore of the stars. The winking red star Algol was regarded by the Arabs as the most evil of all the stars. Lovecraft made it the seat of the adversary in his story *Beyond the Wall of Sleep*. In the story *Polaris*, the faithful and unvarying Pole Star becomes a kind of celestial conscience that spans thousands of incarnations of a soul tormented by his sense of failure and guilt.

Conditions on the surfaces of the planets were unknown in Lovecraft's time, allowing him free reign to imagine any conditions he wished. Mars was believed to be a cold, dry world, but Lovecraft had by the age of seventeen already dismissed the theory of astronomer Percival Lowell that its red surface was crossed by channels of water, and that green patches were visible between them. Venus was usually presented in popular literature as a jungle world, and no one could have guessed how hot Venus was at its surface, so Lovecraft naturally made Venus a jungle world in his story *Within the Walls of Eryx*, co-written with Kenneth Sterling. Lovecraft placed various alien races on some of the moons of the outer planets, and he built an entire mythology around recently discovered Pluto, which he called Yuggoth and associated with the Mi-Go. He speculated in his fiction about an undiscovered planet beyond the orbit of Pluto, which he named Kynath, and would have been fascinated by the recent discovery of several large bodies beyond Pluto.

He even gave his fantasy free reign regarding the far side of the Moon, which he playful referred to as the "dark side" in *The Dream-Quest of Unknown Kadath*. As an amateur astronomer, Lovecraft knew full well that the Moon does not have a dark side—all sides of the Moon receive an equal amount of light and darkness—but just as the myth of the great cataract that falls off the edge of the world beyond the Pillars of Hercules has reality in the dreamlands, so does the myth of the Moon's dark side, which in Lovecraft's fiction is the gathering place of Earth's cats, and coveted by the giant cats of Saturn. In folklore and myth, the cat is a lunar animal. It made sense for Lovecraft to give his talking cats the power to leap from the rooftops to the Moon, since the Moon was their natural place.

No planets had been observed around other stars while Lovecraft was alive, simply because not even the most powerful telescope of his day was up to the task of seeing them, but it was not difficult to postulate that many of the stars visible in our night sky have planetary systems similar to that of our Sun. In *The Dreams in the Witch House* Lovecraft described the home planet of the Elder Things, in a star system with three suns of different colors, all three of which were sometimes in the sky at the same time, casting three differently colored shadows in three directions from anyone standing under them.

Lovecraft based the climax of his story *Beyond the Wall of Sleep* around a nova, or new star, that appeared in the heavens near Algol in the year 1901. In the story, this new star was the returning alien soul that had been trapped in the body of Catskills hillman Joe Slater until his death. The story was written in 1919, but Lovecraft set it in 1901 to take advantage of this rare celestial event. Only a passionate amateur astronomer such as Lovecraft would ever have imagined basing a horror story on a nova. In the story, the nova flares immediately after Slater's death. This made no sense, as Lovecraft must have been well aware, since even had the alien soul been able to traverse space in an instant, it would have taken many years for the light of the exploding nova to reach the Earth. It's another example of Lovecraft's playfulness where astronomical matters were concerned.

Aldebaran *

A red or orange star, also known as Alpha Tauri, in the constellation Taurus, that is mentioned by Lovecraft in two of his stories. It was suggested to Randolph Carter by the bearded priests Nasht and Kaman-Thah that the Kadath he sought might not even be in the dreamlands surrounding the Earth, but might lie in some unguessed dreamlands around a planet that circles the star Aldebaran, or the star Fomalhaut. August Derleth placed the city of Carcosa on a planet circling Aldebaran, but this was not done by Lovecraft, for whom Aldebaran was merely a red star in the night sky.

(*Polaris; The Dream-Quest of Unknown Kadath*)

Algol *

A red star the light of which brightens and dims periodically. It is what is known as an eclipsing binary star—two stars revolve around a common center, and approximately every three days, the dimmer stellar body, Beta Persei B, passes in front of the brighter, Beta Persei A, causing Algol to dim as seen from Earth for a period of around ten hours. There is a third star in this system, Beta Persei C, but it plays no part in this regular dimming. The name "Algol" means "the ghoul" or, more loosely translated, "the demon." It has the most evil reputation of any star in the night sky. The Arab astronomers reviled it for the ill-fortune its rays carried when in significant astrological aspect in the horoscope of a man.

Algol is the location of an evil light-being referred to by Lovecraft in his story *Beyond the Wall of Sleep* only as the "oppressor." It was attacked by another light-being seeking vengeance for a past wrong on February 22, 1901. The being, which called itself a Nemesis, had been until then trapped in the body of an ignorant hill-country man from the Catskills named Joe Slater. When Slater died, the entity was released into the cosmos to fulfill its delayed vengeance against the oppressor dwelling in the star Algol. The arrival of the Nemesis at Algol manifested itself in the form of a nova, or new star, which burst into existence near Algol in the year 1901. Novas are not actually new stars, but explosions of existing stars, which cause them to become visible for the first time due to their increased brightness, but ancient astronomers did not know this and assumed that they were new stars being born.

Lovecraft, who was a keen amateur astronomer, had nothing to say in his story about the limitation of the speed of light, which would have delayed the observation from Earth of the nova that burst forth near Algol until approximately ninety-three years after its occurrence. However, the entity that inhabited Joe Slater demonstrated from remarks it made to the narrator of Lovecraft's story that it could travel through time. It must be assumed that when it left the flesh of the dying man Slater, it traveled not only through space toward Algol, but back through time, so that its battle with the oppressor took place in the past, but was witnessed in the present by astronomers on Earth as a nova on the same night that Slater died.

(*Beyond the Wall of Sleep*)

Arcturus *

Described as winking "ruddily" just before dawn above a cemetery on a low hill. Most stars do not wink—atmospheric disturbances cause them to appear to flicker even though their light remains constant. This is more apt to occur when the star is near the horizon, as its light passes through more intervening air. The exceptions are variable stars, such as Algol, which actually do increase and decrease in brightness, although this change in magnitude is more gradual than a winking or flickering.

(*Polaris*)

black planets

In *The Haunter of the Dark*, the poet Robert Harrison Blake refers to the "ultimate void of the black planets." At the time he makes the reference, he is under the telepathic influence of an avatar of Nyarlathotep, a creature that cannot bear any amount of light, so it is reasonable to assume that the black planets are the home of this creature, which was called to Earth through the black stone known as the Shining Trapezohedron. It may be speculated that these planets circle a dead star that emits no light.

(*The Haunter of the Dark*)

dark star

A star beyond our galaxy, the central cavern of which is inhabited by a race of intelligent beings that have dealings with the Mi-Go. By "dark," Lovecraft presumably means that the star has exhausted all its nuclear fuel and has gone cold. The brains of a number of these beings were kept by the Mi-Go in metal cylinders in Vermont.

(*The Whisperer in Darkness*)

Dionaean Plateau

A plateau on the surface of Venus riddled with holes that are rumored to conceal an unknown alien species.

(*In the Walls of Eryx*)

Erycinian Highland

A plateau on Venus that is also known as Eryx, which contains a remarkable maze formed from transparent walls that are completely invisible to the human eye.

(*In the Walls of Eryx*)

Hali, Lake *

A misty lake upon an alien planet in the Hyades star cluster, upon the shore of which is located the fabulous city of Carcosa. Further along the lake is the city of Yhtill. This unnamed planet has twin suns, and more than one moon. Lake Hali is mentioned by

Robert W. Chambers in his 1895 story collection *The King In Yellow*, and it was from this source that Lovecraft derived the name. Chambers got the name from the 1891 story *An Inhabitant of Carcosa* by the writer Ambrose Bierce, who used it for a character, not a place.

(*The Whisperer in Darkness*)

Jupiter *

One of the outer moons of Jupiter, which is not specified by Lovecraft in *The Shadow Out of Time*, had a race of intelligent beings six million years in the past. It was visited by the time-traveling Yithians in their cosmos-spanning search for new knowledge. The outer moons are those that lie beyond the orbit of Callisto, the outermost of the four Galilean moons, large moons observed by Galileo in 1610, which were for centuries the only moons of Jupiter known. Lovecraft may have intended Himalia, discovered in 1904; Elara, discovered in 1905; Pasiphië, discovered in 1908; or Sinope, discovered in 1914.

The fourth moon is said in *Beyond the Wall of Sleep* to be the home of a proud race of insect-philosophers. Probably the moon Ganymede is intended—it is the fourth moon in order from Jupiter of those discovered prior to 1919, the year Lovecraft wrote his story. In 1892 the small moon Amalthea was discovered inside the orbit of the innermost of the four Galilean moons, Io, making Ganymede the fourth moon of those known to Lovecraft. The assumption is often made that Lovecraft's fourth moon is Callisto, but Lovecraft was an amateur astronomer and would have been well aware of the existence of Amalthea.

In *Through the Gates of the Silver Key* mention is made of "an untellable secret from the close-glimpsed mists of Jupiter." This reference is to the planet Jupiter itself, which is covered in thick cloud bands. No indication is given as to what this secret might be, but it may have involved the Great Red Spot, a vast anti-cyclonic storm on Jupiter that has been raging for many centuries, and was visible to Galileo when he first examined Jupiter through his telescope.

(*The Shadow Out of Time; Beyond the Wall of Sleep*)

Kynarth

A world on the edge of our solar system, that lies beyond the orbit of Pluto.

(*Through the Gates of the Silver Key*)

Kythanil

A double planet that at one time revolved around the star Arcturus. It was the home of a race that flew across the gulf of space to Earth and settled in ancient Hyperborea, where they worshipped Tsathoggua. By "double planet" Lovecraft probably meant a planet with a moon that is almost as large as the planet itself.

(*Through the Gates of the Silver Key*)

Mars *

The surface of this planet is occupied by sprawling "cyclopean ruins." In making this revelation, Lovecraft anticipated those who claim that there is a great stone face lying on the Martian surface, and that it is surrounded by pyramids and other structures. Astronomers dismiss these more recent speculations as misinterpretations of photographic information.

(*Through the Gates of the Silver Key*)

Mercury *

This planet will be inhabited in the future by an intelligent species of bulbous vegetable beings who will be taken over by the time-spanning minds of the Great Race of Yith in one of their periodic migrations of self-preservation. The Yithians will go to Mercury from Earth after leaving the bodies of the race of intelligent beetles that will arise on Earth following the passing away of mankind.

(*The Shadow Out of Time*)

Moon *

In *At the Mountains of Madness*, Lovecraft indicated that the material that formed the Moon had been wrenched from the South Pacific by some unspecified cataclysm. The theory that the Moon was formed from material torn away from the Earth was quite popular among scientists, as a way of accounting for why our planet, alone among the smaller rocky planets of this star system, should have such a large satellite. In the same story it is said that the scientist Danford, whose mind was shattered when he looked back at the mountains of madness in Antarctica while fleeing from the city of the Elder Things in an airplane, sometimes mutters about "the moon-ladder," but there is no explanation as to what he may intend by this cryptic term.

In *The Doom That Came to Sarnath*, the alien race that inhabited the gray stone city of Ib, in the land of Mnar, was said on the brick cylinders of Kadatheron to have descended to Mnar in the distant past one night while wrapped in a mist, along with their city and the lake on the margin of which it was situated. Long after the destruction of Ib by the men of Sarnath, the stone idol of the god of Ib, Bokrug the water-lizard, was worshiped in the high temple at Ilarnek at the phase of the gibbous Moon.

The Dream-Quest of Unknown Kadath relates that the gods of Earth like to dance on mountaintops under the moonlight. The zoogs gave Randolph Carter a flask of moon-wine, a highly intoxicating alcoholic liquor brewed on the Moon. The cats of Earth's dreamlands leap from tall spires to the Moon, and frolic on its far side, which Lovecraft inaccurately referred to as its "dark side." There is no dark side of the Moon—both the side turned to us and the far side are by turns illuminated and dark as the Moon revolves around the Earth. The seas of the dreamlands are plied by black galleys from the cities on the far side of the Moon, which are inhabited by inhuman moon-beasts. These moon-beasts employ the almost-human inhabitants of the plateau of Leng as their agents in dealings with men.

(*At the Mountains of Madness; The Doom That Came to Sarnath; The Dream-Quest of Unknown Kadath*)

Neptune *

The brains of two beings from this planet were kept in metal cylinders by the Mi-Go of Vermont. Lovecraft hints at the strangeness of the appearance of these creatures, but gives no details. The surface of Neptune is spotted by white fungi.

(*The Whisperer in Darkness; Through the Gates of the Silver Key*)

Polaris *

The Pole Star links the souls of two men across a span of 26,000 years. In the time of the northern kingdom of Lomar it occupied the celestial pole, and in our own time it has returned to this position in the heavens. A man of Olathoë, a city in Lomar, betrayed his people by falling asleep on guard duty beneath the rays of this star, resulting in the slaughter of his city by an attacking army. In the America of the present another man, into whom the soul of the guard has reincarnated, suffers each night beneath the accusing, icy gaze of Polaris, aware of his crime in his former life but unable to make amends.

According to Joshi (*A Dreamer*, p. 109) this story was inspired by a dream Lovecraft had in the spring of 1918, in which Lovecraft found himself hovering as a disembodied awareness above a strange city of "many palaces and gilded domes" that lay between ranges of "gray, horrible hills." Lovecraft transformed his dream city into the Olathoë of his story.

(*Polaris*)

Shaggai

A planet more distant than Yuggoth—which we know as Pluto—where the Haunter of the Dark, who is an avatar of Nyarlathotep, stopped on its long flight across space on leathern wings from the black planets to our Earth. Lovecraft mentions in *The Shadow Out of Time* an "unknown trans-Plutonian planet" within our solar system, but eighteen million years in our future. Perhaps Shaggai is that unnamed planet. Or it may be that Shaggai lies entirely outside the solar system.

(*The Haunter of the Dark; The Shadow Out of Time*)

Stronti

A world in one of the twenty-eight galaxies beyond our Milky Way that are accessed by the race on Yaddith using light-beam or light-wave envelopes. It is one of the worlds beyond our galaxy visited by Randolph Carter while he inhabits the alien body of a wizard of Yaddith named Zkauba. Two other worlds visited by Carter in the same manner are Mthura and Kath. Carter mentions no details about these worlds.

(*Through the Gates of the Silver Key*)

Terra Nova

The only human settlement on the planet Venus. At the time the events related in the story *In the Walls of Eryx* occur, this town has existed for seventy-two years. Since Venus is presently uninhabitable, we must assume that this story is set in the distant future, or in some alternative reality.

(*In the Walls of Eryx*)

trans-Plutonian planet

A planet beyond the orbit of Pluto that will be the habitation of a race of half-plastic entities some eighteen million years in our future. We know of them only because they are visited by the time-travelers of the Great Race of Yith.

(*The Shadow Out of Time*)

Venus *

An intelligent race will evolve on Venus in the distant future, long after the human race has ceased to exist. The time-traveling Yithians visited future Venus in their projected minds to inhabit the bodies of this race and to acquire their collective knowledge.

(*The Shadow Out of Time*)

Yaddith

In *The Diary of Alonzo Typer*, Yaddith is mentioned in a note written in low Latin by the wizard Claes van der Heyl on a piece of dried reptilian skin. The note is wrapped around a strange key found by the occultist Alonzo Typer in 1935, in the old deserted farmhouse of the van der Heyl clan, in the decaying village of Chorazin, located near Attica in the state of New York. The wizard wrote, "may the Lords of Yaddith succor me," when referring to his dreaded use of the key.

Yaddith is a distant planet inhabited by an alien race. In *Through the Gates of the Silver Key* a member of that race, the wizard Zkauba, found himself unwillingly forced to share his inhuman body with the consciousness of Randolph Carter, who took command of it and used it in an effort to find his way back to his own body.

(*The Diary of Alonzo Typer; Through the Gates of the Silver Key*)

Yekub *

The alien planet in a distant galaxy that is the home of the worm-like race, to which the mind of George Campbell was transported when he gazed into the depths of a crystal cube in the Canadian woods. Its blue sun casts a sapphire light over its surface. This name was not invented by Lovecraft, but appears in the portion of the collaborative story *The Challenge From Beyond* that was written by Robert E. Howard.

(*The Challenge From Beyond*)

Yith

The planet of origin of the Great Race, described by Lovecraft as "that black, aeon-dead orb in far space." The Yithians were able to explore the distant past of their home world by the use of their mental time traveling.

(*The Shadow Out of Time*)

Yuggoth

The planetoid we know as Pluto. It is inhabited by the alien race of fungoidal crustaceans called the Mi-Go, who dwell in great windowless cities of black stone and grow fungus for their food in lightless gardens. This fungoidal race worships Nyarlathotep on Yuggoth, and also Yog-Sothoth, whom they call "the Beyond-One." An earlier vanished race built cyclopean bridges on Yuggoth that span rivers of flowing black pitch, but the Mi-Go have no record of their appearance or nature, although their works endure. Yuggoth is the most recent of the planets colonized by the Mi-Go—in *The Whisperer in Darkness* it is referred to as "the youngest child" of the star-spanning empire of the Mi-Go, the origin of which lies beyond "the Einsteinian space-time continuum or greatest known cosmos."

It may have been the earlier unknown race that colonized the Earth before the beginnings of terrestrial life, and placed the god Ghatanothoa in a crypt beneath the fortress atop Mount Yaddith-Go on the continent of Mu, which has since sunk beneath the waves of the Pacific. Lovecraft referred to them only as the "Yuggoth-spawn" and the "Elder Ones." If so, it may also have been this earlier race that fashioned the Shining Trapezohedron on Yuggoth before that stone was carried to Earth. These beings Lovecraft called the Old Ones. Both these works are usually attributed to the Mi-Go. However, the Lovecraft scholar S. T. Joshi is of the opinion (*Selected Papers on Lovecraft*, p. 39) that Ghatanothoa was brought to Earth and worshipped by the earlier race, which may have been indigenous to Yuggoth.

In *The Horror in the Museum*, the ten-foot tall amphibious creature with six legs named Rhan-Tegoth that was conveyed to London by George Rogers from northern Alaska originally came from Yuggoth, or at least Rogers believed this to be the case. Rogers spoke of "lead-gray Yuggoth, where the cities are under the warm deep sea." In *Medusa's Coil*, Marceline de Russy threatened to call up with magic "what lies hidden in Yuggoth."

(*The Whisperer in Darkness; Out of the Aeons; The Haunter of the Dark; The Horror in the Museum; Medusa's Coil; Through the Gates of the Silver Key*)

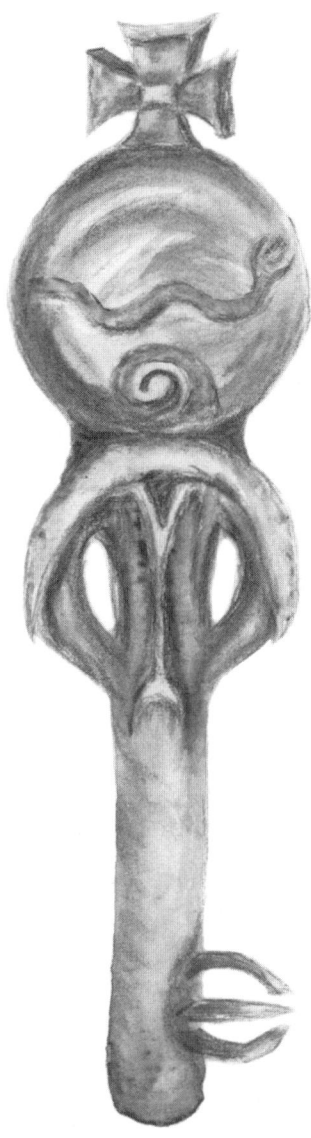

The Key to the Eighth Gate

8th Astral Gate: Cancer—The Crab

Sun passes through Cancer: July 20—August 10

Constellation is represented by a crab or crayfish.

Right Pillar: Al Tarf (Arabic: *al-tarf*—The End). Astronomical designation: Beta Cancri. Astrological nature: Saturn-Mercury. Influence: Magnitude: 3.5—a binary. Color: orange. Sun crosses: July 20. Location: southern foot of the crab. Comments: Little lore is given for this star.

Left Pillar: Acubens (Arabic: *al-Zubanah* –The Claws). Astronomical designation: Alpha Cancri. Astrological nature: Saturn-Mercury. Influence: malevolent and poisonous. Magnitude: 4.2—a binary. Color: white. Sun crosses: August 4. Location: arm of the southern claw. Comments: This star was once the brightest in Cancer.

The astral gate of Cancer lies between the star of its right pillar, located on the southern foot of the Crab, and the star of its left pillar, on the arm of the southern claw. The sun enters the gate by crossing the longitude of Al Tarf, the star of the right pillar, around July 20. The solar transition of this wide gate takes fifteen days. The Sun exits the gate around August 4, when it crosses the longitude of the star of the left pillar, Acubens.

The key to the Eighth Gate opens the constellation Cancer, the dimmest of all the zodiacal constellations, allowing entry into that part of the walled city of the *Necronomicon* that concerns the alien worlds dreamed by Lovecraft. Use it for divining information or receiving dreams about the astral landscapes and cities of other planets.

Seal of the Eighth Key on the Eighth Gate

Ritual of Opening Cancer

Face the direction of the compass ruled by the Eighth Gate, which is southwest by south—that is, slightly to the left of the southwest point. Visualize before you the closed gate in the southern wall of the city of the book so that it is more than large enough for you to walk through without awkwardness.

With the visualized image of the gate clear in your mind and projected upon the astral plane in the direction southwest by south, speak this invocation to Yog-Sothoth, which has the same general form for all the gates:

> Guardian of the Gate! Defender of the Door! Watcher of the Way! Who art the stout Lock, the slender Key, and the turning Hinge! Lord of All Transition, without whom there is no coming in or going out, I call thee! Keeper of the Threshold, whose dwelling place is between worlds, I summon thee! Yog-Sothoth, wise and mighty lord of the Old Ones, I invoke thee!
>
> By the authority of the dreaded name, Azathoth, that few dare speak, I charge thee, open to me the gateway of Cancer, the Crab, that lies between the blazing pillar Al Tarf on the right hand and the blazing pillar Acubens on the left hand. As the solar chariot [or, lunar chariot] crosses between these pillars, I enter the city of the *Necronomicon* through its Eighth Gate. Selah!

Visualize the key of the Eighth Gate in your right hand some six inches long and made of cast silver. Feel its weight, texture, and shape as you hold it. Extend your right arm and use the key to draw upon the surface of the gate the seal of the key, which should be visualized to burn on the gate in a line of white spiritual fire. Point with the astral key at the center of the gate and speak the words:

> In the name of Azathoth, Ruler of Chaos, by the power of Yog-Sothoth, Lord of Portals, the Eighth Gate is opened!

Visualize the gate unlocking and opening inward of its own accord upon a shadowed space. On the astral level, walk through the gateway and stand in the darkness beyond. Focus your will upon the alien place distant among the stars that you wish to scry or enter in a dream oracle. Open your mind to receive impressions, and if directions for scrying or obtaining a dream vision are given, follow them. In a more general sense, this ritual and this gate may be used to scry any location on any distant planet, both in normal space and on higher dimensional levels.

After fulfilling the purpose for which this gate was opened, conclude the ritual by astrally passing out through the gate and visualizing it to close. Draw the seal of the Eighth Key on the surface of the gate with the astral key you hold in your hand, and mentally cause it to lock itself shut, as it was at the beginning of the ritual. Speak the words of closing:

> By the power of Yog-Sothoth, and authority of the supreme name Azathoth, I close and seal the Eighth Gate. This ritual is well and truly ended.

Allow the image of the gate to grow pale in your imagination and fade to nothingness before you turn away from the ritual direction.

The Ninth Gate

Ninth Gate
Books

In the Necronomicon mythos, books fulfill the function of conveying forgotten or secret information from the past to the present. They are a bridge across time with a span that may be as short as a few weeks or months in the case of diary records, or as long as millions of years when it concerns texts recorded by alien races that predate humanity. This is a crucial role, since many of the stories depend for their resolution on ancient secrets or arcane magical formulae lost to history.

In Lovecraft's stories, there are certain books that should not exist, and if they do exist, that should never be read. To open them is to risk insanity and death. These are always the books most highly treasured by a few individuals for whom the forbidden is an irresistible lure. An archetypal scene that in many ways typifies the books of the mythos occurs in the story fragment *The Book*, written in 1935, which appears to be based on another of Lovecraft's dreams. A man discovers a moldering, worm-eaten Latin manuscript book in a rundown second-hand bookshop, and recognizes in it something both potent and dangerous. The sinister proprietor of the shop is only too happy to part with it, and asks for no payment, but makes a sign with his hand to turn aside its evil.

> There was a formula—a sort of list of things to say and do—which I recognized as something black and forbidden; something which I had read of before in furtive paragraphs of mixed abhorrence and fascination penned by those strange ancient delvers into the universe's guarded secrets whose decaying texts I loved to absorb. It was a key—a guide—to certain gateways and transitions of which mystics have dreamed and whispered since the race was young, and which lead to freedoms and discoveries beyond the three dimensions and realms of life and matter that we know. Not for centuries had any man recalled its vital substance or known where to find it, but this book was very old indeed.

Although this unnamed manuscript book is not the *Necronomicon*, it expresses the central attraction of Alhazred's work. It is "black and forbidden," containing "guarded secrets" to dimensional portals of which "mystics have dreamed" since the human race was young, secrets that lead beyond the "realms of life and matter that we know." Such books are ancient treasure troves for the mind, the finding of which always carries a heavy price, particularly for those who attempt to make personal use of their secrets.

The ancient bookshop, in which the dread tome is discovered, is itself a kind of time capsule of a period centuries in the past. It is very much the place an antiquarian such as Lovecraft would visit in his dreams. By entering such a shop, the lover of books steps back in time. The shop "reaches back endlessly through windowless inner rooms and alcoves," all of them piled with stacks of moldering, worm-riddled books that touch the ceiling, and containing bins filled with more carelessly tumbled books. It was perhaps in such an astral bookshop that Lovecraft dreamed the first vision of his *Necronomicon*.

There are several types of books that figure prominently in the mythos. The grimoires are book of magic signs, rituals, and chants for the purpose of opening occult doorways, or having commerce with inhuman intelligences such as the Old Ones. The ancient histories tell of lost civilizations and forgotten gods that were on the Earth before the evolution of humanity. Their contents may have been set down by alien scribes, such as the early chapters of the Pnakotic Manuscripts, which were written by members of the Great Race of Yith, or may have been drawn from the akashic library by a psychic medium such as Rudolf Yergler, author of the *Chronicle of Nath*. Another type of book are the diaries in their various forms where events are recorded, sometimes for the benefit of future generations within the world of the story, but always for the benefit of the reader, as the advancement of the plot depends on them. From what we know of the *Necronomicon* based on those few fragments that Lovecraft quoted in his stories, it is a combination of ancient history and grimoire.

Lovecraft mingled in his mythos the titles of real books and imaginary books with a complete lack of discrimination. Which is which is not always self-evident, and the confusion is enhanced by Lovecraft's tendency to attribute imaginary contents to real texts. It is easy to get the impression that Lovecraft was an expert on books dealing with esoteric topics. Nothing could be further from the truth. His own interests lay in astronomy, architecture, genealogy, history, and various sciences—he knew almost nothing about occult books in an overt sense. He drew many of the names of the books he refers to from the ninth edition of the *Encyclopaedia Britannica*, and in one letter to a friend bemoaned his own lack of background knowledge in this area, since it would lend his stories greater plausibility. He was afraid that readers would easily see that he was simply dropping names from the encyclopedia.

He was not completely lacking in knowledge of occult matters, however. He had read some material on Madame Blavatsky and her new religion of Theosophy, a bit about the lost continents of Atlantis and Mu, and was at least aware of the existence of Aleister Crowley, for whom he expressed aversion. The story that his wife knew Crowley is not true, but it is entirely possible that she knew people in Crowley's wider circle. Lovecraft was writing in the heyday of the Astrum Argentum and the Ordo Templi Orientis, Crowley's occult organizations. The Hermetic Order of the Golden Dawn was operating under the leadership of S. L. MacGregor Mathers' widow, Moïna. Theosophy was doing a booming business under Blavatsky's successor, Annie Besant, and spiritualism was at the height of its popularity, as evidenced by Houdini's keenness to publish books debunking it.

Lovecraft studied spiritualism in preparation for ghostwriting a book with C. M. Eddy to be published under Harry Houdini's name, which was to have been titled *The Cancer of Superstition*. Houdini had already had a book cobbled together in 1924 on the same subject, *A Magician Among the Spirits*. Houdini's death in 1926 prevented Lovecraft from putting his newly acquired knowledge to use. However, his study of spiritualism shows that his understanding of occult matters was growing throughout his lifetime. Had he lived twenty more years, he might have been quoting from Mathers' translation of the *Book of Abramelin the Mage* and Crowley's *Book of the Law*.

Aklo Writings

A written record referred to by the occult investigator Alonzo Typer in reference to a malignant spiritual presence he encountered on April 17, 1935, at the deserted van der Heyl farmhouse, in the village of Chorazin, near Attica, New York. The unseen presence was described by Typer as "appallingly evil and definitely nonhuman." He wrote that it "towers like a colossus, bearing out what is said in the Aklo writings." In the attic of the old house Typer found a book containing "variations in the Aklo formulae" that he had not previously known to exist. Within the book was the "third Aklo ritual" by which the unseen spiritual presences in the house might be rendered tangible and visible.

(*The Diary of Alonzo Typer*)

Al Azif

This is the original Arabic title for the *Necronomicon*. The title signifies the night noises of desert insects, which were said by the Bedouins to be the howling of demons. In his *History of the Necronomicon*, Lovecraft indicated that no copies of the original Arabic text survive.

(*The History of the Necronomicon*)

Albertus Magnus *

The complete works of Albertus Magnus were published in Latin under the title *Opera Omnia* at Lyons in 1651 by Peter Jammy in twenty-one folio volumes. In *The Case of Charles Dexter Ward*, this substantial set formed part of the library of the necromancer Joseph Curwen, and is described as "Peter Jammy's set of Albertus Magnus."

(*The Case of Charles Dexter Ward*)

Ars Magna et Ultima *

A Latin work by Raymond Lully. It formed part of the library of Joseph Curwen.

(*The Case of Charles Dexter Ward*)

Azathoth and Other Horrors

A book of "nightmare lyrics" composed in childhood by the precocious genius Edward Pickman Derby, and published when he was eighteen. His childhood friend, Daniel Upton, referred to the writings as "Edward's demoniac poems." Some of them were written when Derby was only seven years old.

(*The Thing on the Doorstep*)

book of Azathoth

The ancient witch Keziah Mason tells Walter Gilman that he must accompany the Black Man of the witches to the throne of Azathoth, at the center of ultimate chaos, where he must sign his name in blood in the book of Azathoth, and take on a secret name as a member of the witch coven. The book of Azathoth appears to be the prototype for all the books of pacts that appear in the transcripts of the European witch trials, in which the witch makes her mark in her own blood in a book proffered by the Devil at the sabbat, as a binding contract with the forces of evil. The majority of witches were women, but men were also witches, and followed the same procedure in joining the coven and pledging fidelity to the Devil, who appeared at the sabbat in the form of the Black Man—a man robed in black whose face was concealed.

(*The Dreams in the Witch House*)

Book of Dzyan *

A supposed ancient text written in the Senzar language, it is mentioned by Lovecraft in several places in his fiction. Madame H. P. Blavatsky, the founder of the Theosophical Society and an accomplished trance medium, claimed to have read part of it, and published the fragment at the beginning of her 1888 work *The Secret Doctrine*. The *Stanzas of Dzyan*, as they are alternatively called, are in the form of seven brief chapters with numbered paragraphs, most of which consist of no more than a single sentence. It is claimed to be the teaching of the Sons of the Fire-Mist, a hierarchy of beings who projected their minds from Venus into the primitive minds of the ancient Lemurian race in order to elevate and civilize them. Lovecraft made a single reference to these mysterious super-beings, calling them the "Children of the Fire Mist" in his short story, *Through the Gates of the Silver Key*.

In the very first sentence of her earlier but no less monumental 1877 work, *The Veil of Isis*, Blavatsky wrote in a guarded way concerning the book that contained their teachings. "There exists somewhere in this wide world an old Book—so very old that our modern antiquarians might ponder over its pages an indefinite time and still not quite agree as to the nature of the fabric upon which it is written." A little further in her text she made reference to a time frame of 70,000 years in connection with "the Oriental Kabalists," but it is not clear if we are to assume this to be the age of the *Book of Dzyan*. Elsewhere, in the first sentence of *Isis Unveiled*, she was a little more precise about the surface upon which the book is penned. "An Archaic Manuscript—a collection of palm leaves made impermeable to water, fire, and air, by some specific unknown process—is before the writer's eye."

Blavatsky was coy about the physical reality of the *Book of Dzyan*. In her preface to the Secret Doctrine, she wrote:

> It is more than probable that the book will be regarded by a large section of the public as a romance of the wildest kind; for who has ever even heard of the book of Dzyan?
>
> The writer, therefore, is fully prepared to take all the responsibility for what is contained in this work, and even to face the charge of having invented the whole of it.
>
> (Blavatsky, *Sec. Doc.*, vol. 1, p. viii)

There is another possibility, which the dreamer Lovecraft might have regarded as an interesting speculation—that the psychic and trance medium Blavatsky read the stanzas of the *Book of Dzyan* on the astral level, in the akashic records. The akashic records are a great storehouse that holds the accumulated wisdom of all of human history, and of the history of many other intelligent beings as well. If so, then when Blavatsky wrote that she had the book before her eye, she would not necessarily have been lying. A book written on palm leaves could not have survived over 70,000 years (unless preserved by some occult force), but once written, even if that writing took place on some plane of reality other than the physical plane we inhabit, it would be forever present in the library of the akashic records.

(*The Haunter of the Dark; The Diary of Alonzo Typer*)

Book of Eibon *

Three editions of this work are known to exist, the oldest in the Latin language bearing the title *Liber Ivonis*; another in Norman French that is titled *Livre d'Eibon*; and the English edition. The author of the work is unknown. The *Book of Eibon* was the invention of Lovecraft's friend, Clark Ashton Smith, but Lovecraft made reference to it a number of times in his stories.

(*The Diary of Alonzo Typer; Out of the Aeons; The Dreams in the Witch House; The Thing on the Doorstep; The Shadow Out of Time; The Haunter of the Dark*)

Book of Hidden Things

A grimoire mentioned by Claes van der Heyl in a note left wrapped around an ancient key in the van der Heyl farmhouse in the village of Chorazin, near Attica, New York. He wrote, "That which I have awaked and borne away with me, I may not part with again. So it is written in the *Book of Hidden Things*."

(*The Diary of Alonzo Typer*)

Book of Thoth

Alhazred wrote in the *Necronomicon* of those "who have dared to seek glimpses beyond the Veil, and to accept HIM as guide, they would have been more prudent had they avoided commerce with HIM; for it is written in the Book of Thoth how terrific is the price of a single glimpse." The guide referred to by Alhazred is 'Umr At-Tawil, the Most Ancient One, whose name is rendered "the Prolonged of Life."

Thoth was the Egyptian god of wisdom, and the scribe who recorded the result of the weighing of the heart of the newly dead to determine its worth. He is pictured with the head of an ibis, writing on a clay or wax tablet with a reed pen. The early Christian writers demoted Thoth to the status of a demon, and credited him with the invention of gaming with dice. Later, when playing cards were introduced to Europe,

Thoth was also said to be their inventor. The Greeks when they came to rule Egypt created a hybrid god known as Thoth-Hermes. They attributed to this god many occult secrets, which were recorded in numerous books. The best of these are what we know today as the Hermetica.

(*Through the Gates of the Silver Key*)

book, worm-riddled

The narrator of the unfinished story, *The Book*, finds a worm-riddled manuscript book written in medieval Latin in a decaying second-hand bookstore near the river. The title page and the early leaves are missing. It is described as "a key—a guide—to certain gateways and transitions" that lie beyond normal three-dimensional reality. He recites the ninth verse from a formula in the book near its end, "a sort of list of things to say and do," and transitions through the first dimensional gateway. As a consequence, he acquires a familiar spirit that scratches outside his attic window. His perception of reality is forever changed, for he now sees not only the present but also the past and future of things.

This unfinished story reads like the transcription of one of Lovecraft's dreams. The narrator is given no name, no place nor time. The ancient bookstore with its "ceiling-high shelves full of rotting volumes reached back endlessly through windowless inner rooms and alcoves" is very much a dream vision.

(*The Book*)

brick cylinders of Kadatheron

An ancient record that speaks of the descent to the Earth from the Moon of the people of the gray stone city of Ib. One night they came down through the mist along with their city and a vast lake. They settled in the land of Mnar. The writing on the cylinders states that these creatures were green-skinned, had bulging eyes, flabby lips, and were without voices.

(*The Doom That Came to Sarnath*)

Chronicle of Nath

A work by the "German mystic and alchemist" Rudolf Yergler, based in part on the writings attributed to Hermes Trismegistus. In it, mention is made of the Year of the Black Goat when a shadow from outside came to Nath, a shadow that might only be dispelled by one who could look upon its true shape and survive the ordeal.

(*The Tree on the Hill*)

Clavis Alchimiae *

Clavis Philosophiae et Alchymiae, a Latin work on alchemy by Robert Fludd, was first published at Frankfurt in 1632 by William Fitzer. The entire print run was destroyed by the actions of the militia shortly after it issued from the press. Fludd managed to get the work reprinted the following year, and it is these copies that survive as the first edition of the work, one of which was seen in Joseph Curwen's library at Providence, Rhode Island, in 1746.

(*The Case of Charles Dexter Ward*)

Commoriom myth-cycle *

The high priest of Atlantis, Klarkash-Ton, wrote down and preserved the myths of Commoriom, the capital city of Hyperborea (Greenland). The name of the high priest was Lovecraft's tribute to his friend, the writer Clark Ashton Smith, who invented Commoriom for his own fiction. Smith used the term "Commoriom myth-cycle" in a letter to Lovecraft dated February, 1931.

(*The Whisperer in Darkness; At the Mountains of Madness*)

Cryptomenysis Patefacta *

Book on ciphers by John Falconer, subtitled *The Art of Secret Information Disclosed without a Key*, that was printed at London in 1685 by Daniel Brown. In the book, Falconer gave methods for conveying secret information by means of signs and gestures, such as the Egyptian hieroglyphics and a finger alphabet. An analysis of the writings of Johannes Trithemius, the author of *Steganographia*, closes the work. Falconer also wrote *Rules for Explaining and Decyphering all Manner of Secret Writing*, published at London in 1692. The *Cryptomenysis Patefacta* is mentioned in passing in *The Dunwich Horror* amid a list of various authorities on cryptography. Lovecraft probably derived the reference from the ninth edition of the *Encyclopaedia Britannica*.

(*The Dunwich Horror*)

Cultes des Goules *

A work by the Comte d'Erlette. It was characterized by Lovecraft as "infamous." In *The Haunter of the Dark*, a copy is discovered by Robert Harrison Blake in the abandoned Church of Starry Wisdom at Providence, Rhode Island. This book was originally the invention of the writer Robert Bloch, who corresponded by letter mail with Lovecraft.

The name of the character Robert Blake is a tongue-in-cheek reference by Lovecraft to his friend, Robert Bloch.

(*The Shadow Out of Time; The Haunter of the Dark*)

Daemonolatreia *

Book by the French Roman Catholic inquisitor Nicolas Remy (1530–1612), who according to the prevailing custom of his day went under the Latinized version of his name, Remigius. Published at Lugduni in 1595, it concerns the nature of witches and demons, and how they are to be rooted out and opposed. In *The Festival*, reference is made to the "shocking *Daemonolatreia* of Remigius, printed in 1595 at Lyons." In *The Dunwich Horror*, Dr. Henry Armitage, the chief-librarian at Miskatonic University, calls for the *Daemonolatreia* of Remigius along with the dreaded *Necronomicon* while searching frantically for some magic formula that will combat Wilbur Whateley's monstrous invisible brother.

(*The Festival; The Dunwich Horror*)

De Furtivis Literarum Notis *

A book on ciphers by Giovanni Battista della Porta (1535–1615) that was published in 1563. The Latin name means "On Concealed Characters in Writing."

(*The Dunwich Horror*)

De Lapide Philosophico *

Tractatus de Lapide Philosophico, published in 1611, is a work on alchemy by Johannes Trithemius (1462–1516). In 1746 it was seen in the library of Joseph Curwen at Providence, Rhode Island.

(*The Case of Charles Dexter Ward*)

De Vermis Mysteriis *

An occult text written by "old Ludvig Prinn" that Lovecraft described as "hellish." The writer Robert Bloch first referred to this apocryphal text under the English title *The Mysteries of the Worm*, but it was Lovecraft who translated the title into Latin.

(*The Haunter of the Dark; The Diary of Alonzo Typer; The Shadow Out of Time*)

Diary of Alonzo Typer

A small book of "tough paper" leaves approximately six inches tall by three and a half inches wide, bound between thin metal plates. Its handwritten script relates the events leading up to Typer's mysterious disappearance.

(*The Diary of Alonzo Typer*)

Eltdown Shards *

An ancient record that tells of the coming to the Earth of the Great Race from Yith some 600 million years ago. The Eltdown Shards were invented by Richard F. Searight, who corresponded with Lovecraft. In *The Challenge from Beyond*, Lovecraft wrote that the shards are pieces of clay dug up in southern England from "pre-carboniferous strata." They were translated around 1912 by the Reverend Arthur Brooke Winters-Hall, a clergyman of Sussex, England, and the translation was published by him at his own expense. It is frequently quoted by occultists.

(*The Shadow Out of Time; The Diary of Alonzo Typer; The Challenge from Beyond*)

"Image du Monde" *

"L'Image du monde" ("The Image of the World") is a poem written by the French priest of the Catholic Church, Gauthier de Metz, around the year 1246. It concerns the creation of the universe and the nature of the world, and was quite popular during the Middle Ages. One of its chapters treats astrology. In the Nameless City reference is made to "infamous lines from the delirious *Image du Monde*." As is often the case, Lovecraft has used the name of a real work of literature, but has attributed to it a sinister reputation that is not deserved.

(*The Nameless City*)

India, book from

A book from India obtained by Harley Warren in 1919 was written in unknown letters similar to those on the parchment that Randolph Carter discovered in an old oak box that contained the silver key. It is intimated that this book may have been responsible for Warren's death, when he descended down the stone stair of the crypt at Big Cypress Swamp in Florida.

(*The Statement of Randolph Carter*)

Key of Wisdom *

An alchemical text by Artephius, thought to have been written in the twelfth century. *Liber qui Clavis majoris sapientiae dicitur* by Artephius was published in the fourth volume of *Theatrum Chemicum* in 1613 at Strasbourg. Who Artephius may have been is not know with certainty, but some scholars believe Artephius was the Arab alchemist Al Toghari, who died around 1119. This book was observed to be in the personal library of Joseph Curwen at Providence, Rhode Island, in 1746.

(*The Case of Charles Dexter Ward*)

Liber Damnatus

A grimoire mentioned by the necromancer Joseph Curwen in a letter to Simon Orne, written on the first of May, circa 1750. The reference concerns an instruction given by the evoked Old One, Yog-Sothoth, as to the details of ritual work intended to insure the future resurrection of Curwen after his death. "And IT said, that ye III Psalme in ye Liber-Damnatus holdes ye Clauicle. With Sunne in V House, Saturne in Trine, drawe ye Pentagram of Fire, and saye ye ninth Uerse thrice. This Uerse repeate eache Roodemas and Hallow's Eue; and ye Thing will breede in ye Outside Spheres."

A clavicle is a key. With the Sun in the fifth astrological house and Saturn in a trine aspect with the Sun, Curwen is to draw a pentagram of elemental fire. A pentagram of fire is not a blazing pentagram, but a pentagram drawn in a certain way that distinguishes its elemental nature. In modern magic, as it descends from the teachings of the Hermetic Order of the Golden Dawn, each of the four elements, and the quintessence or fifth element of Spirit, has its own unique pentagram. They are all identical in shape, but are unique in the way they are drawn. He is then to speak the ninth verse of the third psalm of *Liber Damnatus* three times. This is to be done on Roodmas and Halloween. By Roodmas, Lovecraft almost certainly had May-Eve, or Beltane (April 30), in mind. Roodmas is actually September 14, but it is often associated by pagans with April 30, which is six months away from Halloween (October 31), on the opposite side of the wheel of the year. The "Outside Spheres" are the celestial spheres beyond the known Ptolemaic universe—beyond the eighth sphere of the fixed stars.

(*The Case of Charles Dexter Ward*)

Liber Investigationis *

Liber Investigationis Magisterii is the Latin version of an alchemical text by Geber, the Latinized name for the Persian alchemist Abu Musa Jabir ibn Hayyan (721–815). The book was observed in the Providence, Rhode Island, library of the necromancer Joseph Curwen in 1746.

(*The Case of Charles Dexter Ward*)

Liber Ivonis *

This was one of the moldering grimoires discovered by the writer Robert Blake on the shelves of the vestry room in the abandoned Church of Starry Wisdom, in Providence, Rhode Island. It is said to be the title of the Latin version of the *Book of Ebon*.

(*The Haunter of the Dark*)

Magnalia Christi Americana *

A work written by Cotton Mather that is also know under its English title *The Ecclesiastical History of New England*. In *The Unnamable* Lovecraft referred to "that demoniac sixth book which no one should read after dark." The work consists of seven books in total, published in one volume at London in 1702, but divided into two volumes when republished in Hartford in 1820. Part of it concerns the Salem Witch Trials. An edition of this work was in Lovecraft's personal library.

(*The Unnamable; Pickman's Model*)

Mesnard's edition *

The works of Hermes Trismegistus "in Mesnard's edition" are said to be present in the Providence, Rhode Island, library of Joseph Curwen in the year 1746. The edition referred to is perhaps *Hermis Trismegisti*, Traduction par J. Mesnard, 8 volumes, Paris (edited by Didier), no date.

(*The Case of Charles Dexter Ward*)

Monograph of Eli Davenport

This rare monograph contains a record of oral folklore from Vermont prior to the year 1839, drawn from the memories of the oldest residents of that state. It hints at the existence of a race of monstrous creatures in the remote hills, both on the highest forested peaks, and in the deep valleys between them. Even the wolves were said to shun these regions. Davenport mentions a strange "buzzing voice" heard in these woods.

(*The Whisperer in Darkness*)

Nameless Cults *

A book by the German writer Friedrich von Junzt (1795–1840) that bears the title *Unaussprechlichen Kulten* in its original language. As the title implies, it concerns the nature of various curious cults that worshipped forgotten alien beings regarded by them as gods or demons. Both the book and its author are the creations of writer Robert E. Howard, a close friend of Lovecraft who is most famous for his character Conan the Barbarian.

In his 1931 story *The Children of the Night*, Howard wrote that von Junzt was one of the few men who could read the *Necronomicon* in the original Greek translation—not "who had read" it, but "who could read" it, the implication being that to read the Greek version of the text was to unhinge the reason of most men. And indeed, Taverel, one of the characters of the story, remarks of von Junzt, "I'm convinced the man is mad." Howard wrote in his story of that same year, *The Black Stone*, that von Junzt was found dead with the marks of taloned fingers on his throat, in a locked and bolted room, with the pages of an unpublished manuscript scattered and torn all around his corpse. The German's close friend, the Frenchman Alexis Ladeau, pieced the manuscript back together and read it, but was so horrified by its contents that he immediately burned it and cut his own throat with a razor. Fortunately for students of obscure lore, the earlier work by von Junzt did not meet a similar fate but was published, and became *Nameless Cults*, which is sometimes called the *Black Book*.

Howard indicated in the *Children of the Night* that the book contains information on the cults of Cthulhu, Yog-Sothoth, Tsathoggua, Gol-goroth, Bran, and other dark gods. According to Howard, the most puzzling aspect of *Nameless Cults* is the frequent recurrence of the theme of keys. Von Junzt made reference to keys in various incongruous contexts, such as when he referred to the infamous Black Stone of Hungry. It is obvious that normal physical keys are not intended, but keys in a symbolic sense that open dimensional locks.

Howard composed a detailed false history for the work similar to the pseudo-history Lovecraft created for his own *Necronomicon*. *Nameless Cults* originally came into print at Dusseldorf in 1839. Fewer than a dozen copies are known to exist. Bridewell published an English translation in 1845. So horrifying was the work that the Golden Goblin Press of New York felt compelled to censor it when they did a reprinting of the Bridewell translation in 1909. Copies of the book were quite rare and difficult to obtain. An edition of the work is kept in a locked vault at the library of Miskatonic University. Many of these details are mentioned by Lovecraft in his story *Out of the Aeons*, where he refers to the book as "that monstrous blasphemy."

(*The Shadow Out of Time; Out of the Aeons*)

Necronomicon

The *Necronomicon* is at the center of Lovecraft's fiction. It weaves all four threads of the mythos together into a single cord by appearing in stories of all four types—those involving gods and monsters from beyond the Earth, those concerned with explorations of the dreamlands, stories about witchcraft and black magic, and stories that deal with degeneration, decay, and death.

Lovecraft did not invent the *Necronomicon*—he dreamed it. The title came to him in a dream, as did the image of the book repeatedly. He came to recognize the mythic power of the book and its mysterious title, which he did not understand when first he dreamed them, and began to insert them into his fiction at frequent intervals. Of all the dream grimoires and evil books mentioned in Lovecraft's stories, none is more ominous, more feared, or more highly prized, than the *Necronomicon*.

The manner in which the *Necronomicon* appears to Lovecraft provides the silver key of insight into his fiction. The underlying core of his work was not contrived or calculated, but sprang forth spontaneously from his dreams and nightmares. His writings were an effort to exorcise these haunting dream visions by placing them into fictional settings that he controlled, rather than being controlled by them as he was while he lay in sleep. For example, the night-gaunts of his childhood terrors, which returned to torment him again and again, where used in *The Dream-Quest of Unknown Kadath* to carry his alter ego, the dreamer Randolph Carter, through the air to Kadath, which was otherwise unreachable.

Lovecraft wrote a detailed fictional history of the book, as an aid to his memory when he chose to insert references to it into his stories. The book was penned by the mad Arab poet, Abdul Alhazred, at the city of Damascus prior to the year 738, which is the year of the poet's disappearance and presumed death. It was written during Alhazred's last years, and in his old age. Lovecraft gives the year of the book's composition as *circa* 730.

How Alhazred went mad is never revealed, but it would be natural to assume that some great mental and emotional shock unseated his reason, if indeed he was mad. He may have been sane, but dismissed as mad by those of his contemporaries who read what he wrote, and were unable to comprehend how a sane man could have written it. At any rate, his mind was clear enough to produce the *Necronomicon*, so his insanity, if it existed at all, was of a selective kind.

The original Arabic name for the book was *Al Azif*. Lovecraft wrote in 1927 in his *History of the Necronomicon* that the Arabic word *azif* means the sound made by nocturnal insects, which was assumed by the Arabs to be the howling of demons in the darkness of the desert night.

The book did not achieve the Greek title of Lovecraft's dream until it was translated from Arabic into Greek by Theodorus Philetas of Constantinople in the year 950. The book, which was of course in manuscript at the time, was prohibited in 1050 by Michael, Patriarch of Constantinople, and all known hand-made copies of it were gathered together and burned. At least one copy escaped the fire. Over the intervening century from the date of its translation, all known copies of the Arabic text had been lost, so Michael had reason to hope that the work had been utterly obliterated by the flames. This hope was vain, however.

Olaus Wormius translated the Greek text into Latin in 1228. In his preface, Wormius confirmed that the original Arabic text was no longer to be found. Both the Latin and Greek translations were suppressed in 1232 by Pope Gregory IX. The Greek translation of Theodorus was printed in Italy at some time between the years 1500 and 1550. The Latin translation of Olaus was printed twice, in a beautiful fifteenth-century blackletter edition published in Germany, and in a seventeenth-century edition that was probably printed in Spain. Neither of these later editions bore any internal indications of their place of origin or publishing house, so their dates and the cities in which they were printed remain conjectural.

Note that the Latin translation was printed a century or so before the printing of the Greek translation, even though the Greek translation is almost three centuries older. Lovecraft wrote that the last Greek copy of the text known to exist perished in a fire at Salem in 1692, the year of the infamous witch trials at Salem-Village.

The English mathematician and magician, John Dee (1527–1608) made an English translation of the *Necronomicon* that was never published. Wilbur Whateley possessed an incomplete manuscript copy of Dee's translation damaged by rats and worms, that had been handed down to him from his grandfather, old Wizard Whateley. Only fragments of Dee's original manuscript exist today.

Of the two extant printed Latin editions, an example of the fifteenth-century German printing was in Lovecraft's time housed under lock and key in the British Museum. It may be presumed to now reside in the British Library. A copy of the seventeenth-century Spanish printing is kept at the Bibliothèque Nationale at Paris. Other copies of the seventeenth-century edition are housed in the Widener Library at Harvard, and in the world-renowned collection of esoteric texts in the library of Miskatonic University at Arkham. Another copy is in the library of the University of Buenos Ayres.

Lovecraft wrote that there are rumors of a fifteenth-century copy in the private collection of a certain celebrated American millionaire. Perhaps he had William Randolph Hearst (1863–1951) in mind, but this is only conjecture on my part. A less well-supported rumor placed a Greek printing of the *Necronomicon* in the library of the Pickman family of Salem, but if it ever really existed, it vanished when the artist, Richard Upton Pickman, disappeared in 1926.

In the uncompleted story *The Descendant*, a young Englishman named Williams with an interest in the occult buys a copy of the German black-letter edition of the Latin translation from a Jewish bookseller in Clare Market. It is described as having a bulky leather cover with a brass clasp. The price asked by the Jew is slight, even though an old bookseller with a bent back in Chandos Street has previously informed Williams that there are only five copies known to exist, and all of them are kept carefully locked away by library custodians. There is the implication that the Jew knows more about the book than he lets on, and has sold it to Williams out of some secret malice.

It was correct of the authorities and the churches to suppress the *Necronomicon*, Lovecraft wrote in his history of the book, because the reading of it leads to "terrible consequences" that he did not enumerate. Because of its universal suppression, few among the general public were aware of the book's existence prior to its inclusion in Lovecraft's fiction. An exception is the writer Robert W. Chambers, who based his apocryphal two-act play, *The King In Yellow*, on the effects caused by reading the *Necronomicon*. In Chambers' stories the mere reading of the second act of this play induces madness and despair, with fatal consequences.

Without having a copy of the *Necronomicon* to read, it is impossible to know all of what is in it, since Lovecraft quoted only a few brief passages from the text. To judge by these quotations, it concerns the history and nature of the Old Ones, and of the other great beings and races that inhabited the Earth before the evolution of mankind, along with practical instructions on the art of necromancy, and on opening the gateway of Yog-Sothoth.

(*At the Mountains of Madness; The Dreams in the Witch House; The Diary of Alonzo Typer; Out of the Aeons; The Call of Cthulhu; The Case of Charles Dexter Ward; The Dunwich Horror; The Festival; The Haunter of the Dark; The Horror in the Museum; The Hound; Medusa's Coil; The Shadow Out of Time; The Thing on the Doorstep; The Whisperer in Darkness; Through the Gates of the Silver Key; The Descendant; History of the Necronomicon*)

Notebooks of Claes van der Heyl

Two occult diaries in low Latin that cover the years from 1560 to 1580, written in a crabbed hand by Claes van der Heyl, the ancestor of Dirck van der Heyl, of the village of Chorazin, near Attica, New York. They were found in 1935 by occultist Alonzo Typer, the first book in a carved chest in the attic of the abandoned and decaying old van der Heyl farmhouse, the second in a desk in a little locked room of that same house.

A clasp of blackened silver held the first book closed. Between its yellowed pages was a loose leaf upon which was drawn the color image of a being described by Typer as "a monstrous creature resembling nothing so much as a squid, beaked and tentacled, with great yellow eyes, and with certain abominable approximations to the human form." It is referred to by Typer as the Ancient One, the Nameless One, and the Forgotten One who is Guardian of the Ancient Gateway.

In the second diary, reference was made to the city of Yian-Ho, "that lost and hidden city wherein brood eon-old secrets, and of which dim memories older than the body lurk behind the minds of all men." The second diary was a key to understanding the contents of the first diary. From them, Typer learned the Chant that would evoke the Nameless One, but he was troubled that the Chant offered no means to control it.

(*The Diary of Alonzo Typer*)

Old Book

A book kept by the priests of Nath, mentioned by the mystic and alchemist Rudolf Yergler, in his *Chronicle of Nath*. In the Old Book is the prophecy that one who can look upon the true shape of the shadow that came to the Earth from Outside, and survive the ordeal, will have the power to send the shadow back from whence it came.

(*The Tree on the Hill*)

papyri of Democritus

A terrible work of "ancient blasphemies" mention in the story *The Green Meadow*. Democritus was a Greek philosopher. There is nothing particularly blasphemous in his work, at least by modern standards, although it may have seemed so to his contemporaries.

(*The Green Meadow*)

papyrus of Ilarnek

An ancient record that recounts the discovery of fire by the green-skinned, frog-like race that descended from the moon to the land of Mnar, along with their gray stone city of Ib and a large lake of misty green water. Ib was destroyed by the human inhabitants of the city of Sarnath, built on the shore of the same lake not far from Ib.

(*The Doom That Came to Sarnath*)

Papyrus of Ancient Meroë

An ancient Egyptian text that describes strange forms of life that existed when the world was young—forms that men would not consider living things.

(*The Green Meadow*)

People of the Monolith *

A book by Justin Geoffrey, whom Lovecraft described as "the notorious Baudelairean poet." After paying a visit to the Black Stone of Hungry in 1926, he died screaming in a madhouse. This book and its author were created by Robert E. Howard for his 1931 story *The Black Stone*, and were mentioned by Lovecraft only once.

(*The Thing on the Doorstep*)

Pnakotic Manuscripts

Also known as the Pnakotic Fragments, this document predates the human race. A copy of it was kept in the ancient city of Pnakotus, in what is now the Australian outback, where the Great Race of Yith that built the city fifty million years ago housed its main library. The first five chapters of the work detail the history of the Great Race. It is illustrated, and at least eight fragments exist in modern times, because the eighth is said to contain a long ritual. Tsathoggua is mentioned in the text. The work passed through ancient Lomar and Hyperborea, and various scribes added to its contents, until it fell into the hands of sinister human cults that worship and collaborate with the Great Race even to this day. The last copy of the work in the dreamlands resides at the city of Ulthar.

A drawing in the part of the manuscripts that is too ancient for anyone to read depicts how the Other Gods set their seal upon the granite of the Earth in antediluvian times. They did so again at the request of the gods of Earth, who were angered by men living on a slope of the mountain Ngranek in the dreamlands. The Other Gods blasted it with fire, and now the mountain overlooks only "sheer crags and a valley of sinister lava ."

(*The Shadow Out of Time*; *The Other Gods*; *The Dream Quest of Unknown Kadath*; *The Whisperer in Darkness*; *The Diary of Alonzo Typer*; *Out of the Aeons*)

Poligraphia *

A Latin work on cryptography by the Abbot Johannes Trithemius (1462–1516). The *Polygraphiae*, published in 1508, became the most popular work on ciphers and codes used during the Renaissance, and even down to modern times. The Cipher Manuscript that served as the basis for the formation of the Hermetic Order of the Golden Dawn in 1888 was composed using a system described in the *Polygraphiae*. Trithemius also wrote a Latin work titled *Steganographia* that was more obscure during the Renaissance than his *Polygraphiae*, because it was thought to be a grimoire for the summoning of spirits by magic, but it has since been demonstrated to be another work on cryptography disguised as a grimoire (although, in point of fact, it might equally be regarded as a grimoire disguised as a cryptographic text—Trithemius was the most accomplished magician of his age). Lovecraft would have done better to have referred to the much more mysterious *Steganographia*, rather than to the prosaic *Polygraphiae*, but he had almost no knowledge of these texts or their contents.

(*The Dunwich Horror*)

Qanoon-e-Islam *

An Arabic book title designed to conceal the identity of a copy of Abdul Alhazred's *Necronomicon*, which resided in the library of the necromancer Joseph Curwen. This was probably a Latin copy of the *Necronomicon* with a false cover, although it is tempting to wonder if the false Arabic title concealed an Arabic copy.

Qanoon-e-Islam is an actual book in English published in London in 1832, the full title of which is: *Qanoon-e-Islam, or the Customs of the Moosulmans of India; comprising a full and exact account of their various rites and ceremonies, from the moment of birth till the hour of death*. It was written by Jaffur Shurreef, a Muslim of India, and translated into English by G. A. Herklots.

(*The Case of Charles Dexter Ward*)

Regnum Congo *

A Latin work by Pigafetta, based on the notes of the sailor Lopex. A copy described in *The Picture in the House* resided in an ancient farmhouse on a rural road not far outside Arkham. It was published at Frankfurt in 1598. Bound in leather, it had metal fittings and was illustrated with more than a dozen plate engravings by the brothers De Bry. The book was purchased in London by the Salem merchantman Ebenezer Holt, and traded to the unnaturally long-lived owner of the farmhouse in 1768. A lightning strike upon the house in November, 1896, destroyed this copy of the work along with its owner.

This obscure book actually exists. According to S. T. Joshi, who wrote an essay on the topic titled "Lovecraft and the Regnum Congo" (Price, pp. 24–9), Lovecraft derived his references from the 1863 work *Evidence As To Man's Place In Nature* by Thomas M. Huxley. Figure 1 in Huxley's work shows the engraving by the De Bry brothers of palm trees from *Regnum Congo*, which is described in Lovecraft's story. The author of *Regnum Congo* was the Venetian writer Antonio Pigafetta (1491–1535). Pigafetta sailed with Magellan around the world, and wrote about his experiences in *Relazione del Primo Viaggio Intorno Al Mondo* (*Report on the First Voyage Around the World*), parts of which were published at Paris in 1525.

The full Latin title of the book referred to by Lovecraft is: REGNUM CONGO: *hoc est VERA DESCRIPTIO REGNI AFRICANI QUOD TAM AB INCOLIS QUAM LUSITANIS CONGUS APPELLATUR, per Philippum Pigafettam, olim ex Edoardo Lopez acroamatis lingua Italica excerpta, num Latio sermone donata ab August. Cassiod. Reinio. Iconibus et imaginibus rerum memorabilium quasi vivis, opera et industria Joan. Theodori et Joan. Israelis de Bry, fratrum exornata. Francofurti, MDXCVIII.*

(*The Picture in the House*)

R'lyehian script

R'lyehian is the language of the drowned city of R'lyeh, where dead Cthulhu waits dreaming in his stone house for the stars to once again come right in the heavens. The writing on the parchment that accompanied the silver key inherited by Randolph Carter was in this language, which the spawn of Cthulhu brought to Earth from space "countless ages ago." The text concerned the manner of traveling through time and space via dimensional portals while remaining in the body.

(*Through the Gates of the Silver Key*)

Seven Cryptical Books of Hsan

This arcane text is mentioned by the dream explorer Randolph Carter as of little use to his purposes. Barzai the Wise, resident of the dream city of Ulthar, knew about them.

(*The Dream-Quest of Unknown Kadath*; *The Other Gods*)

Tablets of Nhing

A text consulted by the wizard Zkauba on the planet Yaddith, concerning what to do about persistent and troubling dreams of an alien being named Randolph Carter on a distant planet of the future known as Earth. The Tablets of Nhing may have had an oracular function similar to the texts of the I-Ching.

(*Through the Gates of the Silver Key*)

Thesaurus Chemicus *

An alchemical tract by Roger Bacon written in Latin, that was published at Frankfurt in 1620. The same work had been published earlier in 1603 at Frankfurt under the title *Rogeri Baconis angli de arte chymiae scripta* (Thorndike, vol. 2, p. 680). The 1620 edition was in Joseph Curwen's library at Providence in 1746.

(*The Case of Charles Dexter Ward*)

Traite des Chiffres *

Traicté des chiffres, ou secretes manieres d'escrire by Blaise de Vigénère was published at Paris in 1586. He is best known for his innovation of the Vigénère Table, a method of letter substitution that uses a square of twenty-six alphabets, each written horizontally one above the other, each corresponding to a single letter. The sequence of letters in each row of the table is shifted one letter from the row above. Words could be keyed into this table in various ways to produce ciphers. There is an obvious correspondence between de Vigénère's Table and the Tables of Commutations (Right Table and Averse Table) of the Jewish Kabbalah. These tables were published in bk. 3, ch. 25 of the *Three Books of Occult Philosophy by Henry Cornelius Agrippa* (see Agrippa, pp. 541–2).

(*The Dunwich Horror*)

Turba Philosophorum *

This is one of the essential texts of medieval alchemy. It was present among the books in the library of the necromancer Joseph Curwen, residing at Providence in 1746.

A. E. Waite translated it from Latin into English in 1896, but Curwen would have owned the Latin text. Waite remarked in his preface: "The *Turba Philosophorum* is indisputably the most ancient extant treatise on Alchemy in the Latin tongue, but it was not, so far as can be ascertained, originally written in Latin; the compiler or editor, for in many respects it can scarcely be regarded as an original composition, wrote either in Hebrew or Arabic" (Waite, p. i).

(*The Case of Charles Dexter Ward*)

Whispers

This magazine of supernatural horror published the story *The Attic Window* in its January, 1922, issue. The story was written by the narrator of Lovecraft's *The Unnamable*, Randolph Carter, who is a thinly veiled representation of Lovecraft himself.

(*The Unnamable*)

Wild Marvells of Science *

A book of natural history by Morryster, which from its spelling may perhaps be dated to the sixteenth century. Lovecraft derived his passing reference to this apocryphal work in his story *The Festival* from an 1891 story by Ambrose Bierce titled *The Man and the Snake*, in which Bierce quoted a passage from Morryster. Morryster is also an entry in the unabridged edition of Bierce's *The Devil's Dictionary* (though not in the more popular abridged 1911 edition), where Bierce has written "Morryster, see Tree." Under the entry for "Tree" Bierce quoted a passage from *Trauvells in ye Easte* by Morryster. These works by Morryster do not exist.

(*The Festival*)

Witch-Cult in Western Europe *

A book by the English woman Margaret A. Murray, published in 1925, that sets forth the startling claim that the men and women executed for the practice of witchcraft in Europe during the witch-persecution of the sixteenth and seventeenth centuries were not deluded individuals, but were members of the remnant of a secret pagan religion that worshipped Diana, goddess of the Moon. At first greeted with great acclaim, the book quickly fell out of favor, and suffered intense criticism that destroyed its author's reputation as a serious scholar and anthropologist—undeservedly, as the book is well researched, despite its daring and unconventional conclusions.

Concerning Murray's book, the protagonist of Lovecraft's story *The Horror at Red Hook*, police detective Thomas F. Malone, observed:

> He had not read in vain such treatises as Miss Murray's *Witch-Cult in Western Europe*; and knew that up to recent years there had certainly survived among peasants and furtive folk a frightful and clandestine system of assemblies and orgies descended from dark religions antedating the Aryan world, and appearing in popular legends as Black Masses and Witches' Sabbaths. That these hellish vestiges of old Turanian-Asiatic magic and fertility cults were even now wholly dead he could not for a moment suppose, and he frequently wondered how much older and how much blacker than the very worst of the muttered tales some of them might really be.

There is no presumption in Murray's book that the pagan cult of witches surviving in rural parts of Europe had its origins in "Turanian-Asiatic magic and fertility cults" as Lovecraft suggested. Murray believed that the Dianic cult, as she called it, was the "ancient religion of Western Europe" (Murray, p. 12). This speculation was added by Lovecraft himself—that not only is witchcraft the survival of a pagan cult of goddess worship, but that its roots go back further than ancient Rome, and are more remote than the Mediterranean Basin.

Lovecraft identified the cultists as Yezidis, devil worshippers of Kurdistan, and the goddess of this fertility cult as Lilith, demon-queen of Hell who has her roots in ancient Sumer. To further bridge the gap between Lilith and the witches, he quoted an ancient Greek incantation to the goddess of witches, Hecate, but omitted the name of the goddess from the incantation so that it would apply to Lilith. This connection between Hecate and Lilith is not so far-fetched as might first appear. The two have many qualities in common. Both are associated with the Moon, the dead, woman's mysteries, and with the sacrifice of children. Hecate and Lilith were explicitly linked by Lovecraft in his description of a vast cavern beneath the earth:

"Satan here held his Babylonish court, and in the blood of stainless childhood the leprous limbs of phosphorescent Lilith were laved. Incubi and succubae howled praise to Hecate, and headless moon-calves bleated to the Magna Mater."

(*The Horror at Red Hook*)

yellowed papyrus

An opium dreamer found this document in the dream city of Zakarion. It is filled with the thoughts of the dream-sages of that city, who have never been born into mortal bodies in the waking world. They wrote much about the world of dreams, including lore concerning a golden valley with a sacred grove and temples, and a high, vine-covered stone wall having a small bronze gate. Beyond the gate, some of the dream-sages wrote there were wonders, but others warned that through it lay only disappointment.

(*Ex Oblivione*)

Zobnarian Fathers

The Zobnarian Fathers are the authors of wisdom texts that were held in the city of Olathoë, in the lost northern land of Lomar.

(*Polaris*)

Zohar *

This mammoth collection of Kabbalistic commentaries on the Torah is the central work of the Kabbalah, a Jewish system of mysticism and magic. *Sefer ha-Zohar* was written in Spain between the years 1280–6 by Moses de Leon (died 1305). Lovecraft mentions it in passing with other esoteric books in the library of Joseph Curwen, calling it "the cabbalistic Zohar."

(*The Case of Charles Dexter Ward*)

The Key to the Ninth Gate

9th Astral Gate: Leo—The Lion

Sun passes through Leo: August 10—September 16

Constellation is represented by a male lion.

Right Pillar: Regulus (Greek: Prince, or Little King). Also know as Cor Leonis (Latin: Heart of the Lion). Arabic name: *qalb al-'asad*—Heart of the Lion. Astronomical designation: Alpha Leonis. Astrological nature: Jupiter-Mars. Influence: generosity, nobility, leadership. Magnitude: 1.3—multiple star system. Color: white. Sun crosses: August 22. Location: the breast of the lion. Comments: this is one of the four Persian royal stars, and was associated by the ancient Persians with the summer solstice.

Left Pillar: Zosma (Greek: The Girdle). Arabic name: *al thahr al-'asad*—The Lion's Back. Astronomical designation: Beta Leonis. Astrological nature: Saturn-Venus. Influence: melancholy, regret, despair, disgrace, danger from poison. Magnitude: 2.6—multiple star system. Color: white. Sun crosses: September 9. Location: the rump of the lion. Comments: The Saturn influence brings out the worst qualities of Venus.

The astral gate of Leo lies between the star of its right pillar, located on the breast of the lion, and the star of its left pillar, on the lion's rump. The sun enters the gate by crossing the longitude of the great star Regulus, star of the right pillar, around August 22. The solar transition of this wide gate takes eighteen days. The sun exits the gate around September 9, when it crosses the longitude of the star of the left pillar, Zosma.

The key to the Ninth Gate opens the constellation Leo, allowing entry into that part of the walled city of the *Necronomicon* that concerns occult or esoteric books, both those that exist in this world and those that exist only on the astral planes. Use it for reading the information contained in their pages via scrying and dreams.

Seal of the Ninth Key on the Ninth Gate

Ritual of Opening Leo

Face the direction of the compass ruled by the Ninth Gate, which is southwest by west—that is, slightly to the right of the southwest point. Visualize before you the closed gate in the western wall of the city of the *Necronomicon* so that it is more than large enough for you to walk through.

With the visualized image of the gate sustained in your mind and projected upon the astral plane in the direction southwest by west, speak this invocation to Yog-Sothoth, which has the same general form for all the gates:

> Guardian of the Gate! Defender of the Door! Watcher of the Way!
> Who art the stout Lock, the slender Key, and the turning Hinge! Lord of

All Transition, without whom there is no coming in or going out, I call thee! Keeper of the Threshold, whose dwelling place is between worlds, I summon thee! Yog-Sothoth, wise and mighty lord of the Old Ones, I invoke thee!

By the authority of the dreaded name, Azathoth, that few dare speak, I charge thee, open to me the gateway of Leo, the Lion, that lies between the blazing pillar Regulus on the right hand and the blazing pillar Zosma on the left hand. As the solar chariot [or, lunar chariot] crosses between these pillars, I enter the city of the *Necronomicon* through its Ninth Gate. Selah!

Visualize the key of the Ninth Gate in your right hand some six inches long and made of cast gold. Feel its weight, texture, and shape as you hold it. Extend your right arm and use the key to draw upon the surface of the gate the seal of the key, which should be visualized to burn on the gate in a line of white spiritual fire. Point with the astral key at the center of the gate and speak the words of opening:

In the name of Azathoth, Ruler of Chaos, by the power of Yog-Sothoth, Lord of Portals, the Ninth Gate is opened!

Visualize the gate unlocking and opening inward of its own accord upon a shadowed space. On the astral level, walk through the gateway and stand in the darkness beyond. Focus your attention on the book described by Lovecraft that you wish to view or read, or upon the library or other place where you know the book you desire is located. Open your mind to receive impressions of the book, and use your will to project your intention to read its pages across the astral realms. Knowledge of its contents will be given in the form of scrying or dreams. In a more general sense, this ritual and this gate may be used to scry the contents of any astral book, and even to call into your possession a desired book that has material existence.

After fulfilling the purpose for which this gate was opened, conclude the ritual by astrally passing out through the gate and visualizing it to close. Draw the seal of the Ninth Key on the surface of the gate with the astral key you hold in your hand, and mentally cause it to lock itself shut, as it was at the beginning of the ritual. Speak the words of closing:

By the power of Yog-Sothoth, and authority of the supreme name Azathoth, I close and seal the Ninth Gate. This ritual is well and truly ended.

Allow the image of the gate to grow pale in your imagination and fade to nothingness before you turn away from the ritual direction.

The Tenth Gate

Tenth Gate
Talismans

Objects such as amulets, talismans, tokens, charms, icons, and the like were thought to acquire potency in magic by virtue of their substance, their shape or pattern, their associations, and by having occult force, which may be blind or intelligent, infused into them. These factors are frequently combined to further heighten the power of such objects, numerous examples of which appear in the Necronomicon mythos.

Some materials were considered in that branch of occultism known as natural magic to be inherent attractors and reservoirs of various kinds of magical energies. For example, silver was thought to possess the properties of the Moon by virtue of its shining whiteness, and gold the properties of the Sun due to its bright yellow color. It is no accident that Randolph Carter's famous silver key is made of the metal of the Moon—the Moon is the ruler of dreams and visions.

There was no need for the witch or wizard to do anything to these and similar natural substances in order to give them occult virtues—they possessed these virtues due to their own natures. Herbs of this kind were used in natural magic to heal the sick. Stones with occult virtues were employed to attract love, to convey eloquence, to find hidden treasure, and so on. Such natural substances were placed into charms or talismans to render their working more effective. It was common for wizards to insert small pieces of dried root beneath the stone of a ring for occult purposes.

Stone has been intuitively recognized throughout history to act as a reservoir for occult potential. In ancient times rough standing stones known as menhirs were used to mark places of ritual and to define ritual spaces. Stonehenge is the best known of the stone circles of Europe, but there are many others with stones arranged in various patterns such as ovals, spirals, and lines. Lovecraft makes numerous mentions of stone circles and lines of standing stones, such as the circle in the northern Maine woods, and the lines of stones on the island in the Miskatonic River. Equally important to Lovecraft was the color of the stones. Black, white, and green stones have special significance in the mythos.

Not only substances but shapes can be repositories for certain magic energies. The Stone Age tribes of Europe used standing stones as much for their upright, elongated forms, which possessed phallic significance, as for their composition. Rounded artificial hills, such as those described in the story *The Mound*, were worshipped as breasts of the Earth goddess both in Britain and in America. The symbolic significance of caves should be obvious—they are the mouth, or womb, of the Earth, to be ritually penetrated, just as Randolph Carter penetrated the Snake-Den in *The Silver Key* in order to pass over the boundary of our everyday waking reality.

A talisman or charm can be empowered by inscribing upon it a specific form or symbol conducive to its intended function. The action of a charm designed to embody the virtues of a specific astrological planet will be enhanced by having the symbol of that planet carved into its surface, and if the substance of the charm is naturally resonant with that planet, its working will be even stronger. For example, Mars is the planet of strife and combat, but also of boldness and courage. The color of Mars is red; the metal of Mars iron or steel. By inscribing the symbol of Mars on the blade of a dagger, and filling the lines of the symbol with red pigment, the working of the charm as an attractor and repository of the occult virtues of Mars is greatly enhanced.

Sometimes objects acquire occult energies merely because they are near those energies for prolonged periods of time. Houses that are used for ritual magic may pick up the energies of those rituals, and years later long after those rituals have ceased, they may cause visitors to feel uneasy or frightened due to the uncanny residue of magical force. Those who sleep in such houses often experience nightmares, or hear disembodied noises or voices. A book of spells known as a grimoire can acquire over time a kind of talismanic energy due to the ritual environment in which it is used, and the potently focused thoughts and emotions of those who employ it. Years later this occult potential will still be sensed by anyone who handles or reads the book. Personal objects of powerful witches and magicians are prone to pick up energies of this kind, due to their close contact with their possessors during ritual work.

The effect is massively heightened when a witch or wizard sets out to deliberately infuse magical virtue into an object. The energy projected into the object may be in the form of what is known as a blind force—an unthinking occult potential that is neither good nor bad in itself, but is simply energy analogous on the esoteric level to electricity. The elemental forces are often used by magicians in this way. The potency of elemental fire, for example, which has the qualities of forcefulness, decisiveness, quickness, and impetuosity, can be projected, concentrated, and infused into a charm designed to embody the occult virtues of elemental fire. By contrast, the potency of elemental water, which has the qualities of dreaminess, reflection, emotionalism, and receptivity, can be infused into a charm intended to embody the virtues of this element.

The occult energy infused into a talisman or charm need not be a blind force. It may also be an intelligence—an astral being with conscious awareness and a self-identity that has either been created or summoned by the witch to inhabit the talisman. In past centuries, magicians often infused servant spirits known as familiars into rings and medallions, so that they could carry the spirits with them and call them forth at need. Spirits were sometimes made to reside within mirrors, where they usually functioned as oracles. The alien force that is bound up with the black, faceted stone know as the Shining Trapezohedron is such a being—in *The Haunter of the Dark* the black stone is used to summon this intelligence, which is then asked to reveal occult secrets. Spirits were also bound into objects or structures to act as guardians, and to prevent the intrusion of undesirables.

In Lovecraft's stories, the distinction between demons and aliens is not always clear. A creature who would have been looked upon as a demon by a witch of old Salem such as Keziah Mason might not be regarded in this way by a professor of Miskatonic University. Many creatures of the mythos such as the Old Ones transcend our normal reality, making this distinction between spiritual and corporeal difficult to quantify. Wilbur Whatley's hybrid brother was so unnatural, he was invisible to human sight, and the Mi-Go are composed of such otherworldly stuff that when killed, they simply evaporate to nothingness. Those of past centuries would naturally have regarded such beings as demonic.

Neither is there a clear distinction between magic and alien science. There are certain signs and marks that control various alien creatures in ways that appear to be magical. If there is a mechanism at work other than magic, it is not apparent to the limited human mind. In *The Shadow Over Innsmouth*, the Deep Ones were said to have been kept at bay by the Kanaky islanders of the Pacific with marks on stones that resembled a type of swastika. The Elder Sign is a kind of hand gesture used to ward off the evil of the Old Ones and associated malign influences. In *The Dreams in the Witch House*, Gilman saves himself from the witch Keziah Mason by holding up a silver crucifix.

Whether the use of such symbols is merely a shared superstition, or has tangible force on some transcendent level of reality, is never resolved in Lovecraft's writings. In the famous words of the science fiction writer, Arthur C. Clark, "Any sufficiently advanced technology is indistinguishable from magic." It might be added that from the practical standpoint of the inferior species, which is the human race in Lovecraft's mythos, such advanced technology might as well be magic, for all the difference it makes, since we can never understand it in other than a magical sense.

amulet, jade

Around the neck of a corpse in a five-centuries-old coffin in Holland, two young English grave robbers find a jade amulet. The corpse was reputed to have been that of a ghoul (that is, a robber of graves) in life, who had once taken "a potent thing from a mighty sepulchre." One of the men describes the amulet: "It was the oddly conventionalised figure of a crouching winged hound, or sphinx with a semi-canine face, and was exquisitely carved in antique Oriental fashion from a small piece of green jade." The expression on the face of the carving bears a disquieting malevolence that savors of death. It should be noted that the bones of the corpse exhibit signs of having been crushed by the powerful jaws of some great beast.

The grave robbers recognize the amulet from hints they have read in the *Necronomicon*. It is the soul-symbol of the corpse-eating cult that dwells on the plateau of Leng, which in this story is placed in Central Asia. Alhazred wrote that the features on the carving were drawn from "some obscure supernatural manifestation of the souls of those who vexed and gnawed at the dead." The amulet was in the shape of a small three-dimensional statuette, not a flat piece of jade. Around its base ran an inscription, the letters of which neither of the grave robbers recognized from their occult reading. On the bottom of the base a skull was engraved, like a kind of maker's mark.

The two young dilatants steal the amulet and carry it to England to place in their private collection of items taken from graves. Occasionally they burn candles before it in a sort of mock ritual observance. What they do not realize is that the separation of the amulet from the neck of its possessor awakens a nemesis in the shape of a giant spectral hound. They are also haunted by the ghost of the Dutch ghoul. After one of the young men, named St. John, is torn apart by the vengeful canine spirit, the other, who is never named, tries vainly to return the amulet to its ancient grave in an effort to avert the same fate, but the amulet is stolen in Rotterdam before he can replace it. Later he reads of the thieves having been torn apart, and under a strange compulsion of the mind, returns to the cemetery to dig up the corpse of the old Dutch ghoul. There he finds the amulet, hanging around the neck of the corpse.

(*The Hound*)

black stone

A carved black stone found by Henry Wentworth Akeley in the woods on Round Hill, east of Townshend, in Vermont, that is some two feet high and a foot across. Its angles are cut in an alien geometry that defies analysis. On its surface are unknown hieroglyphics, some of which may be recognized as "ideographs" that also appear in the *Necronomicon*. It is an ancient artifact of the Mi-Go. Akeley speculates in *The Whisperer in Darkness* that the inscription concerns "the Yog-Sothoth and Cthulhu cycles—which are hinted at in the *Necronomicon*." The Mi-Go had a talent for carving curious black stones into planes with alien geometry—it was they who made the black stone known as the Shining Trapezohedron. Akeley is confident that the black stone he found on

Round Hill has been fashioned on Yuggoth, a way station for the Mi-Go in this star system, where there are cities of terraced towers built of the same black stone.

Concerning another different black stone, Old Sophy, the ancient negro servant at the Louisiana plantation of Antoine de Russy, asserts that she had "done got de black stone outen Big Zimbabwe in ol' Affriky!" She uses this stone as an altar in her rites of worship—she is referred to as a witch-woman in *Medusa's Coil*. Old Sophy mentions dancing around a crocodile stone in Big Zimbabwe by moonlight. The stone she brought to America may have been this stone.

(*The Whisperer in Darkness; Medusa's Coil*)

crucifix

Walter Gilman saves himself from the clutching hands of the witch, Keziah Mason, who seeks to throttle him with her powerful fingers, by thrusting into her face a silver Christian crucifix he is wearing around his neck on a chain of nickel. The sudden shock of this sacred symbol startles the witch. Lovecraft wrote, "At sight of the device the witch seemed struck with panic, and her grip relaxed long enough to give Gilman a chance to break it entirely." Gilman wraps the chain of the crucifix around her neck and uses it to strangle her to death.

Gilman had received the crucifix from the devoted Catholic Joe Mazurewicz, a fellow tenant of the Witch House, and he in his turn had been given the silver crucifix and chain by Father Iwanicki of St. Stanislaus' Church. Mazurewicz explicitly told Gilman that the holy symbol had been "blessed by the good Father Iwanicki" before it passed into Mazurewicz's hands. Whether it was the blessing by a priest of the crucifix, its right-angled geometric shape, its religious associations with Christ, Gilman's sudden-found faith in its power, or its silver composition that distressed Keziah enough to break her grip on Gilman's throat, Lovecraft does not indicate.

The distinction between a crucifix and a Christian cross is worth mentioning. A crucifix is a Christian cross with an image of the crucified body of Jesus upon it. Since the image of the body of Christ may be assumed to represent Christ more directly than the abstract symbol of the cross alone, superstitious Catholics are inclined to ascribe a greater power to the crucifix than to the naked cross.

(*The Dreams in the Witch House*)

cyclopean symbol

After Barzai the Wise dares to climb to the summit of the mountain Hatheg-Kla to look upon the dancing gods of Earth, the Other Gods blast the mountain as a warning to the curious who might follow him, searing into its naked rock a "cyclopean symbol" some fifty cubits across "as if the rock had been riven by some titanic chisel." The same symbol is to be found in that part of the Pnakotic Manuscripts that is too ancient to be read.

(*The Other Gods*)

Dragon's Head and Tail *

The two astrological symbols known as *caput draconis* or Dragon's Head (☊) and *cauda draconis* or Dragon's Tail (☋) appear in *The Case of Charles Dexter Ward* as part of the occult incantation to Yog-Sothoth that raises the dead from their essential salts, or reduces them to their salts once again. The Dragon's Head is used to raise up the dead; the Dragon's Tail is used to lay them down once again.

These signs were appropriately chosen by Lovecraft. The Dragon's Head is the ascending node of the Moon, the place in the heavens where the apparent circle traced by the orbit of the Moon crosses from below to above the apparent circle traced by the Sun; and the Dragon's Tail is the descending node of the Moon, the place in the heavens where the path of the Moon crosses from above to below the path of the Sun. These nodes do not mark the Moon itself, but empty points in space where the paths of the Moon and Sun intersect.

The nodes of the Moon, which are always directly opposite each other, represent a kind of occult dance between the Moon and Sun, in which sometimes the Moon is above the plane of the Sun, and sometimes below. The nodes, are not stationary but wind around the heavens as the relationship between the paths of Sun and Moon change relative to each other. As a rule of thumb, in medieval and Renaissance astrology charts the ascending node was considered to exert a favorable influence, and the descending node an unfavorable influence.

(*The Case of Charles Dexter Ward*)

Elder Seal

A symbol or glyph that according to the *Necronomicon* is engraved on stones in the lost city of the Elder Race on the high plateau of Antarctica, and also on stones of the city on the sunken island of R'lyeh were Cthulhu and his spawn lie dreaming. Precisely what this seal looks like is a matter for conjecture. Lovecraft never described it in his stories, but he drew it in 1930 in one of his letters to fellow writer Clark Ashton Smith—in that thumbnail sketch he made it resemble the naked branch of a tree, a central stem with five angled twigs extending from it. August Derleth described the Elder Seal in his story

The Lurker At the Threshold in the form of an eye, but it may be presumed that Lovecraft knew better what it looked like than Derleth. It is not called the Elder Seal in the *Necronomicon*, but is referred to as "their seal"—the seal of the invisible Old Ones.

(*The Dunwich Horror*)

Elder Sign

A hand gesture made as a cultic sign of recognition, and perhaps to ward off the Old Ones. In the *Necronomicon* Alhazred makes reference to "the evil that defieth the Elder Sign." There is more than one elder sign, although only one is widely known and used. In *The Last Test*, the Atlantean priest Surama "made an elder sign that no book of history records." *Through the Gates of the Silver Key* speaks of "vaporous brains of the spiral nebulae" who know Yog-Sothoth, the keeper of the gates, only as an "untranslatable Sign."

If this sign of Yog-Sothoth is a form of the Elder Sign, then it may be that the power of the Elder Sign lies in its ability to close the gates of Yog-Sothoth. By inversion, the sign would open the gates—in the poem "The Messenger" the Elder Sign is said to be that which "sets the fumbling forms of darkness free." It is possible that these two forms of the Elder Sign are hand gestures that represent the nodes of the Moon, known as the Head of the Dragon and the Tail of the Dragon. The glyphs of the nodes are used in *The Case of Charles Dexter Ward* in conjunction with the name "Yog-Sothoth" to raise up dead men from their essential salts, and to return them to their salts once again.

(*The Descendant; The Dream-Quest of Unknown Kadath; Through the Gates of the Silver Key; The Last Test; The Haunter of the Dark; The Book; The Messenger*)

Grey Eagle's charm

A disk of dark and lustrous unknown alloy about two inches in diameter, bearing an image of Yig the serpent god on one side and an image of Cthulhu on the other. It hangs upon a thong of leather through a perforation on its rim, and is magnetically attracted to objects of the same metal that composes it. The charm was the family heirloom of Grey Eagle, a chief of the Wichita Indian tribe who was some one hundred and fifty years old, his life having been strangely prolonged by the power of the charm. The Indian chief never knew that what he thought of as a magic charm was not of this planet, and was the ceremonial metal of the copper-skinned alien race of subterranean K'n-yan.

(*The Mound*)

Key, green

An ancient key made of some frosted, greenish, unknown metal described as similar to brass that had corroded and become covered in verdigris. The key is said to be of ponderous bulk, with a coffin-shaped end, and a handle in the shape of a non-human image the exact nature of which cannot be discerned. It was found in 1935 by the occultist Alonzo Typer, hidden in the drawer of a desk in a small locked room of the deserted ancestral home of the van der Heyls, in the New England village of Chorazin. The key was wrapped in a piece of newspaper dated October 31, 1872. Inside the newspaper was a second wrapping of some dried, reptilian skin that bore crabbed Latin writing in the hand of Claes van der Heyl, a wizard who had lived at the end of the sixteenth century.

In the note, the wizard declared that he had traveled to the lost and forbidden city of Yian-Ho in the flesh, something no other human being had ever accomplished, and had acquired there the secrets of the primal ones, which he would never reveal. He declared that the key was to a lock given to him in Yian-Ho, that must be placed on the "vestibule of That Which is to be found." The reference was to a vault beneath the house that guarded an entrance to passages beneath the earth. Upon the door of that vault was a lock in the same unknown greenish metal as the key, covered with strange occult hieroglyphics.

The key was hidden away on Halloween, 1872. Alonzo Typer, descendant of the van der Heyl bloodline, made use of it in 1935 on April 30—Walpurgis Night. It may be that the sabbat of Halloween is when the lock on the vault was sealed, and the sabbat of Walpurgis is when the lock was opened. These dates are six months apart, on opposite sides of the year. The opposite dates suggest sealing and loosing, but also a going in and a coming out. It was the fatal destiny of Typer to release that which his ancestor had sealed and imprisoned beneath the house, so that it could make its way to the well in the circle of standing stones on the hill, thereby returning to its original place, and lifting the curse from the bloodline of the van der Heyls. Since the body of Typer was never found, it may be speculated that the monster took Typer with it into the well.

(*The Diary of Alonzo Typer*)

Monolith

In the story *Dagon*, the monolith is a massive white granite stone, artificially shaped, that is covered with unknown hieroglyphic writing made up of symbols representing sea creatures such as "fishes, eels, octopi, crustaceans, molluscs, whales," as well as several other species unknown to the modern world. Also depicted in bas-relief carvings on the stone are amphibious beings similar to men, but possessing webbed hands and feet, wide frog-like mouths, and bulging eyes, who worship large stones. The monolith was brought to the surface when a new island rose from the floor of the sea due to volcanic activity in the South Pacific Ocean. A shipwrecked man landed his lifeboat on the island in time to see a gigantic amphibious being arise from the water and embrace the monolith as though in a kind of adoration or worship, making certain "measured sounds."

There is another very similar, but larger, monolith, in *The Call of Cthulhu*. This also is a single block of carved stone, which was exposed in the spring of 1925 when the island of R'lyeh temporarily rose from the floor of the Pacific Ocean at the coordinates S. Latitude 47° 9', W. Longitude 123° 43'. This monolith, described as rising from the sea like a great pillar, was also covered with hieroglyphics, and was situated on the top of a mountain where dreaming Cthulhu had his fortress house of stone. The influence of the earlier story *Dagon* on the later tale is obvious. It may be that the monolith on R'lyeh had the function of magnifying Cthulhu's telepathic commands, which he was able to send around the world once his city arose from the depths and the intervening miles of ocean water were no long an obstacle to his projected thoughts.

(*Dagon; The Call of Cthulhu*)

Shining Trapezohedron

Lovecraft wrote of this great gemstone that it was "a window on all time and space." In geometry, a trapezohedron is a polyhedron with regularly alternating kite-shaped sides, a form of anti-prism. Different regular trapezohedrons are distinguished by their number of facets. The Shining Trapezohedron referred to in *The Haunter of the Dark* was described by the protagonist as a "crazily angled stone" that was egg-shaped, or irregularly spherical, and some four inches in size. It was nearly black in color, but with red striations visible in its depths through its polished, irregularly shaped facets. This indicates that it was a distorted trapezohedron, or perhaps a symmetrical form that was modeled upon a higher geometry than is used in this world.

It was fashioned on Yuggoth (another name for the planetoid Pluto), probably by the Mi-Go although this is not explicitly stated, and carried to the Earth by the Old Ones. The crinoid Elder Things of Antarctica valued it highly and placed it into a specially constructed "strangely-adorned metal box." The asymmetrical box with its hinged lid was of a yellowish metal, and covered with bas-relief images of alien beings. The Trapezohedron did not rest in the bottom of this box, but was suspended in space within it by means of a metal band around its equator that was attached to the upper edge of the interior of the box by seven radiating spokes.

Long after the crinoids abandoned their great city, the serpent-men of Valusia found the box amid its ruins. In the land of Lemuria it passed into the keeping of men, but it was lost beneath the waves with the sinking of Atlantis. A Minoan fisherman chanced to haul it up from the bottom of the sea in his net, and sold it to an Egyptian merchant. The pharaoh Nephren-Ka of Egypt recognized its value and built a temple above the windowless crypt where he kept the jewel. He had the audacity to use the Trapezohedron, and for this transgression his name was stricken from all monuments and scrolls, and the temple pulled down upon the sealed crypt with the box that held the jewel still within it.

In 1843, the American archaeologist Enoch Bowen dug it from its resting place, and the following year brought it to Providence, Rhode Island. He founded the occult order known as the Church of Starry Wisdom in Providence. It was devoted to worship of the Trapezohedron, and the thing it summoned, with ritual blood sacrifice. He placed the box in the shuttered steeple of a soot-blackened, gothic revival stone church on Federal Hill, the meeting place for his cult, which he purchased in July of 1844. In the center of the floor of the tower room stood a strangely angled stone pillar some four feet tall and two feet across. This supported the metal box that held the great jewel. It was surrounded by seven chairs, behind each of which stood a monolithic image sculpted in black-painted plaster.

The Trapezohedron was used to call into our world a being known as the Haunter of the Dark, thought to be an avatar of Nyarlathotep, but the action of the stone was inhibited by light. For this reason, while the cult was active, the tower room in the church was kept tightly shuttered with opaque screens. At its height in 1863, the cult boasted over two hundred members. Toward the end of 1877 hostility toward the cult had grown so intense over the mysterious disappearance of children that 181 cult members fled Providence for their lives in the face of an enraged Irish mob. Thereafter the church remained abandoned.

After the Trapezohedron resulted in the death of the overly inquisitive writer and painter Robert Blake in 1935, it was taken from the church steeple by Doctor Ambrose Dexter and cast into the deepest part of Narragansett Bay.

(*The Haunter of the Dark*)

sign of doom

A symbol inscribed by the high priest of the city of Sarnath, Taran-Ish, upon the altar of chrysolite just before his death from extreme fear, on the night that the statue of the water-lizard god Bokrug, god of the amphibious people of Ib, was stolen from the temple at Sarnath, where it had been placed as a spoil of war after the destruction of Ib by the men of Sarnath.

(*The Doom That Came to Sarnath*)

sign of Koth

An occult symbol that dream travelers sometimes see affixed above the great open door of a black tower at twilight, in the city of the gugs. It was discovered by the friend of Randolph Carter, Dr. Marinus Bicknell Willett, carved by Joseph Curwen above a door in the crypts where he conducted his abhorrent experiments in necromancy. Randolph Carter had at some previous time spoken ominously to Willett about the meaning the symbol possessed in the dreamlands, and had drawn it on paper for the doctor, but Willett did not reveal what things Carter had told him.

(*The Case of Charles Dexter Ward; The Dream-Quest of Unknown Kadath*)

silver key

A mysterious object in the shape of an antique key of tarnished silver, almost five inches in length, covered with arabesques that have occult significance. It was passed down as a legacy through the family of Randolph Carter, along with a parchment written in an unknown language, both contained in a box of carved oak blackened with age that was bound with rusty iron. Randolph Carter asserted to his friends that it would open the successive doors of the "mighty corridors of space and time." He believed it connected in some way with the lost city of Irem, and with a hand chiseled into the keystone of a great arch in that city. He was able to determine that the writing on the parchment was a translation of R'lyehian, the native language of the spawn of Cthulhu. To open dimensional gates with the key, it is rotated nine times while chanting certain words.

(*The Silver Key; Through the Gates of the Silver Key*)

standing stones

A circle of great standing stones, with a single menhir in the center, occupied the grassy, moss-covered crown of a hill behind the abandoned house of the van der Heyl family, in the village of Chorazin, near Attica, New York. The occultist Alonzo Typer described the stones as "neither brown nor gray, but rather of a dirty yellow merging into an evil green." The texture of the stones he describes as like that of a scaled serpent, "cold and clammy." Near the menhir was a stone-rimmed opening that resembled a well. The native Iroquois Indians loathed and shunned the stones.

Edward Pickman Derby speaks in *The Thing on the Doorstep* of a circle of standing stones in the deep woods of northern Maine, near the town of Chesuncook, which he describes as "Indian relics." They mark the entrance to the pit of the shoggoths, which is reached by descending six thousand steps. The coven of Ephraim Waite held their sabbat gatherings in this pit beneath the stone circle.

Near the town of Arkham, rows of moss-covered standing stones are to be found on the unnamed island in the midst of the Miskatonic River, the origins of which are said in *The Dreams in the Witch House* to be "obscure and immemorial." It is presumed by most of the folk of Arkham that they were set up by the Indians. The stones are clearly visible from the Garrison Street bridge, if one looks northward up the river at the island.

The strangely regular domed hills around Dunwich are crowned by circles of standing stones. The people of the town remember the time old Wizard Whateley shrieked the name "Yog-Sothoth" in one such ring of stones, with "a great book open in his arms."

In *The Whisperer in Darkness*, Henry Wentworth Akeley takes a photograph of a circle of standing stones atop a hill in Vermont, which Albert Wilmarth, a professor at Miskatonic University, examines. The circle is described by Wilmarth as "druid-like" and the grass around the stones is much beaten down and worn away, as though by the tread of many feet, although no footprint is visible in the photograph. The hill is in a remote location, as evidenced by the completely uninhabited vista of low, forested mountains behind it.

(*The Diary of Alonzo Typer; The Thing on the Doorstep; The Dreams in the Witch House; The Dunwich Horror; The Whisperer in Darkness*)

swastika *

The swastika was not invented by the Nazis, but is an ancient Hindu symbol of good fortune. The Vikings used it to represent the fiery meteor of Thor's hammer. It is more generally considered to stand for the blazing disk of the Sun. Examples of it have been found in rock carvings dated to the Neolithic period. There are two forms that rotate in opposite directions, but opinions vary as to which is lucky and which unlucky, with some cultures making no distinction between the two. The shape of the arms also varies considerable from place to place.

This sign of the lost Old Ones painted on small beach stones was found by Captain Obed Marsh of Innsmouth scattered all over the ground when he visited for the last time the South Sea island "east of Othaheite" where the Kanaky natives had close dealings with the Deep Ones. Natives on neighboring islands had driven the inhabitants away due to their unnatural practices. The sign of the Old Ones had been used by the Kanakys to control the Deep Ones and ensure that the Deep Ones did not turn against them.

(*The Shadow Over Innsmouth*)

White Stone

The Salem witch Keziah Mason testified at her trial for witchcraft before Judge Hathorne about a white stone in a dark valley beyond Meadow Hill, near Arkham, where witches gathered at midnight and drew "lines and curves" to open portals between worlds. In modern times, the white stone is still to be found in the shadowed ravine, the ground surrounding it strangely barren of plant life. The common people of Arkham believe that witch sabbats are held at the stone on Walpurgis Night, at which children are sacrificed.

(*The Dreams in the Witch House*)

The Key to the Tenth Gate

10th Astral Gate: Virgo—The Virgin

Sun passes through Virgo: September 16—October 31

Constellation is represented by a winged virgin who carries stalks of ripe wheat in her hands.

Right Pillar: Spica (Latin: *spicum*—The Spike), meaning a spike, or stalk, of ripe wheat. Astronomical designation: Alpha Virginis. Astrological nature: Venus-Mars. Influence: promotes success in the arts, sciences, religion and law, but may signify isolation or loneliness. Magnitude: 1. Color: brilliant white—binary star. Sun crosses: October 16. Location: the left hand of the Virgin. Comments: This is the only bright star in Virgo, for which reason it was called by the Coptic Egyptians Khoritos (Solitary).

Left Pillar: Syrma (Greek: Train of the Dress). Astronomical designation: Iota Virginis. Astrological nature: Mercury-Mars. Influence: the occult, secret wisdom, concealed truths. Magnitude: 4.1. Color: white. Sun crosses: October 29. Location: the hem of the Virgin's dress. Comments: The dress of the Virgin conceals the Mysteries.

The astral gate of Virgo lies between the star of its right pillar, located on the left hand of the virgin, and the star of its left pillar, which is on the hem of her dress. The Sun enters the gate by crossing the longitude of Spica, the star of the right pillar, around October 16. The solar transition of this gate takes thirteen days. The Sun exits the gate around October 29, when it crosses the longitude of the star of the left pillar, Syrma.

The key to the Tenth Gate opens the constellation Virgo, allowing entry into that part of the walled city of the Necronomicon that concerns the talismans and magical objects dreamed by Lovecraft. Use it for divining information about these talismans.

Seal of the Tenth Key on the Tenth Gate

Ritual of Opening Virgo

Face the direction of the compass ruled by the Tenth Gate, which is west by south—that is, slightly to the left of due west. Visualize before you the closed gate in the western wall of the city of the book so that it is more than large enough for you to walk through without awkwardness. You should see it as a real city gate in a city wall.

With the visualized image of the gate clear in your mind and projected upon the astral plane in the direction west by south, speak this invocation to Yog-Sothoth, which has the same general form for all the gates:

> Guardian of the Gate! Defender of the Door! Watcher of the Way! Who art the stout Lock, the slender Key, and the turning Hinge! Lord of All Transition, without whom there is no coming in or going out, I call thee! Keeper of the Threshold, whose dwelling place is between worlds, I summon thee! Yog-Sothoth, wise and mighty lord of the Old Ones, I invoke thee!
>
> By the authority of the dreaded name, Azathoth, that few dare speak, I charge thee, open to me the gateway of Virgo, the Virgin, that lies between the blazing pillar Spica on the right hand and the blazing pillar Syrma on the left hand. As the solar chariot [or, lunar chariot] crosses between these pillars, I enter the city of the *Necronomicon* through its Tenth Gate. Selah!

Visualize the key of the Tenth Gate in your right hand some six inches long and made of cast iron. Feel its weight, texture, and shape as you hold it. Extend your right arm and use the key to draw upon the surface of the gate the seal of the key, which should be visualized to burn on the gate in a line of white spiritual fire. Point with the astral key at the center of the gate and speak the words:

> In the name of Azathoth, Ruler of Chaos, by the power of Yog-Sothoth,
> Lord of Portals, the Tenth Gate is opened!

Visualize the gate unlocking and opening inward of its own accord upon a shadowed space. On the astral level, walk through the gateway and stand in the darkness beyond. Hold in your mind the talisman or magical object of the mythos you wish to scry or better understand. Open your mind to receive any impressions that may arise. In a more general sense, this ritual and this gate may be used to gain guidance and information on the making of any talisman, so that its working will be effective.

After fulfilling the purpose for which this gate was opened, conclude the ritual by astrally passing out through the gate and visualizing it to close. Draw the seal of the Tenth Key on the surface of the gate with the astral key you hold in your hand, and mentally cause it to lock itself shut, as it was at the beginning of the ritual. Speak the words of closing:

> By the power of Yog-Sothoth, and authority of the supreme name Azathoth, I close and seal the Tenth Gate. This ritual is well and truly ended.

Allow the image of the gate to grow pale in your imagination and fade to nothingness before you turn away from the ritual direction.

The Eleventh Gate

Eleventh Gate
Oddities

Lovecraft was a life-long fancier of the strange. He liked being around not only things old, but things old and dead. Family trees of the long deceased fascinated him. Old houses with horrifying histories attracted him. He had a particularly fondness of graveyards that shows itself in many of his stories. As a young man he made frequent nocturnal visits to the graveyard at the Cathedral of St. John, Episcopal, in Providence. He liked to walk the streets alone at night and breathe in the atmosphere of genteel decay. Almost the entire short story, *The Unnamable*, is set in the old burying-ground at Arkham, where Lovecraft's alter ego Randolph Carter, and Carter's friend Joel Manton, spend a quiet afternoon seated on a tomb, discussing various local horrors.

The affinity which Lovecraft felt for the grotesque and uncanny may have arisen in part from his feelings of alienation as a boy. His father went insane and had to be locked into a mental institution when Lovecraft was only three years old. He lived as a madman for another five years, finally dying in 1898. By that time Lovecraft's mother had begun to show symptoms of insanity. She became convinced that her son Howard avoided other people and walked the streets alone at night because he was ashamed of his hideously deformed face. While Lovecraft cannot be considered handsome, he is scarcely deformed, yet his mother's constant reiteration of hideous deformity must have made a deep impression on the boy.

Lovecraft was by nature rather odd. He was a precocious genius who learned to read by the age of three, and was translating difficult Latin poetry at age ten. Although his formal schooling was disrupted by periodic nervous breakdowns, which forced his removal from school for extended periods, he acquired an education of sorts by reading the dusty old tomes in the library of his maternal grandfather, Whipple Van Buren Phillips. He was especially drawn to eighteenth-century works of literary criticism and essays. The writing style, speech mannerisms, and attitude of eighteenth-century England became a kind of mania for him, which he only shook off with difficulty as an adult. He would salt his prose with quaint expressions and archaic spelling, and took to referring to himself as the "Old Man." He thought of himself as an ancient, even while still in his twenties and thirties. It was a harmless affectation, but a curious oddity.

Another quirk of his character was the determination to live his life as an English gentleman, even though he was not English, and did not have the wealth to ignore the necessities of earning a living. Lovecraft steadfastly called himself an amateur writer throughout his life, often corrected or expanded the works of others without compensation, or for such scant payment that he might as well have done it for free, and refused to be businesslike about placing his stories for publication or demanding the fees that were past-due to him from publishers and those who hired him to do ghostwriting assignments. Indeed, his determination not to be financially successful as a professional writer was almost perverse, and bordered on the self-destructive.

It was probably not a case of Lovecraft refusing success, but more a matter of him being constitutionally incapable of acting in the ways necessary for a successful professional writer. Still, at times it seemed that he was willfully thwarting attempts by his friends to help him. A few casual words of discouraging criticism might cause him to put a story into a drawer for years, and not even seek to have it published. He wrote only two novels, *The Case of Charles Dexter Ward* and *The Dream-Quest of Unknown Kadath*, neither of which was published during his lifetime. There was nothing wrong with either novel. Both were published to acclaim after his death. Yet Lovecraft simply would not, or could not, make the necessary effort to place them with book publishers. The imp of the perverse sat on his shoulder, counseling him to avoid success at all costs.

Much of the richness of the Necronomicon mythos stems from the oddities, otherworldly in their strangeness, that impart an indescribable atmosphere to the stories. Lovecraft's great strength was his originality. He wrote to please himself, and never tried to imitate other horror writers, but he sometimes left homages to their work in his fiction in the form of borrowed terms and references, which he modified for his own purposes. These curious little details are scattered like jewels throughout the mythos. They reveal some of the influences upon Lovecraft's mind that helped shape the mythos, but they are also part of what makes the mythos so unique.

aether *

The aether (or ether) is a concept held by astronomers prior to the twentieth century to explain how light could propagate through the airless void between the stars. Since light was presumed to be a wave, and it was believed that waves could only travel through some sort of physical medium, space was hypothesized to be filled with an invisible, tenuous substance similar to a very thin fluid that was termed "the aether." The revelations of Albert Einstein concerning the nature of relativity marked the end of the concept of an interstellar aether in modern science.

Lovecraft mentioned the aether in *The Whisperer in Darkness* as something the wings of the Mi-Go push against when they fly through space: "The things come from another planet, being able to live in interstellar space and fly through it on clumsy, powerful wings which have a way of resisting the aether." The same reasoning would no doubt explain how winged Cthulhu, and how the winged race of the Elder Things, were able to fly through space. The aether is also present in *The Dream-Quest of Unknown Kadath* when Randolph Carter sails off the edge of the ocean of the dreamlands through the void to the far side of the Moon.

Sometimes Lovecraft employed the term more loosely to represent a glowing fog or mist, and in a few cases it is difficult to separate the two meanings, since both seem to apply. The aether in *The Strange High House in the Mist* is on a material level simply a sea mist, but yet it is also the medium that conveys the god Nodens on his seashell to the door of the old cottage atop the cliff, and seems almost to have a life of its own.

(*The Whisperer in Darkness; The Crawling Chaos; The Diary of Alonzo Typer; Hypnos; Celephaïs; Fungi from Yuggoth; The Nameless City; The Strange High House in the Mist*)

Akariel

The carven sea gate of the dream city Thalarion, the City of a Thousand Wonders, that is ruled by the eidolon (idol) of the god Lathi. Those who pass through the gate into the city, and look upon the graven image of the god, are never heard from again beyond the city walls.

(*The White Ship*)

Akurion

A great gray rock that in times past stood up from the misty surface of the green lake of the lost city of Ib, in Mnar. Only marshes now remain on the ground the lake once occupied. The rock was near the shore, not far from the green stone seawall of the city of Sarnath that bordered the lake before the destruction of that city some ten thousand years ago. Akurion was used by the men of Sarnath to gauge the level of water in the lake, which varied greatly, in spite of the lack of streams flowing into or out from the lake.

(*The Doom That Came to Sarnath*)

ankh *

The ankh, or *crux ansata*, more commonly known as the Egyptian cross, is a cross that terminates at the top in an elongated loop. It is a symbol representing life, and it appears frequently in ancient Egyptian art. The ankh is generally regarded as a fortunate symbol, or symbol of blessing, although some narrow-minded Christians associate it only with the pagan religion of Egypt and on this basis regard it as a sign of evil magic.

In *The Haunter of the Dark*, when the writer Robert Harrison Blake first enters the great stone church in Providence, Rhode Island, known as the Church of Starry Wisdom, he finds that the usual Christian cross above the altar has been replaced by the *crux ansata*. This is hardly surprising since the church had been purchased by Professor Enoch Bowen to serve as the center for his esoteric cult of Starry Wisdom, to house the ancient occult relic known as the Shining Trapezohedron, which the archeologist had carried back from a tomb he had excavated in Egypt.

(*The Haunter of the Dark*)

avatars *

An avatar is a lower incarnation or expression of a higher being. The term derives from Hinduism, and signifies in a literal sense a descent. The exalted higher gods sometimes descended to lower planes in order to accomplish specific tasks. In order to make this descent, they took on vessels more in keeping with the nature of the lower planes. The concept of avatars was one of the basic teachings of Theosophy, and it was probably from his readings about Theosophy that Lovecraft picked up the term.

In Lovecraft's stories, the Old Ones such as Shub-Niggurath and Nyarlathotep are almost without form as we know it in their purest expression, but at times they adopt more constrained bodies in order to function on our material world. Nyarlathotep in particular has numerous avatars. Robert Harrison Blake believed that the being known as the Haunter of the Dark, which manifested through the Shining Trapezohedron in the Church of Starry Wisdom at Providence, Rhode Island, was an avatar of Nyarlathotep. When it came to Blake at the end of the story, he saw that it had black wings and a three-lobed eye.

Blake wrote that in ancient Khem (Egypt) Nyarlathotep even took the form of a man. This is supported by Lovecraft's story *Nyarlathotep*, where the god appears in the form of an Egyptian showman. In *The Dream-Quest of Unknown Kadath*, Nyarlathotep shows himself to Randolph Carter as a youthful Egyptian pharaoh in prismatic robes, a regal figure with a proud carriage and smart features who has the "languid sparkle of capricious humour" in his eyes. He warns Carter to pray that Carter may never meet him again in his "thousand forms."

Another avatar of Nyarlathotep is the fabled Black Man who presided over witches' sabbats. The Black Goat of the sabbat is an avatar of Shub-Niggurath, and the two often are spoken of together in this context.

(*The Haunter of the Dark; Nyarlathotep; The Dreams in the Witch House; The Dream-Quest of Unknown Kadath*)

balustraded terrace

When Walter Gilman is cast from sleep across space by the magic of the witch Keziah Mason, he finds himself lying on a terrace in an alien city beneath a sky resplendent with the mingled colors of three suns. The strangely shaped buildings of the city two thousand feel below stretch away to the limits of his vision, and other terraces are ranked above the one he occupies. Around the edge of the terrace is a metal balustrade as high as his chest, ornamented with metal figurines some four and a half inches tall in the shape of the crinoid Elder Things—a ribbed barrel torso with radiating arms. So thin is the attachment of these ornaments than when Gilman grips one of them, it breaks off in his hand. He notices gaps in the row of figurines along the top of the balustrade, where others have been broken off in the past.

He hears a noise behind him and turns to see the witch and her familiar, accompanied by three Elder Things, entering the room to which the terrace is attached. The sight of the living Elder Things, identical in every detail to the small metal image in his hand, is too much for Gilman, who falls unconscious. He awakens in his own room, and later discovers on his table the uncanny metal icon he had broken from the balustrade in his dream. Is it merely a decoration, or does it have some larger significance? Was it chance that it came loose in Gilman's hand, or was he intended to break it off?

The description of Gilman on the terrace is strangely evocative. We are to assume that Gilman was transported by Keziah to one of the planets of a distant star system ruled by the Elder Things, either in the present or in the past. The gaps in the ornaments along the balustrade have an ominous significance, for they indicate that others before Gilman have been carried through dimensional portals to the same terrace, and that they, too, have broken off its delicate decorations as they clutched at them in horror, fighting vertigo while gazing across the vast city below.

(*The Dreams in the Witch House*)

bead, metal

In the collaborative story *The Night Ocean*, an artist vacationing on Ellston Beach finds in the sand a large metal bead of unusual design. Its minute carving shows a "fishy thing" against a backdrop of seaweed. The bead was probably dropped by one of the amphibious race that comes out of the ocean and onto the beach under moonlight. These beings seem to resemble the sea-dwelling race in Lovecraft's story, *The Temple*, although they are not well described in either tale.

(*The Night Ocean*)

cataract *

Beyond the twin Basalt Pillars of the West, in the dreamlands, the waters of the western ocean fall off the edge of the world, forming a "monstrous cataract" that bears most ships to their doom. The exceptions are the black galleys of the moon-beasts, which are able to continue into the void on their voyages to the far side of the Moon. Lovecraft drew on actual folklore of the ancient world, which told of ships that dared to sail from the Mediterranean between the Pillars of Hercules into the unexplored western sea, only to fall of the edge of the world in a great waterfall. In the dreamlands, the fantasies and fears of waking life become reality.

(*The White Ship; The Dream-Quest of Unknown Kadath*)

cats *

Lovecraft had a peculiar reverence for cats, which finds expression in some of his stories. In *Imprisoned with the Pharaohs*, cats are mentioned among the sacred animals mummified by the Egyptians so that they "might return some day to greater glory."
He created a special city in the dreamlands, Ulthar, where the crime of killing a cat is punished by death. At the beginning of *The Cats of Ulthar* he wrote, "For the cat is cryptic, and close to strange things which men cannot see. He is the soul of antique Aegyptus, and bearer of tales from forgotten cities in Meroë and Ophir. He is the kin of the jungle's lords, and heir to the secrets of hoary and sinister Africa. The Sphinx is his cousin, and he speaks her language; but he is more ancient than the Sphinx, and remembers that which she hath forgotten."

In *The Dream-Quest of Unknown Kadath*, cats are said to be able to leap from the tops of houses to "cryptic realms" on the dark side of the Moon, where they frolic together and "converse with ancient shadows." The only foes they fear are the very large cats of Saturn, who covet the Moon's dark side for their own, and sometimes contest for it with Earth's cats. The cats of Saturn are in league with the evil toad-beasts of the moon, and hate the cats of Earth. Because Randolph Carter was kind to a kitten, the cats carried Carter off the Moon and back to Earth's dreamlands, saving him from the wrath of Nyarlathotep.

(*Imprisoned With the Pharaohs; The Cats of Ulthar; The Dream-Quest of Unknown Kadath*)

clock, coffin-shaped

A tall, coffin-shaped clock with four hands and strange hieroglyphics on its dial and the front of its case that no one can decipher occupies a niche in a room in the house of Etienne-Laurent de Marigny, in the French Quarter of New Orleans. It is the size of a large grandfather clock, but the case is wider. The hands of the clock do not keep any earthly time, nor is the ticking of the clock any earthly rhythm, but is described as a "cosmic rhythm which underlies all mystical gate-openings." De Marigny was the friend of Randolph Carter, and after Carter was declared dead, served as his executor. Carter was not dead, but came to inhabit and control the alien body of a wizard of the planet Yaddith, which he brought back to Earth via a dimensional portal and disguised as the eastern swami Chandraputra.

Carter indicates in *Through the Gates of the Silver Key* that the clock had been sent to de Marigny by the yogi that Harley Warren used to talk about, the yogi who declared himself alone of all men to have visited Yian-Ho on the plateau of Leng, and to have returned with items from that forbidden city. The implication is that the clock comes from Yian-Ho. The clock, Carter asserts, had been made by those who know much about the First Gateway. The First Gate is the gate of dreams unlocked by the silver key, which leads from Earth space and normal time to "that extension of Earth which is outside time." When the wizard, named Zkauba, regains control of his body, he flees into the case of the clock and vanishes, presumably back to Yaddith. The clock can be used as a gateway through space and time by those who know how to read it.

(*Through the Gates of the Silver Key*)

colors, poisonous

In *The Colour Out of Space*, during the 1880s a meteorite falls to earth near the well of the farmer Nahum Gardner, whose farm occupies a valley west of Arkham, Massachusetts. When scientists from Miskatonic University gather a sample and return it to the university for tests, they discover that it displays under the spectroscope "shining bands unlike any known colours of the normal spectrum." The soft material is alien, dissimilar to anything on the Earth. It radiates a constant heat, as though from some inner radioactivity. Over the span of a few days the sample evaporates to nothingness.

When the scientists return to the Gardner farm for more, they learn that the meteorite has shrunk. In the center of its dwindling mass they find a colored globule. The color is indescribable, but resembles the spectral bands of the meteorite fragment tested earlier. When tapped with a hammer, the glassy globule pops into nothingness. The next day, when the scientists come back yet a third time for more samples, they learn that during the night the meteorite attracted multiple lightning strikes, which utterly destroyed it. Nonetheless, the alien color lingers in Gardner's well, and in the mists that hang above it.

In some strange way the well has become poisoned, causing unnatural growth in plants and animals watered by it, tainting them so that they are unfit to eat, and driving insane the human beings who drink from it. Eventually it kills everything on the farm.

A circle of death expands from the well over a period of four decades into an area of five acres, which comes to be known locally as the blasted heath. This gray zone grows larger each year as the poison continues to spread from the well beneath the ground. The alien colors themselves seem to be poisonous, or a part of the poison.

Lovecraft derived this concept of colors so alien, they were not a part of the normal visible spectrum, from the story *The Damned Thing* by Ambrose Bierce. In Bierce's story, an alien creature is colored with colors that are beyond the usual human range of perception, rendering the creature effectively invisible to human sight. Lovecraft's alien colors in *The Colour Out of Space* are not invisible, but the mind cannot quite grasp them or assign any familiar qualities to them. Wilbur Whateley's invisible hybrid brother in *The Dunwich Horror* also owes much to Bierce's story.

(*The Colour Out of Space*)

coven *

Covens are groups of witches. The traditional number of a coven is said to have been thirteen, but the number often varies as members join or leave the group. One witch serves as priestess, the embodiment of the Goddess, and the other twelve form the circle around her. In some modern covens the witches take turns serving as priestess. Sometimes a male member fulfils the role of priest, the embodiment of the God of the witches.

Lovecraft's presentation of witchcraft was wholly negative. There is no such thing as a good witch in the Necronomicon mythos. He based his references to witchcraft upon the writings of Christian demonologists, both Protestant and Catholic. Much of his concept of witches, their sabbat meetings, and their sacrifices comes from the writings of Cotton Mather, and also from his study of the Salem witch persecutions. Lovecraft had read *The Witch-cult in Western Europe* by Margaret A. Murray and used some of her material in his stories—his references to the Black Man of the sabbat are drawn in part from Murray's book—however, his reading of Murray did not soften his traditional prejudice against witchcraft.

In *The Thing on the Doorstep*, the coven of witches to which Ephraim Waite belonged met in the pit of the shoggoths in northern Maine, beneath a circle of standing stones near the town of Chesuncook.

(*The Thing on the Doorstep*)

crystal cube

A race of worm-like beings in distant galaxy scattered crystal cubes across space in order to learn more about other galaxies, which they could not reach with their starships. By chance, one of these cubes fell to Earth in the distant past, during the occupation of our planet by the Great Race from Yith, the space and time spanning beings who inhabited with their naked minds alone an ancient earthly species of rugose cones.

No race in the universe is more knowledgeable than the Great Race. They recognized the danger this cube posed to all who looked within its illuminated depths—that their minds would be captured and transported to the distant world of the worm-like race, and their bodies stolen by the disembodied minds of these hostile aliens, sent to Earth through the cube to investigate our world and determine whether all life on it should be destroyed.

The Yithians did not destroy the cube, for they valued knowledge above all else, but they built for it a darkened shrine and hid the cube within it so that none of their race would look upon it. Over time, the chaos of warfare caused the arctic city of the temple to be destroyed, and the cube to be lost. Fifty million years ago the Great Race left to inhabit the distant future of the Earth, leaving the crystal cube behind them.

The ancient cube is picked up from the ground by George Campbell while camping in the Canadian woods. His mind is exchanged through the cube with the mind of one of the worm-like beings on their distant planet Yekub, where his human mind in its alien body acts decisively to seize control of their god, and thus becomes supreme ruler of their world. Meanwhile, the alien mind inhabiting his human body in the Canadian wilderness falls into bestial madness and perishes.

(*The Challenge from Beyond*)

cycles, prehistoric

Mention is made in the *Necronomicon* of the "Yog-Sothoth and Cthulhu cycles." These seem to refer to the two separate periods during which the Old Ones under Yog-Sothoth, and the octopi spawn under Cthulhu, dominated the Earth. Cthulhu and his spawn were subdued by the Elder Things, after much warfare, and were forced to go into suspended animation on the Pacific island of R'lyeh when the stars went wrong in the heavens. Eventually R'lyeh sank beneath the waves. The invisible Old Ones, or at least one branch of them, were driven underground by the advanced technology of the Great Race, who locked them into the earth behind massive trap doors.

(*The Whisperer in Darkness; The Call of Cthulhu; The Shadow Out of Time*)

eidolon *

A word chosen by Lovecraft to describe the idol of the god Lathi, ruling deity of the dream city of Thalarion. It is a curious word with multiple meanings, which is certainly why Lovecraft selected it. "Eidolon" is a Greek word meaning "an image, an idol," but also "an apparition," "a ghost," and even "an ideal." In Theosophy it was used for the astral double of a recently dead human being, a kind of simulacrum of the deceased rather than the actual soul or spirit of the deceased. Theosophists believed that the eidolons of the dead are always present around us, but under ordinary circumstances do not see us any more than we are able to see them. However, the strong desire of those at a séance, coupled with the psychic abilities of the presiding medium, can sometimes summon these eidolons to the material level of reality and manifest them to ordinary human vision. Theosophists regarded this as a form of necromancy. Lovecraft was familiar with Theosophical doctrines and may have drawn the word from this source.

(*The White Ship*)

Esoteric Order of Dagon

A secret religion founded in the Massachusetts fishing community of Innsmouth by the South Sea trader Obed Marsh for the worship of the god Dagon, the goddess Hydra, and their children, the amphibious race known as the Deep Ones. No exact year is given for its founding, but it was established around 1838. It used the former old Masonic Hall on New Church Green for its church. The priests of the religion wore upon their heads a strangely shaped golden tiara given to the order by the Deep Ones.

Those admitted to the order were required over time to take three oaths. The first oath of silence bound them not to speak about the order. The second oath of loyalty bound them to support the works of the order, and for this support they were rewarded by the Deep Ones. The third and final oath compelled them to take a Deep One in marriage and to have hybrid children from this union, who would go to live beneath the sea when they matured. At first Marsh and his followers balked at the third oath, but after the Deep Ones demanded it, they were forced to accede.

In February 1928, the Federal government raided Innsmouth and destroyed many of its older buildings along the harbor, using the cover story that the raid was to combat smuggling. A submarine sent torpedoes downward into the deep-sea trench off Devil Reef in an effort to destroy the city of the Deep Ones, Y'ha-nthlei. The Esoteric Order of Dagon may have ended at this time—or it may merely have gone into hiding.

(*The Shadow Over Innsmouth*)

essential salts *

In Lovecraft's Necronomicon mythos, the human body may be reduced by alchemical means to its essential salts—what remains after its more volatile components have been driven off. Once the essential salts are refined from the corpse, it is possible at any later date to reconstitute them into the living creature from whence they came by means of a ritual formula that is found in the *Necronomicon*. The use of essential salts for calling up the spectre of a dead ancestor is mentioned in 1702 by Cotton Mather in his

Magnalia Christi Americana (bk. 2, ch. 12). Mather referred to the alchemist Borellus as his source. According to Mather, Borellus asserted that the process was lawful and did not involve any necromancy. Lovecraft quoted Mather's paraphrase of Borellus at the beginning of his novel *The Case of Charles Dexter Ward*:

> The essential Saltes of Animals may be so prepared and preserved, that an ingenious Man may have the whole Ark of Noah in his own Studie, and raise the fine Shape of an Animal out of its Ashes at his Pleasure; and by the lyke Method from the essential Saltes of humane Dust, a Philosopher may, without any criminal Necromancy, call up the Shape of any dead Ancestour from the Dust whereinto his Bodie has been incinerated.—*Borellus*

The quotation from Mather's book indicates that the process involved the calling forth of a visual image of the living creature to whom the salts had belonged. It was an act of natural magic, which was not considered unlawful by many authorities, but Lovecraft made it into a necromantic process.

(*The Case of Charles Dexter Ward*)

familiars *

In the story fragment *The Book*, a man finds a worm-riddled manuscript book in an old bookstore and recites a formula from it that opens the first gateway leading beyond the ordinary three-dimensional reality of normal consciousness. As a consequence, he acquires a familiar spirit—"For he who passes the gateways always wins a shadow, and never again can he be alone." The recitation of the magic formula evoked the familiar from some other reality and bound it to the man.

Familiars appear elsewhere in Lovecraft's tales. The Salem witch Keziah Mason, in the story *The Dreams in the Witch House*, had as her familiar the rat-like creature with the human face and hands called Brown Jenkin, which Lovecraft patterned after descriptions of familiars given by Cotton Mather. They were often said to resemble small animals, but with various distortions or deformities, and unnatural in their behavior. The familiar acted both as servant and guardian to its master.

(*The Book; The Dreams in the Witch House*)

flutes *

Lovecraft had a minor obsession with the sound of flutes—not the modern transverse flutes played from the side with which we are familiar today, but Eastern wind instruments of the kind that might be heard in Arab or Asian folk music. The sound of flutes occurs numerous times throughout his body of work, sometimes accompanies by drumming, and always it is characterized as horrid or abominable.

In *The Dreams in the Witch House*, Gilman resists accompanying Keziah Mason to the throne of Azathoth "where the thin flutes pipe mindlessly." Even so, he has memories of his dreams in which he hears echoes of "monstrous, half-acoustic pulsing, and of the thin, monotonous piping of an unseen flute," suggesting that the decision is not fully his to make.

In the story *Nyarlathotep*, the narrator hears "the muffled, maddening beating of drums, and thin, monotonous whine of blasphemous flutes from inconceivable, unlighted chambers beyond Time; the detestable pounding and piping whereunto dance slowly, awkwardly, and absurdly the gigantic, tenebrous ultimate gods, the blind, voiceless, mindless gargoyles whose soul is Nyarlathotep." It is obvious that he hears the music at the center of chaos, just as Gilman heard it. There is no indication who may be playing the music, or what its source may be.

Near the beginning of *The Dream-Quest of Unknown Kadath*, reference is made to "that last amorphous blight of nethermost confusion which blasphemes and bubbles at the centre of all infinity," otherwise known as Azathoth, and to the "muffled, maddening beating of vile drums and the thin, monotonous whine of accursed flutes." The blind, voiceless, and mindless Other Gods, whose soul and messenger is Nyarlathotep, dance to this music. Further on in the same work, in the windowless stone monastery on the plateau of Leng, Randolph Carter is treated to the music of such a flute played by the High-Priest Not To Be Described, a lumpish figure on a golden throne robed in yellow silk, with a yellow mask concealing his face. The musical instrument he plays is characterized as a "disgustingly carven flute of ivory."

The horror occasioned by the sound of flutes would be inexplicable if it did not evoke the primal sound at the black throne of Azathoth. Chaos is formless, but holds in potential all forms. It is wet clay awaiting its shape, and the music is the shaping instrument. Hence, in *The Festival* when the narrator attends a ritual of black magic, and hears the droning of a flute, the changing of the key of the music precipitates "a horror unthinkable and unexpected," which causes him to faint, and drives him insane.

In *The Haunter of the Dark*, the Lord of All Things whose name must not be spoken aloud, Azathoth, is said to be lulled by the "thin monotonous piping of a demoniac flute held in nameless paws." The identity of the flute player is not explicitly stated, but it is usually assumed to be Azathoth himself. Certainly it is Azathoth who is the source of this music, either directly or by proxy.

Lilith is worshipped to the sound of flutes in *The Horror at Red Hook*. In the story *The Moon-Bog*, bog-wraiths lead human beings to their doom to the detestable piping of unseen flutes, accompanied by the beating of drums, in the same way snake charmers of India are supposed to mesmerize cobras with flute music (they do not—snakes are deaf).

In *The Rats in the Walls*, an indication is given as to who is playing the flutes. The half-mad narrator alludes to "grinning caverns of earth's centre where Nyarlathotep, the mad faceless god, howls blindly in the darkness to the piping of two amorphous idiot flute-players." These are perhaps the same flute players who entertain Azathoth on his black throne, if indeed this god does not play the flute with his own hands. The caverns of the Earth's center may be assumed to be a metaphor for the center of ultimate chaos, which has no geographical location in our universe. Since the narrator of Lovecraft's tale is temporarily insane when he has this vision, his description is not to be trusted.

(*The Dreams in the Witch House; Nyarlathotep; The Dream-Quest of Unknown Kadath; The Festival; The Haunter of the Dark; The Horror at Red Hook; The Rats in the Walls*)

Footprints

The footprints of Wilbur Whateley's invisible brother, who is said to resemble in shape the Old One who was his father, are described in the *Dunwich Horror* as round and as large as a barrelhead, with lines radiating from a single point, like the lines of a palm-leaf fan.

The prints of the blind and invisible race from beyond our universe that was cast from the surface of our world into deep caverns by the coming of the Great Race from Yith were made in the form of five circular marks, each three inches across, arranged in the shape of a pentagram. This pattern occupied approximately a square foot of area, and was formed in groups of three. This invisible race, referred to in *The Shadow Out of Time*, appears to have been the same Old Ones with whom old Wizard Whateley and his hybrid grandson Wilbur had dealings at Dunwich. It may be argued that these prints are not the same as those made by Wilbur's brother, but Wilbur's brother was a hybrid who was half human and half Old One. His footprints may have differed from those of the Old Ones.

In *At the Mountains of Madness*, the prints of the Elder Things discovered in the Antarctic by the Miskatonic Expedition of 1930–1931, impressed into pre-Cambrian slate when it was no more than fresh mud, were about a foot across, triangular in shape, and striated.

The footprint of the secretive Mi-Go from Yuggoth, who mine for metals in the hills of Vermont, is described in *The Whisperer in Darkness* as "hideously crab-like" and around the size of a normal human print. From a central pad project on each side saw-toothed nippers.

In *The Dream-Quest of Unknown Kadath*, the dream explorer Randolph Carter once asked a group of lava-gatherers on the slope of Mount Ngranek if the night-gaunts leave webbed footprints. They denied this to be so.

Footprints in the form of split hooves, like those of a goat, appear in a number of stories. In *The Unnamable*, one such footprint is impressed into the chest of Randolph Carter during a graveyard encounter with an inhuman creature.

When in *The Hound*, two English decadents rob a five-hundred year old grave in Holland and carry back to their home in England a jade amulet in the shape of a crouching hound, they discover in the soft earth under their library window a series of footprints "utterly impossible to describe."

In *The Dreams in the Witch House*, Brown Jenkin, the familiar creature of the Salem witch Keziah Mason, leaves bloody tracks across the floor that have the shape of four tiny human hands, after it finishes killing Walter Gillman by gnawing his still-beating heart out of his chest.

In *The Festival*, a man led through the snowy streets of Kingsport by a throng of silent, robed figures to the old church on Central Hill sees no footprints in the snow, not even those of his own feet; but later when he is found floating half-dead in Kingsport Harbor, he is told that his footprints in the snow show that he must have become lost in the dark on the road outside of town, and wandered off the cliffs at Ornage Point, before ever reaching Kingsport.

(*The Dunwich Horror; The Shadow Out of Time; At the Mountains of Madness; The Whisperer in Darkness; The Dream-Quest of Unknown Kadath; The Unnamable; The Hound; The Dreams in the Witch House; The Festival*)

Gate, Ultimate

In the Necronomicon mythos, the gates are portals of transition between levels of reality, which may be separated distantly in time and space, or may overlap and exist simultaneously in the same location, the way two notes of music can exist upon the air at the same time. Certain places on the Earth are favorable for the formation of these gates, and as a result they have acquired religious significance. Randolph Carter called them places of "a dark polarity and induced gate." In ancient times the locations were marked by rings or rows of standing stones, such as those on the small island in the Miskatonic River not far from Arkham, or by sacrificial altar stones such as the one on top of Sentinel Hill outside of Dunwich, or by stone pillars. There are also gateways in caves beneath the earth. One such place is the cave known as the Snake-Den in the hills outside of Arkham, where Randolph Carter vanished with his silver key on October 7, 1928. At the back of this cave is a particular stone called by Carter the "mystic pylon."

The gates are presided over by Yog-Sothoth, a being that straddles all dimensions, existing everywhere simultaneously, and for this reason controls all portals between worlds. They can be opened by means of incantations and ritual magic, and are more easily opened at certain dates of the year, such as May-Eve or Halloween. Certain crafted devices, such as the Shining Trapezohedron once possessed by the forgotten Egyptian pharaoh Nephren-Ka, or the large silver key passed down to Randolph Carter by his ancestor, or the coffin-shaped clock with four hands owned by Carter's friend, Etienne-Laurent de Marigny, can facilitate the opening of the gateways of Yog-Sothoth, but they are of no use to those lacking the knowledge of how to activate them. For example, the silver key must be held up to the setting Sun, and rotated in a specific way in the air nine times, and on the final rotation certain syllables must be correctly intoned on the breath into the opening void.

Randolph Carter used his silver key to pass through two special gates. The First Gate led him back to his childhood and his childhood dreams. The second gate, called the Inner Gate or Ultimate Gate, led him "from earth and time to that extension of earth which is outside time," in the vast cavern of the Ancient Ones, and to that dread guide spoken of by Alhazred in the *Necronomicon*, who guards the Ultimate Gate—he who is called the 'Umr at-Tawil, the Most Ancient One, the Prolonged of Life. The Ancient Ones occupy pedestals in an oddly curved line that is "neither semicircle nor ellipse, parabola nor hyperbola," but is akin to the lines drawn by the witch Keziah Mason on her jail cell the day she vanished from Salem Jail. Such lines bend space and time, and transcend three-dimensional reality.

With the aid of the dreaming Ancient Ones and the guidance of the 'Umr at-Tawil, Carter used the silver key in combination with a ritual he instinctively knew to open the Ultimate Gate in the wall of the cavern of the Ancient Ones. The opened gate allowed Carter to pass through solid rock as though it were warm water. Beyond the gate he realized that he was not a single being, but countless beings at different points of time and space existing simultaneously in a transcendent reality. Whereas the passage of the First Gate moved Carter backward in time, the passage of the Ultimate Gate caused Carter to transcend time and experience all times at once.

(*Through the Gates of the Silver Key*)

Gem of Nath

This small, amber-colored crystal "cut in devious angles impossible to classify" has the power of revealing the true forms that lie beneath the material shadows of things in our world when a person gazes through it. It is said to be "curiously warm and electric" to the touch. The ancient gem was part of the collection of precious stones at a museum of unspecified location, although the curator of the museum could not have had any conception of its power.

In the *Chronicle of Nath* by the German mystic Rudolf Yergler, it is written that in the Year of the Black Goat a shadow from beyond the Earth that feeds on the souls of men comes to the Earth, promising those it entrances with the illusion of liberation in the alien Land of the Three Suns. By peering through the Gem it is possible to see the shadow's true shape, and the man who can do this and remain sane can send the shadow back to the "starless gulf of its spawning" until the next time the Year of the Black Goat comes.

The Gem was used by the esoteric writer Constantine Theunis for this purpose in 1938, after the shadow from Outside had manifested to his friend, Single, at 10 AM on June 23 of that year in the form of a strange tree growing on a hill seven miles south of Hampden, Idaho, in the region of the Blue Mountain Forest Reserve known as Hell's Acres. June 23 is the day after the summer solstice. Single had taken photographs of the tree, and Theunis later constructed a kind of *camera obscura* in a black box in order to view the photographs through the Gem, which he borrowed from the museum. The Gem was fixed to an opening on one side of the box, and the photograph was placed on the opposite side. In this way, Theunis was successful in sending the shadow back to the starless gulf, although it put him in the hospital. He used the Gem to make a pencil sketch of the shadow, which had the true shape of a giant hand, even though it appeared to normal human vision to be a tree.

(*The Tree on the Hill*)

hieroglyphics

Alien hieroglyphic writing appears several times in Lovecraft's stories. In *Dagon*, the cyclopean monolith on the risen island consisted of aquatic symbols in the shapes of "fishes, eels, octopi, crustaceans, molluscs, whales and the like." Some of the marine creatures in the symbols did not resemble any life forms known to modern science.

The Dreams in the Witch House features near the end of the story a carving in bluish stone of one of the Elder Things, with undecipherable hieroglyphics written on its base, which was owned by the witch Keziah Mason.

A bas-relief stone carving by Henry Anthony Wilcox that depicts Cthulhu bears hieroglyphic writing in the story *The Call of Cthulhu*. Wilcox, a student at the Rhode Island School of Design, dreamed of the hieroglyphics engraved on the stones of the city of R'lyeh, under the influence of Cthulhu's telepathic dream projections.

The large black stone removed from Round Hill, east of Townshend, Vermont, by Henry Wentworth Akeley in *The Whisperer in Darkness* was covered with unknown hieroglyphics. Akeley's friend, Albert Wilmarth, recognizes some of the symbols from the *Necronomicon*.

The parchment that accompanied the silver key inherited by Randolph Carter was covered in hieroglyphics. According to Colonel Churchward, an expert on lost Mu, they were not Naacal, or the hieroglyphics of Easter Island. However, according to Carter's friend, Etienne-Laurent de Marigny, they did resemble the writing in the book Harley Warren received from India in 1919.

In *Out of the Aeons*, a two-foot-long scroll less than four inches wide containing a single vertical line of hieroglyphics was found inside an iridescent cylinder of Yuggothian metal that lay inside a crypt on an island heaved up from the floor of the Pacific Ocean in 1878. Both the cylinder and the mummy discovered beside it in the crypt were sold by the Orient Shipping Company to the Cabot Museum of Archaeology at Boston in the following year. The hieroglyphics resemble some that appear in the book *Nameless Cults* by von Junzt.

(*Dagon; The Dreams in the Witch House; The Call of Cthulhu; The Whisperer in Darkness; Through the Gates of the Silver Key; Out of the Aeons*)

Innsmouth look

A change of appearance in those men and women of the town of Innsmouth who are the offspring of intermarriage between human beings and the amphibious race of Deep Ones. It only begins to show itself in maturity, but is easily noticeable in the early thirties. It is characterized by creases in the sides of the neck that are the beginnings of gill slits, and by a narrow head, bulging eyes that seldom blink, and cease to blink entirely at a more advanced stage, a flat nose, a receding forehead and chin, underdeveloped ears, a wide mouth with thick lips, and a gray-blue skin complexion. The hair of the head and face begins to fall off with patches of skin. The hands and feet enlarge and the fingers shorten and curl close to the palm. The posture becomes hunched. Eventually in most but not all cases the look progresses to such an extent that those afflicted can no longer pass for human and must hide themselves away until around age seventy, when the change reaches a stage that allows them to dwell permanently beneath the surface of the sea.

(*The Shadow Over Innsmouth*)

insect-philosophers

A race of insect-philosophers crawls "proudly" over the surface of the fourth moon of Jupiter, which for Lovecraft was probably Ganymede, although Callisto is often supposed to be the moon he intended.

(*Beyond the Wall of Sleep*)

iridescent cylinder

A hollow cylinder some four inches long and seven-eighths of an inch in diameter, made of an iridescent metal impervious to acids and impossible to analyze. Van Junzt in his *Nameless Cults* identified the substance as *lagh* metal, brought to this planet from Yuggoth by the Mi-Go. Its outer surface was covered in engraved figures with a strange geometry and unknown hieroglyphics. It was fitted with a tight cap of the same metal, which when removed revealed a tightly rolled scroll some two feet in length composed of a thin, bluish-white membrane, that was wrapped around a slender rod of the same metal. According to van Junzt, the scroll was made of *pthagon* membrane, the inner skin of the extinct yakith-lizard of lost Mu. A single line of undecipherable hieroglyphics extended down the center of the scroll in a thin column that was penned or painted onto the scroll with a gray pigment. These hieroglyphs resembled those found in *Nameless Cults*, and consisted of a protective magic formula against the demon Ghatanothoa.

(*Out of the Aeons*)

ivory head

When the British freighter *Victory* is sunk in the Atlantic Ocean by a German U-boat in 1917, one of the dead crew found clinging to the deck rail of the U-boat has in his possession a small but beautifully carved piece of ivory in the shape of a youth's head crowned with a laurel wreath. The olive-skinned seaman is not English, but of some Mediterranean country. The first officer of the German submarine takes the carving for his own when the body is cast into the sea.

Almost at once sickness falls upon the crew of the U-boat, and they are troubled by apparitions of the British dead. They come to believe that the submarine is cursed by the presence of the ivory talisman. Bad luck and madness plague the boat. An explosion in the engine room cripples the controls, preventing the boat from surfacing. When the remnants of the crew mutiny, the commander shoots them and ejects their bodies through the air lock. Soon after, his first officer goes insane and demands to be released from the boat, to which the commander agrees merely to be rid of him.

The boat drifts and settles into the ruins of a great submerged city that the commander assumes must be Atlantis. In the city is an immense temple carved from the solid rock face of a cliff, and on the façade of the temple are statues of a radiant god whose features are identical to those of the ivory head. The god represented by the ivory head, who is evidently housed within the undersea temple, is not identified by Lovecraft, but may perhaps be Phaëthon, son of Helios, who was cast down into the sea when he was about to burn up the world with his father's fiery chariot. Phaëthon is mentioned in Plato's account of Atlantis, as presented in the book *Atlantis: The Antediluvian World* by Ignatius Donnelly (see Donnelly, p. 7), with which Lovecraft was familiar.

(*The Temple*)

lagh metal

This metal is not found in the mines of Earth. Long ago it was carried to this planet from Yuggoth (Pluto) by the Elder Ones, who may be the Mi-Go, or are possibly the earlier race that inhabited Yuggoth before the coming of the Mi-Go. At any rate, the Mi-Go used it to fashion the metal cylinders into which they put the living and conscious brains they extracted from human beings in Vermont. This cylinder metal is not named—Lovecraft called it only "a metal mined in Yuggoth"—but it is very likely *lagh* metal.

(*Out of the Aeons; The Whisperer in Darkness*)

lions, Winged

A pair of winged lions carved from diorite occupy a round plaza at the end of a colonnade in the ruins of the ancient city of Sarkomand. Between them there is a darkness that marks the entrance to the subterranean staircase leading to the Great Abyss.

(*The Dream-Quest of Unknown Kadath*)

L'mûr-Kathûlos

This person or place is mentioned only once, in Lovecraft's story *The Whisperer in Darkness*, in the midst of a long list of obscure names of persons and places. Its meaning is unknown. Lovecraft scholars have attempted to find meaning in the resemblance of its parts to the words "Lemuria" and "Cthulhu" but this is no more than conjecture.

(*The Whisperer in Darkness*)

magnetic cylinder

A cylinder of lustrous yellow Tulu-metal, strongly magnetic to objects of its own alloy, and covered with strange figures and unknown hieroglyphics in bas-relief, was discovered buried in an artificial earthen mound on the plains of Oklahoma in 1928. It was about a foot long and four inches in diameter. Among the figures on the cylinder were images of Cthulhu and Yig. It had a cap that unscrewed, to reveal a roll of yellow paper-like material written over in green ink. The scroll, dated 1545, contained the testament of Pánfilo de Zamacona y Nuñez, a member of the Spanish expedition of Francisco Coronado into the wilds of North America. Zamacona was captured by the mound people of Oklahoma and taken below to their blue-litten world of Xinaián (K'n-yan).

(*The Mound*)

mole

Joseph Curwen, resurrected from the dead by a necromantic ritual involving his essential salts, bore on his chest a "very peculiar mole or blackish spot." This was the skin blemish known as the Devil's Mark, impressed upon his body by the finger of the lord of the witches' sabbat, who was known as the Black Man. It was a sign of fidelity and obedience. The Devil's Mark was supposed to be completely insensitive to pain.

Lovecraft pretended to quote from the transcript for August 8, 1692, of the Salem witch trials concerning this mark: "Mr. G. B. (Rev. George Burroughs) on that Nighte putt ye Divell his Marke upon Bridget S., Jonathan A., Simon O., Deliverance W., Joseph C., Susan P., Mehitable C., and Deborah B." After searching through the Salem transcripts for 1692 I find no mention of a Joseph C. It was the practice in the Salem witch trail transcripts to write the last names out in full, not to abbreviate them with the initial letter. I also find no mention of the Devil's Mark, although there is mention of accused witches making a red mark with their finger in a book.

(*The Case of Charles Dexter Ward*)

moon-ladder

In *At the Mountains of Madness*, a graduate student of Miskatonic University named Danforth makes the mistake of looking back as he is flying away from the mountains of Antarctica that support the ice-encased city of the crinoid Elder Things. He is driven temporarily insane, and begins to babble. One of his babblings is the "the moon-ladder." This is never explained by Lovecraft.

Moon-ladders are a part of the mythology of various peoples. For example, in Bantu mythology, the spider on the moon weaves a thread that links the moon with the Earth, allowing the Moon Princess to descend upon it "rung after silvery rung" with her retinue (Knappert, p. 48). In one of the Native American legends about Coyote, a crafty animal god, Coyote makes a ladder and climbs up to the moon, from which he uses his bow and arrows to rearrange the stars into the constellations.

(*At the Mountains of Madness*)

moon-Wine

A wine favored by the Zoogs that is uncommonly heady and powerful. Randolph Carter uses it to loosen the tongue of Atal, priest of Ulthar, concerning the forbidden secrets of the gods of Earth known as the Great Ones.

(*The Dream-Quest of Unknown Kadath*)

pineal gland

The scientist Crawford Tillinghast builds a machine designed to stimulate latent but normally unused senses, allowing human beings to perceive the world of strange creatures that always surrounds us, but remains unnoticed. The stimulation of the pineal gland causes an extension of the faculty of normal sight, and opens an interdimensional vista of floating jellyfish-like creatures that pass through solid objects as men of flesh pass through air.

Lovecraft derived this lore on the pineal gland from Western occultism, where this gland is supposed to be associated with the third eye in the forehead between the eyebrows, the opening of which allows spiritual vision. Those who have activated their third eye can see into the astral realms that surround us, and can view the strange inhabitants of these realms. Among the beings dwelling in the astral world are the larvae, floating but mindless semi-formed spiritual creatures that arise from obsessions and strong or repeated emotions. The jellyfish-like things seen in the story *From Beyond* were probably based on Theosophical teachings about larvae.

(*From Beyond*)

powder of Ibn Ghazi

A magic powder that allows Wilbur Whateley to view the shape of his invisible brother when blown on his breath over his brother's body. The scholar of Miskatonic University, Dr. Henry Armitage, used it in a mechanical sprayer to reveal the same shape of the creature on Sentinel Hill.

(*The Dunwich Horror*)

secret portal

Abdul Alhazred wrote in the *Necronomicon* that each tomb has a secret portal guarded by a Herd that feasts on the things growing out of the decaying corpse. The secret portal is probably a dimensional gateway, although the reference may be to ghouls, who have the ability to slip in and out between our world and the dreamworld. Arguing against this interpretation is the detail that the Herd feasts on things growing from the corpse, not on the corpse itself. This inclines me to believe that the secret portal is nonphysical, and that the Herd is made up of spiritual beings.

(*Through the Gates of the Silver Key*)

Seven Caves of Chicomoztoc *

Chicomoztoc ("place of the seven caves") is the womblike place of racial origin in the mythology of the Aztecs of central Mexico. Within it are seven linked caves that can be accessed through a single opening. Its physical location is a mystery the solution of which explorers have sought in vain for centuries.

(*The Electric Executioner*)

Tekeli-li! Tekeli-li! *

A piping cry produced by the vocal organs of shoggoths, in imitation of the speech of the Elder Race who were their creators. It is mentioned by Edgar Allan Poe at the end of his novel, *The Narrative of Arthur Gordon Pym of Nantucket*, when Pym hears this strangely evocative cry from sea birds off the coast of Antarctica.

(*At the Mountains of Madness*)

Tharp

The name of a year in the dreamland of Sona-Nyl, called the "immemorial year of Tharp." It is probably one in a repeating cycle of years used in this place, where there is said to be "neither time nor space," but the other years in the cycle are not named.

(*The White Ship*)

Theosophy *

Lovecraft had a fascination for Theosophy, a kind of love-hate relationship with it. On the one hand, his scientific, rational mind dismissed its teachings as so much piffle, but on the other hand, he was drawn to the descriptions of alien races and vast periods of spiritual evolution. He made use of several bits and pieces of Theosophical lore. Lovecraft's reference to the Children of the Fire Mist is based on the Sons of the Fire-Mist, who are mention in the *Stanzas of Dzyan* at the beginning of H. P. Blavatsky's *Secret Doctrine*, and on further comments about them made by W. Scott-Elliot in his 1904 work *Lost Lemuria*. Lovecraft referred to the *Book of Dzyan* several times. This is an apocryphal work upon which Blavatsky claimed to have based her Theosophical teachings. A portion of it is printed at the start of her *Secret Doctrine*.

Lovecraft also made direct mention of Theosophy on a number of occasions. In *The Shadow Out of Time* he referred to "Hindoo tales involving stupefying gulfs of time and forming part of the lore of modern theosopists." In *The Call of Cthulhu*, Old Castro "remembered bits of hideous legend that paled the speculations of theosophists and made man and the world seem recent and transient indeed." The reporter for the Boston newspaper the *Pillar*, Stuart Reynolds, is said in *Out of the Aeons* to have a "smattering of theosophical lore."

(*The Shadow Out of Time; The Call of Cthulhu; Through the Gates of the Silver Key; The Haunter of the Dark: The Diary of Alonzo Typer; Out of the Aeons*)

Thon and Thal

The twin harbor beacons that guard the entry to the port city Baharna on the isle of Oriab, in the Southern Sea of the dreamlands. They are not described, but may be presumed to be tall lighthouses.

(*The Dream-Quest of Unknown Kadath*)

tiara

The ornate jewelry of the Deep Ones is not designed to fit the human body, but various pieces were given to the people of Innsmouth as gifts. A few of them were sold and found their way into museums such as the museum at Miskatonic University in Arkham. Among these fugitive pieces is a tiara that is the prize exhibit of the Newburyport Historical Society. Cast in an unidentifiable gold alloy, it is unnaturally large, with a high front, and shaped for an irregular, elliptical head unlike any human head. The surface is deeply engraved with geometric designs and images of marine creatures, among them monsters half-fish and half-frog.

A drunken Innsmouth man had pawned the tiara at a pawnshop in State Street, Newburyport, in 1873. Shortly thereafter he was killed in a brawl. The tiara was labeled "of probable East-Indian or Indochinese provenance." The Marsh family of Innsmouth offered to buy back the piece as soon as they learned of its acquisition by the Historical Society, but in spite of the high price they offered for it, the Society refused to part with it. The offer to purchase the tiara is made by the Marshes on a regular basis, but the Historical Society is firm in not wishing to part with its prize catch. It is worth noting that the pastor of the Esoteric Order of Dagon in the former Masonic Hall at Innsmouth wears an almost identical tiara as part of his religious regalia.

(*The Shadow Over Innsmouth*)

Tsath-yo

A language spoken once in Hyperborea that was millions of years older than the coming of the spawn of Cthulhu to R'lyeh. It was the original language in which a spell had been written that enabled Randolph Carter to travel through space and time in his own body. This spell was on a parchment that Carter received as a legacy along with a large silver key, but the hieroglyphics of the spell on the parchment were not in the original language of Tsath-yo, but a translation in the later R'lyehian tongue Carter made use of the translated text.

(*Through the Gates of the Silver Key*)

Tuaregs *

The Tuaregs (or Touaregs) are a race of nomadic herders of the central Sahara desert, in Africa. They are referred to as the "blue men of the desert" because their robes are dyed indigo blue. Lovecraft wrote that they were rumored among archaeologists to be descended from the primal race of lost Atlantis. The enigmatic Surama, resurrected by Doctor Alfred Clarendon through the use of a necromantic ritual, pretended to be of this race, but was probably a priest of Atlantis.

(*The Last Test*)

Tulu-metal

A lustrous metal magnetic to itself but not to other metals, that was brought to Earth from beyond the stars by Cthulhu along with an alien race resembling American Indians that still inhabits blue-litten K'n-yan, a vast cavern deep in the interior of this planet. Lovecraft described the metal as "heavy, darkish, lustrous, and richly mottled." All the Tulu-metal that exists was contained in the statues and figurines carried across space with this race. For a period in the race's history, the Tulu-metal was alloyed with common Earth metals and made into coins that served this race as currency.

(*The Mound*)

Whippoorwills *

Birds fabled by the people of Dunwich to wait around the houses of those who are dying in an attempt to capture their released souls. If the singing of the birds become clamorous, it is a sign that the dead person's soul has been taken, but if it dies away, it is a sign that the soul has escaped. This bit of folklore was not invented by Lovecraft but was current in New England during his lifetime.

(*The Dunwich Horror*)

White Ship

A mysterious galley that appeared from the south to carried Basil Elton, keeper of the North Point lighthouse at Kingsport, on a voyage across the seas of the dreamlands.

(*The White Ship*)

Year of the Black Goat

In the *Chronicle of Nath* by Rudolf Yergler it is written that in the Year of the Black Goat a shadow comes from the starless gulf that spawned it to feed on the souls of men. It is a shadow that should not exist on the Earth, and has no form known to the eyes of Earth. A man who can gaze upon the true shape of the shadow and live can send it back from whence it came, until the cycle of years brings the Year of the Black Goat around once again. Its true shape is revealed by gazing at its semblance through an amber crystal known only as "the Gem," which is cut with strange angles.

The Year of the Black Goat occurred in the spring of 1938. The shadow was seen on June 23 of this year, which is the day after the summer solstice, so it seems probable that the Year of the Goat begins on the summer solstice. However, Lovecraft gave no exact indication of how long the cycle of years may be that will bring the Year of the Black Goat around once again, but only referred in a vague way to "thousands of eons."

(*The Tree on the Hill*)

Yr and Nhhngr

These words are not explained, but they occur together in *The Dunwich Horror*, where Wilbur Whateley writes in his diary, "I shall have to learn all the angles of the planes and all the formulas between the Yr and the Nhhngr." It is possible that they refer to occult names for months of the year. Lovecraft's story borrows some of its inspiration from Arthur Machen's story *The White People*, in which a precocious young girl who is keeping a diary writes, "I must not write down the real names of the days and months which I found out a year ago, nor the way to make the Aklo letters." Reference is made in *The Dunwich Horror* to the Aklo language, indicating a link between Lovecraft's tale and the story by Machen.

(*The Dunwich Horror*)

The Key to the Eleventh Gate

11th Astral Gate:
Libra—The Balance

Sun passes through Libra: October 31—November 22

Constellation is represented by a scale or balance with two weighing pans—at one time this constellation was regarded as the claws of Scorpio.

Right Pillar: Zubenelgenubi (Arabic: *al-zuban al-janubiyyah*—The Southern Claw). Astronomical designation: Alpha Libri. Astrological nature: Saturn-Mars. Influence: revenge, retribution, violence. Magnitude: 2.8. Color: pale-yellow—binary star. Sun crosses: November 7. Location: the southern pan of the balance. Comments: Sometimes referred to as the Price to be Paid.

Left Pillar: Zubenelschemali (Arabic: *al-zuban al-samaliyyah*—The Northern Claw). Astronomical designation: Beta Libri. Astrological nature: Jupiter-Mercury. Influence: good fortune, honor, wealth. Magnitude: 2.6. Color: pale-emerald. Sun crosses: November 13. Location: the northern pan of the balance. Comments: Sometimes called the Price to be Received.

The astral gate of Libra lies between the star of its right pillar, located on the southern pan of the balance, and the star of its left pillar, on the northern pan of the balance. The Sun enters the gate by crossing the longitude of Zubenelgenubi, the star of the right pillar, around November 7. The solar transition of this narrow gate takes six days. The sun exits the gate around November 13, when it crosses the longitude of the star of the left pillar, Zubenelschemali.

The key to the Eleventh Gate opens the constellation Libra, allowing entry into that part of the walled city of the *Necronomicon* that concerns curiosities, oddities, and enigmas dreamed by Lovecraft. Use it for divining information or receiving dreams about the strange or unique things in the mythos that seem to stand apart.

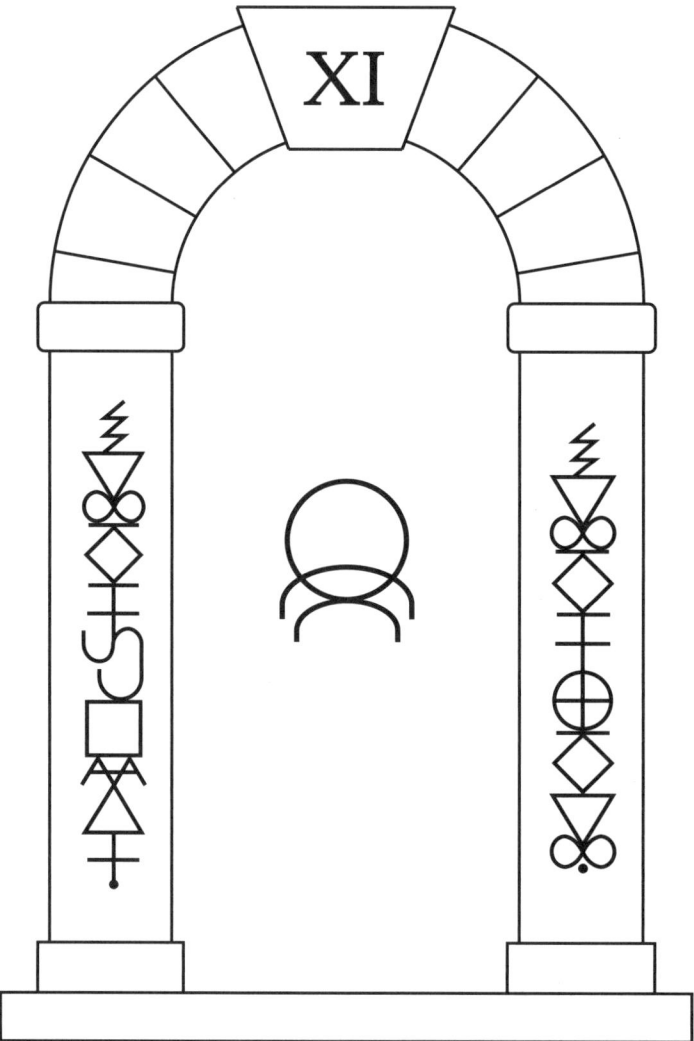

Seal of the Eleventh Key on the Eleventh Gate

Ritual of Opening Libra

Face the direction of the compass ruled by the Eleventh Gate, which is west by north—that is, slightly to the right of due west. Visualize before you the closed gate in the western wall of the city of the book so that it is more than large enough for you to walk through without awkwardness.

With the visualized image of the gate clear in your mind and projected upon the astral plane in the direction west by north, speak this invocation to Yog-Sothoth, which apart from a few details has the same general form for all the gates:

> Guardian of the Gate! Defender of the Door! Watcher of the Way! Who art the stout Lock, the slender Key, and the turning Hinge! Lord of All Transition, without whom there is no coming in or going out, I call thee! Keeper of the Threshold, whose dwelling place is between worlds, I summon thee! Yog-Sothoth, wise and mighty lord of the Old Ones, I invoke thee!
>
> By the authority of the dreaded name, Azathoth, that few dare speak, I charge thee, open to me the gateway of Libra, the Balance, that lies between the blazing pillar Zubenelgenubi on the right hand and the blazing pillar Zubenelschemali on the left hand. As the solar chariot [or, lunar chariot] crosses between these pillars, I enter the city of the *Necronomicon* through its Eleventh Gate. Selah!

Visualize the key of the Eleventh Gate in your right hand some six inches long and made of cast bronze. Feel its weight, texture, and shape as you hold it. Extend your right arm and use the key to draw upon the surface of the gate the seal of the key, which should be visualized to burn on the gate in a line of white spiritual fire. Point with the astral key at the center of the gate and speak the words:

> In the name of Azathoth, Ruler of Chaos, by the power of Yog-Sothoth, Lord of Portals, the Eleventh Gate is opened!

Visualize the gate unlocking and opening inward of its own accord upon a shadowed space. On the astral level, walk through the gateway and stand in the darkness beyond. Hold in your thoughts whatever curiosity described by Lovecraft that you seek to understand more fully. Open your mind to receive impressions, and if directions for scrying or obtaining a dream vision are given, follow them. In a more general sense, this ritual and this gate may be used to scry and understand any singular or unique formation, object or instrument on the physical, the astral, and even the mental planes.

After fulfilling the purpose for which this gate was opened, conclude the ritual by astrally passing out through the gate and visualizing it to close. Draw the seal of the Eleventh Key on the surface of the gate with the astral key you hold in your hand, and mentally cause it to lock itself shut, as it was at the beginning of the ritual. Speak the words of closing:

> By the power of Yog-Sothoth, and authority of the supreme name Azathoth, I close and seal the Eleventh Gate. This ritual is well and truly ended.

Allow the image of the gate to grow pale in your imagination and fade to nothingness before you turn away from the ritual direction.

The Twelfth Gate

Twelfth Gate
Abominations

An attempt to examine in detail the abominable things in the Necronomicon mythos is met with a tangible difficulty. Lovecraft preferred to suggest his horrors rather than to define them, believing that the horror conjured up in the depths of the imagination is greater than any a writer could explicitly set down on the page. His use of adjectives to suggest rather than to describe is so much of a hallmark of his writing style that it has become a cliché imitated by other writers more for humor than as a homage. Words such as "eldritch," "cosmic," "cyclopean," "tenebrous," "gibbous," "blasphemous," "unholy," "rugose," "squamish," "noisome," and "loathsome" occur with great frequency in his stories. He usually reserved such adjectives for his greater abominations, the horror of which defies human description, but the lesser evils are couched in more prosaic terms that allow them to be considered by mere mortals.

Much that is abominable in the mythos is connected with graveyards, tombs, and corpses. Lovecraft dreamed of descending into graves, beneath which were flights of stone steps leading to endless catacombs of the dead and the undead. His story *The Statement of Randolph Carter* is directly based on such a dream. Graveyards in his imaginary New England are sometimes riddled beneath with tunnels by which inhuman things gain access to dead flesh and bones. Necromancy, the magic dealing with body parts and substances of corpses, and with the animation of the dead, is a favorite topic.

Another source of the abominable lies in the descriptions of alien creatures that shock the human mind with their sheer uncouth otherness. Sometimes Lovecraft used the device of comparing the parts of these horrific alien beings with familiar and detested objects, such as insect eyes, bat wings, snake skin, and tentacles. This was a common technique of the demonologists of past centuries, and of artists who attempted to depict demons in woodcuts and paintings. If a thing is completely beyond description, wherein lies the horror? True horror comes from the imagination, but the imagination must have something to work upon.

A third kind of abomination that touched Lovecraft very deeply was the abomination of human sexual perversion, degeneration, and madness. The 1924 story *The Loved Dead*, which Lovecraft wrote in concert with Clifford Martin Eddy, concerns the subject of necrophilia. When it was published in *Weird Tales*, it caused an uproar of condemnation that threatened to end the magazine, yet paradoxically this publicity helped circulation numbers and gave the magazine a much-needed boost. It was a daring topic, even for Lovecraft, yet the mythos stories are filled with things almost as bold.

Lavinia Whateley's sexual union with Yog-Sothoth or another of the Old Ones in the story *The Dunwich Horror*, arranged by her abusive, domineering father old Wizard Whateley, gives rise to the birth of unholy hybrid twins, one of whom appears partially human in early childhood, and the other of which has no human or Earthly traits of any kind.

In *Facts Concerning the Late Arthur Jermyn and His Family*, a man commits suicide after he has slowly realized that one of his maternal ancestors was a hybrid white ape, and thus that he himself is not wholly a human being, but is part animal. This revelation is so shaming and repulsive that he falls into a self-loathing that has the grandeur of Greek tragedy, in which he is unable to tolerate his own existence for even an instant longer than the span necessary to take his own life.

The Martense clan of the story *The Lurking Fear* is noteworthy for having achieved the greatest degree of human degeneration ever described in fiction. At one time a proud merchant family from New Amsterdam living in a lonely mansion in the Catskill Mountains, through centuries of vicious inbreeding they became wretched subhuman creatures; naked, hairy, more numerous than rats, dwelling in a warren of tunnels beneath the ruins of the mansion, and sustaining themselves on the flesh of human corpses.

Cannibalism was a favorite theme to which Lovecraft returned repeatedly. The feeding on human flesh was for him one of the sure signs of a descent into abomination that had passed beyond the point of any possible redemption or salvation. Another theme of unredeemable abomination was ritual human sacrifice, particularly the sacrifice of infants, which occurs among the degenerate cults and witch covens that worship creatures of darkness such as Lilith in her true form and Nyarlathotep in his various avatars.

One aspect of Lovecraft's multifaceted genius was his ability to draw upon his deepest phobias and obsessions, his worst nightmares, and set them forth in his stories in all their horror with an unflinching clarity that has almost no match among the writers of his time. The effect is sometimes nauseatingly potent, as the vomit of the subconscious that should always remain hidden is exposed to the light of awareness. Yet without it, his mythos would lack much of its compelling seduction. Lovecraft's horrors are somehow more real than the horrors of his fellow pulp writers of the 1920s and 30s, for the very reason that he did not contrive them, but pulled them forth from his soul leaving bloody and torn roots.

Abyss

A place that lies beyond the final dimensional gateway and all the multitude of possible worlds, a negation of being that is inhabited by nameless devourers. Only the 'Umr at-Tawil, described by Alhazred as "the Most Ancient One or the Prolonged of Life," can lead the foolish seeker to this ultimate oblivion.

(*Through the Gates of the Silver Key*)

black fever

A slow-acting but excruciatingly painful and fatal disease not of this Earth that was drawn down from beyond the stars by Surama, a former priest of lost Atlantis. Surama was restored to life from his mummified state by a necromantic ritual performed in North Africa by the medical researcher Doctor Alfred Clarendon. Before the sinking of their continent, the Atlanteans established a colony in what is now North Africa, which is why the mummy of the priest was entombed there. Surama promised Clarendon wisdom and power if he would spread the disease, but Clarendon found himself intoxicated by the sheer evil of infecting healthy living beings and watching them slowly die. In the end, Surama grew disgusted with the pettiness of Clarendon's imagination and abandoned him.

(*The Last Test*)

black galleys

A race of fungous and amorphous blasphemies called moon-beasts (sometimes called "moon-things") inhabit the far side of the Moon, but sail the seas of Earth's dreamlands in sinister black galleys, trading rubies for gold and slaves. The galleys are primarily slave ships. Because they are so hideous to look upon, the moon-beasts conceal themselves below decks when they come into a port in the dreamlands such as Dylath-Leen. Their agents in dealings with human beings, the enslaved horned-men of Leng, take care of all trading details. It is the moon-beasts who work the oars of the galleys, not the slaves. The galleys sometimes take the slaves to an island in the Cerenerian Sea called the Nameless Rock, where they are unloaded and tortured. These evil vessels have the extraordinary ability to sail off the edge of the world past the great cataract in the west, and through the gulf that separates the Earth from the Moon. The slaves that are transported to the Moon serve as beasts of burden or as food for the moon-beasts.

(*The Dream-Quest of Unknown Kadath*)

black goat *

A black cock and a black goat are mentioned in *The Dreams in the Witch House* in connection with a witch sabbat conducted by Keziah Mason in a black valley—probably the ravine beyond Meadow Hill near Arkham. They were destined for blood sacrifice, to be coupled with the sacrifice of a human infant.

Daniel Morris, who was descended from the wizard Nicholas Van Kauran on his mother's side, and who was widely known as Mad Dan, used to sacrifice a black goat on Halloween at the top of Thunder Hill, as is written in the story *The Man of Stone*.

In the *Chronicle of Yath*, a psychic text written by the German mystic and alchemist Rudolf Yergler, mention is made of the "year of the Black Goat" when a shadow that should not exist came down to Earth to feed on the souls of the men of Nath. The year of the Black Goat rolls around again in 1938, when the shadow is fought and defeated by the occultist Constantine Theunis, as described in Lovecraft's story *The Tree on the Hill*.

The Whisperer in Darkness relates that the Mi-Go who meet in Lee's Swamp, at the base of the western slope of Dark Mountain, in Virginia, with their cult of human worshippers, chant the titles of the Black Goat of the Woods, and the Black Goat of the Woods with a Thousand Young. These are titles of Shub-Niggurath.

The black goat was a common fixture of descriptions of European witches' sabbats from the fourteenth to the sixteenth centuries. Sometimes witches were said to copulate with the goat, but it was assumed to be the Devil in disguise by the Inquisitors of the Roman Church, not an ordinary animal.

(*The Dreams in the Witch House; The Man of Stone; The Tree on the Hill; The Whisperer in Darkness*)

black mass *

The black mass is a very specific occult ritual that is a parody of the high mass of the Catholic Church. It deliberately seeks to degrade and defile the ritual of the mass by perverting its elements—the mass is celebrated on the naked body of a whore instead of on an altar, the wine is urine or blood, the host feces or turnip, the priest who celebrates the mass is a defrocked priest, the cross in hung upside down, the words are recited backward, and so on. The purpose of this defilement of the high mass of the Church is to exalt the Devil and thereby win his aid in a specific action.

Genuine performances of the black mass were quite rare, and most frequently were done more as a decadent entertainment than with any serious expectation of infernal assistance. The Inquisition sometimes accused witches of performing the black mass, but in most cases the grounds of such accusations are unsound. Pagan celebrations performed by witches at their sabbats were not black masses. Witches were usually of low birth, whereas black masses, on those rare occasions when they actually took place, were enacted by educated persons of higher birth.

In *The Diary of Alonzo Typer*, members of the notorious van der Heyl family were said to have dabbled in the black mass "and cults of even darker significance"—presumably cults devoted to the worship of the Old Ones.

The clandestine assemblies of rural folk descended from "dark religions antedating the Aryan world," religions that are "hellish vestiges of old Turanian-Asiatic magic and fertility cults," are said in *The Horror at Red Hook* to appear in popular legends as black masses and witches' sabbats. Lovecraft here intimated that the actual practices at these gatherings were stranger and more horrible than anything described in the legends.

Lovecraft again mentioned "Black Masses and Witches' Sabbaths" together in *Medusa's Coil* when he described the portrait of Marceline de Russy that was painted by Frank Marsh, which contained in the background a scene of some nightmarish rite of black magic from the ancient world, and which depicted the horror of Marceline's true form. The painting itself was burned in the fire that destroyed the house containing it, but the ghost of the painting survives.

(*The Diary of Alonzo Typer*; *The Horror at Red Hook*; *Medusa's Coil*)

black throne

Azathoth, the mindless god, "rules all time and space from a black throne at the centre of Chaos."

(*The Dreams in the Witch House*)

blasted heath

West of Arkham, Massachusetts, in the bottom of a spacious valley on the old road not far removed from the town of Bolton was a circular patch of withered ground of some five acres in extent, which was said to be "like a great spot eaten by acid." The ground was covered with a fine gray ash that never seemed to blow away on the wind. It has the look of a patch of ground burned over, but no forest fire had ever burned there. The locals avoided it. Settlers could not be induced to establish farms anywhere near it. Nothing would grow there. Curiously, the trees and undergrowth some distance away from this blighted spot flourished with unnatural luxuriance and denseness. The blasted heath lay on the north side of the old road, but a portion of it was apparent on the other side of the road as well, suggesting that it was expanding. In the midst of it were the ruins of the old Gardner farm, and in the midst of those ruins an old well.

A local man, Ammi Pierce, related the story that in the 1880s a meteorite fell to earth on the farm of Nahum Gardner. It attracted the lightning, which utterly destroyed it, but not before it leaked some alien gas or essence into the Gardner farm's well. The water of the well became poisoned in a particularly insidious way—animals that drank it, or plants watered with it, grew more rapidly than was natural, but there was a sickness in their growth that made them unfit to eat. When human beings drank the water, or ate of things watered with it, they went slowly insane and their bodies deteriorated. It may be that the blasted heath continues to expand to this day, but if so, it does so underwater, for the valley was flooded and became part of the reservoir that serves the good people of Arkham.

(*The Colour Out of Space*)

brain cylinders

The Mi-Go dwelling in secret at Round Hill in Virginia had the ability to cut out the brain of a man and insert it into a fluid-filled metal cylinder, so that the brain remained conscious, and was able to see, hear, and speak by means of electrodes connected with machines that simulated these human senses. Brains preserved in this way were nearly deathless. The cylinders were of no metal recognized on Earth, about a foot high, and slightly less in diameter. On the curved front of the cylinders were three sockets for hooking up the sensory machines. The Mi-Go used this method to convey the brains of other species through space from star system to star system. It was necessary because the bodies of these beings were too frail to survive the journeys.

(*The Whisperer in Darkness*)

Brown Jenkin

This horrific little sprite is the familiar of the witch Keziah Mason, who while under sentence of execution for witchcraft in 1692 escaped from Salem Jail by slipping through an inter-dimensional portal. She created this gateway by drawing in blood on her cell wall certain lines and curves that point out "directions leading through the walls of space to other spaces beyond." She seemed to vanish from the face of the earth, but she returned periodically to work her mischiefs, and Brown Jenkin was her helper. At the time of her disappearance, her jailor went mad and began to babble about a "small white-fanged furry thing" that skuttered out of her empty cell when he opened the door to check on her.

(*The Dreams in the Witch House*)

charnel gardens

The shore of Xura, the Land of Pleasures Unattained, which lies in the dreamlands, appears from a distance at sea to be a pleasant place of "flowery meadows and leafy woods," but a closer approach reveals the stench of decaying corpses hanging over the land. Randolph Carter referred to its "charnel gardens." It must be assumed that something in the scent or touch of the flowers, or in the water, or in the air of that accursed place, is deadly.

(*The White Ship; The Dream-Quest of Unknown Kadath*)

corpse-eating cult

On the plateau of Leng there exists a cult of corpse-eating necromancers. They wear around their necks small green-jade amulets carved in the shape of a crouching hound with a malevolent expression on its semi-canine face. The mad Arab, Abdul Alhazred, wrote about this cult in veiled terms in his *Necronomicon*. The amulets are bound to the very souls of the necromancers who wear them.

(*The Hound*)

effluvium of K'thun

This material is mentioned only once, in the story *The Horror in the Museum*, as part of a rambling, abusive curse. "Fool! Spawn of Noth-Yidik and effluvium of K'thun! Son of the dogs that howl in the maelstrom of Azathoth!" From context is would seem to be some loathsome bodily secretion or excretion of a reviled being named K'thun.

(*The Horror in the Museum*)

feasts of Nitokris

When the narrator of *The Outsider* realizes that he is a walking corpse, he learns to enjoy his condition, and revels in "the unnamed feasts of Nitokris beneath the Great Pyramid," which are feasts on the flesh of the dead. Nitokris (or Nitocris) is the ghoul-queen who rules the catacombs beneath the pyramids with her undead husband, the pharaoh Khephren.

(*The Outsider; Imprisoned with the Pharaohs*)

giant penguins

Beneath the deserted city of the Elder Things in Antarctica live a race of giant, blind albino penguins that stand six feet tall. They inhabit the subterranean sea beneath the city and provide food for the shoggoths that sometimes pass through the tunnels that connect the cavern with the abandoned buildings.

(*At the Mountains of Madness*)

gyaa-yothn

Genetically modified beasts used as beasts of burden by the subterranean race of blue-litten K'n-yan. The are described as "great floundering white things" that have black fur growing on their backs and a small horn extending from their foreheads. Evidence of some human strain in their composition is revealed by their faces, which have a humanoid appearance. They are carnivorous, and feed on the slave-class of K'n-yan, a race of degenerate human beings bred to be almost mindless. Wild gyaa-yothn had first been discovered in Yoth, the vast red-litten cavern that lies below the cavern of K'n-yan. Originally they had possessed reptilian characteristics, but they were crossbred with human slaves to be more mammalian in appearance, and were domesticated by the men of K'n-yan.

(*The Mound*)

Herd

The Herd is described by Alhazred in the *Necronomicon* as standing guard over the secret portal that exists within every tomb, and thriving on the things that grow out from the corpse.

(*Through the Gates of the Silver Key*)

horned skull

Under the eaves in the attic of the deserted house beside the old burying-ground in Arkham, the writer Randolph Carter discovered a cache of monstrously deformed bones. The skull was humanoid in appearance but had four-inch horns. Carter gathered up the bones and placed them into an open space in the tomb in the old burying-ground behind the house, which was the tomb of the former owner of the house, who had died in 1710. Ancient records revealed that the bones had belonged to an illegitimate child of the man's daughter, who was identified as the mother of the monstrous baby by a defect in one of its eyes, which was also in one of the mother's eyes.

The girl was hanged by the horrified and superstitious people of Arkham, and her unnatural child was locked away in the attic of the house under the care of her father. Even after its death from starvation and neglect, following the death of its grandfather in 1710, the ghost of the creature continued to haunt the old abandoned house and the surrounding houses of the town. In 1793 a boy who entered the old house was driven mad by what he saw there. Lovecraft's story implies that the monstrous child was a hybrid birth resulting from a union between the daughter of the owner of the old house and something inhuman.

The crack in the brickwork of the grandfather's tomb, into which Carter inserted the bones of his grandson, was caused by the root of a willow tree that had grown up and engulfed the unmarked tombstone of his daughter, which was close to his gravesite. The willow sprouted the year the girl was buried in her unmarked grave, and later the expanding trunk of the tree half-surrounded the stone. It was upon the very tomb in which Carter had placed the deformed bones that Carter and his friend Joel Manton were sitting when attacked at twilight by the ghost of the creature. They were knocked unconscious and carried a mile by the ghost, or whatever unnatural thing it may have been, which deposited them in a field beyond Meadow Hill. Both men had claw wounds on their bodies, and Carter's skin received the impress of a cloven hoof.

Manton, who saw the creature, described it as "a gelatin—a slime yet it had shapes, a thousand shapes of horror beyond all memory. There were eyes—and a blemish." It seemed to come from both the attic window of the house and the fissure in the brickwork of the tomb, perhaps reuniting itself with its bones. Lovecraft mentioned that the place where the two unconscious men were deposited had once been the location of a slaughterhouse. The significance of this detail is not obvious, unless it may be assumed that the girl, who was a drunkard, is supposed to have had a sexual coupling with a beast such as a goat or bull.

(*The Unnamable*)

Hound, Winged

These disembodied beasts served the wizards of the corpse-eating cult of the plateau of Leng as familiar spirits and guardians. In some mystical way that was never clearly explained by Lovecraft, the essence of one of these monstrous creatures was bound up with the soul of the wizard who wore its jade talisman, called the "soul-symbol," around his neck. They resemble nothing on the Earth, but look somewhat like a giant hound with wings on its back. It may be that the hounds of Leng are manifestations of the souls of the wizards in animal form. Alhazred wrote in the *Necronomicon* that the "sinister lineaments" of the hounds are shaped by the souls of those who gnaw the dead—that is, by the wizards of the corpse-eating cult of Leng who wore the soul-symbols.

It is a common theme in Western magic that magicians have the power to project their astral forms through space, and that they can, if they wish, mold their astral bodies into the shapes of beasts such as wolves. Indeed, this is one explanation given for the worldwide myths of the werewolf and other were-animals. The winged hound may well be an astral projection of the soul of the ghoul, living or dead, who wears its jade amulet around his neck. The souls of wizards were believed to persist after death in their places of burial because they were stronger or more vital than the souls of ordinary human beings.

(*The Hound*)

Hounds of Argos *

Psamathe, daughter of King Crotopus of the town of Argos, had an affair with the god Apollo and gave birth to a son, whom she named Linus. In fear of her father's wrath, she set the baby out to die, but the king learned of his daughter's indiscretion, had her executed, and fed the infant to his dogs. In fury, Apollo sent the monster Poene (Punishment) to devour all the children of Argos.

(*The Electric Executioner*)

Howler

A monstrous howling thing with four human hands in place of paws, and a human face. It was the issue of the witch Goody Watkins, hanged in 1704, though what its father may have been Lovecraft did not speculate. It or its ghost continues to inhabit the upstairs room of the old Watkins cottage on the Brigg's Path to Zoar. Its resemblance to Brown Jenkin should be noted.

(*Fungi from Yuggoth*)

Hybrids

Beneath the mansion of Robert Suydem, alchemist and worshipper of the demoness queen of Hell, Lilith, were found four woman chained in cells with infants at their breasts of inhuman aspect. When these unnatural and deformed babies were carried into the light, they quickly died. Lovecraft intimated in *The Horror at Red Hook* that they were the product of matings between demons and the unfortunate women, all of whom were completely insane when released from their prisons by the police.

Wilbur Whateley of the story *The Dunwich Horror* was the product of a union between Yog-Sothoth and Lavinia Whateley, the daughter of old Wizard Whateley. As he matured, his inhuman side became dominant and began to transform his body into something monstrous and not wholly of this dimension of space.

Perhaps the most notable example of hybrids is the children of the marriages between the people of Innsmouth and the Deep Ones, which the people of Innsmouth were obligated to enter into by the terms of the third oath they swore in the church of the Esoteric Order of Dagon. At birth the babies seemed completely human, but as they grew older, amphibious characteristics began to show themselves, until around the age of seventy years they were able to live permanently in the depths of the ocean and left the land forever, or to return only at rare intervals.

The unfortunate Arthur Jermyn killed himself after learning that he was descended from a hybrid offspring resulting from the union between an Englishman and a hybrid white ape of Africa—herself the result of an ancient cross-breeding between true apes and a true human beings. Even though he was far removed from this taint, in a genetic sense, Jermyn could not live with the knowledge of it.

In *The Curse of Yig*, a woman named Audrey Davis, traveling with her husband from Arkansas in 1889 through the Indian Territory to settle in Oklahoma, angers the god of serpents by killing four baby rattlesnakes. Later, she gives birth to four offspring that are partly humanoid and partly serpentine. The one that survives cannot speak, but merely writhes on its belly and hisses.

The beasts of burden in blue-litten K'n-yan that are known as gyaa-yothn are the result of deliberate cross-breeding between something reptilian found in Yoth, the cavern world below K'n-yan, and enslaved human beings used by the people of K'n-yan for meat animals. Such a genetic mix was only possible due to the advanced alien science of the race of K'n-yan.

In *Pickman's Model*, the ghouls are in the habit of stealing human babies and substituting in their place ghoul babies to be bred up as humans, for the purpose of cross-breeding with humans and thereby keeping the blood of the ghouls, who are related to humans, healthy and strong.

A young woman in the story *The Unnamable* has a sexual union with a beast, or some sort of bestial creature, and gives birth to a child with horns that is not human, and must be hidden away in the attic all its life.

(*The Horror at Red Hook; The Dunwich Horror; The Shadow Over Innsmouth; Facts Concerning the Late Arthur Jermyn and His Family; The Curse of Yig; The Mound; Pickman's Model; The Unnamable*)

Last Void

A place beyond the Ultimate Gate that is "outside all earths, all universes, and all matter."

(*Through the Gates of the Silver Key*)

Noth-Yidik

The insult "Spawn of Noth-Yidik and effluvium of K'thun!" is hurled at an unbeliever of Rhan-Tegoth by the proprietor of a London wax museum, George Rogers, self-appointed priest of Rhan-Tegoth. It is obviously a deadly insult, and probably harks back to the mythology of the planetoid Yuggoth, which is the world we know as Pluto, as that was the origin of Rhan-Tegoth. However, there is not enough information given to conjecture its precise meaning.

(*The Horror in the Museum*)

pit of the shoggoths

A place outside normal space where the mind of Ephraim Waite, in the body of Edward Pickman Derby, went to practice black magic with his coven. It lies at the bottom of six thousand steps. Access it had through a ring of standing stones in the woods of northern Maine. Lovecraft referred to it as "the unholy pit where the black realm begins and the watcher guards the gate." Reference is made in the sonnet "Night Gaunts" in *Fungi from Yuggoth* to "nether pits," which contain a foul lake where the "puffed shoggoths splash in doubtful sleep."

(*The Thing on the Doorstep; Fungi from Yuggoth*)

shantak-birds

Larger than an elephant, with a head shaped somewhat like the head of a horse, the shantak-bird has slippery scales instead of feathers. The servants of Nyarlathotep use them as transportation. These birds, though shunned by men, are valued for their enormous and richly flavored eggs, which are sought by gourmands because of their exotic taste. The great father of all shantak-birds is said to be housed beneath the central dome of the palace of the Veiled King at the onyx city of Inquanok, in the dreamlands. The shantak-birds are rumored to be unwholesome. It is best not to look upon them, and for this reason the father of shantak-birds is fed in the dark. It is said to send forth queer dreams to those who merely pause and gaze curiously at its domed dwelling place.

(*The Dream-Quest of Unknown Kadath*)

soul-bottles

The Terrible Old Man of Water Street in Kingsport knew some kind of magic, which he may have picked up in his voyages to the Far East, that enabled him to trap souls in bottles, and to use those souls for his servants and guardians. When a trio of young men tries to rob him one night, they are all killed by these spirit familiars. The Old Man receives communications from the spirits within the bottles by means of small lead weights suspended inside the bottles on strings, so that they strike against the sides of the glass to make tapping sounds. The souls trapped in the bottles appear to be those of the Terrible Old Man's seagoing companions, for some of their names are "Jack, Scar-Face, Long Tom, Spanish Joe, Peters, and Mate Ellis."

(*The Terrible Old Man; The Strange High House in the Mist*)

stench

The Old Ones are reputed in the *Necronomicon* to be identifiable by their strong and unique stench, even though they walk the earth invisible. When Earl Sawyer of Dunwich visited the farm of Old Whateley, he smelled just such a stench in the tool shed that had served as the temporary shelter for Wilbur Whateley's unnamed invisible brother, who resembled his father, an Old One. Sawyer averred that he had smelled a similar odor in the stone circles on the hills around Dunwich, and in 1917 smelled it coming from the sealed upper story of the Whateley house. Luther Brown, the hired boy of farmer George Corey, is the only one to describe the smell. He said that it "smells like thunder." This suggests that it is a smell similar to burnt sulfur, which is also know as brimstone. It is to be noted that a foul smell of brimstone is one of the accompaniments of demonic manifestation, according to the Renaissance demonologists.

(*The Dunwich Horror*)

Tcho-Tcho people *

A race of short, hairless humanoids described by Lovecraft as "wholly abominable." He did not explain why, but it may have been their practice of cannibalism. They were invented by the writer August Derleth in his 1933 story *The Thing that Walked on the Wind*, where they are said to be a race of people in Burma who have produced "forbidden and accursed designs."

(*The Shadow Out of Time; The Horror in the Museum*)

three-lobed burning eye

The avatar of Nyarlathotep known as the Haunter of the Dark, which was called to Earth through the Shining Trapezohedron by the Church of Starry Wisdom, was described by Robert Harrison Blake: "I see it—coming here—hell-wind—titan blue—black wing—

Yog-Sothoth save me—the three-lobed burning eye" The term "three-lobed" probably refers to the pupil of the eye. Humans have a circular pupil. Cats have a vertical pupil. Goats have a horizontal pupil. The thing that came for Blake may have had a pupil with three projections, giving the pupil a roughly triangular shape. The iris of the eye was probably red. Given the aversion of this creature to any light, it may be that its eye was hypersensitive.

(*The Haunter of the Dark*)

Upas-tree

A large species of tree, an example of which grows in the valley of Nis. Its leaves are fatal, though whether by ingestion or by skin contact, Lovecraft did not reveal.

(*Memory*)

Well, bottomless

In the windowless monastery on the plateau of Leng is a domed chamber that contains the golden throne of the High-Priest Not To Be Described. At the foot of the high stone dais the throne occupies, six blood-stained altars surround a gaping circular pit that may reach down to the Vaults of Zin. Into this black well the dreamer Randolph Carter pushed an acolyte of the High-Priest.

A similar bottomless well is to be found in a domed hall on the rocky island in the northern sea of the dreamlands that serves as a way station for the black galleys of the moon-beasts. The vaultings of the dome are covered with grotesque carvings. On the far side of the hall is a small and strangely wrought bronze door that Carter feared to open, although he had no explicit reason not to open it.

(*The Dream-Quest of Unknown Kadath*)

Yazidis *

An ancient Persian cult that was widely believed to worship the Devil as their god. They have been hated and persecuted by their Muslim neighbors for centuries, causing their numbers to dwindle. Most of their evil reputation is undeserved, as their rituals are no more evil or abhorrent than those of other religious cults. However, there is some truth in the belief that they worship the Devil. The Yazidis worship the first archangel known as Malek Taous (more properly *Tawûsê Melek*, the King Peacock), leader of six other archangels who preside over the world. Malek Taous, who is represented by the image of a peacock with its tail fanned, has the alternative name "Shaytan," the name for the Devil in the Koran. However, Yazidis never speak this name.

According to Yazidi myth, Malek Taous was created first by God from his own illumination, followed by the other six lesser archangels. God ordered Malek Taous not to bow down before the other archangels. Later, God formed Adam, the first man, from dust gathered by the other six, and breathed life into his body. God ordered all seven archangels to bow down and worship Adam. The lesser six archangels complied, but Malek Taous refused on the grounds that he was formed from the light of God, whereas Adam was made only from the dust of the earth. For this defiance, God praised Malek Taous and appointed him leader of all the angels and God's representative on the Earth.

The Yazidis pray to the Sun at sunrise and sunset, facing the Sun as they pray. At noon they pray facing Lalish, a small valley sixty kilometers northwest of Mosul, in northern Iraq, where the tomb of their prophet Sex Adi is located. They worship small bronze images of a peacock, but assert that they are not worshipping the images themselves but the archangel Malek Taous through the images. Their religious text is known as the *Black Book*.

Lovecraft rather uncharitably presented Yazidis as illegal Kurdish immigrants who worshiped the demoness Lilith, queen of Hell, in the district of Red Hook, in the city of New York, and sacrificed abducted children to her.

(*The Horror at Red Hook*)

y'm-bhi

Lifeless zombies of the resurrected corpses of human slaves, used for slave labor in the subterranean world of blue-litten K'n-yan. Some are headless, or strangely disfigured by surgical grafts.

(*The Mound*)

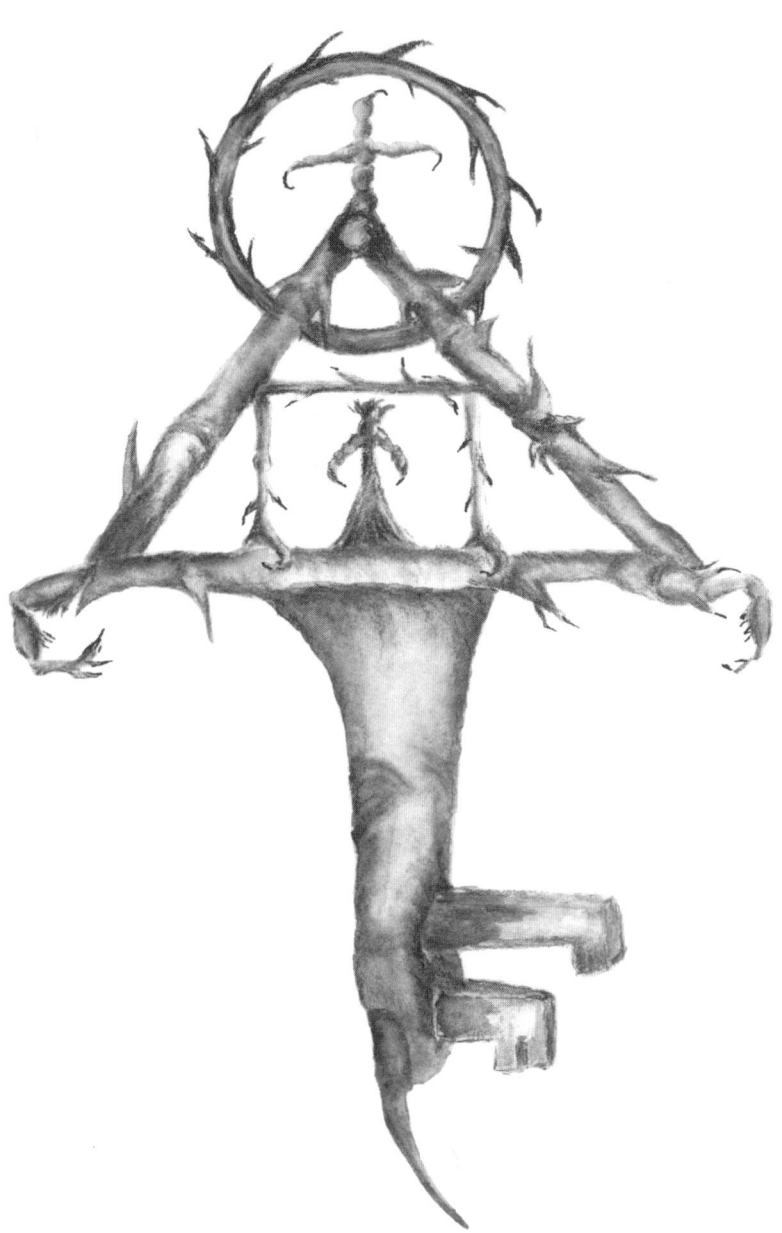

The Key to the Twelfth Gate

12th Astral Gate: Scorpius—The Scorpion

Sun passes through Scorpius: November 22—November 29

Constellation is represented by a scorpion.

Right Pillar: Antares (Greek: Rival of Mars). Arabic name: *kalb al akrab* (Heart of the Scorpion)—in Latin: Cor Scorpii. Astronomical designation: Alpha Scorpii. Astrological nature: Mars-Jupiter. Influence: honor and success, but the danger of overconfidence. Magnitude: 1—binary star. Color: fiery red. Sun crosses: December 1. Location: the heart of the scorpion. Comments: One of the four Persian royal stars, called the Watcher of the West.

Left Pillar: Shaula (Arabic: *Al Shaulah*—The Sting). Astronomical designation: Lambda Scorpii. Astrological nature: Mercury-Mars. Influence: desperate and dangerous actions, accidents, disasters. Magnitude: 1.6. Color: white. Sun crosses: December 15. Location: sting of the scorpion. Comments: This unfortunate star is usually treated in conjunction with its close neighbor, Lesath, which has similar associations. Together these stars were known as the Two Releasers.

The astral gate of Scorpius lies between the star of its right pillar, located in the heart of the Scorpion, and the star of its left pillar, located on the sting of the Scorpion. The Sun enters the gate by crossing the longitude of Antares, the star of the right pillar, around December 1. The solar transition of this gate takes fourteen days. The Sun exits the gate around December 15, when it crosses the longitude of the star of the left pillar, Shaula. Note that the time frame of the crossing of this gate is completely outside the timeframe of the crossing of the constellation itself, due to its irregular shape.

The key to the Twelfth Gate opens the constellation Scorpius, allowing entry into that part of the city of the book that concerns the abominations of the Necronomicon mythos.

Seal of the Twelfth Key on the Twelfth Gate

Ritual of Opening Scorpius

Face the direction of the compass ruled by the Twelfth Gate, which is northwest by west—that is, slightly to the left of the northwest point. Visualize before you the closed gate in the western wall of the city of the book as though it were a real gate in a real city wall.

With the visualized image of the gate clear in your mind and projected upon the astral plane in the direction northwest by west, speak this invocation to Yog-Sothoth:

> Guardian of the Gate! Defender of the Door! Watcher of the Way!
> Who art the stout Lock, the slender Key, and the turning Hinge! Lord of

All Transition, without whom there is no coming in or going out, I call thee! Keeper of the Threshold, whose dwelling place is between worlds, I summon thee! Yog-Sothoth, wise and mighty lord of the Old Ones, I invoke thee!

By the authority of the dreaded name, Azathoth, that few dare speak, I charge thee, open to me the gateway of Scorpius, the Scorpion, that lies between the blazing pillar Antares on the right hand and the blazing pillar Shaula on the left hand. As the solar chariot [or, lunar chariot] crosses between these pillars, I enter the city of the *Necronomicon* through its Twelfth Gate. Selah!

Visualize the key of the Twelfth Gate in your right hand some six inches long and made of cast silver. Feel its weight, texture, and shape as you hold it. Extend your right arm and use the key to draw upon the surface of the gate the seal of the key, which should be visualized to burn before the bars of the gate in a line of white spiritual fire. Point with the astral key at the center of the gate and speak the words of opening:

In the name of Azathoth, Ruler of Chaos, by the power of Yog-Sothoth, Lord of Portals, the Twelfth Gate is opened!

Visualize the bars dissolving and the gate opening inward of its own accord upon a shadowed space. On the astral level, walk through the gateway and stand in the darkness beyond. Hold in your mind whatever abomination or horror of the mythos that you wish to scry or experience later in an oracular dream. Open your mind to receive impressions of the atrocity. In a more general sense, this ritual and this gate may be used to scry or receive oracles concerning all evil or unnatural works of black magic.

After fulfilling the purpose for which this gate was opened, conclude the ritual by astrally passing out through the gate and visualizing the bars reforming. Draw the seal of the Twelfth Key over the surface of the gate with the astral key you hold in your hand, and mentally cause it to lock itself shut, as it was at the beginning of the ritual. Speak the words of closing:

By the power of Yog-Sothoth, and authority of the supreme name Azathoth, I close and seal the Twelfth Gate. This ritual is well and truly ended.

Allow the image of the gate to grow pale in your imagination and fade to nothingness before you turn away from the ritual direction.

The Thirteenth Gate

Thirteenth Gate
Rites and Incantations

There are a surprisingly large number of references to technical details of ritual magic in the Necronomicon mythos, given that Lovecraft knew next to nothing about the subject and always professed a complete disdain for it. The actual practice of ceremonial magic may never have appealed to him, but he felt the allure of its glamour in spite of his protestations to the contrary. Magic shows up again and again in his stories. It is a puzzle why a man who claimed to regard all occultism, and indeed all religion, as no more than pernicious superstition, should have devoted so much of his energies to writings about magic.

In my opinion, Lovecraft was a creative artist torn between two attracting poles. On the one hand, he celebrated a philosophy of rationalism and materialism that exalted the latest discoveries of astronomy, chemistry, geology, archaeology, and the other sciences. But on the other hand, there was a romantic part of him that was powerfully moved against its will by the irrational and fantastic, the weird and uncanny. The rationalism lay on the surface and was Lovecraft's consciously professed belief. The irresistible attraction towards the fantastic and occult was hidden and rooted much deeper. Lovecraft would probably have denied its very existence. It sprang from the same fathomless black well as his strange dreams, which he could only exorcise and gain control over by writing them down.

He did his best to be plausible when writing about the procedural aspects of magic, but bemoaned his lack of background knowledge that forced him to rely on articles in the ninth edition of *Encyclopaedia Britannica*. In a letter to Clark Ashton Smith he asked, "Are there any good translations of any mediaeval necromancers for raising spirits, invoking Lucifer, & all that sort of thing?" (Lovecraft, *Sel. Let.* vol. 2, p. 28).

Lovecraft never did find his way directly to the grimoires. His study of ritual magic was made up largely of secondary sources such as A. E. Waite's 1898 *Book of Black Magic and Pacts* and Lewis Spence's 1920 work *Encyclopaedia of Occultism*. He had done some superficial studying of astrology and spiritualism, but only to debunk these subjects for Houdini, who hired Lovecraft as his ghostwriter. Houdini paid Lovecraft $75 for an article critical of astrology, which seems to have been lost, but Houdini died before his planned exposé of spiritualism, *The Cancer of Superstition*, in the process of being put together by Lovecraft and C. M. Eddy, could get well off the ground.

In spite of the bit of folklore that Lovecraft's wife, Sonia Greene, whom he met in 1921 and married in 1924, had been a friend, or even a former lover, of Aleister Crowley in 1918 when Crowley visited New York, there is no hard evidence to connect her with the infamous Great Beast so prominently featured in the newspaper scandals of the time. Lovecraft thought the publicity surrounding Crowley excessive but knew little or nothing of his teachings, and, had he been exposed to them, would undoubtedly have dismissed them as fantasies. He was almost as ignorant of the doctrine of Theosophy, although later in his life Lovecraft began to read more on the subject. The sheer cosmic scope of the history of the world that was part of the teachings of Madame Blavatsky appealed to him.

Magic usually appears in Lovecraft's stories for malignant purposes, such as cursing and ensnaring the souls of the innocent, or raising the dead back to life, or summoning the Old Ones from beyond the spheres. Occasionally the wise professors of Miskatonic University use their extensive theoretical knowledge of the occult to combat its abuses, fighting elemental fire with elemental fire, as it were. In *The Dunwich Horror*, Wilbur Whateley's inhuman, invisible brother is banished by magic before he can be used to bring about the end of all life on this planet, and in *The Case of Charles Dexter Ward*, the evil necromancer Joseph Curwen has the same spell that was used to raise him up from his essential salts turned against him, returning him once again to dust.

Lovecraft seems to have regarded magic, at least within the context of the Necronomicon mythos, as a kind of blind force that could be worked for good or evil, depending on the intention of the person wielding it, but which was most often turned to evil uses. Magic is always unsavory in the mythos—there is something vaguely tainted about it, and about those who are drawn to study it, with only a few exceptions. One exception is Randolph Carter, who had descended from a long line of magicians but who never used magic maliciously. Yet in the end, even Carter is caught up in the coils of magic and undone by it. The fascination for magic in Lovecraft's stories is usually a siren song from which comes little good but a great deal of harm. Those who study it, as did Charles Ward and Arthur Gilman, have a kind of fatalism draped around their shoulders. Their passion for the occult is their doom.

The other type of magician in the mythos is the wicked wizard who always uses magic for evil purposes. His lust is for both forbidden knowledge and personal power, and he pursues his mania to the exclusion of all moral considerations. In *The Thing on the Doorstep*, Ephraim Waite, the wizard of Innsmouth, destroyed his own daughter so that he could preserve and extend his term of life, and he was perfectly prepared to destroy Edward Derby in the same manner. The necromancer Joseph Curwen performed a rite that ensured his resurrection after death by his descendant, Charles Ward, even though it involved impressing that descendant with a predisposition for the study of the occult that would dominate and destroy his life.

If Lovecraft's use of magic is sometimes for the greater good, the same cannot be said about his use of witchcraft, which is invariably evil and demonic. Modern Wiccans will find little to like in his treatment of the Craft. Lovecraft adopted the same attitude toward witches as that of Cotton Mather, whose book *Magnalia Christi Americana* he had in his personal library. Witches in the mythos are minions of the Black Man of the sabbat, who is none other than an avatar of Nyarlathotep. They take the form of hunched stereotypical crones, or evil and seductive lamia who use their wiles to ensnare men. Wizards also form part of their covens, but the wizards involved with witches are invariably evil in the mythos. Lovecraft does not seem to have conceived the possibility of a good witch.

The innovation he brought to the concept of magic was to integrated it with higher dimensional geometry. The portal magic of Keziah Mason is based on the alien mathematics of the Old Ones, or perhaps of the Elder Things, with whom Keziah has commerce. Ephraim Waite met with other witches in the pit of the shoggoths beneath stone ruins in northern Maine, where he acquired knowledge that was to him magic, but was to the alien creatures who taught him a kind of science. Over the millennia of human history, mankind has acquired the use of only a small portion of this science of uncouth geometries, which the limited human intellect comprehends as a kind of magic. The great alien races that lurk and watch on the borders of our world possess much more of it, and what they hold is vastly more powerful.

Aklo *

Aklo is a language mentioned several times in Lovecraft's stories. The term originates in the story *The White People*, by Arthur Machen. In that story a character writes in a diary, "I have a great many other books of secrets I have written, hidden in a safe place, and I am going to write here many of the old secrets and some new ones; but there are some I shall not put down at all. I must not write down the real names of the days and months which I found out a year ago, nor the way to make the Aklo letters, or the Chian language, or the great beautiful Circles, nor the Mao Games, nor the chief songs."

In *The Dunwich Horror*, Wilbur Whateley writes in his diary, "Today learned the Aklo for the Sabaoth, which did not like, it being answerable from the hill and not from the air." Aklo is evidently the language in which an incantation must be chanted to be effective. The Sabaoth is that special day of the year on which the chant may be used.

Wilbur Whateley studied the incantation at age three and a half, for use on the final sabbat that would open the gate of Yog-Sothoth to admit the Old Ones—probably the witches' sabbat of May-Eve, or Walpurgis Night, is intended, since that is the sabbat on which Wilbur himself was engendered. Wilbur was not fond of the Aklo, because it required a response from his monstrous invisible brother, who would occupy Sentinel Hill at the time, not from the Old Ones who spoke from the air above the hill. Wilbur was worried about this because he feared his brother did not have much in the way of an "earth brain" with which to make the correct responses. The being who was summoned by Wilbur with magical incantations, and who gave to him the Aklo Sabaoth—the sabbat ritual in the Aklo language—told him that he might be "transfigured" when he conducted the ritual.

In *The Haunter of the Dark*, the writer Robert Harrison Blake solves a cryptogram written in the Aklo language. "The text was, he found, in the dark Aklo language used by certain cults of evil antiquity, and known to him in a halting way through previous researches." Mention is also made of the "Aklo writings" in *The Diary of Alonzo Typer*, where the writings hint at a malevolent intelligence beyond time and beyond the universe that is allied to power outside the Earth.

(*The Dunwich Horror; The Haunter of the Dark; The Diary of Alonzo Typer*)

Candlemass *

Lovecraft wrote that the citizens of Dunwich celebrated the festival of Candlemass on February 2 under another name. That name must have been Imbolc. It is one of the pagan cross-quarter days of the year, falling directly between the winter solstice and the spring equinox.

(*The Dunwich Horror*)

Dho formula

A magic chant taught to Wilbur Whateley by his grandfather, Wizard Whateley, when the boy was three and a half years old. Using it, Wilbur was able to psychically glimpse an inner city said to be located at the two poles—which suggests that it is perhaps a city inside the Earth that is accessed from the poles. Wilbur wrote in his diary that he might be able to "break through" with the Dho-Hna formula.

(*The Dunwich Horror*)

Dhol chants

Magic incantations associated with the inhuman residents of the plateau of Leng.

(*The Horror in the Museum*)

"Dies Mies Jeschet" *

Charles Dexter Ward uses the incantation "Dies Mies Jeschet Boene Doesef Douvema Enitemaus" as the culmination of a ritual to raise the dead. Lovecraft probably derived this from an extract from the writings of the French occultist Eliphas Lévi that was quoted in A. E. Waite's 1886 work *The Mysteries of Magic*. It appeared in the second part of Eliphas Lévi's 1855–6 work *Dogma et Rituel de la Haute Magie* (bk. 2, ch. 15), which was first published in English in 1896 as *Transcendental Magic* (see Lévi, p. 320), but it seems likely that Lovecraft got it from Waite's compendium, not from Waite's source.

Lévi reproduced this incantation, calling it the "Grand Appellation of Agrippa." By this he meant that it was taken from the Latin edition of the *Opera omnia* (*Complete Works*) of the German magician Henry Cornelius Agrippa. However, it is not part of Agrippa's writings, but instead appears in a brief epitome of various forms of divination by Georgius Pictorius Villinganus that is appended to the first volume of the Latin *Opera* of Agrippa.

The incantation is used when performing a divination to identify a guilty person by means of a turning sieve. This was a popular form of divination during the Renaissance. A round metal sieve for sifting flour was held by the pinchers of a large pair of tongs, or the blades of a large pair of shears, so that the widely spread tongs or shears gripped the round, smooth barrel of the sieve on its outer sides. Two people supported the handles of the tongs or shears, each with a single fingertip. This was a delicate arrangement, and the slightest tremor of the hands naturally caused the sieve to slid down as the tension of the tongs or blades of the shears slackened momentarily.

The mysterious incantation "Dies, Mies, Jeschet, Benedoefet, Dowima, Enitemaus" was uttered to invoke the spirit of the sieve, and then a series of suspects were named. When the name of the guilty party was spoken, it was believed that the sieve would rotate slightly as it slid partway down on its tenuous supports. Pictorius commented on the words of the incantation that they were "understood neither by those who speak them nor by others." Eliphas Lévi, as translated by A. E. Waite in *Transcendental Magic*, echoed this statement when he wrote of the words, "We make no pretence of understanding their meaning; possibly they possess none, assuredly none which is reasonable, since they avail in evoking the devil, who is the sovereign unreason."

Lovecraft, reading Waite's comments in *The Mysteries of Magic*, and not having any notion that the incantation was used in sieve divination by common country folk, assumed that the incantation had a greater significance. He divided the word "Boenedoesef" into two words, "Boene" and "Doesef," thereby extending the incantation to seven words. The reason for this division is not hard to find—in the Latin *Opera* of Agrippa (vol. 1, p. 597), the word is broken over two lines of text, and for this reason is hyphenated as "BENE-DOEFET." If the hyphen were overlooked, or if it were pale or missing entirely from the copy, it would be inevitable that the single word be mistaken for two words. This must have been the case in Lovecraft's source text.

(*The Case of Charles Dexter Ward*)

Emanation of Yoth

Spell in the *Book of Ebon*, which Daniel Morris contemplated using against Arthur Wheeler.

(*The Man of Stone*)

esbat *

A minor convocation of witches, or in Lovecraft's fiction, of devil worshippers.

(*The Diary of Alonzo Typer*)

Evoë *

The intoxicated followers of the Greek god Dionysos invoked the god by repeatedly shouting the phrase "Io! Evoë!"

(*The Electric Executioner*)

Feast of the Foxes

An occult ritual conducted on top of Thunder Hill in the state of New York by Daniel Morris, the descendant of the notorious wizard Nicholas Van Kauran.

(*The Man of Stone*)

Gorgo *

A cult of Kurdish devil worshippers of the Yazidi clan, who were apprehended by federal authorities at Red Hook, in the state of New York, used this barbarous name in their chant of evocation to the demoness Lilith: "O friend and companion of night, thou who rejoicest in the baying of dogs and spilt blood, who wanderest in the midst of shades among the tombs, who longest for blood and bringest terror to mortals, Gorgo, Mormo, thousand-faced moon, look favourably on our sacrifices!"

Lovecraft derived this text directly from the invocation to Hecate, under her alternative title "Bombo" (more properly "Baubo"), recorded by St. Hippolytus of Rome (*c.* 170—*c.* 236) in the fourth book of his *Philosophumena* (bk. 4, ch. 35): "Come infernal, terrestrial, and heavenly Bombo, goddess of the broad roadways, of the crossroad, thou who goest to and fro at night, torch in hand, enemy of the day. Friend and lover of darkness, thou who doest rejoice when the bitches are howling and warm blood is spilled, thou who art walking amid the phantoms and in the place of the tombs, thou whose thirst is blood, thou who doest strike chill and fear in mortal hearts, Gorgo, Mormo, moon of a thousand forms, cast a propitious eye on our sacrifice."

(*The Horror at Red Hook*)

Great Rite

A ritual that Daniel Morris, a descendant of the infamous wizard Nicholas Van Kauran, asserted was to be conducted atop Thunder Hill in the state of New York to "open the gate."

(*The Man of Stone*)

Green Decay

A curse that occurs in the *Book of Eibon*. Daniel Morris, a descendant of the infamous wizard Nicholas Van Kauran, found it in the book, which had belonged to his uncle Hendrik Van Kauran, having been passed down from Nicholas to his grandson William Van Kauran, who carried the book across the Atlantic to the United States. The curse is said to have unpleasant consequences with regard to the appearance and odor of the person on whom it is cast. Morris contemplated using it on the sculptor, Arthur Wheeler, because he believed the sculptor was having an affair with his wife.

(*The Man of Stone*)

Halloween *

Also known as Hallowmass, Hallow Eve, and Samhain, a pagan festival. It was on Halloween that Lavinia Whateley and her infant son, Wilbur, who was sired by one of the Old Ones, conducted a bonfire ritual while naked on the top of Sentinel Hill, near

Dunwich. In *The Thing on the Doorstep*, a witches' sabbat is held on Halloween in the pit of the shoggoths, the entrance to which is in cyclopean ruins in the woods north of Chesuncook, Maine.

(*The Dunwich Horror*; *The Diary of Alonzo Typer*; *The Thing on the Doorstep*)

"Hel, Heloym, Sother" *

In Lovecraft's story *The Horror at Red Hook*, a demonic incantation is read upon a wall by a police inspector:

> HEL · HELOYM · SOTHER · EMMANVEL · SABAOTH · AGLA · TETRAGRAMMATON · AGYROS · OTHEOS · ISCHYROS · ATHANATOS · IEHOVA · VA · ADONAI · SADAY · HOMOVSION · MESSIAS · ESCHEREHEYE.

Lovecraft characterized this incantation in the story as "Hebraised Hellenistic Greek" and wrote that it suggested "the most terrible daemon-evocations of the Alexandrian decadence." By this he meant the period during which the Greeks ruled Egypt from the Egyptian city of Alexandria—a period during which the magic of Greece was melded with the magic of ancient Egypt. In a letter written in October of 1925 to Clark Ashton Smith, Lovecraft admitted "I bedeck my tale with incantations copied from the 'Magic' article in the 9th edition of the *Britannica*, but I'd like to draw on less obvious sources if I knew of the right reservoirs to tap." He made an attempt at translating the words: "O Lord God Deliverer; Lord-Messenger of Hosts: Thou-art-a-mighty god-forever; Magically fourfold assemblage; And anointed one, together and in succession!" The actual text in the *Britannica* article reads as follows:

> The magician relies on the power of divine Hebrew names, such as the *shem hammephorash* or the name Jehovah in its true pronunciation, with which Solomon and other wonder-workers of old did marvellous things. He draws powerful spells from the Kabbalah of the later Jews, with its transposed letters and artificial words, —using for instance the name *Agla,* formed from the initials of the Hebrew sentence —"Thou art a mighty God for ever." But in compelling the spirits he can use Hebrew and Greek in admired confusion, as in the following formula (copied with its mistakes as an illustration of magical scholarship in its lowest stage)—"Hel Heloym Sother Emmanuel Sabaoth Agla Tetragrammaton Agyros Otheos Ischyros Athanatos Jehova Va Adonai Saday Homousion Messias Eschereheye!"

Daniel Harms points out in *The Necronomicon Files* (p. 95) that Lovecraft lifted the incantation from the *Encyclopaedia Britannica* without ever really understanding its use, which was the finding of treasure. More specifically, it is said by William Howett in volume two of his 1863 *History of the Supernatural* (pp. 31–2) to be part of a Catholic Church exorcism ritual to release from the clutches of demons a spirit that is bound to the earth to haunt the locality of its hidden treasure. This may have been its stated use, but it could be used for many other purposes, since it is really no more than a string of bastardized Hebrew divine names mixed with Greek words of power. These names and words are to be found frequently scattered throughout the grimoires.

For example, in the grimoire known as the *Fourth Book of Occult Philosophy*, the Hebrew divine names El, Elohim, Zebaoth, Adonay, Jah, and Saday occur in a list of what are termed "the ten general names." The *Magical Elements* of Peter de Abano has grouped together as a portion of one conjuration "Hagios, O Theos, Ischyros, Athanatos." In the Second Conjuration of the *Goetia*, we find the Greek words of power "O Theos, Ischyros, and Athanatos," as well as the Hebrew name "Emmanuel," and the Greek form of the Hebrew name of God, Tetragrammaton, which was extremely popular in incantations in the grimoires.

In texts of magic, the spelling of words and names often varied greatly, or became corrupted by copying errors. The corrected spelling of the incantation used by Lovecraft would be as follows:

> El · Elohim · Soter · Emmanuel · Tzabaoth · AGLA · Tetragrammaton · Agyros · O Theos · Ischyros · Athanatos · Jehovah · Yah · Adonai · Shaddai · Homousion · Messias · Asher Eheieh.

El is a Hebrew name meaning "The Mighty One" that is used as a divine termination in the names of angels, such as Raphael and Michael. In magic, its addition to a name was considered to empower that name with divine force. In this context it means "of God" or "with God." *Elohim* means "Lord." *Soter* is Greek for "Savior." *Emmanuel* means "God is with us" and was equated with God. *Tzabaoth* (often spelled *Sabaoth*) signifies "Hosts," meaning the angelic hosts of heaven. *AGLA* is an acronym for the Hebrew phrase meaning "Thou Art Mighty Forever, O Lord." *Tetragrammaton* is the Greek substitute for *Yahweh* (*YHWH*) and simply means "Name of Four Letters." *Agyros* may perhaps mean "Shining" or "Enlightened." The Greek *O Theos* means "the One God"—the definite article *O* signifies "One." The Greek *Ischyros* means "Strong." The Greek *Athanatos* means "Eternal." *Jehovah* is another form of *Yahweh* that was used by Christian Europeans. *Yah* is the first half of *Yahweh* (*YH*). *Adonai* means "Lord." *Shaddai* is an ancient name for God that means "Almighty." The Greek *Homousion* means "One Substance." *Messias* is an older form of the Greek *Messiah*, from the Hebrew *Mashiach*, and means "Anointed One." *Asher Eheieh* is a partial form of *Eheieh Asher Eheieh*, which means "I Am That Which I Am."

Since these are simply names and words of power that are called upon, they have no connected meaning that can be translated as a coherent text, so Lovecraft's attempt was doomed to failure. On the other hand, since they are general names and power words, they may well be used for various purposes of practical magic, the exorcism of a soul that haunts a hidden treasure being only one possible use.

(*The Horror at Red Hook*)

Kamog

The secret coven name of the black magician of Innsmouth, Ephraim Waite. It was used in the pit of the shoggoths, down the six thousand steps, below the cyclopean ruins with their standing stones in the northern Maine woods where the coven was accustomed to meet and work their evil magic.

Secret names are used by modern witches and magicians to differentiate their everyday personalities from their magical personalities. They are often given by a teacher to a student, but may also be chosen by the witch. In a symbolic sense, the giving of a new name is a rebirth into a new identity. When priests and nuns take up their avocation, they take on new names to mark the beginning of their lives in Christ. Ritual magicians take a magical name or motto that is used within the brotherhood or occult lodge to which they belong.

The transcripts of the European witch trials indicate that sometimes, though not always, witches adopted or were given a coven name to be used at the sabbat gatherings. The Devil in the form of the Black Man might baptize the witch in blood at the sabbat and give her a new name, but at other times the members of the coven selected their witch names amongst themselves. Margaret A. Murray wrote that this practice was confined to Scotland (Murray, p. 85), but Montague Summers stated, "The giving of a new name seems to have been very general" (Summers, p. 85).

(*The Thing on the Doorstep*)

long chant

An invocation that opens the dimensional gate of Yog-Sothoth to admit the Old Ones to our earthly reality, or at least permits them to extend their power into our world. It is found on page 751 of the complete English edition of the *Necronomicon*. Old Whateley the wizard on his death bed instructed his unnatural grandson, Wilbur, to make use of it, but since Wilbur's copy of the English edition was incomplete, he was forced to go to Miskatonic University at Arkham in an attempt to consult the Latin edition in the library in an effort to learn the content of the missing text.

(*The Dunwich Horror*)

long ritual

A ritual recorded on the eighth of the Pnakotic Fragments, used to restore life to Rhan-Tegoth, a mummified amphibious creature from "lead-gray Yuggoth, where the cities are under the warm deep sea" who was worshipped on our planet in the dim past as a god.

(*The Horror in the Museum*)

May-Eve *

Another name for this festival is Walpurgis Night, April 30, when it is reputed that witches gather on high places for their greatest sabbat of the year. Tremors were felt in the ground on this date in 1915 by the people of Dunwich and Aylesbury. It seems probably that Wilbur Whateley and his invisible brother were engendered on May-Eve, 1912, since Wilbur was born nine months later, February 2, 1913.

(*The Dunwich Horror; The Diary of Alonzo Typer*)

Naacal formula

In *Out of the Aeons*, a protective occult formula was composed in the hieratic Naacal language by T'yog, high priest of Shub-Niggurath and guardian of the Copper Temple in K'naa, at the inspired direction of the Mother Goddess he served. It was designed to protect him from the petrifying effects of looking upon the god Ghatanothoa in his crypt atop Mount Yaddith-Gho. T'yog intended to use it to banish Ghatanothoa from the kingdom of K'naa in the land of Mu. The formula was written on a scroll of pthagon membrane, which according to the *Nameless Cults* of von Junzt is the inner skin of the extinct yakith-lizard, and was rolled inside an engraved cylinder of the *lagh* metal that had been carried across space by the Elder Ones from Yuggoth. *Lagh* metal cannot be mined on our planet. Von Junzt asserted that the creation of this magic charm took place in 173,148 BC.

The Naacal language is mentioned in *Through the Gates of the Silver Key* in connection with Harley Warren, friend of Randolph Carter who vanished beneath the earth into an open crypt, never to emerge. It is called the "primal Naacal language of the

Himalayan priests." It was the study of works in this language that led Warren to enter the crypt.

It should be noted that although the Naacal formula was invented by Lovecraft, the Naacal language is spoken about in the books of James Churchward (1852–1936). According to Churchward, writing in his 1926 book *The Lost Continent of Mu*, an Indian priest taught him to read the lost Naacal language from several ancient tablets in the priest's possession.

(*Out of the Aeons; Through the Gates of the Silver Key*)

Nahab

The secret coven name of the Salem Village witch, Keziah Mason, spoken at sabbat gatherings.

(*The Dreams in the Witch House*)

parchment of the silver key

A parchment bearing a spell that was enclosed with the silver key left as a legacy to Randolph Carter. The spell was written in the R'lyehian tongue, the hieroglyphic language carried to the Earth by the spawn of Cthulhu, which settled on the Pacific island of R'lyeh. It was only a translation of a more ancient Hyperborean language of Tsath-yo, which was millions of years older than the R'lyehian translation. The spell was sought by Carter to enable him to travel back to the Earth with his own body, from which his mind had been displaced.

(*Through the Gates of the Silver Key*)

"Per Adonai Eloim" *

The following necromantic invocation was spoken by Charles Dexter Ward for the purpose of raising his long dead ancestor back to life.

> Per Adonai Eloim, Adonai Jehova,
> Adonai Sabaoth, Metraton On Agla Methon,
> verbum pythonicum, mysterium salamandrae,
> cenventus sylvorum, antra gnomorum,
> daemonia Coeli God, Almonsin, Gibor,
> Jehosua, Evam, Zariathnatmik, Veni, veni, veni.

This was probably copied by Lovecraft from Arthur Edward Waite's compendium of Lévi's occult writings, *The Mysteries of Magic: A Digest of the Writings of Eliphas Lévi*, where it appears in Latin on p. 162. It derives from the second volume of Lévi's *Dogme et Rituel de la Haute Magie* (the second volume was first published in French in 1856). Waite eventually got around to translating this whole work by Lévi into English under the title *Transcendental Magic* (1896). He rendered Lévi's original Latin of the invocation into English (Lévi, p. 320):

> By Adonaï Eloïm, Adonaï Jehova, Adonaï Sabaoth, Metraton On Agla Adonaï Mathon, the Pythonic word, the Mystery of the Salamander, the Assembly of Sylphs, the Grotto of Gnomes, the demons of the heaven of Gad, Almousin, Gibor, Jehosua, Evam, Zariatbatmik: Come, Come, Come!

Lovecraft made several mistakes, such as omitting the fourth "Adonai," writing "God" in place of "Gad," and misspelling "Almousin" as "Almonsin" and "Zariatbatmik" as "Zariathnatmik." But then, in his novel *The Case of Charles Dexter Ward* he did indicate that the invocation used by Ward is only a "very close analogue" of that given by Lévi, so perhaps these minor differences were deliberate.

(*The Case of Charles Dexter Ward*)

sabbat *

A major convocation of witches, or in Lovecraft's fiction, of devil worshippers. The most important sabbats named by Lovecraft are Halloween (October 31) and Walpurgis Night (April 30).

In *The Dreams in the Witch House*, the old witch Keziah Mason takes the university student to a sabbat presides over by Nyarlathotep, who wears the form of the fabled Black Man of the sabbat. In *Medusa's Coil*, the portrait of Marceline de Russy, who is the reincarnation of some ancient evil, shows in the background a witches' sabbat.

(*The Diary of Alonzo Typer*; *The Dreams in the Witch House*; *Medusa's Coil*)

Seven Lost Signs of Terror

Symbols discovered by the occultist Alonzo Typer by studying the two handwritten diaries of Claes van der Heyl, which he found in the old van der Heyl farmhouse, in the New England village of Chorazin. They are used to coerce into obedience any dweller in the cosmos "or in the unknown darkened spaces." Their use appears to be similar to that of the curses used by goetic magicians to compel the obedience of demons.

(*The Diary of Alonzo Typer*)

Three Words

Joseph Curwen demanded of a fourteenth-century Frenchman that he had raised from his essential salts whether the order for a massacre executed by Edward, the Black Prince, at the town of Limoges in 1370 "was given because of the Sign of the Goat found on the altar in the ancient Roman crypt beneath the Cathedral, or whether the Dark Man of the Haute Vienne had spoken the Three Words." The sign of the goat was probably the inverted pentagram, the points of which mark the two ears, two horns, and beard of a goat's head. The Dark Man, otherwise known as the Black Man, was a mysterious figure in European witchcraft who presided over the great gatherings of witches known as sabbats. Lovecraft identified him with Nyarlathotep. The Three Words must be the words of some incantation, but Lovecraft left no hint as to which three words he intended.

(*The Case of Charles Dexter Ward*)

Voorish sign

The term "voor" was borrowed by Lovecraft from the story *The White People* by Arthur Machen. In Machen's story, "voor" is a word in an occult language, and seems to means a twilight or gloaming—something that obscures. The story concerns the diary of a young girl. In this diary, the girl writes of "the kingdom of Voor, where the light goes when it is put out, and the water goes when the sun takes it away." She uses the term in a more general sense when she writes of a winter countryside, "it all looked black, and everything had a voor over it." She describes the winter sky as "like a wicked voorish dome." Elsewhere, she writes, "I saw the terrible voor again on everything."

Lovecraft adopted the term to refer specifically to the Voorish sign, a magic hand gesture used by Wilbur Whateley to see his hybrid brother, who is invisible to ordinary human sight. Wilbur wrote in his diary, "I can see it a little when I make the Voorish sign or blow the powder of Ibn Ghazi at it."

(*The Dunwich Horror*)

Words of Fear

Described as "hideous and unutterable," they were discovered in 1935 by Alonzo Typer in the diaries of Claes van der Heyl, at the old van der Heyl farmhouse, in the village of Chorazin, New York. They are to be used in conjunction with the Seven Lost Signs of Terror to compel the creatures of the "unknown darkened spaces" to obedience.

(*The Diary of Alonzo Typer*)

Yellow Sign *

It is linked with Hastur, and with a cult of men in league with "monstrous powers from other dimensions" who are dedicated to tracking down and doing injury to the Mi-Go. Precisely what the Yellow Sign may be Lovecraft does not reveal.

The Yellow Sign was created by the writer Robert W. Chambers for his series of short stories collected under the anthology title *The King In Yellow*. In Chambers' short story *The Yellow Sign*, the lover of the narrator finds an onyx clasp that is inlaid with the Yellow Sign—a kind of seal or sigil that the narrator of the story characterizes as "a curious symbol or letter in gold. It was neither Arabic nor Chinese, nor as I found afterwards did it belong to any human script" (Chambers, p. 98). The Yellow Sign is described in the second part of the infamous two-act play, *The King In Yellow*, the reading of which drives men insane. After reading the second act of the play, the narrator and his lover discuss the onyx clasp "inlaid with what we now knew to be the Yellow Sign" (Chambers, p. 101).

(*The Whisperer in Darkness*)

The Key to the Thirteenth Gate

13th Astral Gate: Ophiuchus—The Serpent-Bearer

Sun passes through Ophiuchus: November 29—December 18

Constellation is represented by a man holding in his hands a great serpent, the body of which is sometimes shown wrapped around his waist or between his legs.

Right Pillar: Ras Alhague (Arabic: *Ras al Hawwa*—Head of the Serpent-charmer). Astronomical designation: Alpha Ophiuchi. Astrological nature: Saturn-Venus. Influence: mental discipline, healing through knowledge. Magnitude: 2.1. Color: sapphire-blue. Sun crosses: December 16. Location: forehead of the Serpent-charmer. Comments: The wisdom of the serpent is potent when harnessed, but dangerous—medicines easily become poisons.

Left Pillar: Sinistra (Latin: Left). Astronomical designation: Nu Ophiuchi. Astrological nature: Saturn-Venus. Influence: sinister actions, malice, depravity. Magnitude: 3.3. Color: white. Sun crosses: December 21. Location: left hand of the Serpent-charmer. Comments: The left hand is the hand of darkness.

The astral gate of Ophiuchus lies between the star of its right pillar, located on the forehead of the Serpent-bearer, and the star of its left pillar, on the left hand of the figure. The Sun enters the gate by crossing the longitude of Ras Alhague, the star of the right pillar, around December 16. The solar transition of this gate narrow takes five days. The Sun exits the gate around December 21, the winter solstice, when it crosses the longitude of the star of the left pillar, Sinistra.

The key to the Thirteenth Gate opens the constellation Ophiuchus, allowing entry into that part of the walled city of the *Necronomicon* that concerns the practical techniques of ceremonial magic described by Lovecraft. Use it for divining information or receiving dreams about these methods of ritual working.

Seal of the Thirteenth Key on the Thirteenth Gate

Ritual of Opening Ophiuchus

Face the direction of the compass ruled by the Thirteenth Gate, which is due north. This is the only gate in the northern wall of the city. Visualize it closed before you so that it is of a dimension that you may easily walk through it without awkwardness.

With the visualized image of the gate clear in your mind and projected upon the astral plane in the direction due north, speak this invocation to Yog-Sothoth, which has the same general form for all the gates:

> Guardian of the Gate! Defender of the Door! Watcher of the Way!
> Who art the stout Lock, the slender Key, and the turning Hinge! Lord of

> All Transition, without whom there is no coming in or going out, I call thee! Keeper of the Threshold, whose dwelling place is between worlds, I summon thee! Yog-Sothoth, wise and mighty lord of the Old Ones, I invoke thee!
>
> By the authority of the dreaded name, Azathoth, that few dare speak, I charge thee, open to me the gateway of Ophiuchus, the Serpent-bearer, that lies between the blazing pillar Ras Alhague on the right hand and the blazing pillar Sinistra on the left hand. As the solar chariot [or, lunar chariot] crosses between these pillars, I enter the city of the *Necronomicon* through its Thirteenth Gate. Selah!

Visualize the key of the Thirteenth Gate in your right hand some six inches long and made of cast electrum—an untarnishing, silvery alloy of the seven planetary metals. Feel its weight, texture, and shape as you hold it. Extend your right arm and use the key to draw upon the surface of the gate the seal of the key, which should be visualized to burn on the gate in a line of white spiritual fire. Point with the astral key at the center of the gate and speak the words:

> In the name of Azathoth, Ruler of Chaos, by the power of Yog-Sothoth, Lord of Portals, the Thirteenth Gate is opened!

Visualize the gate unlocking and opening inward of its own accord upon a shadowed space. On the astral level, walk through the gateway and stand in the darkness beyond. Open your mind to receive impressions of whatever magical method or procedure caused you to work the ritual, and pay attention to any intuitions or mental images that arise. More information may come to you later in oracular dreams. In a more general sense, this ritual and this gate may be used to investigate any technical procedure of practical magic, such as the composition of rituals, the making of charms, the wording of invocations, and so on.

After fulfilling the purpose for which this gate was opened, conclude the ritual by astrally passing out through the gate and visualizing it to close. Draw the seal of the Thirteenth Key on the surface of the gate with the astral key you hold in your hand, and mentally cause it to lock itself shut, as it was at the beginning of the ritual. Speak the words of closing:

> By the power of Yog-Sothoth, and authority of the supreme name Azathoth, I close and seal the Thirteenth Gate. This ritual is well and truly ended.

Allow the image of the gate to grow pale in your imagination and fade to nothingness before you turn away from the ritual direction.

Mythos Works by Lovecraft

Listed here are works by Lovecraft containing elements that may be considered in the broadest terms part of the Necronomicon mythos. It may be argued that some of the stories are not part of the mythos, lacking as they do any obvious ties to the *Necronomicon* or the Old Ones, or other central mythos devices. However, in my opinion they are linked to the mythos, even if tenuously, by such things as theme and atmosphere. This is not a complete list of Lovecraft's writings, but concerns only stories dealing with the weird, with cosmic horror, and with things strange and unnatural. Lovecraft also wrote poems, most of them while he was quite young. Only the poems that pertain to the mythos are included in this list.

The indicated year of writing is the year in which a work was completed; the year of publication is the year in which it first saw print. The composition of a few works straddles two or more years, such as *The Dream-Quest of Unknown Kadath*, begun in October of 1926 but completed in January of 1927. The individual poems of *Fungi from Yuggoth* were written between December of 1929 and January of 1930, and groups of the poems were published in various years—I have supplied the year of publication for the sonnet cycle as a whole.

Some of the stories are collaborations with other writers, but in most of these cases, the major portion of the text was produced by Lovecraft, and almost always the mythos elements have been inserted by Lovecraft. The collaborations are an important part of the Necronomicon mythos and cannot be overlooked. It may be useful here to go through these stories indicating how much of each should be credited to Lovecraft.

The Green Meadow and *The Crawling Chaos* were both based on the dreams of Winifred V. Jackson (penname: Elizabeth Berkeley), which she described to Lovecraft, who then wrote them up in final story form. The dream that gave rise to *The Green Meadow* was very similar to a dream that Lovecraft himself had experienced. Lovecraft wrote all of the introduction to the *Green Meadow*, which was not part of Jackson's dream. Of *The Green Meadow*, Lovecraft wrote in a letter, "it is practically my own work all throughout." These two stories are the only collaborations to which Lovecraft affixed his name (the pseudonym Lewis Theobald Jun.) as co-author.

The Horror At Martin's Beach, written with his future wife Sonia Greene, was predominantly Lovecraft's work.

The stories *Ashes, The Ghost-Eater, The Loved Dead,* and *Deaf, Dumb, and Blind* were revisions by Lovecraft of first drafts written by C. M. Eddy. Lovecraft's influence shows most strongly in *The Ghost-Eater,* although *The Loved Dead* is a remarkable work that expresses Lovecraft's characteristic alienation from the norms of humanity.

Imprisoned with the Pharaohs (later given in various anthologies its original title, *Under the Pyramids*) is almost entirely Lovecraft's story, both in conception and execution, even though it was published with only Harry Houdini's name on it. The owner of *Weird Tales,* J. C. Henneberger, asked Lovecraft early in 1924 to make a story out of Houdini's ridiculous claim that while visiting Egypt he had been tied up by thieves and cast into a tomb as a test of his abilities, and had used his talents to escape. Lovecraft never believed the story, but used it as the jumping-off place for his own curious tale.

Lovecraft based *Two Black Bottles* on a detailed synopsis by Wilfred Blanch Talman, but he added dialogue and changed the story around, putting his own stamp on it.

The stories co-authored with Zealia Bishop, *The Curse of Yig, The Mound,* and *Medusa's Coil,* are among Lovecraft's best and are almost wholly Lovecraft's work, although there is more of Bishop in *Medusa's Coil,* the weakest of the three stories. In the case of *The Mound,* Bishop expressed to Lovecraft her story idea in only two brief sentences—Lovecraft wrote the whole thing.

The Last Test and *The Electric Executioner* were extensive revisions that Lovecraft made to existing stories that had already been published by Adolphe de Castro. Both revisions were published in *Weird Tales.*

The Trap, written with Henry S. Whitehead, is believed to be three-quarters Lovecraft's work.

Hazel Heald is another collaborator who did little more than supply Lovecraft with plot concepts, which he transformed into complete stories. *The Man of Stone* was based on an outline by Heald. Lovecraft claimed that he had written almost all of *The Horror in the Museum* because Heald's synopsis was so poor, he could not use it. The same was the case with *Winged Death, Out of the Aeons,* and *The Horror in the Burying-Ground*—Heald supplied no more than a vague idea or two. Of these stories with Heald, *The Horror in the Museum* and *Out of the Aeons* are pure Lovecraft in concept as well as execution.

Through the Gates of the Silver Key is an important mythos story. Lovecraft's collaborator, E. Hoffmann Price, was a fan of Lovecraft's work who pressed Lovecraft to produce a sequel to his story *The Silver Key* and offered his version. Lovecraft extensively revised it. Price later claimed that Lovecraft had only left about fifty words of his original draft unchanged, but he retained Price's basic story concept.

The Tree on the Hill and *The Disinterment*, written with Dwane W. Rimel, are closer to what would be considered genuine collaborations. Of the two, Lovecraft's contribution is more obvious in *The Tree on the Hill*, particularly in the latter half of the work.

R. H. Barlow was a writer with some real talent of his own. Lovecraft thought well enough of him to name Barlow his literary executor, entrusting Barlow with his papers after his death. *The Night Ocean*, the most mythos-themed of the several collaborations he wrote with Barlow, was a story Lovecraft admired. It is mostly Barlow's work, although Lovecraft revised it and added his touches here and there.

The Diary of Alonzo Typer is an extensive revision by Lovecraft of an original draft by William Lumley, which Lovecraft did without compensation, purely as a favor to Lumley.

Lovecraft almost doubled the length of *In the Walls of Eryx* when he revised the draft of Kenneth Sterling.

The Challenge From Beyond is a special case. It was not one of Lovecraft's usual ghost-writing jobs, but was written in company with four other talented contributors to *Weird Tales*, as a kind of stunt for *Fantasy Magazine*. The story was going nowhere until Lovecraft took it up. He gave it direction, and contributed around half of the text.

It is easy to become overwhelmed by the sheer number of mythos works, and to forget which contains what, even when we restrict the list to works by Lovecraft alone, omitting those by other contemporary and later writers. To increase the practical value of this list of Lovecraft's mythos writings, a brief summary of the contents of each work has been added after its dates as an aid to memory.

The Alchemist—written 1908; published 1916.

In revenge for the unjust slaying of his beloved father by a French count, an alchemist possessed of the secret of life haunts the fortress of the family for six centuries, killing in turn each male descendant of the count when the descendant reaches his thirty-second year.

Ashes (with Clifford Martin Eddy Jr.)—written 1923; published 1924.

The research chemist Professor Arthur Van Allister develops a liquid capable of reducing any material other than glass to a pile of soft white ash. With a view to selling it to the military as a weapon, he tries it on a rabbit, and then decides that he needs a human subject.

"*Astrophobos*"—written 1917; published 1918.

In this poem, which Lovecraft published under his pseudonym Ward Phillips, Lovecraft contemplates the beauty of a star in the northern heavens near the constellation Ursa

Major. He begins to see pastoral visions, but gradually the visions become corrupted and a sense of dread grows within him concerning the distant lands of the "star of madness."

At the Mountains of Madness—written 1931; published 1936.

Miskatonic University sponsors an expedition to Antarctica that discovers the ice-covered city of the Elder Things, along with a number of frozen but perfectly preserved bodies of the city's alien inhabitants.

"Azathoth"—written 1922; published 1938.

A prose poem in which an unnamed dreamer in a drab, gray city is lifted out of his body by an emanation from the stars, and deposited on a green shore fragrant with flowers.

The Beast in the Cave—written 1904–5; published 1918.

In this early story, which Lovecraft revised for publication in 1918, a man lost in Mammoth Cave encounters a beast that has been stalking him in the darkness and succeeds in wounding it with a thrown piece of rock.

Beyond the Wall of Sleep—written 1919; published 1919.

When a hill man of the Catskill Mountains region commits violent murder and is placed in an insane asylum, one of the interns of the institution investigates and discovers that he is leading a double existence—the ignorant laborer Joe Slater by day while awake, and by night in his dreams an inhuman being of blazing light who restlessly seeks to avenge some wrong done against him by an equally alien enemy.

The Book (unfinished)—written 1933; published 1938.

In this dreamlike story fragment, a man finds a worm-eaten manuscript book in Latin in a decaying bookstore by the river, and takes it home to recite an occult formula near its end that opens the first gateway beyond the three-dimensional world of ordinary consciousness, so that he thereafter sees not only the present reality of things, but simultaneously their past and future.

The Call of Cthulhu—written 1926; published 1928.

A geological upheaval in the South Pacific Ocean causes R'lyeh to rise to the surface. From within his stone tomb Cthulhu sends forth mental projections, calling those of his cult to the island to open the door and release him.

The Case of Charles Dexter Ward—written 1927; published 1941.

Obsessed with the past, a young man uses necromancy to resurrect a dead relative with whom he bears a striking resemblance. The resurrected ancestor murders him and impersonates him, so that he can resume his interrupted experiments in necromancy.

"The Cats"—written 1925; published 1936.

A poem that describes a modern city, as viewed through the eyes of its night-roaming alley cats, who come in a great legion to wipe out the exotic rabble of immigrants praying to their strange gods. In the end, when all is dead, only the cats remain. Lovecraft wrote this poem while living in New York. It mentions "bleak Arkham bridges."

The Cats of Ulthar—written 1920; published 1920.

An elderly couple in the city of Ulthar in the dreamlands hate cats. They kill the kitten of a young boy in a caravan passing through the city. All the cats of the city vanish for a night, and when they return the next day, the bones of the couple are discovered in their cottage, picked clean of flesh. The authorities of Ulthar pass a law that, henceforth, no one in the city may kill a cat.

Celephaïs—written 1920; published 1922.

A Londoner rediscovers the dreams of his childhood, and wanders the land seeking the dream city of Celephaïs, in the valley of Ooth-Nargai. He finds it at the end of his mortal life, but continues to reign eternal in Celephaïs as Kuranes, king of Ooth-Nargai.

The Challenge from Beyond (with C. L. Moore; A. Merritt; Robert E. Howard; Frank Belknap Long)—written 1935; published 1935.

While camping in the Canadian woods, George Campbell comes upon a strange cube of rock crystal with an inscribed disk embedded within it, and when he gazes into it, his consciousness is transported into the body of a worm-like being on the distant, alien world called Yekub. He kills the lord of science and the priests, seizes the sphere that is the god of the worm-like race, and thereby becomes their king.

The Colour Out of Space—written 1927; published 1927.

A meteorite falls to earth on a farm outside Arkham, releasing an iridescent gas into the well. The crops and livestock watered from the well, and the family tending the farm, at first exhibit a kind of fevered growth, but this soon turns to corruption. The family goes mad and dies, and the abandoned farm becomes a shunned place as the poison in the well gradually spreads in an ever-widening circle throughout the countryside.

Cool Air—written 1926; published 1928.

An alchemist cheats death by preserving his body against decay through the modern marvel of air conditioning, while animating it by the force of his will.

The Crawling Chaos (with "Elizabeth Berkeley" [Winifred Virginia Jackson])—written 1920; published 1921.

An opium overdose provokes a vision of the angry waves of the sea eating away at a promontory of red land, the point of which is occupied by a house of marble.

The Curse of Yig (with Zealia Bishop)—written 1928; published 1929.

The curse befalls Walker Davis and his wife, Audrey, in the spring of 1889, while they are on their way from Arkansas to settle in Oklahoma. When Audrey kills a brood of newborn rattlesnakes on the trail, the Indian god of all serpents, Yig, is angered, and on Halloween night visits the couple in their cabin. Walker is killed, Audrey driven mad so that thereafter she hisses and writhes on her belly like a serpent, but the worst part of the curse is the thing Yig engenders inside Audrey's womb.

Dagon—written 1917; published 1919.

During the First World War, a passenger on a ship captured by the Germans manages to escape in a small boat, and makes his way in a life raft to a new island that has been heaved up from the floor of the Pacific. Exploring the island, he finds a white stone monolith covered with strange hieroglyphs and pictographs, then watches as a giant creature emerge from the ocean's depths to adore the stone.

Deaf, Dumb, and Blind (with Clifford Martin Eddy Jr.)—written 1924; published 1925.

Richard Blake of Boston, a veteran of the Great War who in 1918 suffered injuries that rendered him deaf, dumb, blind, and paralyzed, but who is nonetheless a celebrated poet, is found dead at his typewriter in the old Tanner house, which is reputed to be haunted. Before dying, he managed to type an account of his last thoughts and impressions.

The Descendant (unfinished)—written 1927; published 1938.

A young man takes a room at Gray's Inn, London. His neighbor is an elderly eccentric who covers his ears and howls whenever the church bells ring, but never speaks about his strange behavior, until he learns that the young man has bought a copy of the *Necronomicon* from a London bookseller. He then reveals himself to be Lord Northam, proprietor of Northam Keep on the coast of Yorkshire, and as a warning to the young man, begins to relate the story of his life—at which point the fragment ends.

The Diary of Alonzo Typer (with William Lumley)—written 1935; published 1938.

A journal found in the ruins of a large country house in the village of Chorazin, near Attica, New York, details the paranormal investigation carried out in the house by the occultist Alonzo Typer, prior to its sudden collapse and Typer's disappearance.

The Disinterment (with Duane W. Rimel)—written 1935; published 1937.

A man who has contracted leprosy in the Philippines simulates his own death with the help of his close friend, an unorthodox medical researcher, in the hope that his friend will be able to find a cure while he remains hidden from the knowledge of the outside world. To his horror, he discovers that while he has lain helpless, his friend has made him the subject of one of his unnatural experiments.

The Doom That Came to Sarnath—written 1919; published 1920.

The men of Sarnath destroy the alien city of Ib and steal the statue of its god, only to suffer a terrible doom at the hands of the ghosts of Ib.

The Dream-Quest of Unknown Kadath—written 1926–7; published 1948.

Randolph Carter embarks on a dream quest to find the mountain called Kadath in the Cold Waste, on top of which is the palace of the gods of Earth.

The Dreams in the Witch House—written 1932; published 1933.

Walter Gilman is a student of Miskatonic University studying mathematics and folklore who delves too deeply into the trans-dimensional mysteries of the Salem witch Keziah Mason, and finds himself compelled against his wishes to take part in the sabbat sacrifice of a child.

The Dunwich Horror—written 1928; published 1929.

The hybrid product of a union between a human woman and Yog-Sothoth seeks to use a ritual in the *Necronomicon* to open the gateway between worlds that will allow the entry of the Old Ones into our reality, so that they can fulfill their purpose—the cleansing of the Earth of all biological life, and its elevation to a higher sphere. He is aided by his monstrous invisible twin brother, whose form favors that of their alien father.

The Electric Executioner (with Adolphe de Castro)—written 1929; published 1930.

An American traveling by train through Mexico in 1889 encounters a madman intent on killing everyone on Earth before the return of the god Quetzalcoatl. His chosen method is an electrocution device of his own invention.

The Evil Clergyman—written 1933; published 1939.

This is another of Lovecraft's dreams, which he wrote down in a letter to a friend. An occult investigator spends the night in the attic room of a clergyman who had a reputation for black magic, only to suffer a visitation of the ghost of the clergyman that causes the investigator to undergo an uncanny transformation.

Ex Oblivione—written 1920; published 1921.

An opium dreamer seeks to find the latch to a small bronze gate in a stone wall in a golden valley of his dreams, hoping that the doorway will lead to an even more radiant dream country that he can dwell in forever.

Facts Concerning the Late Arthur Jermyn and His Family—written 1920; published 1921.

Arthur Jermyn is fascinated by the discoveries of his great-great-great grandfather, Sir Wade Jermyn, an African explorer who in the eighteenth century found the ruins of a lost stone city in the Congo that was rumored to have been inhabited by a race of hybrid white apes. Arthur continues to research his family history, and pursue his ancestor's African discoveries, until a final revelation relating to his family bloodline drives him to commit suicide.

"Festival"—written 1925; published 1926.

This poem, originally published in *Weird Tales* under the title "Yule Horror," describes a druidic Yuletide celebration involving ritual cannibalism beneath strangely animated trees.

The Festival—written 1923; published 1925.

A man returns to Kingsport on the winter solstice to honor the custom of his clan to meet once every hundred years in festival on that date. He is led by a throng of silent, robed figures into catacombs under the ancient church on Central Hill, beneath which is a great cavern.

From Beyond—written 1920; published 1934.

Crawford Tillinghast builds a machine designed to stimulate latent senses in human beings that will allow them to see the things that inhabit the world around them, but remain invisible and unfelt by the five ordinary physical senses. The machine has the unexpected side effect of rendering human beings perceptible to these extradimensional creatures.

Fungi from Yuggoth—written 1929–30; published as a set 1943.

This long poetical work, in thirty-six sonnets, is Lovecraft's most important mythos poetry. Each sonnet is a miniature narrative in itself. Some reference his prose writings, such as the sonnet "Nyarlathotep," which relates the dream vision that gave rise to the short story *Nyarlathotep*. "The Book" tells the same events as those in the story fragment *The Book*.

The Ghost-Eater (with Clifford Martin Eddy Jr.)—written 1923; published 1924.

A man traveling in Maine from the town of Mayfair to the town of Glendale get caught by a thunderstorm on a forest trail while passing through the Devil's Woods, and is forced to seek shelter in a lonely house. The tenant of the house offers him a room for the night, which the traveler gratefully accepts, but he discovers that he is not the only one who wants to sleep in the bed.

The Green Meadow (with "Elizabeth Berkeley" [Winifred Virginia Jackson])—written 1918–9; published 1927.

A diary written in Greek is found within a meteorite. It is written on paper that has no known counterpart on the Earth, and tells of a strange awakening in a land of green trees and blue water, and of a Green Meadow across the water to which the writer floats, a place where young men are infinitely old.

The Haunter of the Dark—written 1935; published 1936.

A writer of fiction vacationing at Providence is strangely drawn to a blackened stone church, which he learns was formerly the meeting place of a cult known as the Church of Starry Wisdom. Central to the beliefs of this cult is an artifact found in a ruined temple in Egypt that is known as the Shining Trapezohedron. This black jewel-like stone allows a being to be summoned from outside time and space, a being that shuns all light but is possessed of deep occult knowledge that it will communicate to its worshippers, in return for sacrifices.

He—written 1925; published 1926.

A poet wandering through Greenwich Village in New York in search of remnants of the old city is led by an elderly man in a black cloak down winding alleys and beneath low archways to an ancient house, where he is shown vistas of the past and future.

Herbert West—Reanimator—written 1921–2; published 1922.

Six tales related by a friend of the brilliant but deranged medical student Herbert West, describing his various experiments in bringing the dead back to life.

History of the Necronomicon—written 1927; published 1938.

This fanciful history of the *Necronomicon* and its author, Abdul Alhazred, was written by Lovecraft as a way of keeping the references he made to the book free from contradiction. It was passed around to his friends in manuscript form, and was only published after his death.

The Horror at Martin's Beach (with Sonia H. Greene)—written 1922; published 1923.

This story was co-written by Lovecraft and his future wife, Sonia Greene. The newborn offspring of some unknown deep-dwelling sea species, which in spite of its infancy is none the less over fifty feet in length, is captured, killed, and put on display at Martin's Beach for the amusement of tourists. The boat on which it is displayed mysteriously breaks from its moorings during a storm and is lost. Subsequently, the mother of the infant sea monster exacts a cunning and terrible revenge.

The Horror at Red Hook—written 1925; published 1927.

In tunnels beneath Red Hook, a working class district of New York City, the demon queen Lilith is worshipped with child sacrifices by the vestiges of a Turanian-Asiatic fertility cult.

The Horror in the Burying-Ground (with Hazel Heald)—written 1934; published 1937.

An undertaker who dabbles in alchemy concocts an embalming fluid that preserves life but simulates death, causing those who are injected with it while still living to grow stiff and appear lifeless, but to regain the use of their limbs after the passage of time.

The Horror in the Museum (with Hazel Heald)—written 1932; published 1933.

The occult enthusiast George Rogers brings to his wax museum in London the frozen corpse of a monstrous creature discovered in northern Alaska. He proceeds to nourish it back to life with freshly spilled blood, and worships it as a god.

The Hound—written 1922; published 1924.

Two decadent English dilatants who amuse themselves by robbing graves steal a jade amulet in the shape of a crouching hound from the tomb of a fifteenth-century Dutch necromancer. They are haunted by the ghost of the dead man, and stalked by the shadow of an enormous black hound.

Hypnos—written 1922; published 1923.

A mad sculptor who is also a dreamer embarks on a dream quest for knowledge and power with the aid of strong drugs, but what he finds in the realm of nightmares so terrifies him that for the remainder of his life he shuns sleep.

Imprisoned with the Pharaohs (with Harry Houdini)—written 1924; published 1924.

The escape artist Harry Houdini commissioned Lovecraft to ghostwrite this story of Houdini's adventure in the catacombs beneath the Pyramids, where Houdini encounters the enormous beast that was the model for the original Sphinx. It was originally titled *Under the Pyramids* by Lovecraft.

In the Walls of Eryx (with Kenneth Sterling)—written 1936; published 1939.

This science fiction story concerns a mysterious transparent maze built on Venus by a lost civilization that had once flourished on that planet. The degenerate remnants of that race take fiendish pleasure in watching the suffering of a human prospector who wanders into the maze, but finds it easier to enter than to leave.

In the Vault—written 1925; published 1925.

The undertaker George Birch inadvertently locks himself into the receiving tomb at Peck Valley Cemetery, where he has stored eight coffins over the winter awaiting burial in the spring when the frost has left the ground. Not all the dead are resting peacefully.

The Invisible Monster: see *The Horror at Martin's Beach*

The Last Test (with Adolphe de Castro)—written 1927; published 1928.

Doctor Alfred Clarendon, a research scientist who is made medical director of San Quentin Penitentiary, begins to infect the prisoners with an excruciating plague, so that he can test the effects of the disease and of the various treatments he devises.

The Loved Dead (with Clifford Martin Eddy Jr.)—written 1923; published 1924.

A man who discovers that being near the corpse at a funeral energizes him and gives him pleasure begins to commit murders, and takes a job in a funeral home in order to gain access to even more corpses.

The Lurking Fear—written 1922; published 1923.

The deserted Martense mansion on top of Tempest Mountain in the Catskills yields its grisly secret to a reporter who visits the mansion to investigate its history of uncanny events. He discovers that the Martense clan has not died out, as everyone assumes, but has multiplied and degenerated due to inbreeding, and lurks in the tunnels beneath the old house and the surrounding countryside.

The Man of Stone (with Hazel Heald)—written 1932; published 1932.

Mad Dan Morris, a descendant of the Van Kauran clan of wizards of the upper Adirondacks, seeks a fitting revenge on the stone sculptor Arthur Wheeler in the belief that Wheeler is having an affair with his wife. He finds a spell in the *Book of Eibon* that will turn a man to stone.

Medusa's Coil (with Zealia Bishop)—written 1930; published 1939.

The son of a southern plantation owner marries a strange woman in Paris and brings her home to the plantation, only to discover that her practice of ancient pagan rituals is based on more than an interest in the occult. She is the reincarnation of a dark goddess whose presence and power manifests itself through her long coil of midnight black hair, which seems to possess a life of its own.

Memory—written 1919; published 1919.

This brief prose poem describes the valley of Nis, in which lie the stone ruins of a nameless ancient city of human beings, long abandoned and overgrown by the jungle.

The Moon-Bog—written 1921; published 1926.

The American millionaire Denys Berry buys a castle beside a bog at Kilderry, County Meath, Ireland. When Berry prepares to have the bog drained, strange wraith-like creatures from the island in its midst exact a terrible vengeance.

The Mound (with Zealia Bishop)—written 1929–30; published 1940.

The account of a Spanish conquistador concerning a great cavern beneath the Indian mounds of the Oklahoma plains. The cavern, called blue-litten K'n-yan by the race of aliens who inhabit it due to the bluish light that pervades it, is a self-contained world, but is not unique, for two other similar vast caverns exist deeper beneath it.

The Music of Erich Zann—written 1921; published 1922.

A university student of metaphysics takes an inexpensive room in an old boarding house on the Rue d'Auseil, and becomes fascinated by the nightly viol music of a tenant in an attic room, an elderly German who improvises wild and unearthly harmonies on his viol that are unlike any the student has ever heard.

The Nameless City—written 1921; published 1921.

An archaeologist excavates a nameless and accursed city that is obliquely alluded to in the *Necronomicon*, digging his way beneath the desert sand to tunnels and rooms that reveal by their proportions and wall murals the inhuman nature of the city's inhabitants. He descends far beneath the ruins, and discovers to his horror that the city is not deserted after all.

The Night Ocean (with R. H. Barlow)—written 1936; published 1936.

This collaborative effort is unusual in that most of it was written by Barlow, not by Lovecraft. An artist goes to Ellston Beach for a seaside vacation, and is frightened by figures moving on the beach who do not seem entirely human.

Nyarlathotep—written 1920; published 1920.

This story is the transcription of one of Lovecraft's recurring nightmares. An Egyptian showman comes to town and puts on a strange display of mingled mysticism and electrical science in the local theater, enthralling his American audience, who find themselves completely under his spell and compelled to follow where he leads them.

The Other Gods—written 1921; published 1933.

A tale of the dreamlands concerning the quest of Barzai the Wise to glimpse the dancing gods of Earth atop the mountain Hatheg-Kla, and of how he was punished for his transgression by the pitiless Other Gods.

Out of the Aeons (with Hazel Heald)—written 1933; published 1935.

The mystery surrounding a strange mummy in the Cabot Museum of Boston, and the undecipherable hieroglyphics on the scroll in the iridescent metal cylinder that accompanied the mummy, which concern Ghatanothoa, a horrifying demon-god of the lost continent of Mu.

The Outsider—written 1921; published 1926.

The lonely inhabitant of a dark castle in an impenetrable forest longs to see the light of the sky above the canopy of trees, and climbs to the top of a black tower of the castle, but upon pushing open a trapdoor in the roof, and ascending through a marble-walled chamber, finds himself standing on the solid surface of the open ground.

Pickman's Model—written 1926; published 1927.

The oil paintings of artist Richard Upton Pickman of Boston shock the art world, not merely because of their horrifying subject matter—ghouls feeding upon the corpses of the dead—but because they have such an uncanny lifelike quality.

The Picture in the House—written 1920; published 1921.

A genealogical researcher traveling by bicycle on a lonely road to Arkham is forced to seek shelter from the rain in an ancient farm house, the owner of which has enjoyed an unnaturally long life due to his peculiar diet.

Polaris—written 1918; published 1920.

A man is tormented by persistent dreams that in the distant past, in another life, he was a resident of the marble city of Olathoë, in the northern land of Lomar, and that he betrayed his city by falling asleep at his post while on watch against the attack of the Inutos, a race of squat yellow fiends who had appeared out of the west to ravage the land.

The Quest of Iranon—written 1921; published 1935.

A youth calling himself Iranon claims to be the son of a king, and says he is seeking to find his lost city of Aira, where he will be crowned king. He wanders from city to city singing songs about the beauty of Aira, city of marble and beryl, but is regarded with scorn or amusement by most the people.

The Rats in the Walls—written 1923; published 1924.

A wealthy American descended from the noble family of the de la Poers returns to England to restore to its former eminence Exham Priory, the baronial mansion of his forefathers, only to discover that his bloodline is tainted by a horrifying legacy that lies hidden in caverns deep beneath the foundations of the ancient house.

The Shadow Out of Time—written 1934–5; published 1936.

Nathaniel Wingate Peaslee, a professor of political economy at Miskatonic University in Arkham, suffers for five years from amnesia, coupled with a strange personality disorder. He gradually recovers the lost memories of that period, and learns to his horror that he has been the victim of a mind exchange with a member of the time-spanning Great Race of Yith that inhabited our earth millions of years in the past.

The Shadow Over Innsmouth—written 1931; published 1936.

While on a sightseeing tour of New England, a young man is drawn to the decaying port of Innsmouth. There he learns its horrifying history—the town is cursed by a pact its inhabitants made in the previous century with the Deep Ones, a race of sea-dwelling amphibians who gave the town wealth in exchange for sacrifices, and the freedom to intermarry and produce hybrid offspring with the townspeople.

The Shunned House—written 1924; published 1928.

The deserted old house on Benefit Street in the city of Providence has stood empty for sixty years due to the unnaturally large number of deaths among its previous tenants. The source of the poisonous influence emanates from beneath the earthen floor of the cellar, where something evil and old lies buried.

The Silver Key—written 1926; published 1929.

Randolph Carter, who has gradually lost the ability to dream under the grinding weight of the banality and materialism of the world, regains it when he discovers a silver key that unlocks the gateways between dimensions of time and space.

The Statement of Randolph Carter—written 1919; published 1920.

An account given to the police by Randolph Carter concerning the disappearance of his fellow occultist Harley Warren, who descended down a flight of stone steps beneath an ancient sepulcher in Big Cypress Swamp late one night, and did not emerge.

The Strange High House in the Mist—written 1926; published 1931.

A man on holiday with his family in Kingsport is drawn to investigate a strange old house perched on the edge of a high sea cliff.

The Temple—written 1920; published 1925.

When a German U-boat sinks a British freighter in the Atlantic in 1917, the first officer takes from one of the dead sailors a small carved ivory head as a keepsake. Bad luck befalls the boat, which the crew attribute to the carving.

The Terrible Old Man—written 1920; published 1921.

The Terrible Old Man is a quaint fixture of Kingsport. A retired sea captain of immemorial years, he lives in a cottage on Water Street, where he keeps a curious collection of bottles from which he receives communications in the form of the tapping of suspended lead weights against the sides of the glass.

The Thing in the Moonlight (with J. Chapman Miske)—written 1927; published 1941.

The description by Lovecraft of one of his weird dreams, to which Miske added a few paragraphs at the beginning and end to turn it into a short story. In the dream, Lovecraft climbs the cleft in a lichen-crusted cliff as the Sun sets behind him, and finds at its top an endless plateau with an antique electric trolley car on a rusting track. He boards the car and waits for the conductor and the motorman, who he watches approach across the plateau under the light of the rising Moon, but to his horror discovers that they are not human.

The Thing on the Doorstep—written 1933; published 1937.

The poet and son of a wealthy family of Arkham, Edward Derby, marries Asenath Waite, of the Innsmouth Waites. Soon after the marriage, his personality changes—whereas before he was timid and vague, he has now become willful and self-assured. His face assumes a characteristic expression that is identical to the expression of Asenath's dead father, Ephraim Waite, who was rumored to have dabbled in black magic.

Through the Gates of the Silver Key (with E. Hoffmann Price)—written 1932–3; published 1934.

A sequel to *The Silver Key*, it explains what happened to the dreamer Randolph Carter after he used his silver key to pass through the Ultimate Gate.

The Tomb—written 1917; published 1922.

Jervas Dudley, a young man of a wealthy New England family, forms an obsession for the ancestral tomb of the Hyde family, to which he is distantly related. He begins to take on the mannerisms of Jervas Hyde, who a century ago was burned to ashes in the Hyde mansion when it was struck by lightning, and so never laid to rest in the family mausoleum.

The Transition of Juan Romero—written 1919; published 1944.

In 1894, gold miners in the American southwest open the dome of a vast cavern that seems to have no bottom. In the night, a rhythmic drumming is heard to emanate from the cavern, similar to the sound of a pagan ceremony. One of the miners and his Mexican servant, Juan Romero, are drawn by the sound to the opening of the cavern, which is lit with redness from below.

The Trap (with Henry S. Whitehead)—written 1931; published 1932.

When a student at a private school in Connecticut is drawn into the fourth dimension through a gateway in the form of an antique mirror created by a seventeenth-century Luciferian and witch, the modern owner of the mirror, a tutor named Canevin, must attempt to free the boy.

The Tree—written 1920; published 1921.

When the Greek sculptor Kalos is murdered by a jealous rival, a strange olive tree grows with unnatural rapidity above his tomb, its roots feeding on his decaying corpse. During a great storm, a heavy limb of the tree falls upon the house of the rival, killing him and destroying his work.

The Tree on the Hill (with Duane W. Rimel)—written 1934; published 1940.

A hiker takes photographs of a strange tree. When he shows them to his friend, the renowned occultist Constantine Theunis, his friend finds a correspondence between the scene photographed and a description in the *Chronicle of Nath* by Rudolf Yergler, where reference is made to the periodic coming of a shadow to the earth that feeds on human souls.

Two Black Bottles (with Wilfred Blanch Talman)—written 1926; published 1927.

A young man travels to the small village of Daalbergen, in the Ramapo Mountains of New England, to receive the inheritance of his recently deceased uncle, the Reverend Johannes Vanderhoof, who was the minister of the village church. He discovers that the sinister old sexton of the church, Abel Foster, had held some hellish occult influence over his uncle's mind that turned his uncle toward evil and caused the church to be shunned.

Under the Pyramids: see *Imprisoned with the Pharaohs*

The Unnamable—written 1923; published 1925.

Seated on a tomb with a friend in the old burying-ground at Arkham, the writer Randolph Carter relates the history of a nearby house, in the locked attic of which had dwelt for decades a monstrously deformed hybrid, the product of a unfortunate union between a girl of the house and some unnatural, bestial thing.

The Very Old Folk—written 1927; published 1940.

One of Lovecraft's dreams, written down in a letter to Donald Wandrei dated Thursday, November 3, 1927. The fifth cohort of the Roman XIIth Legion is assaulted by a supernatural wind summoned by an ancient hill tribe of the Pyrenees during their Sabbath rites.

What the Moon Brings—written 1922; published 1923.

A prose poem in which a man walks through the moonlight to the shore of the sea, where he sees revealed by the ebbing of the tide a city of the dead beneath the waves, and beyond it something vast and terrible that drives him to seek shelter among the dead.

The Whisperer in Darkness—written 1930; published 1931.

The alien race known as the Mi-Go maintain an outpost in the mountains of Vermont, where they gather information about the activities of humanity. They are supported by a network of human spies, drawn from the cult that worships them, and do not take kindly to the attempts of Henry Wentworth Akeley to gather evidence of their existence.

The White Ape—see *Facts Concerning the Late Arthur Jermyn and His Family*

The White Ship—written 1919; published 1919.

    Basil Elton, the keeper of the North Point lighthouse at Kingsport, dreams that he is borne away to many distant cities of the dreamlands in the White Ship.

Winged Death (with Hazel Heald)—written 1932; published 1934.

    A curious tale of academic rivalry and revenge set in Africa. The sociopath Doctor Thomas Slauenwite decides to kill his former friend, Henry Sargent Moore, when Moore accuses him of having stolen the work of another researcher. Slauenwite selects as his instrument of murder a disease-carrying fly that is called the "devil fly" by the Africans.

Bibliography

Aikin, John & others. *General Biography, or Lives Critical and Historical of the Most Eminent Persons of all Ages, Countries, Conditions and Professions.* Ten volumes. London: various publishers, 1799–1815.

Agrippa, Henry Cornelius. *Three Books of Occult Philosophy.* Edited and annotated by Donald Tyson. St. Paul, MN: Llewellyn Publications, 1993.

Chambers, Robert W. *The King In Yellow* [1895]. New York: Ace Books, Inc., undated.

Churchward, James. *The Lost Continent of Mu, Motherland of Man* [1926]. Kempton, Illinois: Adventures Unlimited Press, 2007.

Donnelly, Ignatius. *Atlantis: The Antediluvian World.* Revised edition. New York: Harper and Brothers Publishers, 1949.

Grant, Kenneth. *Outer Gateways.* London: Skoob Books, 1994.

Harms, Daniel, and John Wisdom Gonce III. *The Necronomicon Files: The Truth Behind Lovecraft's Legend.* Boston: Weiser Books, 2003.

Hay, George. *The Necronomicon, or The Book of Dead Names* [1978]. London: Corgi Books, 1980.

Herodotus. *The History of Herodotus.* Translated by George Rawlinson. New York: Tudor Publishing Company, 1947.

Howitt, William. *The History of the Supernatural In all Ages and Nations and In All Churches Christian and Pagan Demonstrating A Universal Faith.* Two volumes. Philadelphia: J. B. Lippincott and Co., 1863.

Joshi, S. T. *A Dreamer and a Visionary: H. P. Lovecraft in his Time.* Liverpool: Liverpool University Press, 2001.

———. *Selected Papers on Lovecraft.* West Warwick, RI: Necronomicon Press, 1989.

Knappert, Jan. *Bantu Myths and Other Tales.* Leiden: E. J. Brill, 1977.

Laycock, Donald C. *The Complete Enochian Dictionary: A Dictionary of the Angelic Language as revealed to Dr John Dee and Edward Kelley.* London: Askin Publishers, 1978.

Lehner, Ernst and Johanna. *Picture Book of Devils, Demons and Witchcraft*. New York: Dover Publications Inc., 1971.

Lévi, Eliphas. *Transcendental Magic* [1896]. New York: Samuel Weiser, 1979.

Lovecraft, H. P. *Selected Letters II: 1925–1929*. Edited by August Derleth and Donald Wandrei. Sauk City, WI: Arkham House Publishers, Inc., 1968.

———. *Supernatural Horror in Literature*. New York: Dover Publications, 1973.

Mathew, John. *Eaglehawk and Crow: A Study of the Australian Aborigines, an Inquiry Into their Origin, and a Survey of Australian Languages*. London: David Nutt, 1899.

Murray, Margaret A. *The Witch-Cult In Western Europe*. Oxford: The Clarendon Press, 1921.

Peck, Harriet Taylor. *Coyote Places the Stars*. New York: Bradbury Press, 1993.

Price, Robert M. (editor). *The Horror of It All: Encrusted Gems from the "Crypt of Cthulhu"*. Mercer Island, WA: Starmount House, 1990.

Shurreef, Jaffur. *Qanoon-e-Islam, or the Customs of the Moosulmans of India; comprising a full and exact account of their various rites and ceremonies, from the moment of birth till the hour of death*. Translated into English by G. A. Herklots. London: Parbury, Allen and Co., 1832.

Spence, Lewis. *An Encyclopaedia of Occultism*. London: George Routledge and Sons, 1920.

Summers, Montague. *The History of Witchcraft and Demonology* [1926]. USA: Castle Books, 1992.

Thorndike, Lynn. *History of Magic and Experimental Science*. Eight volumes. New York: Columbia University Press, 1923–1958.

Waite, Arthur Edward. *The Book of Black Magic and of Pacts: Including the Rites and Mysteries of Goëtic Theurgy, Sorcery, and Infernal Necromancy*. London: G. Redway, 1898.

———. *The Mysteries of Magic: A Digest of the Writings of Éliphas Lévi*. London: George Redway, 1886.

———. *The Turba Philosophorum, or Assembly of the Sages. Also Called the Book of Truth in the Art and the Third Pythagorical Synod* [1896]. New York: Samuel Weiser, 1976.

Index

Abano, Peter de, 373
Afrasiab, 47
Ai, 142, 175, 189, 192, 198
Aira, 233–234, 398
Akariel, 245, 317
Aklo formula, 99
Aklo language, 339, 368
Akurion, 317
Al Azif: see *Necronomicon*
Aldebaran, 227, 229, 254–255
Algol, 254–257
Alhazred, 2, 17, 21, 32–34, 36, 46, 48–51, 58, 62, 78, 80, 85, 90, 99, 116, 121, 143, 164, 181, 202, 210, 222, 270, 274, 282, 287, 300, 303, 329, 335, 347, 351–353, 394
amulet, jade, 299
An Inhabitant of Carcosa (Ambrose Bierce), 258
Anchester, 63, 153, 184–185
Ancient Ones, 19, 329
ankh, 206, 317
Antarctica, 17–18, 22–23, 85, 97, 108, 115, 164–166, 217, 219, 221, 223–224, 233, 240, 259, 302, 305, 334, 336, 351, 388
arachnid race, 19
Aran, 235–236
Arkham, 47, 55–57, 60–61, 68, 76–77, 80, 133, 174–175, 179, 182, 190, 192, 196–197, 200, 204–205, 209, 283, 287, 308–309, 315, 321, 328, 337, 348–350, 352, 375, 389, 397–399, 401
Arkham Sanitarium, 175, 204
Atal, 51–52, 238, 246, 334
Atlantis, 27, 72, 86, 124, 140, 162, 176, 180, 194, 199, 211, 271, 276, 306, 332, 338, 347
Atys, 110
avatars, 132–134, 157, 318, 346
Azathoth, 36, 43, 65, 86, 105, 108, 110–112, 128, 132–134, 136, 147, 159, 171, 215, 229, 236, 251, 267, 272, 295, 313, 326–327, 343, 349, 351, 363, 383, 388
Azathoth and Other Horrors (Derby), 272

Baal, 207
Baharna, 235, 242–243, 247, 337
balustraded terrace, 319
Banof, 177
Barzai the Wise, 37, 52, 85, 238, 246, 288, 301, 397
Basalt Pillars of the West, 68, 158, 233, 235–236, 320
Bedard, Marceline, 181, 201
Bethmoora, 177
Beyond-One, 112, 143, 263
bholes: see Dholes
Big Cypress Swamp, 54, 56, 95, 278, 399
Black Book: see *Nameless Cults*
black fever, 86, 347

black galleys, 158, 161, 221, 233, 235, 238, 243, 260, 320, 347, 358
black goat, 72, 127–129, 135, 137, 220, 275, 318, 329–330, 339, 348
Black Goat of the Woods: see Shub-Niggurath
Black Man, 77, 92, 107, 109, 112, 130, 133–134, 272, 318, 322, 334, 367, 374, 377–378
black mass, 348–349
black planets, 257, 261
black slime, 139, 150
black stone, 28, 117, 184, 202, 257, 263, 281, 286, 299–301, 330
black throne, 36, 110, 159, 326–327, 349
Black Winged Ones, 119, 150
Blake, Robert Harrison, 125, 132, 182, 194, 206, 276–277, 280, 357–358, 368
Blavatsky, H. P., 6–7, 114, 176, 231, 271, 273–274, 336, 366
blind gods: see Other Gods
bog-wraiths, 150, 326
Bokrug, 87, 113, 189, 204, 220, 260, 306
Book of Azathoth, 133, 272
Book of Dzyan, 6–7, 114–115, 273, 336
Book of Eibon, 80, 274, 371, 395
Book of Hidden Things, 274
Book of Thoth, 90, 274
Borellus, 52, 325
brain cylinders, 350
Bran, 52, 281
brick cylinders of Kadatheron, 220, 259, 275
Brown Jenkin, 68, 77, 209, 325, 328, 350, 354
Buddai, 113
Budge, E. A. Wallis, 183
Buo, 53

Camorin, 235
Carcosa, 255, 257–258
Carter, Edmund, 46, 54, 56, 95, 175, 204
Carter, Howard, 183
Carter, Randolph, 53
Carthage, 207
cataract, 68, 158, 206, 211, 233, 235–236, 254, 320, 347
Cathuria, 66, 68, 235–236, 241–242
cats, 161, 167, 233, 244, 246, 255, 260, 320, 358, 389
cats from Saturn, 161, 255, 320
Catskills, 152, 178, 194–195, 208, 255–256, 395
cavern of flame, 72, 78, 233, 236–237
Celephaïs, 73, 86, 128, 157, 190–191, 221, 233, 235–237, 241–244, 317, 389
Cerenerian Sea, 73, 161, 236–237, 242–243, 347
Chandraputra, Swami, 60
Chapman farmhouse, 196
charnel gardens of Xura, 247
Chaugnar Faugn, 114
Chesuncook, 178, 308, 322, 372
Children of the Fire Mist, 114–115, 273, 336
Chorazin, 67, 91, 178–179, 205, 262, 271, 274, 284, 304, 307, 377–378, 391
Chronicle of Nath (Rudolf Yergler), 68, 72, 199, 270, 275, 285, 329, 339, 348, 400
Churchward, Colonel James, 61
city of the Elder Things, 166, 219–220, 259, 351, 388
clock, coffin-shaped, 320
Clulu: see Cthulhu
coleopterous species, 19, 25
colors, poisonous, 321
Commoriom myth-cycle, 140, 276

cone-shaped race, 20
Congo, 71, 287–288, 392
Congregational Hospital, 180, 192
Corey, Abaddon, 61
corpse-eating cult, 221, 300, 351, 353
coven, 178, 209, 272, 308, 322, 356, 374, 376
Crawling Chaos: see Nyarlathotep
Crimson Desert: see Roba el-Khaliyeh
crinoid race: see Elder Race
Crom-Ya, 61
crucifix, 108, 299, 301
crux ansata: see Ankh
Cryptomenysis Patefacta (Falconer), 276
Cthulhu, 1, 17–19, 22–23, 27–29, 35–38, 49, 51, 107, 115–123, 140–141, 150, 163, 182–183, 186, 202, 208, 217, 223, 281, 284, 288, 300, 302–303, 305, 307, 317, 323, 330–331, 333, 336–338, 376, 388
Cultes des Goules (Comte d'Erlette), 80, 276
Cybele, 110, 184

Daemonolatreia (Remigius), 277
Dagon, 76, 92, 121–123, 128, 189, 304–305, 324, 330–331, 337, 355, 390
Damascius, 62
Damascus, 48–49, 51, 181, 282
Dark Mountain, 127, 129, 181, 193, 202, 348
De Furtivis Literarum Notis (Giambattista della Porta), 277
De la Poer, Gilbert, 63
De la Poer, Walter, 63
De Marigny, Étienne-Laurent, 63
De Russy, Denis, 160, 182, 201
De Vermis Mysteriis (Ludvig Prinn), 80, 277
Dee, John, 64

Deep Ones, 4, 19, 75–77, 83, 92–93, 122–123, 128, 154, 181, 189–191, 225, 299, 308–309, 324, 331, 337, 355, 398
Delapore, 65, 184
Demon City: see Thalarion
Demon-star: see Algol
Derby, Edward Pickman, 65
Devil Reef, 76–77, 123, 181, 189, 225, 324
Dho formula, 368
Dhol chants, 369
Dholes, 101, 150–151, 154, 246
Dionaean Plateau of Venus, 257
Dôls: see Dholes
Dorieb, 66, 241
Dragon's Head and Tail, 302
dreamlands, 2, 12, 23, 37, 45, 47, 51, 57–58, 60, 68, 71, 73, 78, 81, 84, 108–109, 128, 151, 154–156, 158, 161, 163, 167, 188, 193, 199, 206, 221, 224, 231, 233–244, 246–247, 249, 251, 255, 260, 282, 286, 307, 317, 320, 337–338, 347, 351, 356, 358, 389, 397, 402
Dudley, Jervas, 66
Dunwich, 18, 20–21, 32, 36, 47, 51, 65, 96–97, 100, 141, 143, 174, 177, 180–182, 196–198, 200, 204, 209, 240, 276–277, 284, 287, 289, 303, 308, 322, 327–328, 335, 338–339, 346, 354–355, 357, 366–368, 372, 375, 378, 391
Dylath-Leen, 161, 237, 244, 347

Easter Island, 61, 182, 206, 330
Egypt, 46, 48–49, 69–70, 72–73, 78–79, 124, 131, 133, 183–184, 186, 206, 275, 306, 317–318, 372, 386, 393
eidolon, 126, 317, 323
effluvium of K'thun, 351, 356
Elder Ones: see Elder Race

Elder Race, 17–18, 20–23, 302, 336
Elder Seal, 302–303
Elder Sign, 299, 303
Elder Things: see Elder Race
Eltdown Shards, 38, 278
Emanation of Yoth, 370
Empty Space: see Roba el-Khaliyeh
Erycinian Highland, 257
Eryx: see Erycinian Highland
Esoteric Order of Dagon, 76, 122, 189, 324, 337, 355
Esquimaux, 186
essential salts, 52, 62, 94, 142, 302–303, 324, 333, 366, 378
Evoë, 370
Exham Priory, 63, 153, 184, 398

familiars, 31, 100, 299, 325, 357
Feast of the Foxes, 370
feasts of Nitokris, 79, 351
five-headed monster, 151
flutes, 36, 132, 150, 157, 161, 325–327
Forgotten One, 124, 285
Fourth Book of Occult Philosophy (Robert Turner), 373
Fishers from Outside, 23, 208, 211
footprints, 55, 163, 327–328

Gallows Hill, 78, 186
gardens of Zokkar, 186
Gate, Ultimate, 328
Gem of Nath, 329
ghasts, 152, 224
Ghatanothoa, 71, 90, 124, 193, 199, 221, 225, 263, 332, 375, 397
ghoul-queen: see Nitokris
ghouls, 2, 70, 82–84, 152–155, 163–164, 185–186, 195, 224, 234, 237, 335, 355, 397

gingko-trees, 235–236
Gnorri, 155, 239
Gnophkehs, 139, 155, 157, 194, 199, 246
Goat with a Thousand Young: see Shub-Niggurath
gods of Earth, 23, 37, 51–52, 59, 84, 108, 134, 155, 164, 187, 237–238, 240–241, 246, 260, 286, 301, 334, 391, 397
Gorgo, 137, 179–180, 370–371
Granny Orne, 187, 192, 205, 209
Great Abyss, 129, 163, 188, 238, 243, 333
Great Ones, 23, 162–163, 238, 240, 334
Great Old Ones: see Elder Race
Great Race of Yith, 19–20, 24, 39, 61, 80, 85, 141, 167, 222, 259, 261, 270, 286, 398
Great Rite, 371
Green Decay, 371
gugs, 37, 152, 154–155, 224, 307
gyaa-yothn, 28, 156, 352, 355

Hadoth, 78, 186
Hali, Lake, 257
Hall School, 193
Halloween, 70, 75, 96, 181, 279, 304, 328, 348, 371–372, 377, 390
Hallowmass: see Halloween
Harms, Daniel, 373
Hastur, 31, 124–125, 128, 130, 379
Hatheg, 37, 52, 85, 238, 301, 397
Hatheg-Kla, 37, 52, 85, 238, 301, 397
Haunter of the Dark, 79, 112, 125, 132, 134, 182–184, 194, 203, 206, 257, 261, 263, 274, 276–277, 280, 284, 299, 303, 305–306, 318, 326–327, 336, 357–358, 368, 393
Hecate, 137, 161, 180, 291, 371
Hell's Acres, 220, 330

Herd, 335, 352

Hermes Trismegistus, 68–69, 101, 275, 280

hidden gods of Kadath: see God of Earth

hieroglyphics, 26, 61, 63, 116, 202, 206, 276, 300, 304–305, 320, 330–333, 337, 397

High-Priest Not to Be Described, 37, 156, 221, 243, 326, 358

Him Who is not to be Named, 129–130

History of the Supernatural (William Howett), 373

horned skull, 352

Houdini, Harry, 69

hound, winged, 353

Hounds of Tindalos, 150, 157, 218

house in the mist, 80, 88, 90, 129, 176–177, 180, 187–188, 192–193, 205, 238, 240, 317, 357, 399

Howard, Robert E., 37, 52, 61, 262, 281, 286,m 382

Howett, William, 373

Huitzilopotchli, 125

Hyades, 257

Hyperborea, 139, 180, 188–189, 259, 276, 286, 337

Ib, 87, 113, 186, 189, 198, 204, 220–221, 259–260, 275, 285, 306–307, 317, 391

Ibn Schacabao, 85

Ilarnek, 175, 189, 192, 198, 220, 260, 285

Ilek-Vad, 57–58, 81, 155, 239, 242

Image du Monde (Gauthier de Metz), 64, 278

Innsmouth, 4, 47, 65–66, 74–77, 92–93, 122–123, 128, 154, 166, 174–175, 181, 189–191, 193, 197, 209, 223, 225, 299, 308–309, 324, 331, 337, 355, 366, 374, 398–399

Inquanok, 162, 221, 239, 243, 245, 356

Inutos, 157, 194, 398

Irem, 49, 85, 130, 191, 202, 210, 307

iridescent cylinder, 60, 63, 331

Isis Unveiled (Helena Petrovna Blavatsky), 176, 273

island in the Miskatonic River, 192, 196, 297, 328

Jaren, 192, 211

Jermyn, Arthur, 71

Jermyn, Sir Wade, 71

Jupiter, 41, 103, 145, 169, 258, 293, 331, 341, 361

Kadath, 23, 37, 45, 51–52, 55, 57–58, 60, 68, 71–73, 78, 83–84, 86, 108–109, 111–112, 119, 128–129, 132, 134, 151–152, 154–159, 161, 163–164, 167, 193, 219, 221, 224, 232–247, 254–255, 260, 282, 286, 288, 303, 307, 316–318, 320, 326–328, 333–334, 337, 348, 351, 356, 358, 385, 391

Kadatheron, 175, 189, 192, 198, 220, 259, 275

Kadiphonek, 194, 199

Kallikanzarai of Greece, 158

Kaman-Thah, 71, 78, 233, 236–237, 255

Kamog, 374

Kanakys: see Walakea, Chief

Ka-Nefer, 72

Kath: see Stronti

Khephnes, 73

Khephren, 70, 72, 79, 151, 166, 183, 351

Kled, 240, 242, 246

King In Yellow (Robert W. Chambers), 7, 124–125, 258, 284, 379
Kingsport, 45, 47, 56–57, 68, 80, 88–89, 174, 180, 187–188, 192–193, 196, 205, 209, 247, 328, 338, 356, 392, 399, 402
Klarkash-Ton, 72, 180, 276
K'naa, 71, 90, 124, 193, 224, 375
K'n-yan, 27–29, 39, 120, 124, 129–130, 137–141, 150, 156, 164, 177, 198, 200, 202, 218, 220–224, 303, 333, 338, 352, 355, 359, 396
Koth, sign of, 60, 155, 241, 307
Koth, Tower of, 241
K'thun, 351, 356
Kukulcan, 135, 140
Kuranes, 73, 86, 157, 233, 237, 244, 389
Kynarth, 258
Kythanil, 259

lagh metal, 331–333, 375
larvae of the Other Gods, 158
Last Void, 355
Lathi: see eidolon
Le Sorcier, Charles, 73
Lee's Swamp, 127, 129, 193, 348
Lemuria, 27, 114, 180, 194, 306, 333, 336
Leng, 37, 124, 139–140, 155–157, 161–163, 210, 219, 221, 225, 233–234, 238, 240, 243, 260, 300, 321, 326, 347, 351, 353, 358, 369
Lerion, 241
Lévi, Eliphas, 74
Libre d'Eibon: see *Book of Eibon*
Liber Ivonis, 274, 280
Lilith, 87, 109, 126–127, 137, 161, 179–180, 291, 326, 346, 354, 359, 371, 394
"L'Image du monde" (Gauthier de Metz), 64, 278

L'mur-Kathulos, 333
Lobon, 127, 137, 143
Lomar, 139, 155, 157, 177, 180, 194–195, 199–200, 211, 246, 260, 286, 291, 397
Lords of Yaddith, 262
Lost Lemuria (W. Scott-Elliot), 114, 336

Magical Elements (Peter de Abano), 373
Magnalia Christi Americana (Cotton Mather), 52, 55, 78, 280, 324–325, 367
magnetic cylinder, 333
Magnum Innominandum, 128–129
man-lizards of Venus, 159
Manuxet River, 191
Marsh, Obed, 74
Martense, Gerrit, 195
Martense, Jan, 195
Mason, Keziah, 77
Mather, Cotton, 78
May-Eve, 34, 75, 96, 141, 181, 193, 279, 328, 368, 375
Meadow Hill, 55, 196, 309, 348, 353
Medusa, 109, 135, 150, 160, 182–183, 194, 201, 208, 211, 223, 240, 263, 284, 301, 349, 377, 386, 395
Mesnard, 68, 280
Mi-Go, 3, 18–19, 22–23, 29–32, 37, 90, 112, 115, 124–125, 127, 129, 134, 139, 143, 181, 193, 199, 202, 218, 224, 254, 257, 260, 263, 299–301, 305, 316, 327, 331–333, 348, 350, 379, 401
Miskatonic University, 54, 61, 64–65, 68, 80, 95, 97–100, 174–175, 197, 209, 220–221, 277, 281, 283, 299, 308, 321, 334–335, 337, 366, 375, 388, 391, 398
Mlin, Tower of, 208

Mnar, 113, 175, 177, 189, 192, 194, 198, 200, 204, 207, 220, 259–260, 275, 285, 317
monograph of Eli Davenport, 280
monolith, 116, 119, 121–122, 244, 286, 304–305, 330, 390
Moon, 12–14, 41, 51, 79, 84, 86, 125, 137, 142, 150, 155, 157–158, 161, 164, 167, 179–180, 198, 207, 210, 220–221, 233, 235, 237–238, 243, 253–255, 257–260, 275, 285, 290–291, 297, 302–303, 317, 320, 326, 331, 334, 347–348, 358, 371, 396, 399, 401
moon-beasts, 84, 155, 157–158, 161, 164, 221, 233, 238, 243, 260, 320, 347–348, 358
moon-ladder, 259, 334
moon-wine, 51, 167, 260, 334
Mormo, 137, 161, 179–180, 371
Most Ancient One: see 'Umr At-Tawil
Mother Hydra, 122, 128
mounds, 27, 29, 164, 198, 396
Mthura: see Stronti
Mu, 61, 71, 90, 124, 130, 193–194, 198–199, 210–211, 218, 224, 249, 263, 271, 330, 332, 375–376, 397
music, 101, 110–111, 132, 140, 161, 188, 203, 210, 242, 245, 247, 325–326, 328, 396

Naacal, 61, 95, 198, 330, 375–376
Nahab, 77, 376
Nameless City, 28, 47, 49, 51, 62, 64, 191, 198, 204, 222, 278, 317, 396
Nameless Cults (Friedrich von Junzt), 63, 124, 281, 331–332, 375
Naraxa, 236, 242
Narg, 66, 236, 241–242

Narrative of Arthur Gordon Pym of Nantucket (Edgar Allan Poe), 336
Narthos, 199, 205, 211
Nasht, 71, 78, 233, 236–237, 255
Nath, 68, 72, 101, 128, 199, 213, 220, 227, 229, 236, 241, 270, 275, 285, 329, 339, 348, 400
Nath-Horthath, 128, 236, 241
Necronomicon (Abdul Alhazred), 2, 202
Necronomicon Files (Daniel Harms & John Wisdom Gonce III), 373
Nemesis of Flame, 162
Nephren-Ka, 78, 184, 186, 206, 306, 329
Ngranek, 51, 163, 242, 286, 327
night-gaunts, 84, 118–119, 129, 155, 162–164, 232, 238, 243, 282, 327, 356
Nir, 238, 244
Nis, 208, 358, 396
Nitocris: see Nitokris
Nitokris, 72, 79, 151, 183, 351
N'kai, 28, 39, 138–139, 149–150, 222
Nodens, 119, 129, 155, 162, 164, 187–188, 238, 317
Norrys, Edward, 185
Not-to-Be-Named One, 28, 129–130, 135–136
Noth-Yidik, 351, 356
Noton, 194, 199
Nug and Yeb, 130, 191, 202, 210
Nug-Soth, 79
Nyarlathotep, 36–37, 73, 77, 86, 92, 107–110, 112, 124–125, 129–134, 136–137, 155–157, 161–162, 164, 179, 183–184, 186, 193, 234, 236, 238, 240, 257, 261, 263, 306, 318, 320, 326–327, 346, 356–357, 367, 377–378, 393, 397

Oaths of Dagon: see Esoteric Order of Dagon
Olathoë, 139, 177, 194, 199–200, 246, 260, 291, 397
Olaus Wormius, 46, 197, 283
old burying-ground, 55, 196, 200, 207, 315, 352, 401
Old Ones, 3–5, 10, 17–23, 25–27, 30–36, 39, 43, 50–51, 54–55, 77, 83, 85, 95–100, 105, 107–109, 115, 117–119, 121, 129, 134–135, 138, 141–143, 147, 155, 171, 181–182, 204, 215, 229, 234, 240, 251, 254, 263, 267, 270, 284, 295, 299, 303, 305, 308–309, 313, 318, 323, 327, 343, 346, 349, 357, 363, 366–368, 371, 374, 383, 385, 391
old people, 27, 164
Olney, Thomas, 187
Ooth-Nargai, 73, 235–236, 242, 244, 389
opal throne: see Ilke-Vad
Orabona, 85
Oriab, 51, 235, 243, 247, 337
Other Gods from Outside, 36–37, 51
Oukranos, 240, 242, 246
Outer Beings: see Mi-Go

papyrus of Ilarnek, 220, 285
papyrus, yellowed, 247, 291
penguins, giant, 351
People of the Monolith (Justin Geoffrey), 286
Pickman, Richard, 81
pit of the shoggoths, 166, 178, 308, 322, 356, 367, 372, 374
Pluto: see Yuggoth
Pnakotic Fragments: see Pnakotic Manuscripts

Pnakotic Manuscripts, 27, 37, 85, 195, 240, 245–246, 270, 286, 302
Pnakotus, 26–27, 217, 222, 286
Pnath, Vale of, 243
Poe, Edgar Allan, 47, 336
Poligraphia: see *Polygraphiae*
Polygraphiae (Johannes Trithemius), 286–287
powder of Ibn Ghazi, 34, 335, 378
primal city, 243
primal tongue: see Tsath-yo
Prolonged of Life: see 'Umr At-Tawil
Providence, 2, 58, 62, 81, 94, 125, 130–131, 173, 175, 182, 184, 204, 206, 239, 253, 276–277, 279–280, 289, 306, 318, 393, 398
pthagon membrane, 332, 375

Quetzalcoatl, 135, 140, 391

Relex: see R'lyeh
Remigius: see Remy, Nicolas
Remy, Nicolas, 277
Rhan-Tegoth, 84–85, 135, 263, 356, 375
R'lyeh, 17, 22, 30, 35–36, 38, 116–123, 183, 186, 223, 288, 302, 305, 323, 330, 337, 376, 388
R'lyehian script, 288
Romero, Juan, 400
Round Hill, 51, 202, 300–301, 330, 350
Rue d'Auseil, 203, 396

sabbat, 77, 92, 107, 133–134, 178–179, 272, 304, 308, 318, 322, 334, 348, 367–368, 372, 374–377, 391
Sabbath: see sabbat
Secret Doctrine (Helena Petrovna Blavatsky), 6–7, 114, 273, 336

Sarkia, 194, 199
Sarkomand, 238, 243, 333
Sarnath, 54, 87–88, 113, 127, 137, 143, 175, 177, 186, 189, 192, 194, 198, 200, 204, 207, 220–222, 259–260, 275, 285, 306–307, 317, 391
Searight, Richard F., 278
Selarn, 243, 246
Serannian, 73, 243–244
serpent-men of Valusia, 306
Seven Caves of Chicomoztoc, 335
Seven Cryptical Books of Hsan, 288
Seven Lost Signs of Terror, 377–378
S'gg'ha, 85–86
Shaddad, 85, 191
Shaggai, 261
Shamballah, 194, 205
shantak-bird, 356
Shining Trapezohedron, 78, 125, 182, 184, 187, 194, 206, 257, 263, 299–300, 305, 318, 329, 357, 393
Ship Street, 80, 187, 192, 205, 209
shoggoths, 19, 22–23, 77, 164–166, 178, 308, 322, 336, 352, 356, 367, 372, 374
Shub-Niggurath, 90, 107, 127–130, 135–137, 139, 318, 348, 375
silver key, 19, 38, 45, 51, 53, 55–61, 63, 68, 81, 85, 89–91, 95, 101, 110, 112, 114–115, 138, 140, 143, 151, 155, 175–176, 180, 188–189, 191, 193, 195–196, 204–205, 211, 219, 221, 223, 225, 239–240, 242, 246, 258–263, 273, 275, 278, 282, 284, 288, 297–298, 303, 307, 321, 328–331, 335–337, 347, 352, 355, 375–376, 386, 398, 400
Sinara, 199, 205, 211
Skai, 244, 246

Smith, Clark Ashton, 72, 79, 138, 156, 180, 202, 274, 276, 302, 365, 372
Snake-Den, 57–58, 205, 298, 328
S'ngac, 86
Snireth-Ko, 86
Sona-Nyl, 68, 244, 336
soul-bottles, 356
spawn of Cthulhu, 17, 22–23, 37, 115, 288, 307, 337, 376
Sphinx, 70, 72–73, 79, 150–151, 166–167, 183, 243, 300, 320, 395
split-hoof, 55
Stanley (Horace Binney Wallace), 47
Stanzas of Dzyan: see *Book of Dzyan*
Starry Wisdom, Church of, 206
Steganographia (Johannes Trithemius), 276, 287
Stethelos, 206–207, 211
Stillwater, 207
stone circle, 33–34, 308
Stonehenge, 184, 297
Stronti, 261
Stygian sea, 223
Summers, Montague, 374
Surama, 86, 162, 176, 303, 338, 347
Swamp Hollow, 207
swastika, 299, 308

Tablets of Nhing, 288
Talman, Wilfred Blanch, 90, 386, 401
Tamash, 127, 137, 143
Tanarian Hills, 73, 236, 242, 244
Tanit, temples of, 207
Tanit-Isis, 182
Taran-Ish, 87–88, 113, 306
Tcho-Tchos people, 357
Tekeli-li, 166, 336
Teloth, 200, 208

Tempest Mountain, 152, 178, 194–195, 208, 395
Temple of the Elder Ones, 239, 245
Terra Nova, 261
Terrible Old Man, 88–90, 187–188, 192–193, 205, 209, 356–357, 399
Tetragrammaton, 372–373
Thalarion, 126, 245, 317, 323
Than, 208
Tharp, 336
Theodorus Philetas, 51, 283
Theosophy, 6, 132, 159, 271, 318, 323, 336, 366
Theunis, Constantine, 330, 348, 400
Thon and Thal, 235, 337
thousand-faced moon, 137, 179, 371
Thraa, 175, 189, 192, 198
Thran, 240, 246
three-lobed burning eye, 357–358
Throk, Peaks of, 246
Thunder Hill, 348, 370–371
Thurai, 246
tiara, 324, 337
Tiráwa, 137, 140
toad-things, 161
Traite des Chiffres (De Vigenere), 289
Trithemius, Johannes, 65, 276–277, 286
Tsadogwa: see Tsathoggua
Tsath, 28, 139, 223, 337, 376
Tsath-yo, 337, 376
Tsathoggua, 23, 28, 39, 138–140, 150, 188, 200, 208, 223–224, 259, 281, 286
Tuaregs, 176, 338
Tulu: see Cthulhu
Tulu-metal, 333, 338
Tutankhamen, 183
T'yog, 90, 375

Uganda, 23, 208
Ulthar, 51–52, 57, 167, 238, 244, 246, 286, 288, 320, 334, 389
Ultimate Gate, 53, 59, 90, 101, 329, 355, 400
Ultimate Gods: see Other Gods
'Umr At-Tawil, 19, 90–91, 274, 329, 347
Unaussprechlichen Kulten: see Nameless Cults
upas-tree, 358
Urg, 243, 246

Van Kauran, Bareut Picterse, 91
Van Kauran, William, 92
Van Kauran, Nicholas, 92
Vaults of Zin, 28, 138, 152, 156, 224, 241, 358
vegetable entities of Mercury, 259
Veiled King, 239, 245, 356
Void, Last, 355
Von Junzt, Friedrich, 63, 281
Voorish sign, 34, 378

Waite, Asenath, 92
Waite, Ephraim, 92
Walakea, Chief, 93
Wallace, Horace Binney, 47
Ward, Charles Dexter, 94
Warren, Harley, 95
Washington Street, 92, 209
Water Street, 80, 88, 187, 192, 205, 209, 356, 399
Webb, William Channing, 186
well, bottomless, 358
West, Herbert, 95
Whateley, Wilbur, 96
whippoorwills, 96, 180, 338
white stone, 72, 121, 196, 309, 390

Widener Library, 209, 283
Wild Marvels of Science (Morryster), 209
Willett, Marinus Bicknell, 60, 62, 94, 241, 307
Winged Ones: see Mi-Go
Winters-Hall, Arthur Brooke, 38, 278
Witch-Cult in Western Europe (Margaret A. Murray), 133
Witch House, 23, 51, 68, 77, 108–110, 112–113, 133–134, 174–175, 192, 196–198, 204, 209–210, 220, 255, 272, 274, 284, 299, 301, 308–309, 318–319, 325–328, 330–331, 348–350, 376–377, 391
Words of Fear, 378
worm-like race, 38–39, 262, 323, 389

Xari, 192, 199, 205–206, 211
Xinaián: see K'n-yan
Xura, 247, 351

Yaddith, 53, 59–60, 101, 124, 151, 193, 199, 224–225, 261–263, 288, 321, 375
Yaddith-Gho, 124, 193, 199, 224–225, 375
yakith-lizard, 332, 375
Yath, 234–235, 243, 247, 348
yath trees, 234
Year of the Black Goat, 72, 220, 275, 329–330, 339, 348
Yekub, 262, 323, 389
Yellow Sign, 7, 31, 379
Yemen, 2, 48–49, 181, 191, 201–202, 210
Yezidis, 291
Y'ha-nthlei, 123, 181, 225, 324
Yhe, 210
Yhtill, 257

Yian-Ho, 210, 221, 225, 285, 304, 321
Yig, 27–29, 120, 130, 135, 137, 140–141, 303, 333, 355, 386, 390
Yithians, 3, 25–26, 39, 61, 80, 217, 258–259, 262, 323
y'm-bhi, 359
Yog-Sothoth, 18–19, 33, 36, 38, 41, 43, 49, 51, 59, 94, 96, 100–101, 105, 107, 110, 112, 132, 141–143, 145, 147, 169, 171, 200, 202, 215, 227, 229, 251, 263, 265, 267, 279, 281, 284, 293, 295, 300, 302–303, 308, 311, 313, 323, 328–329, 341, 343, 346, 354, 358, 361, 363, 368, 374, 381, 383, 391
Yoth, 28, 39, 138–139, 150, 200, 222, 224–225, 352, 355, 370
Yuggoth, 18–19, 30, 32, 37, 84, 100, 112, 124, 134–135, 143, 160, 163–164, 193, 199, 203, 221, 224–225, 254, 261, 263, 301, 305, 317, 327, 331–333, 354, 356, 375, 385, 393
Yuggoth-spawn: see Mi-Go

Zak: see Zar
Zakarion, 247, 291
Zamacona, 130, 333
Zann, Erich, 101
Zar, 247
Zimbabwe, 211, 301
Zkauba, 53, 59–60, 101, 115, 151, 261–262, 288, 321
Zobna, 155, 194, 211
Zobnarian Fathers, 195, 211, 291
Zo-Kalar, 127, 137, 143
zoogs, 167, 246, 260, 334
Zura: see Xura
Zuro, 208

To Write to the Author

If you wish to contact the author or would like more information about this book, please write to the author in care of Llewellyn Worldwide Ltd., and we will forward your request. Both the author and publisher appreciate hearing from you and learning of your enjoyment of this book and how it has helped you. Llewellyn Worldwide Ltd. cannot guarantee that every letter written to the author can be answered, but all will be forwarded. Please write to:

Donald Tyson
℅ Llewellyn Worldwide Ltd.
2143 Wooddale Drive
Woodbury, MN 55125-2989

Please enclose a self-addressed stamped envelope for reply,
or $1.00 to cover costs. If outside the U.S.A., enclose
an international postal reply coupon.

Many of Llewellyn's authors have websites with additional information and resources. For more information, please visit our website at http://www.llewellyn.com.

GET MORE AT LLEWELLYN.COM

Visit us online to browse hundreds of our books and decks, plus sign up to receive our e-newsletters and exclusive online offers.

- Free tarot readings • Spell-a-Day • Moon phases
- Recipes, spells and tips • Blogs • Encyclopedia
- Author interviews, articles, and upcoming events

GET SOCIAL WITH LLEWELLYN

www.Facebook.com/LlewellynBooks

www.Twitter.com/Llewellynbooks

GET BOOKS AT LLEWELLYN

LLEWELLYN ORDERING INFORMATION

Order online: Visit our website at www.llewellyn.com to select your books and place an order on our secure server.

Order by phone:
- Call toll free within the U.S. at 1-877-NEW-WRLD (1-877-639-9753)
- Call toll free within Canada at 1-866-NEW-WRLD (1-866-639-9753)
- We accept VISA, MasterCard, and American Express

Order by mail:
Send the full price of your order (MN residents add 6.875% sales tax) in U.S. funds, plus postage and handling to: Llewellyn Worldwide, 2143 Wooddale Drive
Woodbury, MN 55125

POSTAGE AND HANDLING:

STANDARD: (U.S., Mexico & Canada)
(Please allow 2 business days)
$25.00 and under, add $4.00
$25.01 and over, FREE SHIPPING

INTERNATIONAL ORDERS (airmail only):
$16.00 for one book, plus $3.00 for each additional book.

Visit us online for more shipping options. Prices subject to change.

FREE CATALOG!

To order, call
1-877-NEW-WRLDS
ext. 8236
or visit our website

Alhazred
Author of the Necronomicon
Donald Tyson

H. P. Lovecraft's compelling character, Abdul Alhazred, is brought to life in this epic tale detailing the mad sorcerer's tragic history and magical adventures. Alhazred tells his own life story, beginning with himself as a poor, handsome boy in Yemen who attracts the attention of the king for his divine skill in poetry. As the court poet, young Abdul lives a luxurious life at the palace, where he studies necromancy and magic. But falling in love with the king's daughter leads to a foolish tryst, which is ultimately discovered. As punishment, Abdul is tortured, brutally mutilated, and cast into the desert, known as the Empty Space. Battling insanity, he joins a tribe of ghouls and learns forbidden secrets from a stranger called Nyarlathotep. Thus begins his downward spiral into wickedness. Renamed Alhazred, he escapes the desert and embarks on a quest to restore his body and reunite with his true love. Traveling across the ancient world and fantastic realms, he is hounded by foes and tormented by the demands of his dark lord.

978-0-7387-0892-8, 672 pp., 7 x 10 $29.95

Grimoire of the Necronomicon
Donald Tyson

On the heels of his widely successful trilogy of works honoring H. P. Lovecraft, Donald Tyson now unveils a true grimoire of ritual magic inspired by the Cthulhu mythos. The Grimoire of the Necronomicon is a practical system of ritual magic based on Lovecraft's mythology of the alien gods known as the Old Ones.

Fans of Lovecraft now have the opportunity to safely get in touch with the Old Ones and draw upon their power for spiritual and material advancement. Tyson expands upon their mythology and reintroduces these "monsters" in a new, magical context—explaining their true purpose for our planet. As a disciple, you choose one of the seven lords as a spiritual mentor, who will guide you toward personal transformation. Daily rituals provide an excellent system of esoteric training for individual practitioners. This grimoire also provides structure for an esoteric society—Order of the Old Ones—devoted to the group practice of this unique system of magic.

978-0-7387-1338-0, 216 pp., 7 x 10 $18.95

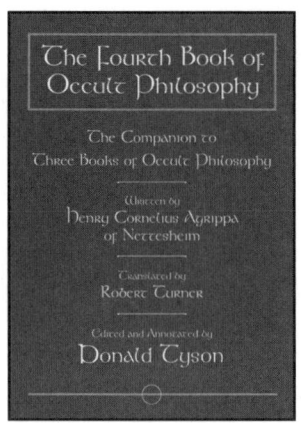

The Fourth Book of Occult Philosophy
The Companion to Three Books of Occult Philosophy
Cornelius Agrippa
Annotated by Donald Tyson

The Fourth Book of Occult Philosophy by Cornelius Agrippa is considered one of the foundation stones of Western magic. The grimoires it contains are among the most important that exist in the Western tradition. For more than three hundred years, this mysterious grimoire has been regarded as difficult or even impossible to understand—until now.

Occult scholar Donald Tyson presents a fully annotated, corrected, and modernized edition of this masterwork that renders it fully accessible to the average reader as well as scholars and skilled magicians. For the first time, these classic works of Western magic are unveiled to everyone seeking to understand them.

978-0-7387-1876-7, 480 pp., 7 x 10   **$37.95**

To order, call 1-877-NEW-WRLD
Prices subject to change without notice
Order at Llewellyn.com 24 hours a day, 7 days a **week!**